Mobile Macromedia Flash® MX with Flash Remoting & Flash Communication Server

About the Authors

Alan Yeung, who recently coauthored *Oracle9i Mobile*, brings years of IT and mobile development experience to this title. Recently, Alan co-founded Where2Net, a software provider of multichannel development tools and web applications, and served as President and CEO. Before that, he held technical and management positions at PointCast, Inc., and Raychem Corporation. Alan's academic background includes an M.B.A from UC Berkeley, a Ph.D. from Stanford University, and a BSChE from the University of Wisconsin. Currently, Alan provides senior-level IT, technical, and management consulting services to U.S. and international corporations.

Nicholas Pang, coauthor of *Oracle9i Mobile*, brings years of mobile and server expertise to this book. Previously, Nicholas served as vice president of product development at Where2Net, where he had hands-on involvement in the design and development of many rich Internet applications using Flash MX, ColdFusion MX, and J2EE servers. Prior to that, he held senior technical and management positions at PointCast, Cadence Design Systems, and Amdahl Corporation. Nicholas has a M.S. in electrical engineering from the University of Wisconsin—Madison and a B.S. in electrical engineering from Arizona State University. Currently, Nicholas provides mobile, web-based application design, CAD, and consumer electronics consulting services to various Japanese and U.S. corporations.

Mobile Macromedia Flash® MX with Flash Remoting & Flash Communication Server

Alan Yeung
Nicholas Pang

McGraw-Hill/Osborne

New York   Chicago   San Francisco
Lisbon   London   Madrid   Mexico City   Milan
New Delhi   San Juan   Seoul   Singapore   Sydney   Toronto

The **McGraw·Hill** Companies

McGraw-Hill/Osborne
2600 Tenth Street
Berkeley, California 94710
U.S.A.

To arrange bulk purchase discounts for sales promotions, premiums, or fund-raisers, please contact **McGraw-Hill**/Osborne at the above address. For information on translations or book distributors outside the U.S.A., please see the International Contact Information page immediately following the index of this book.

Mobile Macromedia Flash® MX with Flash Remoting & Flash Communication Server

1234567890 CUS CUS 0198765432

ISBN 0-07-222645-5

Publisher	Brandon A. Nordin
Vice President & Associate Publisher	Scott Rogers
Editorial Director & Acquisitions Editor	Wendy Rinaldi
Project Editor	Lisa Wolters-Broder
Acquisitions Coordinator	Athena Honore
Technical Editor	Matt Wobensmith
Copy Editor	Mike McGee
Proofreader	Brian Galloway
Indexer	Valerie Robbins
Computer Designers	Tara A. Davis, Kathleen Fay Edwards, Michelle Galicia, Jim Kussow
Illustrators	Jackie Sieben, Lyssa Wald, Michael Mueller, Melinda Moore Lytle
Series Designer	Roberta Steele
Cover Series Design	Greg Scott
Cover Illustration	Akira Inoue/Photonica

This book was composed with Corel VENTURA™ Publisher.

To Stella, who has always been my guiding light.
— *Alan*

To Sophie, my best friend, master chef,
loving wife, and masseur.
— *Nicholas*

Contents at a Glance

Contents

Acknowledgments

Our thanks to Matt Wobensmith, who provided us with lots of insights into Macromedia Flash MX while serving as our technical editor. We also want to thank Stephen Tondre for helping out on the multichannel mobile promotion (m-Promo) application and to super-programmers Sandip Ghosh and Thomas Birkett for creating daVinci Studio.

We'd like to thank our editorial team, including Jim Schachterle and Jeremy Judson, Acquisition Editors, for their inspiration and confidence in us; Athena Honore, Acquisition Coordinator, for keeping us on track; Lisa Wolters-Broder, Project Editor, for guiding us through the editorial process with ease; and Mike McGee, Copy Editor, for vastly improving our book.

I'd like to thank my wife, Stella for her love and patience. Also, I want to thank my sister, Vivien, who inspired me with her dedication and keen mind, and Vincent Tse, who helped me countless times. I am also indebted to my mother for her constant support, and am grateful to Tim Jenks for his insight and humor, not to mention all his help and encouragement. He's indeed both a teacher and friend. I also would like to thank Louis Woo for his unwavering support and confidence in me, and for setting an example for so many. Finally, to Pe-Ling and Fuk-Chin Chen, my in-laws—thank you for all the help and encouragement. I promise to write something less technical next time!

Alan Yeung
San Francisco, California
December 2002

To my wife, Sophie, for all her support, stamina, and love during this long but exciting project. And to my kids, who were very understanding at those times when Daddy needed to focus and concentrate on his writing. As our audience reads this, I'm no doubt off somewhere making up for lost time with them. I also want to thank my parents, and my brothers and sisters, for both their financial and familial support as I worked on this project. Without them, I would not have been able to complete the book. Finally, I'd like to thank Tony Chin, who got me excited about MPEG-4, DivX, Ultra-Wide Band (UWB), and various consumer electronics technologies, some of which are reflected in these pages.

Nicholas Pang
San Francisco, California
December 2002

Introduction

The compelling features and dramatic implications of Macromedia Flash MX and how it can dramatically change the mobile development paradigm tempted us. This book bridges the gap between two strengths—the rich and dynamic nature of Flash client, and the power of server-side and database support to build compelling enterprise applications.

Who Should Read this Book

Our primary audiences are client- and server-side developers who want to use Macromedia Flash MX to build mobile applications and services. For those well-versed in Flash design and ActionScript, this book provides the next step in extending both their web sites and Flash applications into the new world of mobile devices. For server-side coders and mobile developers, this book provides valuable insights into how they can build a Flash front-end to their database with a server back-end infrastructure. The result is a clear and concise path toward creating consumer and/or enterprise mobile solutions that are multimedia in nature, yet easy to build. For ColdFusion developers, in particular, this book offers a unique recipe to add to their ColdFusion know-how and help them master the skills for Flash and mobile development.

How to Use this Book

There are three parts to this book. **Part I** provides a background on mobile application development and an introduction to Macromedia Flash MX in general. It delineates the strengths and features of Macromedia Flash MX and why it is so compelling to adopt Flash for mobile data services. **Part II** describes the key components and skills needed for building rich mobile applications using the Flash MX platform, including its authoring environment, Flash Player, Flash Remoting, ColdFusion MX, and Flash Communication Server. It also teaches you how to manage the complex mobile architecture and platform issues, and discuss ways to support single and multichannel applications. In **Part III**, we pull together the concepts and capabilities to build core Flash applications, including supporting Flash and non-Flash multichannel applications, MP3 Flash Player, and streaming multimedia services.

Part I: Mobile Application Development and Macromedia Flash MX

Chapter 1: Working in the Mobile Environment   In Chapter 1, we discuss what constitutes the Mobile Internet and the environment which mobile developers and designers must work with. We review basic elements of the mobile architecture, including networks, protocols, markup languages, and wireless proxy servers, as well as summarize the opportunities and challenges unique to mobile application development. We review the use of XML and XSL transformations for wireless applications, and introduce the new paradigm that Macromedia Flash MX brings in terms of an application model.

   Chapter 2: Macromedia Flash MX for Mobile Devices   Chapter 2 introduces Macromedia Flash MX—the complete platform for building, deploying, and running rich media applications across multiple channels and devices. We make a case for building mobile applications with Flash, and propose that Flash is more compelling for that purpose than normal web applications. We review the various components of Macromedia Flash MX, including its player, authoring environment, source and output files, and scripting language. We also review the server side support of Flash MX offered by Macromedia—Flash Remoting and ColdFusion MX—and examine the mobile Flash MX architecture advocated by Macromedia. In addition, we look at how other pieces of Macromedia technology can be leveraged for mobile development.

   Chapter 3: Essentials of Dynamic Flash Development   Chapter 3 gives you a quick start on using Macromedia Flash MX to build interactive movies and dynamic applications. We review the roles of client- and server-side developers and Flash designers, and their workflow. Instead of walking through feature after feature, we use the Macromedia Flash MX authoring environment, along with other server-side capabilities, to build our initial Flash MX application—a video store. We illustrate how to use Macromedia Flash and build on existing Flash movies and capabilities. We then extend Flash movies to make them database-driven, server-backed applications that are rich in media, and leverage the Flash client.

Part II: Building Skills for Multichannel Mobile Applications

Chapter 4: Designing Mobile User Interfaces   In Chapter 4, we look at how to design effective user interfaces (UI) for mobile applications using the Macromedia Flash MX authoring environment. We dissect the key issues of building intuitive Flash user interfaces for mobile devices, and review the design and development process, contrasting the workflow for Internet and mobile applications. We will examine ways to enhance usability by looking at the qualities of useful mobile applications and the guidelines used for building them. We review the style guides of designing Flash applications for Microsoft Pocket PCs and the Nokia Communicator Series—which includes page layout, screen size, typography, and so on. We conclude by summarizing the Macromedia Flash MX Core UI components and looking at an example of how to take advantage of them for mobile applications

   Chapter 5: Integrating Animation and Multimedia   Chapter 5 introduces the various animation and multimedia techniques of Macromedia Flash MX. We discuss the basics of audio and video, including the MP3 format and others, and how they can be used in Flash movies—embedded or linked. We go through various animation tools for Flash MX. More importantly, we provide tips about the impact of the multimedia properties on file sizes for delivery to mobile devices, in addition to the impact on the mobile devices' processing power.

Chapter 6: Server-Side Flash   Chapter 6 reviews the choices of server-side scripting that you can make to support Flash. We touch on a few popular server-side scripting languages, introduce Flash Remoting, and discuss the new objects available for use with Flash Remoting to create exciting and compelling Flash application architecture. It covers, in detail, the various Flash MX objects available for use in exchanging XML data with remote servers. Then we introduce you to the powerful Macromedia Flash Remoting module which opened the floodgates to business logic running on ColdFusion, .NET, and J2EE servers. The new Flash MX objects for the client used to integrate with these remote servers are described in depth. Finally, with ColdFusion MX, we cover server-side ActionScript extensively.

Chapter 7: Using Flash Remoting   Chapter 7 discusses how to use Flash Remoting with these server-side capabilities, and introduces you to the exciting world of Web services. We will look at two examples of building mobile Flash applications with a Flash front-end to the popular BabelFish Translator and Google Search Web Service.

Chapter 8: Using ColdFusion MX for Mobile Flash   With ColdFusion MX, Macromedia has made it easy for a developer to integrate Flash MX with such features as ColdFusion components, ColdFusion server-side Flash MX integration, and ColdFusion built-in internationalization support. Additionally, publishing and consuming Web services can be a snap through the use of ColdFusion MX; something made even easier with Dreamweaver MX. In Chapter 8, we examine the architecture and features of this powerful and easy to use server-side scripting platform from Macromedia. With only a few lines of code, components and Web services can be reused, extended, consumed, or published! ColdFusion components (CFCs) represent the most important feature of this release of ColdFusion MX, and drive the behind-the-scenes generation of client proxies and data marshalling for consuming and publishing Web services. All these are done automatically, thus shielding the complexity from developers, who would rather focus more of their time on building the business logic instead.

Chapter 9: Tackling Mobile Architecture and Platform Issues   Chapter 9 reviews the basic tenet of dealing with mobile architecture, setting the stage for our discussion of multichannel application development. We discuss the conventional methodology of delivering and supporting mobile data services using XML and various markup languages, and compare that to the new paradigm unique to Macromedia Flash MX, which uses a rich client–server metaphor. We'll look at ways to tackle platform issues ranging from retrieval of content from different data sources, to the support of different devices, and disclose an improved, back end–driven way to detect different versions of Flash Player, as well as how to detect and manage user sessions in a mobile environment. We cover the personalization and location-based services for delivering compelling mobile content and user experience.

Chapter 10: Planning and Implementing for Compatibility   Chapter 10 addresses the specific issues of handling single and multiple channels, as well as how to support Flash and non-Flash devices. We will dissect the methodology of single- and multiple-channel application development, and show you a typical framework for multichannel application development that will be used as a basis for our discussion. We then contrast how mobile development can be carried out with XML/XSLT, as well as Macromedia Flash MX.

Chapter 11: Flash Communication Server   Chapter 11 covers application design with Flash Communication Server and presents both the client- and server-side objects available for use with Flash Communication Server. We review rich media messaging, real-time collaboration, and streaming media. We look at client-side communications objects like Camera Object, and server-side objects like NetConnection, as well as the seven Flash Communication Server objects. Rich communication applications can easily be built using these new objects with minimal ActionScript code. It gets even easier with the out-of-the-box communication components! We show you how to create the building blocks for a streaming video or video-on-demand application, in addition to the fundamentals of a live web cam application. We conclude by showing you a couple of core examples (building block code) that can be used to build rich multimedia communication applications leveraging FCS and the Flash MX client.

Part III: Creating Macromedia Flash MX Mobile Applications

Chapter 12: Mobile and Multichannel Ad Promotions   Chapter 12 discusses the design and development of a multichannel mobile application for advertising promotions. We create a back end using a relational database management system (RDBMS) and use XML/XSLT to generate markup pages for HTML browsers for PCs, and micro-browsers for mobile devices. We then create a Flash MX application to support PCs and mobile devices that have Flash Player capability. The mobile promotion (m-Promo) application leverages the device detection capability to decide whether to serve up markup pages or SWF files. We conclude by discussing how you can enhance this application or modify it to build enterprise multichannel mobile solutions.

Chapter 13: MP3 Flash Audio Player   Chapter 13 discusses the design and development of an MP3 Player that does more than just play audio: it enhances the Flash Player found in your mobile device. We show you, in detail, how to create a compelling Flash MX application normally reserved for C++ programmers! We do this by utilizing many new features of the Flash MX Player, the Amazon.com Web service, the FreeDB music database, and the complex Tree Flash UI component. Our MP3 Flash MX application is the result of integrating all these features and client-server technologies. We leverage the information stored within the MP3 binary file and use that to call Amazon.com's Web service to get the album details. Additionally, we connect to a music database like FreeDB to get the song titles on the particular album. We conclude by suggesting many different enhancements that the reader can make to our core Flash MX application. We start from the desktop PC version and create versions for the PocketPC and Nokia Communicator form factors.

Chapter 14: Multimedia Communication, Broadcast, and Surveillance   Chapter 14 discusses the design and development of a multimedia communications and broadcast platform that can provide live and recorded videos to PCs and mobile devices. Based on ColdFusion MX and Flash Communication Server, this platform can be extended to create a surveillance application for home or business use.

Appendix A: Glossary   Appendix A consists of terms and definitions used throughout this book.

Appendix B: ActionScript Quick Reference   Appendix B offers a complete listing of Flash ActionScripts.

Appendix C: Tutorial: Relational Databases and SQL   Appendix C contains a quick tutorial on relational database management system and SQL queries.

Appendix D: Online Resources   Appendix D provides a listing of relevant online resources for mobile Flash application development.

The following summarizes the key points you will learn about in each section:

Part I: Mobile Application Development and Macromedia Flash MX

▶ Review the architecture and challenges for mobile development

▶ Explore the Macromedia Flash MX platform

▶ Introduction to multichannel application development for mobile devices

▶ Apply Flash and server-side skills to database-driven applications

Part II: Building Skills for Multichannel Mobile Applications

▶ Learn the rudiments of mobile Flash design

▶ Learn the basics of form factors, device types, and typography

▶ Learn animation and multimedia techniques unique to Flash

▶ Review the basics of server-side scripting and platforms

▶ Learn to use Flash Remoting for mobile Flash development

▶ Use ColdFusion MX to drive Flash clients

▶ Survey the XML/XSLT framework and multichannel applications

▶ Learn to detect mobile devices and Flash Player

▶ Learn to use Flash Communication Server and its core objects

Part III: Creating Flash MX Mobile Applications

▶ Use XML/XSLT, ColdFusion MX, and Flash MX for support of Flash and non-Flash multichannel applications

▶ Master ActionScript and client-side development to consume web services

▶ Build a solution with multimedia streaming and collaboration features with Flash Communication Server

Mobile Application Development and Macromedia Flash® MX

OBJECTIVES

► Explore the architecture, application platforms, and proxy models for mobile data services

► Understand the challenges and opportunities in building mobile applications

► Learn the basics of Macromedia Flash

► Review Macromedia products and strategies for mobile development

► Create a Flash MX application with a relational database and server-side scripts

Working in the Mobile Environment

IN THIS CHAPTER:

Background and Introduction

The Mobile Architecture

Applications and the Proxy Models

Challenges and Opportunities

Summary

I n this chapter, we discuss what constitutes the Mobile Internet and the environment with which mobile developers and designers must work. Before we dive into the details of wireless proxy servers and markup languages, it is useful to have a basic understanding of how web and wireless servers are connected locally or through the Internet, and how they communicate and work together.

Here, we review how the Internet and the wireless Web became what they are today, and we'll pay particular attention to how they impact web and mobile development. Our aim is to introduce the new paradigm that Macromedia Flash MX brings into mobile computing and communications. If you are already familiar with web and wireless server technologies, you may want to quickly skim through this chapter.

Background and Introduction

Like web sites and web applications, the delivery of mobile applications over the Internet has been defined and confined by its infrastructure. As a result, the end-user experience has become subservient to the "transport" methodology, which has led to the use of the "cards and decks" metaphors and different markup languages for the presentation of mobile applications in different devices. First, let's review different computing models and what the mobile Internet requires.

History and Use of the Internet

The Internet started out as an idea born with the Cold War strategy. The goal was to create a method and a distributed communications network that could accept and communicate defense commands and mission information, even in the event of a nuclear attack. The U.S. Department of Defense (DoD) issued a "Request for Proposal," and so the project, ARPANET, named after the Defense Advanced Research Projects Agency (DARPA), was born.

Several faculty members and students at University of California at Los Angeles (UCLA) presented a proposal for a packet-switching network that was distributed in nature and could be extended. The idea was to break up messages into smaller components called packets. Source and destination information is added to the packets for their transport and routing within the network. Each packet—from several hundred to several thousand bytes in size, depending on the system—is sent onto the network individually from the source to its destination. These packets may take different routes to their destination, but once there, they are reassembled into their originating messages. Because the messages are routed through multiple switches, where they can be stored and forwarded depending on traffic and priority, this approach is known as packet switching.

Back in 1969, ARPANET was essentially four switches or computers, known as Interface Message Processors, one each stationed at UCLA, the Stanford Research Institute, the University of Utah, and UC Santa Barbara. These Interface Message Processors, the predecessors of today's web servers, grew from four in 1969 to 37 nodes in 1972. In 1983, DoD spun off the military portion, and partly owing to the simplicity of TCP/IP, more computers and links were added to the network. As a result, a system of networks was formed, spawning what we now know as the Internet. The original protocol for exchanging information between these disparate "servers" was Network Communications Protocol (NCP). Transmission Control Protocol/Internet Protocol (TCP/IP) later replaced NCP in the early 1980s.

Later, the Mosaic browser project at the University of Illinois began to take hold in the Internet community. Through these networks of computers and the use of browser software, you could view pages that were published on a subset of the Internet (the World Wide Web). This browser later became Netscape Navigator, and the protocol used was HyperText Transport Protocol (HTTP).

These early web browsers supported HyperText Markup Language (HTML) and quickly fueled the growth of the Internet's popularity. HTML was a perfect markup language for the World Wide Web since it was quick to learn and easy to use, making it an ideal publishing tool. Subsequently, HTML became the de facto language, and PC browsers became the medium for retrieving and presenting web documents. Also, this approach popularized the web application metaphor in terms of formatting and presenting HTML pages by simply clicking hyperlinks.

In the 1990s, the Internet quickly grew from a repository of web pages to a slick medium for communications, fulfilling its original mission for networked communications through packets. E-mail messages could be sent and received via mail servers (SMTP and POP3), and web and application servers enabled the deployment of database-driven solutions throughout the Internet.

Later in the decade, e-commerce web sites were added to the HTML sites. Relational database management systems (RDBMS) and application servers drove dynamic web sites, generated in real time based on web requests. During this time, web applications founded on page refresh and page download were accepted and firmly put in place.

Toward the end of the 1990s, the world saw another inflection point—the mobile evolution. With mobile devices, you could communicate anytime, anywhere and get web content through the wireless Internet. Although it has been called the wireless Web, the mobile infrastructure is quite different from the World Wide Web, especially in terms of architecture, user interfaces, and use cases.

Next, let's review and contrast them in the context of client/server computing.

From Client-Server to Internet Computing

The client-server model was initially adopted on other older mainframe and server computer networks. The client-server model depends on the request-fulfill relationship between two pieces of software and hardware platforms: the *client* and the *server*.

In a client-server environment, you can deliver information or application program functionalities between the dedicated client-server pair, as illustrated next.

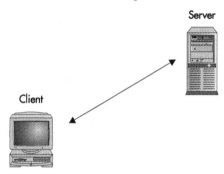

The clients and the applications may sport intuitive user interfaces, purposely built for this use. However, the clients must be defined and may not work with other servers. Additionally, these systems are not readily connected or networked.

The emergence of the Internet allowed web clients within different operating systems and hardware platforms to communicate with any web servers (and clients) as long as HTTP and HTML were supported. This wide area approach brought on the n-tier architecture to modern computing. The era of thin client computing had finally dawned.

For web sites and web applications, the web client is usually a PC-based browser. To receive new information—simply click a web page link. The web client, in the form of a web browser, then makes a HTTP request to the server for the page content. The DNS server, a server to map web and IP addresses, locates the correct web server and relays the request, as shown next. If the page is available, the server will fulfill the request—that is, retrieve the requested file (HTML page) from its file system and return it to the browser. If the request can be fulfilled, the server sends data back to the client. The client can then process, display, and/or store the result.

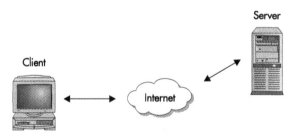

Pervasive or Mobile Computing

The wireless Web is similar to the World Wide Web in that wireless servers and micro-browsers are used to deliver wireless web pages or wireless content to the mobile client devices. Other popular Internet applications, such as e-mail, FTP, and chat, are also supported.

While each of these software types requests information from a server and works with the data returned by the server, the process is slightly different in the mobile world. Mobile devices have inherent constraints in bandwidth and form factors that disallow the use of PC-based browsers. Also, these constraints necessitate new protocols and micro-browsers.

Another noteworthy difference is, of course, the need for signals (packets) to travel across an air interface, either via a wireless LAN or a wireless WAN. These signals must then be converted into protocols suitable for Internet transport or data presentation on the mobile device. Both a proxy and wireless gateway are needed to deliver and receive messages and requests from these mobile devices, as illustrated next.

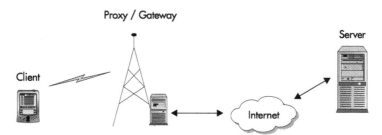

The use of a proxy is needed not just for protocols, but also for content delivery reasons. A vast quantity of information, in the form of web sites, web content, and applications, has been built on HTML. To repurpose this information into a format suitable for mobile devices, many have used different protocols and markups to translate requests and transcode results between the mobile devices and the World Wide Web.

Market Needs and Wants

As mentioned, bandwidth limitations of wireless networks and small form factors for mobile devices are two important issues for mobile application deployment. Wireless coverage, or lack thereof, is another challenge. While the market is beginning to see broadband and always-on wireless services, devices and network technologies with the so-called 2.5 or 3G capabilities still require efficient use of bandwidth, improved usability, and flexible application models to cope with incomplete wireless coverage. Towards this end, building and deploying mobile applications with Macromedia Flash MX may help alleviate some of these shortcomings. We shall revisit these points later in this chapter. For now, let's go over the basics of mobile architecture and see how mobile applications fit into this framework.

The Mobile Architecture

Figure 1-1 shows a typical mobile Internet architecture, which may comprise the following:

▶ **Devices**   A plethora of mobile and wireless devices can be supported, including WAP phones, smart phones, Pocket PCs, Palm PDAs, and telematics.

▶ **Markup languages**   With various devices come many different markup languages, each required to "mark up" or format the pages for presentation on said devices.

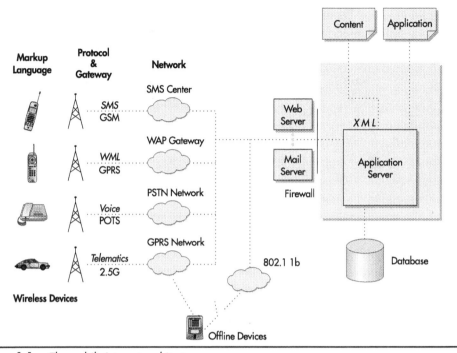

Figure 1-1 *The mobile Internet architecture*

▶ **Protocols** Wireless networking protocols are needed to exchange information (in the form of radio frequency signals, and so on), and to deliver and receive messages and page requests.

▶ **Networks and gateways** Different wireless networks, both WAN and LAN, can be set up to support mobile devices. Besides switching stations and antennae, what matters most to developers are the many gateways and different protocols intended for packet switching and page rendering, including the support for e-mail, short messaging, and voice communications.

▶ **The Internet** Many existing and new communication networks are built on top of the Internet using packet switching. As discussed later, this gives the benefit of always-on and distributed communications.

▶ **Web and application servers** Exposed to the Internet are the servers that act as a bridge between intranets, content, web applications, and data. Enterprise applications and m-commerce sites are just two examples of what could be hosted there.

▶ **Databases** Relational databases can be used for storage of enterprise data, as well as credit card information. In a mobile architecture, you will need the database back end to support sessions, personalization, location-based services (LBS), and mobile commerce.

▶ **Applications and content** E-commerce sites and offline applications are just two of many examples where Web solutions can be deployed to the wireless Web.

E-commerce web sites hosted within the firewall can be enabled to become mobile commerce sites. Offline applications that reside in a Palm PDA or a Pocket PC can be provisioned, with the data synchronized and replicated when a connection is made to the back-end databases.

A typical logic flow for a wireless phone using the Wireless Application Protocol (WAP) may take place as follows:

1. A request for a Wireless Markup Language (WML) page is issued by a WAP phone.
2. The request is transported through the air interface into the WAP gateway.
3. The request is translated into the requisite markup/protocol for the Internet (binary encoding and decoding between gateway and server).
4. The request is then relayed to the web server in accordance with the URL the gateway has resolved.
5. The application server, upon receiving the request through the web server, is now running the web application by retrieving and executing the server side page.
6. The data store, in the form of a RDBMS, will provide dynamic data, and the page is constructed in the right format.
7. Through the Internet, a markup page is then delivered to the gateway, which in turn relays back to the device, using the same protocol and markup as before.

Bear in mind that besides wireless online services, other applications, such as push, offline and mobile Personal Information Management (PIM), may be feasible and could have a different logic flow. They may entail different devices and traverse different networks using various protocols and markup languages. Let's examine these components within the wireless network in more detail.

Devices and Operating Systems

Depending on the network, mobile devices must communicate with the access point of a wireless local area network (LAN) or a wireless WAN through a cellular network. The small footprint, limited size, and computing capabilities can impose severe requirements on how different devices can access information and request services.

Device Browsers and OSs

For the purpose of this book, we shall limit our discussions on small handheld devices that are mobile and (typically) wirelessly connected.

These devices include Pocket PCs with a WinCE operating system and a Mobile Internet Explorer, as well as Palm PDAs with their new Palm OS 5.0 and its own micro-browser. Also included are WAP phones that are enabled to connect to the wireless Web through the so-called Wireless Application Protocol (WAP) and its gateway. These devices use a WAP browser that supports WML. We will also look at smart phones, which are essentially larger, more capable combo phones with PDA and WAP browsers.

Other devices, such as the Blackberry e-mail devices from Research In Motion Limited, as well as regular mobile phones, with its voice interface, can be treated as mobile devices in this context.

Device Constraints

Mobile devices are limited by a number of constraints, including

- ▶ **Battery**   Battery power is a limiting factor for mobile devices, something which has obvious effects on their capacity to process and manage applications. From Palm PDAs to Pocket PCs, you can easily run out of battery power within hours or days if your applications are processor- or memory-intensive.

- ▶ **Memory**   Memory is limited, even in the newer devices. Although many mobile devices have much larger program and RAM memories (32kB of program memory and 8MB RAM), they can't hold a candle to a desktop PC.

- ▶ **Computing power**   The mobile phones of yesteryear used 8-bit microcontrollers with very little memory, perhaps 6kB of RAM. Now, mobile phones and devices may contain 16-, 32-, even 64-bit RISC controllers, if not higher. Even then, the latest Pocket PCs and Palm PDAs, using ARM and other microprocessors, are still clocked at about 200–400 MIPS, making them vastly different from desktop computers.

- ▶ **Form factor**   The size of various devices constitutes different screen sizes, colors, and resolutions in each case. Building mobile applications must take into account the usability issues inherent in these cases.

- ▶ **User interface**   Not only do mobile devices today have limitations in form factors, they are directly impacted by the user interface, or lack thereof, in many devices. You don't have (or want to have) a keyboard, and you may not even want to look at the screen (for example, while you are driving).

Networks and Wireless Services

To build mobile applications and good content, you need to understand the wireless marketplace. While the transport of many mobile applications take advantage of TCP/IP on the wireline side, the wireless segment must travel through the air interface and is subject to the constraints of bandwidth, latency, and coverage.

Because many of today's wireless data communications are coupled with voice services, the development of wireless data services often is subject to the restrictions imposed by the deployment of voice networks. Several technologies look to be the mainstay—for example, cellular radio, as well as air interface technologies, like CDMA. Let's look at how the network works and what the constraints are.

Cellular Radio

Cellular got its name from the physical layout of a wireless Wide Area Network where a pattern of networking resembles a honeycomb, figuratively. Rather than using a single high-power base station to cover a larger area, many smaller stations are distributed across the same area, as shown in Figure 1-2. A vehicle can travel from point A to point B, and the mobile device within this vehicle can communicate through various cellsites. As the vehicle

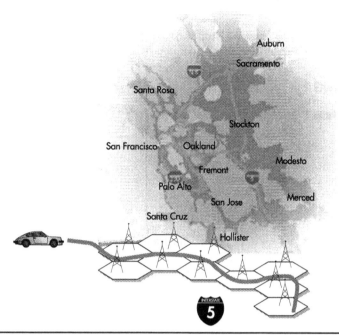

Figure 1-2   *Cellular concepts*

moves toward position B, the wireless communication link is handed off from one cellsite to another. Each cellsite operates on a different frequency to avoid interference between neighboring cellsites. If the cellsites are separated by sufficient distances, however, the frequencies can be reused.

For cellular communications to work, the wireless devices must constantly communicate with the base stations, which are stationary stations whose duties include coordinating all subscriber devices within its cellsite. The base stations also coordinate with a mobile switching center (MSC), which manages activities between base stations as shown next.

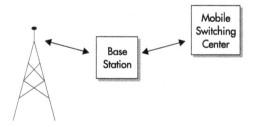

When you make a request for service, this data is relayed to the MSC, and then the gateway using the appropriate web protocols. For wireless access via WAP, the protocols of the bearer network are obviously quite different from those used by the Internet.

Air Interface Technology and the Gs

Perhaps you have heard of 2G, 2.5G, and 3G. Perhaps even 4G. A 2G network generally refers to the wireless infrastructure where second generation digital phone services are supported. This 2G technology is digital and packet switched, and it replaced the analog system that was dubbed 1G. 2G systems can be based on a variety of air interface technologies such as CDMA, TDMA, and GSM. A key issue for 2G data services is that they are not always on. Instead, using WAP for the protocol, users must dial up and suffer a 30–45 second lead time before being connected.

Several air interface technologies exist today for the digital, packet-switched networks, including CDMA, TDMA, GSM, and so on. Rather than going into detail regarding their capabilities and constraints, let's just say the CDMA technology represents the next generation of air interface communications—on which 3G is based.

Protocols and Markup Languages

Protocols and markups are requirements for the transport and presentation of web pages. While wireless protocols may be different from wireline, the legacy of page requests and page rendering was brought to the wireless Web through new standards. Let's look at them.

Protocols

What are protocols? According to the Open Standards Interconnection model from the International Standards Organization (the ISO-OSI model), the networking infrastructure is separated into layers to facilitate development and enhance security. Discrete functions are performed in each layer, and specific protocols have been written to accomplish these functions. The goal is to keep each layer as independent as possible from other layers and to hide the complexities of each layer from other layers as well.

Protocol suites are often referred to as stacks because the layers are stacked on top of each other. Besides speeding protocol development, this simplifies updates and changes because modifications to one layer do not affect the whole stack. Prior to the use of layered protocols, simple changes, such as adding one terminal type to the list of those supported by a non-layered architecture, often required changes to all of the software in the protocol stack.

A *transfer protocol* is a method by which data is sent from one computer to another. Many transfer protocols rely on TCP/IP—a combination of computer identification, data division, and data reorganization. The most common transfer protocols send files (or file requests) from one computer to another. Common transfer protocols include HyperText Transfer Protocol (HTTP) for Web pages, Simple Mail Transfer Protocol (SMTP) for e-mail, and File Transfer Protocol (FTP) for binary and other files.

For wireless applications, WAP is certainly the de facto standard. However, TCP/IP via compact HTML (cHTML) is also popular, especially after the success NTT DoCoMo had with its i-mode wireless data service in Japan.

Markup Languages

As mentioned earlier, markup languages are used to present or publish web content by "marking up" the page using tags. The de facto standard, HTML, was loosely derived from Standardized General Markup Language (SGML), a standard developed by the ANSI in the

1970s and adopted by ISO in 1986. While SGML offers a detailed system for marking up documents and controls the appearance of web documents, HTML was not sufficient for advanced page design and multimedia presentation. Separately, diverging development between Microsoft and Netscape on PC browsers, such as Cascading Style Sheet (CSS) and other extensions, led to new additions and incompatibility in HTML browsing. These also contributed to the fact that HTML is not suitable for the presentation and formatting of wireless web sites and applications.

Wireless Application Protocol

In the 1990s, a new approach was proposed, Wireless Application Protocol (WAP), for mobile development and deployment. WAP is based on XML and uses a gateway between the mobile network and the fixed network to alleviate the problem of slow connections and long latencies as shown next. Unlike TCP/IP, WAP is optimized for wireless networks, and has a tighter integration with the security protocols than is normal on the Internet.

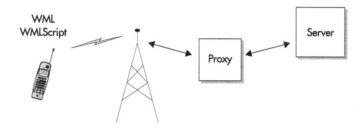

WAP is functional over many networks, including broadcast and paging networks. One problem that WAP addresses is coverage. By removing the acknowledgments protocol inherent in wireless technologies and treating data as messages, WAP has resolved issues related to the connection/disconnection problem.

To solve the latency problems for the Internet side, the WAP gateway acts as a router and proxy, and translates from one protocol to another.

Despite some of the advantages of WAP, it was not an instant success because it required the rewrite of sites, and phones were not generally available. Also, in WAP 1.0 and 1.1, the user interface had been sub par.

Another problem is that there are varying implementations of WAP proxies, some of which follow the HTTP 1.1 standard, and some of which do not. The standard is also unclear on exactly how the system should be implemented. This inconsistent adherence to the WAP standard was found not only between manufacturers but also between models of the same manufacturer, something which could prove problematic to network administrators.

Compact HTML and i-mode

Another markup language for mobile devices (and browsers) is compact HTML (cHTML). Made popular by NTTDoCoMo's i-mode service and adopted by Pocket PCs, cHTML is based on a subset of HTML 2.0, 3.2, and 4.0 with i-mode-specific extensions. These extensions include tags that have special meanings on a phone, such as the *tel:* tag, which is used to hyperlink a telephone number. By clicking the link, users can place a call to the number.

cHTML is based on HTML 3.2, which can be problematic because several attributes used in i-mode browsers were deprecated in HTML 4. Authoring for i-mode, in other words, is the same as authoring in a version different from that used on the Web. As with WML, objects are displayed sequentially from top to bottom. Until CSS is available, there is no way to control positioning in WAP/WML or Pocket PC/WinCE.

XHTML

Because HTML is not easily extensible, a new approach was proposed by the World Wide Web Consortium (W3C) in 1996 to create XML, a simplified version of SGML. Inherited from SGML was a means to allow text editing, page formatting, and data retrieval. Most importantly, XML introduced the concept of formally defining a document type using an explicit nested element structure.

In 1998, the W3C published a draft document entitled "XHTML 1.0" in an attempt to merge HTML 4.0 and XML. XHTML is a family of current and future document types and modules that reproduce, subset, and extend HTML 4. By defining these modules and specifying a mechanism to combine them, a wide range of new devices and applications can be supported. For example, Openwave's Universal Browser (version 5.1) supports both WML and XHTML, and it is anticipated that many future micro-browsers will support the combination of XHTML Basic (W3C), XHTML Mobile (Openwave), and any XHTML flavors.

Servers and Databases

The keystone of the n-tier Internet architecture, web, and application servers acts as the middleware between the plethora of client devices and the data layer, where content and data reside in databases. There are a number of approaches involving servers—integrated or point—that can leverage relational databases to drive personalization, login and session management, Web services, and transcoding.

Web and Application Servers

Web servers receive web requests and deliver files to a web client, whereas web application servers, or simply application servers, process requests and generate those files. Some examples of web servers include Microsoft IIS and the Apache Web Server. By contrast, application servers take on a great deal of processing tasks, including connection to e-mail servers or databases, and the generation of dynamic content in real time (and during run time).

For mobile application development, web and application servers are particularly important as they serve a number of functions, including

- ▶ Device detection
- ▶ Load balancing
- ▶ Caching
- ▶ Database access
- ▶ Data processing

Popular application servers include Apache Tomcat, PHP, ColdFusion, Microsoft IIS (ASP), J2EE (Java/JSP), and so forth. We shall examine the server side in Chapter 6.

Databases

A database server is another frequently-shared resource on a wireless network. Along with application servers, database servers allow developers to create web sites and dynamic content designed to be modified or changed over time. For web applications or news web sites, databases are frequently utilized to facilitate content management.

In the mobile arena, the database is even more critical as it enables session management, personalization, location-based services, and mobile wallets. Similar to wireline applications, a wireless server can send for or update changes to databases and leverage resources across the entire IT infrastructure.

Content and Applications

Finally, a request by a mobile device may involve a request for specific content or application functionality, such as to retrieve a news story, to log in to retrieve critical data, or to download a ring tone. The content may entail a flat file, an XML file, or an HTML page. In the next section, we will examine the differences between static and dynamic applications, as well as always-on, disconnected, sporadically connected, and native applications. Suffice it to say, the data may reside in the database, and the mobile applications in the file system where server pages are stored.

Applications and the Proxy Models

In this section, we take a look at the application and proxy modes where mobile content and applications are supported. For the purpose of this book, we will consider HTML pages not driven by a database and dynamically built by an application server as static content. Any changes on these pages require updating the HTML file in order for it to take effect. These static pages are acceptable for content that doesn't change often, if at all, but they would be nearly unmanageable for a wireless network.

Dynamic applications may include content, commerce, community, and communications. These applications may be driven by databases and are dynamic in context and functionality! In other words, static content includes files from the local file system, whereas dynamic content is created by processing via application servers or by way of dynamic retrieval of data from a database. Now, let's look at various applications and proxy models.

Native, Disconnected, and Online Applications

As shown in Figure 1-3, the traditional software applications, or native applications, may run on a thick or fat client. The OS and the application itself can together deliver the user interface, the application logic, and the processing power to be self-contained. The interactivity, especially regarding the user interface, can be rather compelling. The downside, however, is that these

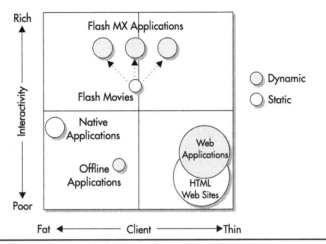

Figure 1-3 *Client-server, rich application models*

applications require a variety of skills to develop and maintain. Even worse, their reusability and scalability are questionable.

On the other hand, the Internet ushers in the era of thin client computing. Depending on whether it entails the original, simple HTML pages or the database-driven applications, the engine that drives the service is a thin client, coupled with an application server and a relational database. Interactions are based on page requests—in other words, almost all interactions are based on clicking a link and requesting a page. User interactivity is relatively low, although animated gifs and applets have made this livelier than ever.

In the era of mobile computing, a new breed is called offline applications. Here, the applications tend to run within a mobile device, which could be a laptop PC or a PDA. When connected to a server or a database, the application may cause the data to be synchronized with the backend and perhaps the master database. Many people call these smart clients since they are neither fat nor thin, and relatively smart!

Finally, Flash movies would fit into all of the preceding models under high interactivity, but would have a relatively broad range of clients, from thin clients to those that are smart and "fat." Although to be fair, it is a plug-in combination with the browser. In the past, most Flash movies were typically not database driven. Now, with Macromedia Flash MX, you can build rich media applications that can leverage a smarter client, yet be backed by a scalable backend server!

The WAP Proxy

For the wireless applications, often called online or always-on applications, there are a number of connection modes using proxy servers that serve a variety of functions for others.

In a typical connection—for example, a dialup or wireless dialup from a laptop to a HTTP gateway—you can envision that no proxy exists between the client and the web server, as shown next. We typically call this the *direct connection* model.

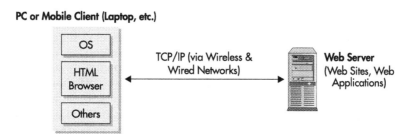

The *proxy connection* model, on the other hand, involves an intermediary, called a proxy server. This proxy server may translate protocols, as well as aggregate content from data sources that support a different protocol as shown next.

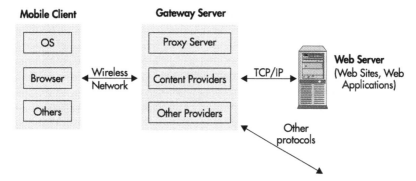

The WAP Programming Model uses this proxy connection model, and consists of a WAP gateway and a Wireless Application Environment (WAE) User Agent. Data flows from the device to the gateway in encoded requests. A WAP gateway translates between the WAP and Internet protocols, and caches information that may be requestd by the client device.

These WAP applications are written in WML and can reside on the WAP gateway or on an application server. WAP also includes WMLScript and Wireless Telephone Application Interface (WTAI) for client support, and additionally may consist of WML encoder, WMLScript encoder, and WAP adaptor for the WAP proxy, as shown next.

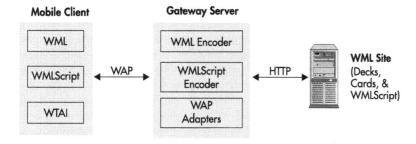

WMLScript, like JavaScript and ActionScript, provides a simple yet fully functional way to offer client-side logic processing. WTAI, meanwhile, acts as an interface to the telephone functions of the device.

While the functionality and steps of the processing are the same for WML and HTML, they have a distinct difference. WAP splits the client processing between the WAP gateway and the client device. The WAP proxy contains an XML processor and can offload the processing between the client and the gateway.

A WML gateway will typically run through a number of steps in a batch mode and cache the content. The request may be sent over the Internet to a server, whose URL has been resolved by the WAP proxy. The response, in the form of web content, is returned to the gateway where it is encoded and forwarded to the User Agent in the device.

Then, the character data is decoded at the gateway into a stream of 16-bit Unicode characters. Afterward, the documents are then parsed using an XML parser and validated against a schema. The resulting data is then formatted and bytecodes are substituted for the WML tags. This translation produces a hierarchy of formatting objects, which are then delivered to the WAP device for page presentation.

The Palm Proxy

Having reviewed WAP, we now turn our attention to the Palm platform and review how it uses a proxy server to deliver wireless content and services. This will become interesting when we contrast this model with the way mobile Flash applications are being deployed and delivered.

Native Palm Applications

To achieve the goals of low bandwidth overhead, reduced battery drawdown, and lower service cost, Palm Computing took a different approach to accessing information on the World Wide Web. The "browsing" metaphor doesn't use the page request and retrieval metaphor typical for an HTML page. Instead, in a manner analogous to clipping an article out of a newspaper, it splits the accessing and processing of content between a proxy and the Palm device, as illustrated next.

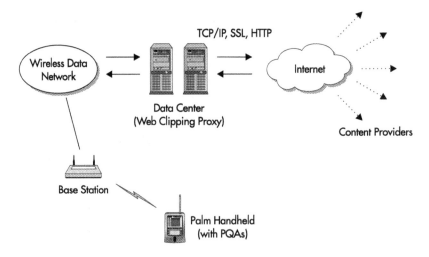

Palm Web Clipping Applications

The concept of "web clipping" is based on minimizing data that is transferred through a wireless network. To accomplish this, Palm Computing conceived two design principles:

1. User interaction is based on simple queries and responses rather than hyperlinks and full page rendering.

2. Support of application partitioning where the query portion is stored locally on the handheld and content should be cached, aggregated, and transcoded at the Palm proxy server.

Because the query portion of the application is stored locally, the user has a richer and more uniform interface to request information from by filling out a form. Once the user submits a query, the resultant page or web clipping is very small. This approach can be used to build rich, interactive applications that are less network-dependent and can display more graphics than typical WAP applications.

Like Flash, web clipping is supported through an add-on (or plug-in) feature over the Palm device. One drawback is that Palm.net users can only access sites stipulated as readable via a Palm Query Application (PQA), and they must download individual PQAs for these applications to work.

Why Is This Significant for Flash?

As you will see later, mobile Macromedia Flash MX applications can take advantage of this concept popularized by Palm, and yet avoid the issues of PQAs and concerns related to protocols and markups in WAP. For example, mobile Macromedia Flash MX applications can deliver the data without going back and forth to the server to call up a new page every time new data are requested.

Because Flash can potentially fit into a thin client, smart client, and even thick client architecture, mobile applications built with Macromedia Flash MX can be very flexible and can deliver the solutions to fit distinct needs and application requirements. Macromedia Flash MX can include functionality from many servers, thus allowing efficient dynamic applications to be delivered over the narrow bandwidth wireless networks.

The Multiclient, Multiserver Model

While various markups and protocols support different devices, there is an increasing number of situations where you must support multiple devices and protocols going through various gateways. The approach is a multiclient, multiserver model where different gateways are connected via different markups and protocols through multiple servers, as shown next.

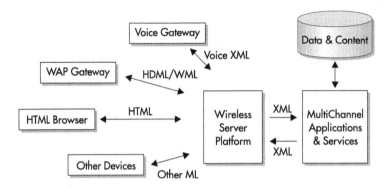

Using a wireless server platform with multiple servers, you can support document presentation and applications via different markup languages. Through XML, your wireless application platform can manage and execute applications and services that are database driven.

By using a multiclient, multiserver model, you can create multichannel applications that can be accessed through different communication channels, markups, and protocols. One advantage of this approach is that you can leverage the integration environment to support the channels and modals you need. The back-end data and application layer are separated from the presentation layer.

Multichannel and Multimodal

Besides different devices (with different markups), you can create applications that can be accessed through different communication channels—for example, Web, wireless, and push. You can also create multimodal applications where you can switch modals or modes during a session—for instance, from text to voice, and back to text. This allows flexibility and versatility to end users, who may want to use voice command while driving.

How do people do application development in this kind of environment? There are a few options:

1. They don't build multichannel. Just single channel.
2. They build two channels and then add more, one at a time.
3. They build and manage multichannel and serve up different markup pages in real time, depending on the properties of the requesting device.
4. They do multiple channels at deployment time.

With Options 1 and 2, each channel is deployed separately and has a unique URL. But this is a maintenance nightmare as you have multiple sources to keep track of. With Options 3 and 4, the goal is to maintain only one source and generate the various channels based on this single source.

XML and XSLT

How do you build multichannel and multimodal applications? By using XML/XSLT! This is because it's mostly a server-based paradigm. In addition to multichannel, because all the servers are driven by the same data structure and managed by the same integrated platforms, you can switch modals, such as from voice to data (WAP, for example) and still access your content or application in the same session with the same server instance.

To expand on the XML content, you basically need the XML to provide a transformation into a suitable markup page or format to present to the requesting device.

What Is XML?

XML stands for "Extensible Markup Language" and is used to exchange structured data over the Internet. XML is also a markup language for documents containing structured information, which holds both content and some indication of what role that content plays. For example, the following is XML data from the public Amazon's XML interface for developers that returns structured data about top-selling products at Amazon.com, such as product name, manufacturer, and other attributes based on keyword search terms:

```xml
<?xml version="1.0" encoding="ISO-8859-1" ?>
<catalog>
    <keyword>oracle9i mobile</keyword>
    <product_group>Books</product_group>
    <product>
    <ranking>1</ranking>
    <title>
        Oracle9i Mobile (Osborne ORACLE Press Series)
    </title>
    <asin>007222455X</asin>
    <author>
        Alan Yeung, Phil Stephenson, Nicholas Pang
    </author>
    <image>
        http://images.amazon.com/images/P/007222455X.01.MZZZZZZZ.jpg
    </image>
    <small_image>
        http://images.amazon.com/images/P/007222455X.01.TZZZZZZZ.jpg
    </small_image>
    <our_price>$34.99</our_price>
    <list_price>$49.99</list_price>
    <release_date>20020628</release_date>
    <binding>Paperback</binding>
    <availability />
    <tagged_url>
        http://www.amazon.com:80/exec/obidos/redirect?tag=2launch-20
        &amp;creative=9441&amp;camp=1793&amp;link_code=xml&amp;
```

```
        path=ASIN/007222455X
    </tagged_url>
    </product>
</catalog>
```

In our example, the content in a *title* (`<title>`...`</title>`) has a different meaning from content in a *list price* (`<list_price>`...`</list_price>`).

Why use XML? XML was created so that richly structured documents could be used over the Web. The XML by itself does not tell a device how to render and present that content to an end user. This is where XSL comes in as described in the next section. By decoupling the content and data from the presentation, the amount of data that needs to be exchanged between remote systems is minimized.

What Is XSL/XSLT?

XSL stands for "Extensible Stylesheet Language" and is a language for expressing stylesheets. Developers can use an XSL stylesheet to express their intentions about how the structured content should be presented. The source content could be transformed into a presentation medium like a PC web browser or a mobile device micro-browser.

XSLT is the language for transforming XML documents into another XML document or another type of document recognized by browsers like WML, XHTML, cHTML, and so on. By applying many different XSLT stylesheets, you can transform a *single* XML document to produce many different markups, as shown next. The transformation would require an XML parser and an XSL engine to complete. This could either be done on your client browser if you have Microsoft Internet Explorer (5.0 or higher) or Netscape Navigator (6.0 or higher), or on the server with an XML parser and an application server like ColdFusion MX.

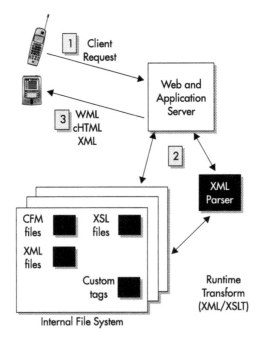

As most mobile devices have slow processors, small memory, and low battery life, we want to minimize the amount of processing required to display the content. Offloading the transformation and processing to the application server is desired. Additionally, different XSLT stylesheets could be applied dynamically to the XML document to serve up the appropriate markup documents automatically. More about this approach used for multichannel design in Chapter 10.

To complete our example, here's the XSLT used to transform our XML document into XHTML:

```
<?xml version="1.0" ?>
<xsl:stylesheet
    xmlns:xsl="http://www.w3.org/1999/XSL/Transform"
    version="1.0">
    <xsl:output method="xml" omit-xml-declaration="yes" indent="yes"/>
    <xsl:template match="/">
    <HTML>
        <BODY>
        <xsl:apply-templates  />
        </BODY>
    </HTML>
    </xsl:template>
    <xsl:template match="catalog">
    <b>
    <xsl:value-of select="product/title" />
    </b>
    <br />
    <img>
        <xsl:attribute name="src">
           <xsl:value-of select="product/small_image" />
        </xsl:attribute>
        <xsl:attribute name="border">0</xsl:attribute>
        <xsl:attribute name="vspace">5</xsl:attribute>
        <xsl:attribute name="hspace">5</xsl:attribute>
        <xsl:attribute name="align">left</xsl:attribute>
    </img>
    <br />
    Author: <xsl:value-of select="product/author" />
    <br />
    ISBN: <xsl:value-of select="product/asin" />
    <br />
    List Price: <xsl:value-of select="product/list_price" />
    <br />
    Our Price: <xsl:value-of select="product/our_price" />
```

```
    <br />
    </xsl:template
</xsl:stylesheet>
```

The resulting XHTML looks like:

```
<HTML>
    <BODY>
        <b>Oracle9i Mobile (Osborne ORACLE Press Series)</b>
        <br />
        <img
src="http://images.amazon.com/images/P/007222455X.01.TZZZZZZZ.jpg"
        border="0" vspace="5" hspace="5" align="left" />
        <br />
        Author: Alan Yeung, Phil Stephenson, Nicholas Pang
        <br />
        ISBN: 007222455X
        <br />
        List Price: $49.99
        <br />
        Our Price: $34.99
        <br />
    </BODY>
</HTML>
```

When viewed on an XHTML browser like the Openwave 5.0 Universal Browser, it resembles the following illustration:

Why are we showing you all this? Because even with markup languages like XHTML on a WAP phone, the presentation is still not rich enough or appealing. How does this apply to Macromedia Flash? Prior to Macromedia Flash MX, Macromedia Flash 5 introduced the XML and XMLSocket objects for loading XML data from remote servers into the Flash client and used ActionScript to parse the XML tree. With Macromedia Flash MX, there is enhanced XML support—a 2000 percent performance gain! And with Flash Remoting (see Chapters 6 and 7), the Macromedia Flash MX client can integrate with any application server and transport protocols (HTTP/HTTPS). More about Macromedia Flash MX is in the next section. A preview of what our example looks like in a Flash player running on a mobile device like the Nokia Communicator is shown next.

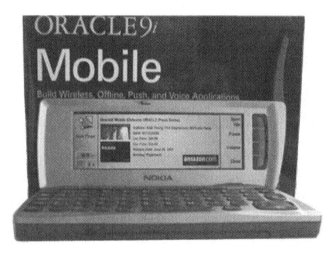

We barely touched on XML and XSLT here. Full details about XML and XSLT can be found on the W3C web site at the following addresses:

- ▶ http://www.w3.org/TR/REC-xml
- ▶ http://www.w3.org/TR/xsl
- ▶ http://www.w3.org/TR/xslt

Challenges and Opportunities

Within the next few years, mobile devices will take over from PCs as the leading client for connection to the Internet. The opportunities are boundless in terms of user scenarios and benefits. Unfortunately, there are also a number of challenges for developers and designers. Let's examine them here.

Any information presented across the Internet to or from wireless devices will be limited by network bandwidth and the display (interface) capabilities of the device. To that end, the bandwidth is limited by both the size and use of the spectrum.

The Mobile Challenges: Cost and Complexity

The mobile Internet is changing quickly. New devices are being rolled out rapidly, and network infrastructure is still very diverse with a remarkable lack of standards. Mobile developers, in fact, have to deal with user interfaces on many handheld devices that are sub par and in need of better usability. Many wireless middleware platforms are still evolving, and issues related to network coverage, bandwidth limitations, and latency further compound the landscape. As a result, building mobile applications has become quite costly and complex. Let's look more closely at the challenges.

Latency

Latency is defined as the amount of time it takes a packet to travel from a client device to its destination (server) and return back to the client device. The more hops a packet has to take (the greater the distance), and the more operations the routers, proxies, and gateway servers have to perform (translation overhead), the greater is the latency.

Besides traffic congestion and translation overhead, other reasons for latency include the extra overhead introduced to a packet when headers are generated to build the packet for its destination. For security concerns, packets are encrypted and decrypted over the course of their transport. This often takes time when packets are transported over many disparate wireless and wireline networks.

NOTE

Two data networks can have similar data speeds but very different latency characteristics.

Bandwidth Performance

Similar to latency, bandwidth performance is related to the data and the network on which it travels. Besides the Internet, the wireless network can experience bottlenecks or network outages. Similarly, headers added to each packet not only increase latency, they also reduce the amount of user data sent as these headers reduce the effective bandwidth.

Coverage

For many enterprises and consumer-facing web sites, one significant hindrance to rolling out true wireless solutions is that coverage is still highly uneven and dispersed. Although you may hear of a purported 90+ percent wireless coverage of the U.S. population, this could mean only a few percent of the entire U.S. land mass and the top 300 or 400 markets. You may find quite a few outages outside larger cities, except for perhaps the most heavily trafficked roadways.

This is one of the reasons why hybrid solutions that work in and out of wireless coverage are becoming popular in many vertical and enterprise applications. We shall cover that further in this book.

NOTE

Having signals for voice coverage doesn't necessarily suggest wireless data coverage is available.

Software

Software platforms for mobile application development still cost too much. Adding to that high price tag is the fact that many of these wireless server platforms are still difficult to build and manage. Companies have invested a lot of money in infrastructure, and they want solutions that will work with the existing infrastructure.

One of the desired ends is a wireless software platform that is standards based. Also, since many web applications are built by scripting level developers, it would be ideal if the wireless software platform can leverage existing skill sets of its developers. Ideally, it would be valuable to have software platforms that can hide or eliminate some of the complexities mentioned previously. This way, developers can concentrate on what they know best: building application logic and implementing solutions.

Opportunities for Mobile Flash

The traditional way of using wireless markup languages and new design style guides has resulted in poor user interface and disappointing user experience. Mobile applications suffer from poor user experience and a mismatch in content format and markup format. These problems are amplified for the mobile application environment when compared to web applications. As a result, many developers are searching for effective means to resolve these issues.

As mentioned earlier, the experience of web applications has been strongly influenced by the frailties of the formats currently in place. With Macromedia Flash MX, you no longer have to build mobile applications that refresh full pages, and which can be dull because they lack graphics and rich media. Yet your rich mobile application will not waste bandwidth by going back and forth needlessly between the client, the proxy, and the server.

Macromedia Flash enables you to build, deploy and run rich dynamic content on wireless devices worldwide:

▶ **Vector graphics rendering engine**   Unlike bitmapped interfaces that must send data for each pixel in a screen, vector-based interfaces need only send the mathematical description of the interface. The result is much smaller files and faster transmission. Another benefit is that vector graphics scale much more easily to a variety of different form-factor mobile devices.

▶ **Compiled and compressed SWF files**   Macromedia Flash runtime code (SWF files) combines code, media, and data into a compact, compiled file format that can be easily delivered.

▶ **Multilingual support**   Having 11 languages allows Flash content to be viewed globally. Flash MX supports Vertical Text and Unicode Standards. New languages supported include Korean, and Traditional and Simplified Chinese.

▶ **No page refresh**   Information exchanged between Flash Player and the application server does not require a page refresh, providing a smooth application experience.

▶ **Framework for ColdFusion, J2EE, and .NET integration**   Integration with ColdFusion, J2EE, and .NET servers through a new, optimized data exchange protocol and application server gateway.

▶ **Application components**   Robust set of UI components enable developers to create advanced Internet applications quickly.

▶ **Flash Communication Server**   A new Flash audio and video server with Real Time Messaging Protocol (RTMP) ushers in a new generation of communication applications for the Internet.

▶ **Persistent state and data**   SharedObjects can be used to store complex object data across or within sessions. SharedObjects also improve application performance by reducing the number of requests made to servers, and the amount of data needed to transmit before a user can begin working. Finally, they enable offline applications that can synchronize data with servers whenever a user is online.

Moreover, by not forcing browsers to redraw an entire page just to present one new bit of information, Flash-centric pages save bandwidth and associated costs.

Solutions built to Macromedia Flash MX support existing 2G network standards and scale into next generation 2.5G and 3G networks. The Macromedia Flash MX applications run on many networks, including CDMA, GSM, TDMA, PDC, and on many devices with Flash Player.

Macromedia Flash MX Application Model

Flash technology can drive the delivery of rich applications to mobile devices, and these applications can be developed and deployed across multiple platforms with much less effort. This maximizes the use of existing content assets while delivering considerable cost savings versus native development.

Instead of a "page request and fulfillment process," typical for HTML, Flash allows the additional flexibility of "data or object request and fulfillment" so file size and transfer can be efficiently handled.

The Macromedia Flash MX application model can be offline-only, online-only, or a hybrid online-offline! Depending on your needs and bandwidth and other constraints, you can tailor the solution to meet the needs. With an offline-only model, the Macromedia Flash MX application runs locally on the mobile device once the SWF/EXE/HTML files are deployed there. There are no other dependencies and the application is self-contained. The application may contain buttons that link to URLs externally via a browser window, if supported by the mobile device.

With an online-only model, the Macromedia Flash MX application runs locally on the mobile device once the SWF/EXE/HTML files are deployed, but content and data to the Flash client comes from remote servers. The data could be in the form of XML or could be the response of consuming a Web service.

Finally, with a hybrid online-offline model, the Macromedia Flash MX application runs locally on the mobile device once the SWF/EXE/HTML files are deployed. The application would normally work with a real-time online connection, but if the connection were lost, it would also work offline with the help of Macromedia Flash MX SharedObjects for storing complex data. When connectivity is eventually re-established, the persistent data could be synchronized back to the remote servers.

Throughout this book, we will discuss the design and development aspects of application development methodology. We will examine the server side components that make Macromedia Flash MX even more exciting when applied to the mobile arena!

Summary

In this chapter, we delineated the framework for which web sites and web applications are built and supported. That, in turn, was incorporated into the world of mobile computing. We made a case for building mobile applications with Macromedia Flash, and proposed that Macromedia Flash is more compelling for that purpose than normal web applications. In Chapter 2, we will show you in detail why that is the case, and why we believe this stands a greater chance of success (for Macromedia Flash to become very successful), as opposed to regular web applications.

Macromedia Flash MX for Mobile Devices

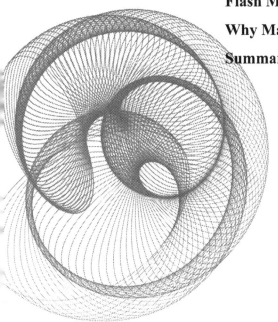

In this chapter, we introduce Macromedia Flash MX—the complete platform for building, deploying, and running rich media applications across multiple channels and devices. We will review the various components of Macromedia Flash MX, including Flash Player, the authoring environment, source and output files, and scripting language. We will also review the server-side support for Macromedia Flash MX—Flash Remoting and ColdFusion MX—and examine the mobile Macromedia Flash MX architecture advocated by Macromedia. Finally, we will discuss Macromedia's overall strategy on linking Macromedia Flash MX with other technologies, and how it may affect your mobile development effort.

What Is Flash?

Macromedia Flash is a platform, a player, a tool, and a standard. It is a platform for building rich, interactive movies and applications for delivery over the Internet. It is a plug-in or ActiveX control software that "plays" animation and rich media on many devices and channels. Also commonly referred to as a high performance runtime for code (SWF file), content, and communication, it is an interface and a tool used by designers and developers to rapidly create web content and applications. And finally, it is a vector-based graphics standard that is widely accepted and implemented for delivering animation and motion graphics. Let us look at how Macromedia Flash came about and why it has become a highly acclaimed platform to build applications on.

The History of Flash

Macromedia Flash has a rather unusual beginning considering that it really started out as a drawing program called Intellidraw—created by Jonathan Gay and his startup company, FutureWave, in the mid-1990s. Written in C++, Intellidraw was an object-oriented framework and leveraged a unique vector graphics technology. Later on, Intellidraw became SmartSketch, a commercially available drawing package. You could use SmartSketch to define the behavior of objects after creating them through graphics design tools. The idea was to build a tool for non-programmers and programmers alike to create animation.

When the World Wide Web gained in popularity, FutureWave soon enhanced the animation capabilities of SmartSketch and built a plug-in software to extend the Netscape browser to play its animation. SmartSketch was renamed FutureSplash Animator, and its plug-in, FutureSplash Player. Next, FutureSplash Player added an ActiveX control for Microsoft's Internet Explorer 3.0, and during the summer of 1996, FutureSplash Animator was used to create a TV-like user experience for MSN.com. Later that year, seeing the unique capability of FutureSplash Animator, its highly compact file format, and the cross-browser support for Netscape and Internet Explorer, Macromedia acquired FutureWave, and FutureSplash Animator was renamed Macromedia Flash 1.0.

With its strength in tools and understanding of web application development, Macromedia gradually built up a loyal following of the Flash platform, adding audio and video support, as well as providing scripting capability. As a result, today Macromedia has become the predominant platform for web animation and rich media applications, having gone through several upgrade cycles to reach Flash Player 6 (MX) and Macromedia Flash MX authoring environment.

Success Factors

To what did Flash owe its success, you may ask. Of course, you will get different answers from many people with different perspectives. Undoubtedly, there were a few key success factors that helped Macromedia Flash become so popular. These include

- ▶ **Timing**   The Internet community was in need of a more efficient graphics and animation format.
- ▶ **Technology**   Macromedia Flash was probably one of the best vector graphics platforms back then, and remains so at the present time.
- ▶ **Execution**   Macromedia did a fantastic job in distributing Flash Player and in making the Flash authoring tool intuitive to use.
- ▶ **Distribution**   Macromedia's remarkable distribution of Flash Player has led to a critical mass of users and developers that are second to none!

Let's look at what vector graphics mean and why Flash was just what the market needed to jazz up the World Wide Web.

Vector Graphics

Earlier on, graphics on the Web derived its lineage from graphic design. Bitmaps were widely used to graphically represent pictures in what's known as "picture elements," or pixels. Each pixel is specified by its color, and because each object of a picture is represented by rows and columns of these pixels, the file size can be quite big, causing your objects to become quite jagged when zoomed in on. Naturally, web graphics (in bitmap, GIF, or JPEG formats) could take a long time to download, and bitmap, especially, also suffered from having an aliased effect, in addition to having a highly bulky format for downloads.

This was when vector graphics burst into the Internet scene. Otherwise known as "outline art," you can simply draw the outline of an object or a shape, assign it with a fill of a certain color, and mathematically, your software would generate the object as a solid item. Your object is now represented as equations that describe its position, line, shape, thickness, size, color, and other parameters. Since blank space is ignored, the resulting vector-based drawings can be very compact, thus allowing fast downloads and efficient presentation on screen by browser software.

A simple example can give you some contrast of size and efficiency. We've created two Flash SWF files—the first using a bitmap image, and the second using a vector graphic image. Both animate the letter "A" by moving it from left to right in a loop, as illustrated next. The size of the first (bitmap-based) SWF file is 1706 bytes, whereas the size of the second (vector graphic–based) SWF file is 250 bytes only. Even with such a simple example, you can see that the savings can be significant. With more complicated animations, the savings are additionally striking, especially for mobile!

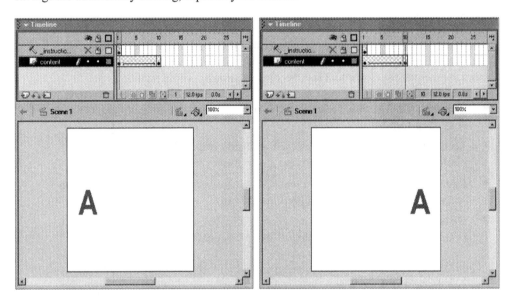

In addition to download efficiency, your animation objects are now scalable with vector graphics. If you expand the graphics, or simply zoom in, the vector-based graphics will show no problems of jagged edges since they are no longer pixel dependent.

The Flash Platform

Many have confused Macromedia's Flash with Director's Shockwave file format. Though they share a branding lineage, both now owned by Macromedia, they are two entirely different technologies. In the broadest sense, Flash is a complete solution. It includes

▶   Macromedia Flash Player
▶   The Macromedia Flash authoring environment
▶   Macromedia Flash source files and delivery formats
▶   The Flash ActionScript scripting language

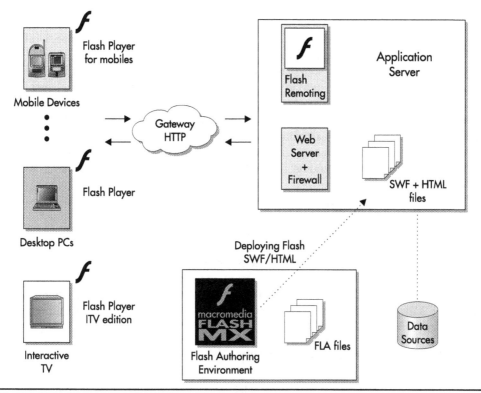

Figure 2-1   *The Macromedia Flash MX platform*

In a nutshell, Macromedia Flash has evolved from an animation tool into a rich media presentation, and is now becoming a rich application platform that leverages its strength of vector graphics and player distribution, as well as its linkage to other server platforms for data-driven applications. Its overall platform is shown in Figure 2-1 above.

Flash Player

As mentioned earlier, Flash Player is a browser plug-in (an ActiveX control in case of MSIE) or a stand-alone Flash movie viewer. From its heyday, Flash Player was designed to both deliver and play graphics and animation through a narrow bandwidth channel over the Internet. In the next few sections, we'll review its features and capabilities.

Small Size

Flash Player is a lightweight plug-in that delivers a lot of punch. From the beginning, it offered rich, streaming multimedia that was browser and operating system (OS) agnostic, coupled with a very manageable download. From Flash 1.0 Player, which weighed in at 80 kB to 150 kB, depending on the platform (PC or Mac), to Flash 6 Player today, which remains no larger than 500 kB, Macromedia has endeavored to keep Flash Player very nimble. What is impressive is that, even in its latest incarnation, Flash Player 6 still allows quick downloads despite all its added-on capabilities, such as video streaming. This is an important asset that helps contribute to its wide distribution. In fact, according to Macromedia, they can support 2.3 million downloads of Flash Player per day, and a new version of Flash Player can achieve 80 percent ubiquity in 12 months.

Cross-Browser and Cross-Platform

Besides its compact size, Flash Player is arguably a more uniform cross-browser interface than HTML itself considering that both Internet Explorer and Netscape Navigator treat it more consistently than other HTML extensions. The add-on for both web browsers comes from Macromedia so there is no ambiguity regarding its implementation, as compared to the messy and diverging extension of the HTML standard offered by Netscape and Microsoft. The same is true across various operating systems (OS) or platforms, such as Windows, Macintosh, Unix, Linux, and so on.

Efficient Use of OS and the Browser Facility

Another key advantage of Macromedia Flash is its rich-client architecture. By tightly controlling the architecture and file format, Macromedia Flash achieves great efficiency in delivering rich content and executing instructions to produce the images, animations, and sound effects, while leveraging the local processing power of the underlying OS and/or browser.

Multimedia

Recent add-ons in Flash Player 6 (MX) include new video support through the adoption of Sorenson Spark technology and client-side capabilities for delivering real-time, peer-to-peer or one-to-many communications. Now, video can be a part of every Flash-enabled web page, just as much as multimedia messaging.

Wide Distribution

While Macromedia was not the first to try to harness the power of vector graphics for web animation, it certainly has been one of the most successful. Part of this success can be attributed to the extensive distribution and availability of Flash Player. As of May, 2002, there were over 430 million users of Flash Player, or approximately 98 percent of all web users worldwide, according to the NPD Online quarterly survey, shown next. In server-side speak, it is the most widely distributed "runtime" in the history of the computer software industry (according to Jeremy Allaire, Macromedia's CTO). Because of this, Flash Player has a strong lead against other popular media players from Apple, Microsoft, and Real Networks.

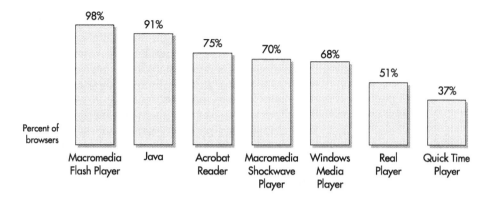

Judging from all the partnership deals as of this writing (see Table 2-1), Flash Player is *everywhere*! Additionally, Flash is the format of choice for Sony's PlayStation, Lucas Arts' Star Wars CD-ROM games, Moxi Digital Entertainment Center, and so on.

Strategic partners in the mobile platform arena include Microsoft (Pocket PC), Symbian, Siemens, and Nokia. For Microsoft, the Pocket PC is destined to become one of the most connected PDAs available. Currently, a version of Flash Player for Pocket PC is distributed to the Hewlett-Packard iPAQ and the Casio Cassiopeia. Pocket PC manufacturers such as Casio have announced their intention to fully support Macromedia Flash Player on future Cassiopeia Pocket PCs and Cassiopeia Windows CE-based devices. Macromedia, meanwhile, is working with Symbian to jointly develop Flash Player for Symbian OS mobile

Partner	Macromedia Flash Player
Microsoft Windows 95, 98, ME, XP (Home and Professional) preinstalled	Default
Apple Mac OS—8.1 and above + hardware, IMac, PB, G3	Default
Microsoft Internet Explorer 5.5, 6.0 (Windows), part of IEAK/OEM	Default
Netscape 6 and Navigator/Communicator	Default
Microsoft Internet Explorer 5.0 (Macintosh)	CD
America Online	Default
RealPlayer	Default
QuickTime	Default
Veon Player	Default
@Home	Default
Web TV/Liberate	Default
NeoPlanet	Default
Prodigy	CD
Corel Linux, Stromix Linux, Mandrake, Caldera Systems	Default

Table 2-1 *Macromedia Flash Player Partners (source: Macromedia)*

phones. Not to be left behind, Sony Ericsson, Nokia, and Psion are already shipping Symbian OS-based devices with Flash support.

Less well-known is the Flash Player included in the Windows CE-based Siemens SIMpad. The SIMpad, a mobile information and communication terminal designed for industrial use, offers an easy-to-use touch screen, virtual keyboard, and Internet browsing at any time without a wired connection. Lastly, Flash Player is available for Nokia 9200 Communicator handsets, including the new Nokia 9210i Communicator and the Nokia 9290 Communicator.

Macromedia Flash may soon be on wireless devices such as 3G Phones. And this isn't just being promoted by Macromedia either. Canon and Hi Corporation in Japan have jointly developed a software engine that allows Macromedia Flash to be displayed on mobile phones. Intended for Java wireless phones, Flash Player is called *K-tai Player* in Japan, and will distribute content as a Java application. The new handset engine works on 2G, 2.5G, and 3G handsets and will play back an animation at up to 15 frames per second. K-tai Players are expected to be made widely available in Japan for NTT DoCoMo, J-Phone, and KDDI Corp., supporting each of their Java requirements.

Given all the excitement of Flash support in various devices, you can expect broad distribution and upgrades of Flash Player across various hardware platforms. The latest version of Flash Player can be downloaded from the Macromedia web site. To evaluate compatibility of your Flash movies and applications, you can still download older versions of Macromedia Flash Player from Macromedia's web site to test out your Flash movies and applications at http://www.macromedia.com/support/flash/ts/documents/oldplayers.htm.

The Flash MX Authoring Environment

The Macromedia Flash MX authoring environment lets you create and publish animation and multimedia files rapidly and easily. Flash's popularity stemmed in part from the fact that it provided what other standards could not: a visual way to design and control the final look of the animation and graphics before publishing them to the Web. Additionally, Flash allows you to load and convert or incorporate a wide range of existing artwork into the Flash experience. For example, Flash's claim to fame was its capability to create (or incorporate) vector-based drawings and buttons, and animate them in accordance with certain behavior that you can easily define and control. Let's review its key features.

Stage and Work Area

Macromedia Flash MX offers a stage where frames of animated graphics are presented (or displayed) by Flash Player, and you create these animations through Flash objects you place inside these frames. The stage can be likened to that in a theater, where actors appear in front of an audience. When a graphic or object is on stage, you as an audience can view it, perhaps with special visual effects, as rendered in the browser. Meanwhile, backstage (or on the side), you have a work area where other actors or objects may be waiting, shielded from the audience (or browser) until it's their turn to appear on stage.

Animation is carried out through actions, motions, and the Timeline. ActionScript is used to create these effects and the Timeline is employed within the authoring environment to design and deploy them, thanks to the playhead and the various tools, menus, and templates offered.

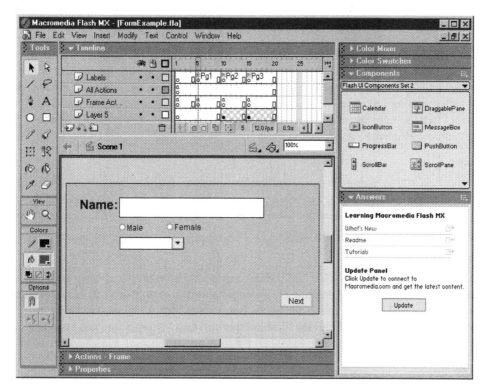

The Timeline

The Timeline is one of the most important parts of the Macromedia Flash interface, and it is what sets Macromedia Flash apart from other graphics tools. When you add an object to the stage, you can control not only how it is displayed, but also when it should appear (and disappear).

In the case of Macromedia Flash, much as in motion pictures, Flash movies are really just a series of frames played back in sequence as the playhead moves along the Timeline (shown next).

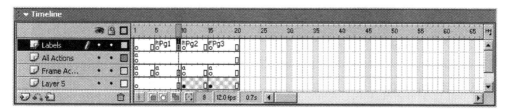

The playhead indicates which frame you are viewing in the movie. To examine the time element of your graphics, click the playhead and drag it back and forth along the Timeline. The changes on the stage can be easily altered for each frame.

Tweening

You can also define keyframes to hold new or changed scenes and define stages. A keyframe is a frame that defines some change in your animation. You can create motions and animation without actually creating all the individual frames by using tweening. Tweening is done when you create starting and ending frames and let Flash figure out where everything should go in between frames, automatically! Tweening minimizes the amount of work required of an animator, but also helps create smaller Flash files.

Layers

Layers allow you to manage your content intelligently and separate objects into different levels when defining their behavior. It's a process similar to how graphic artists create layers of acetate sheets with various cartoon characters and objects. This way, you can easily design and manipulate your images.

Components

Components allow you to quickly build, share, and extend user interfaces using pre-built Flash elements. Components are movie clips with built-in behaviors that can be customized to suit your style. They are used to add interaction and navigation elements to your Flash movies. In Chapter 4, we will review these components in more detail and contrast them with Java Swing GUI controls.

Video

Macromedia Flash MX comes with a very exciting new feature: embedded video. To make this possible, Macromedia teamed up with the video compression technology leader, Sorenson Media, to develop an exclusive Macromedia Flash video codec called Sorenson Spark. Because the Sorenson Spark codec is built into Flash Player 6, Web surfers don't need to download any additional plug-ins or software to view digital video in Flash movies. The Spark codec comes in a Basic and Pro edition. Although Macromedia Flash MX only allows you to encode video files with the Basic edition codec, those who wish to take advantage of the Pro codec can use Sorenson's own Squeeze product.

ActionScript

Besides making it approachable and accessible with a great visual development environment, Macromedia Flash has a scripting language, ActionScript, that allows you to extend its capability. Let's look at that next.

Flash ActionScript

ActionScript, the scripting language of Macromedia Flash MX, allows you to create a movie that behaves exactly as you want it to. To do this, Macromedia Flash built upon its core scripting capability that came of age with Flash 5—a hugely powerful but easy-to-use programming language. With Flash ActionScript, you can add special effects to your movies and applications, yet maintain a minimal file size. You can also program flexibility and complexity into your Flash MX movies, web sites, and applications, or pass data and information back and forth between the movie and the web server with great efficiency.

Like most scripting languages, you don't need to know every ActionScript element to be productive. Rather, with a well-defined goal, you can start building scripts with simple actions. You can incorporate new elements of the language as you learn them, to accomplish more complicated tasks using the new ActionScript Editor IDE, as illustrated next. Like other scripting languages, ActionScript follows its own rules of syntax, reserves keywords, provides operators, and allows you to use variables to store and retrieve information.

ActionScript includes built-in objects and functions and allows you to create your own objects and functions. The ActionScript syntax and style closely resemble that of JavaScript. In addition, Flash Player understands ActionScript written in any previous version of Flash.

ActionScript itself is similar to the core JavaScript programming language. You don't need to know JavaScript to use and learn ActionScript; however, if you do know JavaScript, ActionScript will appear familiar to you. Some of the major differences between ActionScript and JavaScript are as follows:

▶   ActionScript does not support browser-specific objects such as Document, Window, and Anchor.

▶   ActionScript does not completely support all of the JavaScript built-in objects.

▶   ActionScript supports syntax constructs that are not permitted in JavaScript.

▶   ActionScript does not support some JavaScript syntax constructs and statement labels.

▶   ActionScript does not support the JavaScript Function constructor.

We will be discussing Flash MX ActionScript in every aspect wherever it is used in this book.

Flash Formats

You can publish your movie in many alternative formats, including SWF, EXE, HTML, GIF, JPEG, PNG, and QuickTime, as illustrated next. We will only discuss the critical ones here that apply to mobile development.

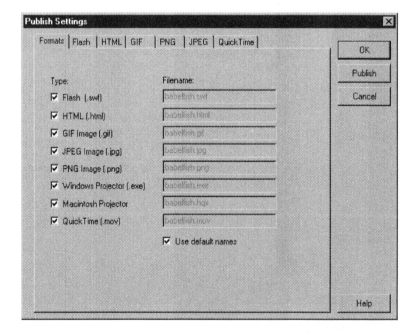

FLA Source Files

The basic format used by Macromedia Flash is FLA. The FLA files hold your original designs, and are compiled into SWF for displaying in the browser. The source file, *.fla*, contains the instructions for multimedia authoring in the Flash authoring environment. Unlike the SWF format, the FLA format is proprietary to the Macromedia Flash MX authoring environment.

SWF and HTML Files

You can publish (and compile) and then deploy Flash files to your server environment to go live. There are a few choices in publishing Flash movies. The format could be stand-alone SWF if it is intended to be viewed through a stand-alone player, or it could be wrapped within an HTML file if it will be viewed through a browser like Internet Explorer and Netscape Navigator. The publishing process takes all of the drawings, fonts, and other content you created in your FLA file and compresses and encodes them into the SWF format. Hence, there is no dependency on certain elements, such as fonts, when your viewer downloads and plays the SWF file. Another highlight is that the SWF file is much smaller and more compact than its parent FLA file, and is thus much quicker and efficient to download for the end user.

NOTE

Although the Macromedia Flash movie has a .swf file extension, which stands for Shockwave Flash, Macromedia Flash was never based on Shockwave, and the SWF file is not in a Shockwave format. Thus, the SWF format should not be confused with the true Shockwave format, which is a DCR file.

The SWF file format is an open and published specification which Macromedia releases with every new version of Flash. According to Macromedia, there are about 200 companies that have licensed the format and who use it for various products, from authoring tools and servers, to applications and embedded devices.

NOTE

The MIME type for SWF files is application/x-shockwave-flash.

As mentioned earlier, Flash is actually a better cross-browser interface than plain HTML because it is consistently treated the same by both major browsers, making it much easier to learn and use. With an HTML wrapper file, your SWF file is played by the embedded (plug-in) Flash player within Internet Explorer or Navigator browser.

Projector Files

Although it is true that most Flash movies are intended for the Web, Flash does include a feature that enables you to create stand-alone Flash-based applications. By using what is known as a *projector*, you can publish your Flash movies as executable (EXE) programs for the Windows platform or as HQX (BinHex) for the Macintosh platform. A projector binds your finished SWF to a bundled version of Flash Player for that platform (Macintosh or Windows) so that the end user does not need to have any additional installed software to play the Flash movie. You could, for example, create a specialized calculator using Flash, and then distribute your creation as a commercial program. Stand-alone Flash-based applications tend to be quite a bit larger than standard Flash movies. The reason for this is quite simple—Flash movies require the separate Flash Player to run, so they don't need all the overhead that a stand-alone program does. In a sense, a stand-alone Flash-based application is really just a complete package that includes both your Flash movie and Flash Player in one. We will look at how the Projector file format plays out as an offline mobile application in a later chapter.

Flash MX: How Does It Work?

We won't go into depth on how Flash FLA and SWF files actually work, but we will explore how the movie is deployed, and how the browser and HTTP request engender the rendering of the Flash movie on your PC browser or your Pocket PC mobile Internet Explorer.

Deploying Flash Movies and Applications

How do you deploy Flash movies? And what happens when you run a Flash movie? Let's find out.

Deploying or publishing Flash movies is actually quite easy. After previewing it in the authoring environment, you can publish and insert your Flash movie into an HTML document, or you can create the SWF file only for playing with a stand-alone Flash Player. The various file formats have already been discussed.

When you publish, the Flash authoring environment does it for you by bundling all your components into a single file. You then move the Flash movie (HTML, SWF) to your folders with your other production HTML or to the production server file system from your development environment. Upon executing the HTML request, your application server will deliver the Flash movie to the browser. The Flash plug-in will then be able to play the Flash movie.

NOTE

Not all mobile devices and versions of Flash Player can play the SWF file stand-alone. For example, with Pocket Internet Explorer on an HP iPAQ device, you may only be able to play the SWF file embedded within an HTML file. Newer versions of Flash Player and OS may remove this restriction.

Running Flash Movies and Applications

When a web surfer visits your site and there is a Flash Player embedded in the browser, your Flash movie will start to play with the Flash plug-in. Essentially, it interrogates the Timeline encoded in the SWF file and reads off what should be displayed in the browser frame by frame.

Additionally, with the Internet Explorer browser in Windows, there is an autoinstall feature that automatically installs a Flash Player if one is not present. You do need to add a bit of HTML on the web page, but the Macromedia Flash MX authoring environment can create the necessary HTML code for you when you publish a Flash movie.

Flash Objects and Object-Oriented Programming

As mentioned, objects have behavior. Early on, Flash itself was object-based. Thus ActionScript is an object-oriented programming (OOP) language designed specifically for animation. Organized around objects rather than actions, data rather than logic, OOP is a concept that changed the rules in computer program development. Historically, a program has been viewed as a logical procedure that takes input data, processes it, and produces output data. The programming challenge was seen as how to write the logic, not how to define the data. Object-oriented programming takes the view that what we really care about are the objects we want to manipulate, rather than the logic required to manipulate them.

SWF Versus SVG

Is SWF the same as SVG (Scalable Vector Graphics)? If not, how are they different? And why?

No, SWF and SVG are not the same, although both are standards for vector graphics for web applications. Both SWF and SVG can enable a visually-enhanced user experience in mobile multimedia messaging over bandwidth-efficient, interactive 2-D graphics technology. In addition, they can deliver fully 3GPP-compliant motion vector graphics from creation through publishing. Flash SWF is a little more compact than SVG, due to its binary format, whereas SVG is a text-based format.

But SWF *is not* the same as SVG, and SWF is not as open a standard as SVG. Macromedia does make it available to the public. Readers interested in learning more are invited to visit the Macromedia site at http://www.macromedia.com/software/flash/open/licensing/fileformat/faq.html.

To create SWF files, you can also use the Macromedia Flash file format (SWF) SDK, which provides a set of tools to write SWF files, documentation of the SWF file format, and code to write SWF files. Several commercial and open source tools exist for generating and parsing SWF files.

Many believe SWF lacks structure. Well, that's not quite correct. While it may not have an XML structure as SVG does, it is quite easy to convert SWF vector graphics into a structured XML document, if necessary. It's true that the design of the SWF recalls the old IFF multimedia format (which is still doing well in some applications), but it continues to work quite well.

The logical question is: should you develop with SWF or SVG? Due to the popularity of Flash Player (the developer and designer base of Macromedia Flash), as well as the technical and marketing muscle Macromedia puts behind SWF, we believe you should seriously consider building mobile applications on SWF, while not ignoring SVG.

The challenges of using either SWF or SVG for mobile development are not due to particular shortcomings of these technologies, but because it remains difficult to repurpose content and applications in order to fit the functional needs of mobile devices. In this book, we will, of course, cover how to use SWF in order to do what cHTML and WML now do in the mobile world!

Server-Side Flash

Why should you bother with server-side Flash? Because you may want to exchange data, build in business logic, or dynamically change content on the fly, using your back-end server and database. If so, what options do you have?

Until Macromedia Flash 5, your options included Flash Generator, or several open source projects for PHP or Java. Now, Macromedia has added a great deal of support. You may have even heard that Macromedia has announced its plan to phase out Flash Generator in favor of Flash MX support with ColdFusion MX. Read on to learn more!

Beyond Generator: Flash Remoting

For once, you will still be able to use the compelling interfaces of Flash to create server-side capability. Flash Remoting is the official technology to link to back-end services, and a serious web application has lots of back-end functionality.

Flash Remoting allows you to expose objects and Web services on an application server as if they were local ActionScript objects. It is similar to Java RMI and .Net Remoting, which are doing similar things in those worlds. You can look at Flash as the front end for web applications, while the back end is provisioned by Web services from multiple sources in a "federated" fashion. Because Flash is supported across multiple devices and platforms, your Flash-enabled applications are distributed for use on various devices from PDAs upwards. In summary, Flash Remoting can fill the missing gap in Flash, enabling true integration with web services. The Flash Remoting architecture is shown next.

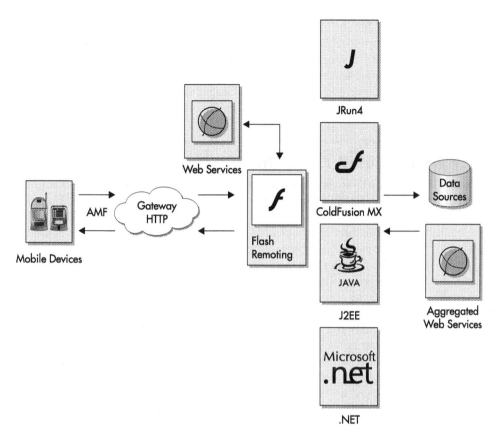

It also allows you to use SOAP Web services directly from the Flash MX client. So you can point to the WSDL file or its URL with ActionScript, and through Flash Remoting and ColdFusion MX, a proxy for that Web service is automatically built that allows you to access the APIs of that Web service from a Flash client. It really is that simple!

Flash Remoting with ColdFusion MX

ColdFusion MX is a major new release of that platform, built on J2EE, that allows developers to use a rapid scripting environment to build server applications that can compile and deploy to any J2EE application server, including your own. There are adapters for ASP.NET and for Java, so you can use Flash as a client with almost any back end.

With Flash Remoting included, ColdFusion MX allows you to connect Web services and application servers to Flash objects in the client. Flash Remoting uses a very efficient binary protocol that runs over HTTP. It is optimized for objects that are created in Flash. If you have a ColdFusion MX component sitting on a server, you can run that on the ColdFusion MX server using a script, or you can import it and use it in Flash as if it were a local Flash object. Thus, it is a very powerful framework for client-server communication.

Flash Remoting is covered in greater detail in Chapter 6, while ColdFusion MX server is discussed in Chapter 8.

Why Macromedia Flash MX for Mobile?

Undoubtedly, Macromedia is very keen on establishing Flash as the premier rich client, especially since it is already quite successful on the Web. We believe Macromedia Flash will even be more successful as a rich client in mobile and wireless devices. Wireless development is complex: there are not enough tools and too many markups, and it is just too difficult to "write once and publish everywhere." Also, wireless development efforts cost too much—especially when you look at wireless servers, point servers, changing standards, lengthy development cycles (partly due to a lack of RAD tools), and the fact that there aren't enough developers with the necessary skills.

We believe those who are building mobile applications will soon find Macromedia Flash very compelling, especially as a front end of a mobile application. The Macromedia Flash architecture is now better suited to interactive applications, making it much easier than ever to build scalable mobile solutions.

Macromedia has made it more compelling in Macromedia Flash MX for mobile development. For example, web designers can automatically optimize content for handheld computers, mobile phones, and other devices using templates.

Flash MX Advantages

The strengths of Flash MX include its broad and pervasive distribution of Flash Players across multiple platforms, not to mention its easy-to-use, strongly supported authoring environment thanks to Macromedia. In addition, the installed base of Flash designer and developers is currently one million strong. Now, with a souped-up ActionScript, the addition of Flash Remoting, and the integration of ColdFusion MX and the Flash Communication Server, it's becoming a development platform. The MX advantages include

▶ **Ease of use**   The Flash MX authoring environment tailors to both designers and developers. Built-in templates allow rapid development in multiple languages, while core tools, the ActionScript editor, and Flash UI components enhance user productivity.

▶ **Its designer/developer base**   Over one million Flash developers and designers have been using Flash for web animation and applications.

▶ **It's the industry standard**   The Macromedia Flash SWF file format is the standard adopted by the industry for building rich applications and web interfaces.

▶ **The wide distribution of Flash Player**   Flash Player has been widely distributed onto 98 percent of PCs connected to the Web, as well as onto other devices like Pocket PCs, Smart Phones, and interactive TVs.

▶ **Its rich media capability**   Flash's capability to enhance user experience is important. It's even more important in the case of mobile applications in capability-constrained devices.

▶ **Support and maturity**   With version 6 and the authoring environment, Flash has received strong backing from its users and, of course, its vendor, Macromedia. After five upgrade cycles, Macromedia Flash MX is very robust and offers a stable and consistent environment for developing and deploying rich applications.

▶ **XML support**   MX has vastly enhanced back-end capabilities that integrate with any application server through XML or URL encoding.

▶ **Speed and compactness**   Macromedia Flash allows content to be developed once and deployed across multiple browsers, platforms, and Internet devices, especially mobile devices with limited computing and storage capabilities.

J2ME Versus Macromedia Flash

For some of you, Macromedia Flash MX may remind you of J2ME (Java 2 Platform, Micro Edition). Yes, indeed, Flash MX can be used to build smart client/server applications for mobile devices, and can even be used to run rich media applications locally, like J2ME applications. However, Flash MX is not quite a full-fledged development platform with virtual machines, whereas J2ME is the compact version of the Java programming platform. Macromedia Flash does have some advantages very similar to J2ME, through consistency across products, code portability, and reliable network delivery.

However, J2ME really comprises a set of profiles and configurations that are defined for different devices, classes, methods, and configuration needs. These configurations and their class libraries tend to make it less approachable for building mobile applications.

So, what's the bottom line? Is Flash a viable alternative to J2ME as a rich Java client? Let's look at a few of these issues:

▶ **Speed**   Java applications can be quite slow even on desktop PCs, and with J2ME, they could tax the devices with slow processing speed, minimal memory, and limited battery life.

▶ **Cross-platform**   While both Flash and J2ME are supposed to be cross-platform, you may come across inconsistencies in how J2ME applications run on different devices, whereas Flash has a small footprint and you can make the performance specific to mobile devices.

▶ **User interface**   For rich interfaces, Java could be quite difficult for developers to build. Building great user experiences onto multiple platforms is a real strength for Flash.

▶   **Availability**   The proliferation of J2ME phones is only beginning. The opposite is true of Flash! One thing to remember about Flash as the rich client is that we've got 98.3 percent ubiquity on the Internet. It's the most widely distributed runtime in the history of computing.

The Macromedia Mobile Strategy

Macromedia Flash MX represents a significant upgrade and signifies a greatly expanded role from Macromedia Flash's initial function as animation software; the big news is its role to drive other pieces of the Macromedia strategy.

As shown in Figure 2-2, Macromedia is pushing to have XHTML and Flash as the de facto standard for mobile and web applications.

XHTML and Flash

HTML is going to be with us for a long time. Flash is great for some things, but it's not good for everything. Believing that designers and developers will use different technologies and tools, Macromedia is pushing to have Flash complement HTML and perhaps XHTML. As HTML evolves into XHTML, the combination of XHTML and Flash will be tighter! Underpinning this effort is obviously the authoring environment of Flash. That dovetails into building a back-end of ColdFusion MX, Flash Remoting, and the Flash Communication

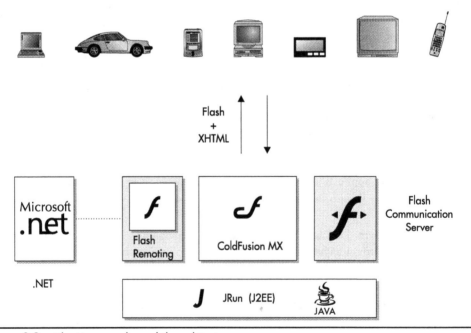

Figure 2-2   *The Macromedia mobile architecture*

Server. This framework, while built on top of a J2EE platform with JRun, will support Microsoft .NET and essentially follow the same path of cross-platform, cross-browser, and cross-server framework support.

The promised payoffs include truly write once, use many times, with both Java and .NET server technologies for both web and mobile applications. Having briefly discussed ColdFusion MX earlier, we'll cover it in greater detail in Chapter 8. For now, let's review what the Flash Communication Server is.

Flash Communication Server

With the Flash Communication Server, Macromedia is introducing a new technology for communications applications. The Flash Communication Server enables two or more people to engage in a real-time communication via text, audio, or video. Real-life examples include net meetings, instant messaging, online chats and communities, customer service, technical support, and training.

The concept is to combine content and communication into a single application environment. Central to this theme are a client (Flash Player) and a server (ColdFusion MX, Flash Remoting, and, of course, Flash Communication Server). Macromedia is pushing to integrate communications into applications, as human interactions and messaging are merged with data-driven Internet applications. Today, there are stand-alone solutions to do some of this, but Macromedia wants to make the back-end programming simpler to implement, and extend the communications aspect to its rich client—Macromedia Flash Player.

We'll cover Flash Communication Server in greater detail in Chapter 11.

The Bigger Picture: Macromedia MX Strategy

Macromedia has evolved its entire product lineup and announced an MX suite that integrates design features with application development support. The suite includes standard user interface components, a model for component reuse, a more advanced object model, programming tools, and a new IDE with debugging and content management features. Some of the key elements are covered in the following sections.

Studio MX

Macromedia Studio MX brings together this widely used set of tools—Flash MX for presentations, Fireworks MX and Freehand for graphic design, Dreamweaver MX for web design, and ColdFusion MX for application development—to create an application integration layer powerful enough to rival the Java-applet model.

The IDE Configurable Model

As content creation and application development converge, Macromedia has developed a workspace and an IDE model across its products. Its tools are now configurable to the different perspectives (designer and developer types), as in the Macromedia Flash MX authoring environment, while preserving a common workflow across those environments.

End-to-End Client-Server Support

Macromedia is also pushing for a fully integrated set of products by combining a rich client with server technology centered around ColdFusion MX, and then a suite of design and development tools that are integrated as Macromedia Studio MX. The idea is that web development is moving towards rich Internet applications, involving content, user interfaces, back-end application logic, and communications. Macromedia wants to wrap these into a single environment to enable a better end-user experience and lower development cost.

A Complete Spectrum from Static Content to Dynamic Mobile Applications

Macromedia is providing a complete spectrum of tools, as well as client-side and server-side technologies for building and deploying web sites and applications. You can start from static content with Dreamweaver MX and Fireworks MX, and move onto rich media and applications using Flash MX. You can also build dynamic web applications with Dreamweaver MX and ColdFusion MX, and take it to the next level of rich client, service-based server-side applications using the Flash Communication Server, Flash Remoting, and JRun.

Summary

In this chapter, we reviewed the features and benefits of Macromedia Flash MX both in general terms and, to some extent, in mobile terms. We also looked at how other pieces of Macromedia technology can be leveraged for mobile development. With a basic understanding of the mobile architecture and strategy for Macromedia Flash, we can now go on to examine the capabilities in detail. You can then be the judge of how well these pieces work together, and whether you want to incorporate some or all of them in building and deploying your mobile services. In Chapter 3, we introduce the methodology of Flash application development, and contrast it with HTML. We also review the basics of building database-driven applications that leverage the rich media capabilities of Macromedia Flash MX.

CHAPTER

3

Essentials of Dynamic Flash Development

IN THIS CHAPTER:

Introduction and Planning

Architecture

Using Flash MX to Create Movies

Incorporating Database and Server Side

Deployment

Summary

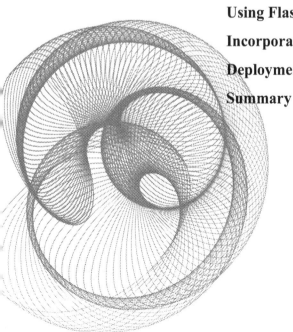

I n this chapter, we give you a quick start in using the Macromedia Flash MX authoring environment to build interactive movies and dynamic applications. Instead of walking through feature after feature (or menu after menu), we are going to forge ahead and use Macromedia Flash MX and other server-side capabilities to build our initial applications.

Our goal is to illustrate a simple way to use Macromedia Flash MX and allow us to build on existing Flash movies and capabilities. It is intended for those who are new to Macromedia Flash, as well as those who prefer to contrast the Macromedia Flash way of building applications with the HTML methodology. Later on, we will extend the Flash movie by turning them into database-driven, server-backed applications that are rich in media, while leveraging the Flash player capabilities.

Introduction and Planning

In this chapter, we will build a rich Internet application—a blueprint online video store with Macromedia Flash MX. We chose a video store because most people are familiar with the use case of an e-commerce store, and the application is relatively sophisticated affording us ample opportunities to illustrate points using Flash MX. Developers and designers can easily follow the workflow and methodology to build their own rich Internet applications. Since this chapter is meant to be an introduction, we will not cover the transactional aspects of an e-commerce site (shopping cart, credit card validation, and so on) at this point.

For the purpose of this book, our approach is prototype driven, which lets you add more features and capabilities later as your skills improve. We will move quickly onto the essential tools and facilities of Macromedia Flash MX, and focus on how to use ColdFusion MX and Flash Remoting at the server side to provision Flash. We will cover:

▶ Flash movies and applications

▶ Video store prototype

▶ Building pages and movies

▶ Testing and deployment

▶ Extending with databases and servers

Definitions: Flash Movies Versus Applications

You may come across many different terms for Flash: Flash movies, Flash documents, even Flash applications. For starters, Flash movies, documents, and applications are not exactly the same. While their definitions may not be universally agreed upon and are still evolving, for the purpose of this book, we regard Flash movies as being the base level SWF files or projector EXE files. They may run solely on a client, without remote data access or server-side execution.

Flash documents are the generic FLA files, whereas Flash applications are broader in scope as they may include all the Flash files: FLA, EXE, and/or SWF files, and are usually all inclusive. More often, Flash MX applications are dynamic in nature and server-driven. In this book, when we regard Flash applications as Internet applications that leverage the rich client in Flash Player, client- and server-side ActionScript, and server-side scripting with ColdFusion MX, J2EE, or .NET.

Roles and Workflow

With different responsibilities, designers and developers have different roles and workflows. As in any development process, dividing tasks among different roles and assigning them to specialists and experts can facilitate the development process (faster to build; easier to debug) and make the application more robust (less costly to support and maintain). For Internet applications based on Macromedia Flash MX, Macromedia is essentially proposing and defining three different roles (see Figure 3-1):

▶ **Server-side developer**   Software engineers or developers working on the server side to create and administer the databases (for example, database schema and SQL queries) and write server-side code (such as CFML, ASP, JSP/Java Servlets, and PHP).

▶ **Client-side developer**   Software engineers or developers writing the ActionScript code for Macromedia Flash MX using the built-in Flash MX ActionScript IDE, Dreamweaver MX, or any text editor.

▶ **Client-side designer**   Designers working in the Macromedia Flash MX authoring environment to create rich client user interfaces including graphics and page/frame design.

These roles may involve three separate individuals or teams, but in some cases, many may hold two, or even all three, roles.

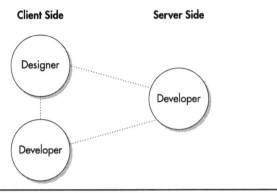

Figure 3-1   *Roles of designers and developers*

Architecture

Let's go into our blueprint application—online Video Store. Besides showing you how to quickly use the Flash MX authoring environment, we are going to look at several examples of using variables, creating dynamic objects, referencing JPGs from remote sources, loading and passing variables, and using Flash MX UI components.

Video Store Prototype

A full-fledged e-commerce web site is rather involved. Here, we will use a simple HTML site as our base or starting reference. There are several reasons for that. First, a simple HTML site can provide initial guidance and visuals for the team to understand the overall architecture, information flow, and application logic. Another reason is to factor out their roles and allow client-side designers, client-side developers, and server-side developers to work together, but also work independently and efficiently. Thirdly, not all team members are well versed in ActionScript or other Macromedia Flash MX capabilities. HTML seems to be a common language to get everyone on the same page. As a result, we will use certain terms and metaphors from HTML programming when we go over the Flash development process in this chapter. This may seem odd for some Flash developers, but it will pay off as we contrast Flash against HTML later on.

As shown in the following illustration, we have four levels or pages in our initial HTML reference web site. The *Main* or Home page contains a list of movie genres to choose from. It may also contain other things like a Search button, ads, and navigational bars. The *Titles* or Genre page displays a list of available movie titles in a particular genre. The *Details* page displays the full description of a chosen movie, including a movie poster, movie synopsis, and so on. Finally, you can also view an embedded QuickTime *Video* trailer within the Flash movie for the particular title.

Main

Titles

Details

Video

These pages serve the following purposes:

▶ **Main Page**   Allows the visitor to pick a movie genre.

▶ **Titles Page**   Allows the visitor to pick a movie title from the chosen genre.

▶ **Details Page**   Allows the visitor to view the description of the chosen movie.

▶ **Video Page**   Displays or plays the video trailer.

Later in this chapter, we will add more features (for example, database driven) and components (such as dynamic ListBoxes and dynamic text) to this Flash MX application.

Static HTML Pages and Flash Movies

We will start by creating a static, stand-alone version of the Flash MX application (movie). We, however, prefer all Flash applications be database driven and dynamic, using client-side and server-side code, but a general introduction is needed here. This will be a two-step process: static Flash application (movie), followed by a dynamic Flash application. For the static Flash application, the data and content are hard-coded into the Flash *.fla* file and a SWF/HTML file generated and placed inside the folder along with other HTML pages of your site. Using a web server, you can serve up Flash movies into a browser on a client machine. No other dynamic data source or server-side scripting is needed in this case after the SWF and HTML are requested by and downloaded to the client (see the next illustration).

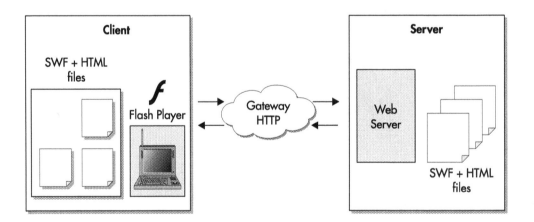

At this point, our prototype is done entirely in Flash MX without server-side code or databases. We then add the server interactions. This is the preferred approach since you may only have a rough idea what kinds of server transactions you want to incorporate until you finish your prototype. Also, having a set of static files (movies) makes it easier to design graphic elements and adjust client-side scripting with the page and movie layout. By contrast, if you spend time coding the back-end server scripts now, you may have to go back and rewrite a big chunk of code later after initial feedback is collected with your prototype.

In addition, you can present this prototype to your user groups (customers and sponsors) to validate the use case. Of course, once you get beyond the prototype phase, you can do a lot more site and page design, along with application logic and data architecture work, parceling out individual assignments to designers, server-side developers, and client-side developers.

Here, for our prototype, the static Flash MX movie, we will extend it to make it dynamic, using ColdFusion MX and Flash Remoting (see the following illustration). We will leverage a relational database management system (RDBMS) to supply the data/content and utilize an application server (ColdFusion MX) to execute the server-side code.

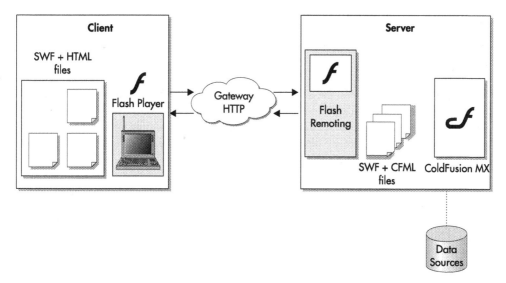

Gathering and Managing Assets

With this prototype, we will not spend time optimizing graphics and fonts for the static Flash application. We will just use the images "as is" along with the QuickTime movie trailers (republished in SWF format) from the original web application folders where they're stored. The poster images in the movie description are in JPEG (*.jpg) format, while trailer videos are in the QuickTime (*.mov) format. We will talk about mobile design style, file types, and typography issues in detail in Chapter 4.

Using Flash MX to Create Movies

We have four "pages" or frames that we will build into one Flash movie. We can, of course, do it using multiple movies but that would involve multiple server requests after the initial movie is downloaded. Since we want this initial cut to be a stand-alone offline Flash application, we will build all pages into one Flash movie and use different timeline for each "page" or frame. Here's the overall structure of our Flash movie.

▶ Stage with different Timeline for each "page" or frame

▶ Basic Layers for objects and ActionScript

▶ Static JPEG graphics

▶ Basic PushButtons

▶ ListBox Flash UI components

▶ Publishing in SWF/HTML

We have already introduced these Flash concepts in Chapter 2, and we will go into style guides in Chapter 4. Hence, we're not going to spend too much time introducing all of the Flash fundamentals, only those required to build this initial application. We will point out the more advanced features when we discuss our dynamic Flash application later in this chapter. Let's build a few of these items using the preceding capabilities.

Timeline

Up front, we have decided to implement this application using one movie and allocating different Timelines or keyframes to each of the four "pages." Here's the breakdown of the keyframes:

▶ **Frame: 1** *Main Page* (frame label is "Main")

▶ **Frame: 5** *Titles Page* (frame label is "Titles")

▶ **Frame: 10** *Details Page* (frame label is "Details")

▶ **Frame: 15** *Video Page* (frame label is "Video")

We could have chosen sequential frames (for example, 1, 2, 3, 4) but for simplicity in displaying the Timeline, we spaced them out (see the illustration that follows).

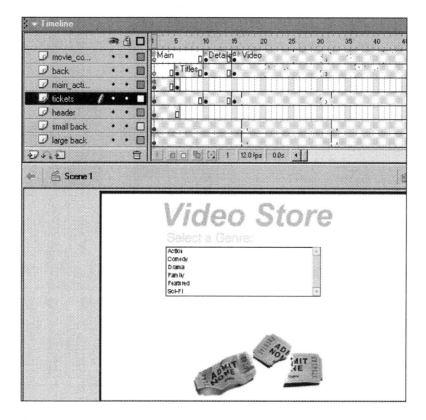

Static Text and Static Images

Let's go through some of the static text and static images we use on various frames before we review the objects needed for navigation and selection.

To build our first keyframe (frame=1) *Main Page*, we have placed two static text objects ("Video Store" and "Select a Genre:") and one static graphic object (tickets image) on the stage. To complete this frame, we also have a fourth object—a ListBox UI component (see *Navigation and Selection* section later in this chapter). Static text objects are the easiest to use. They can be built entirely in Macromedia Flash MX without coding. Just choose the attributes for the position, font, point size, style, color, and so on. You can orient text horizontally, or if you are working with Asian characters, orient the object vertically (static text only). If you want to use your own font, instead of the built-in fonts, Flash MX lets you create a symbol from a font (that you created) so that you can export the font as part of a shared library and use it in other Flash movies. We will cover more on this in Chapter 4.

If you want to "inspect" the attributes or properties of your object, Macromedia Flash MX offers the Property inspector, a screen that lets you edit an object attribute without individually accessing the menus or panels that contain these attributes. This greatly simplifies the review and editing of objects. The Property inspector is context sensitive and its content changes to reflect the particular attributes of the selected object.

For example, the Property inspector screen for the "Video Store" static text object (shown next) illustrates what properties you can change for this object. Similar properties are held for the second static text object, "Select a Genre:".

Besides the two static text objects, we have also included a static image (bitmap object) for the "tickets" image. Simply import it into the movie.

Our second keyframe (frame=5), *Titles Page*, is almost identical to the *Main Page*. The only difference is the static text "Select a Title:" object (the user instructions), the content of the ListBox, and a back PushButton object (see *Back Buttons* section later in this chapter).

The third keyframe (frame=10), *Details Page*, is composed of two static text objects in addition to two static graphic images and two PushButtons, as shown next.

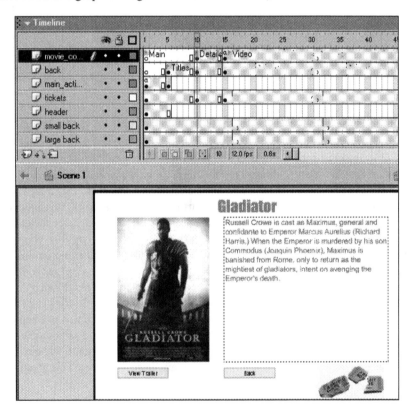

Notice that the last keyframe (frame=15), *Video Page*, is composed of a back PushButton object and an embedded video object that plays a QuickTime movie trailer, as shown next.

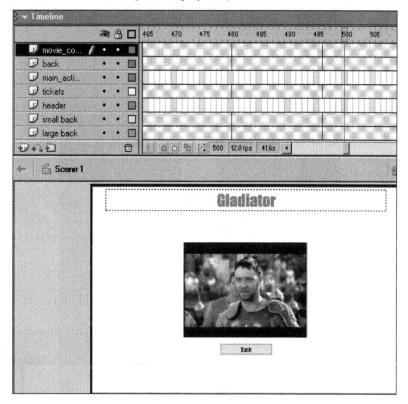

Let's look at these objects in detail next as we move onto navigation and selection using the ListBox and other components.

Navigation and Selection

The prebuilt component library from Macromedia Flash MX allows us to create UI components like drop-down lists and listboxes without coding. You can select these components from the Components palette and drop them into any Flash application, which makes building a user interface quick and easy.

On our first two "pages" or frames (frame=1 and frame=5), we have used a ListBox and populated them with static content. In the *Main Page*, we have all the genres the video store offers, as illustrated in the Property inspector that follows.

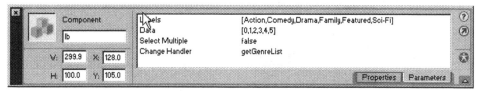

The change handler used here is *getGenreList*. A *change handler* is a function that you specify to be called when a user selects a menu item, a radio button, or a check box. A *click handler* is the equivalent of a PushButton component. The ActionScript code for the getGenreList change handler is shown next:

```
function getGenreList() {
   gotoAndStop("Titles");
}
```

The ActionScript used in our static example is minimal because we're just mimicking the HTML pages.

The *Titles Page* also contains a ListBox, which differs depending on the genre selected. The Action genre is selected in the next illustration, showing the *Titles Page*, followed by its Property inspector screen.

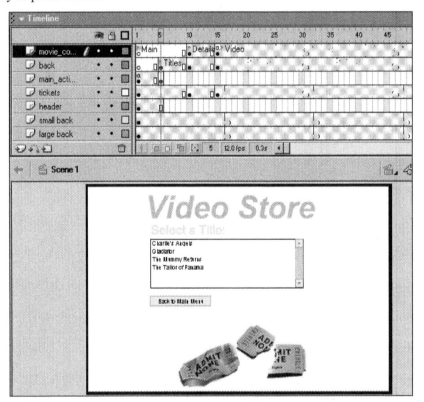

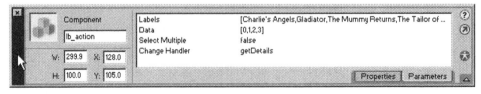

The only thing left to do regarding navigation concerns the back buttons as seen in the *Titles Page*, *Details Page*, and *Video Page*. Since using and implementing the back button is different from that of a browser back button, we will talk about this next.

Back Buttons

The PushButton Flash component lets you add simple push buttons to your Flash movie, and accepts all standard mouse and keyboard interactions. In our static application, we are using the PushButton component (with a click handler) for "back" navigation and for "viewing" the video trailer. The click handler will just call the function associated with the button. For example, the "back" button from the *Titles Page* will return the user to the *Main Page* using the click handler function, *back2Main*, as shown next:

```
function back2Main() {
   gotoAndStop("Main");
}
```

Why couldn't we have used the browser back button instead? For one thing, we could be running this outside of the browser as a stand-alone SWF file or an EXE projector file (Windows) and the browser navigation controls are not available. The browser has its own URL history cache that is *not* linked to the Flash Player. One way to work around this is by using a hidden frame in the browser window and using an embedded Flash movie that can pass history information between it and the main Flash application. This way, the hidden frame will always be updated with new HTML code and is cached in the browser. If the back button is pressed in the browser, the hidden frame goes back to its previous state, and communicates that state to the Flash application. The Flash application then changes its state based on the data sent from the hidden frame.

To do this, a LocalConnection object or the FlashVars property can be used. A LocalConnection object can send strings and entire objects from one movie to another. It can also invoke ActionScript methods in the receiving movie. Using LocalConnection, you can send multiple objects as many times as necessary. The LocalConnection class works even when movies are running in different types of browser. The FlashVars property provides an efficient method of importing variables into the top level of a movie when first instantiated. Placed within the OBJECT or EMBED tag, FlashVars can be used to import root-level variables to the movie. All variables are created before the first frame of the SWF is played. The format of the string is a set of name–value combinations separated by '&'.

ActionScript

The ActionScript used in the static Flash application is very simple. It is only used to move between the various frames or "pages" within the movie. You can get a good idea of how it works just by looking at the simple code snippets used:

```
function getGenreList() {
   gotoAndStop("Titles");
}
```

```
function getDetails() {
   gotoAndStop("Details");
}
function back2Main() {
   gotoAndStop("Main");
}
```

This may look bad at first glance since programmers or developers *never* use GoTo statements in computer programming! Or at least they're discouraged from using them. Think of them as static hyperlinks from one page to the other and it won't sound so bad. You can replicate this code for navigating between frames going forward or backward.

The *gotoAndStop* action sends the playhead to the specified frame in a scene and stops it. If no scene is specified, the playhead is sent to the frame in the current scene.

Testing and Publishing

You can play your SWF file within the Flash MX authoring environment. When and if you are satisfied, you can publish your SWF file and create an HTML wrapper file automatically from the tool. Using commands in the *Control* menu, you can play it using the *Test Movie* command. Two added bonuses of using the Test Movie command versus testing it using a browser after publishing it include

▶ The *Output* window displays error messages and lists of variables and objects.

▶ The *trace* action sends programming notes and values of expressions to the Output window. This is not seen by the user when using a browser to test the SWF/HTML file.

We will go into detail about optimizing your movie for publishing in Chapter 5.

Conclusion

Creating a static Flash application is very time-consuming and can result in an enormous file. A frame is needed for each movie description, for each genre title selection, for each movie trailer, and so on. In our simple example application with about 30 movie titles and five genres, we need a minimum of at least 66 frames (two per movie—one for the movie description, one for the movie trailer). We have shown you how to do each type of frame and you can replicate them for each additional movie title or additional movie genre. Any changes to the content require modifying the FLA and republishing the SWF file. In the rest of this chapter, we will show you how to do it using databases and server-side code so that you can improve performance, ease of maintenance, and interactivity.

Incorporating Database and Server Side

We will now modify our video store static application into one that uses a relational database, ColdFusion MX server-side code, and Flash Remoting. All the data and content will be served dynamically via Flash Remoting—that is, Flash MX client (with ActionScript) communicating directly with ColdFusion MX components.

Using RDBMS

A Relational Database Management System (RDBMS) is a type of Database Management System (DBMS) that stores data in the form of related tables. A table is data arranged in rows and columns. Relational databases are powerful because they require few assumptions about how data is related or how it will be extracted from the database. As a result, the same database can be viewed in many different ways. For a quick tutorial on RDBMS and SQL, see Appendix C.

The database we are using here is simple and straightforward. It contains two tables, *tblGenres* and *tblTrailers*, with the following columns for each.

▶ **tblGenres**   *categoryName* and *categoryID* are minimal requirements. You can extend this table by adding more items (columns) like header images, and so on.

▶ **tblTrailers**   *pkVideoID*, *strVideoTitle*, *strCategory*, *strDescription*, *strPoster*, and *strVideoTrailer* are minimal. You can extend this by adding more items such as smaller images for mobile devices.

Our *tblGenres* database table would look like Table 3-1. Sample entries for our *tblTrailers* database table for *Action* genre would look like Table 3-2.

What are the advantages of using a database? Here are a few key benefits:

▶ You can parcel out the database work and assign each to your database administrator (DBA). This can be easily maintained and supported by them.

▶ Content can be added or deleted from the database and reflected in your Flash application *without* modifying, republishing, retesting, or redeploying your Flash application.

▶ As your content grows, the database grows. But your Flash application does NOT!

▶ The work is *simplified* and *reduced* for all designers and developers involved, as fewer changes are needed and maintenance is minimized.

categoryID	categoryName
0	feature
1	comedy
2	action
3	family
4	drama
5	scifi

Table 3-1   *Genres Table*

pkVideoID	strVideoTitle	strCategory	strDescription	strVideoTrailer	strPoster
49	Minority Report	action	description …	minorityreport.swf	minorityreport.jpg
47	Tailor of Panama	action	description …	tailor.swf	tailor.jpg
46	The Mummy Returns	action	description …	mummy.swf	mummy.jpg
45	Gladiator	action	description …	gladiator.swf	gladiator.jpg
22	Charlie's Angels	action	description …	angels.swf	angels.jpg

Table 3-2   *Action Titles*

What more can a designer and developer ask? Crank up the content and it won't adversely impact the size of your deployed files. Better yet, you don't even have to retest and redeploy!

Dynamic Video Store

Besides implementing our dynamic version of the video store using Flash MX, ColdFusion MX components, and Flash Remoting, we have also decided to use a single main movie in Flash that navigates between the three "pages" and a pop-up movie for the movie trailer. The data and content (genres, titles, movie details, images, and movie trailers) will be served dynamically via Flash Remoting. We will truly *only* have three frames in our movie! Here are the objects used in the "pages":

▶   **Main Page**   Dynamic text (*subHdr* and *header*), ListBox (*lb_dynamic* with change handler *getGenreDetails*), PushButton (*buttonBack*), static graphic. Frame=1.

▶   **Titles Page**   Shares the same page as the preceding but is dynamically modified *lb_dynamic* to change handler *getAllTitles* using ActionScript in addition to setting dynamic text *subHdr* to "Select a Title:" and enabling *buttonBack* to use click handler *back2Main*. Frame=1.

▶   **Details Page**   Dynamic text (*detTitle* and *detDesc*), movie clip (*imgObj* with JPEGs loaded dynamically), and pushbuttons (*buttonVT* with click handler *openVideo* and *buttonDetails* with click handler *back2Titles*). Frame=5.

▶   **Movies Page**   Now a pop-up that is served dynamically based on the database query as in the details page. The *openVideo* function (in *Details Page*) will load the appropriate movie trailer SWF file (embedded QuickTime movie—see *QuickTime Video Publishing* later in this chapter).

NOTE

Labels like subHdr, lb_dynamic, and so on, are instance names. These are unique names that allow you to target movie clip and button instances in ActionScript.

The big picture use case for this is shown in the following illustration.

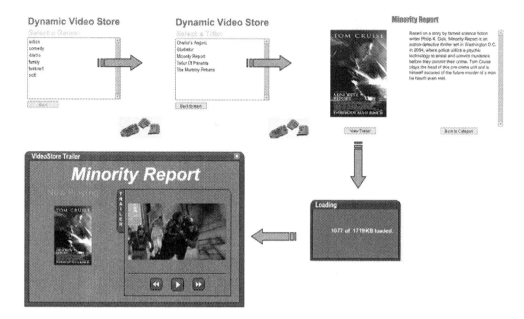

Server-Side ColdFusion MX Components

In order to service calls from the Flash MX client, we are using ColdFusion MX components (details can be found in Chapter 8) via Flash Remoting. Flash Remoting ActionScript is briefly described in the next section and in detail in Chapter 6. We will briefly discuss our ColdFusion MX component, *videostore*, and how to invoke it.

The ColdFusion MX code for our *videostore.cfc* component is shown next:

```
<cfcomponent>
  <cffunction name="getGenre" access="remote" returnType="query">
    <CFQUERY NAME="qry_Genre" Datasource="videostore">
      SELECT categoryName, categoryID FROM tblGenres
      ORDER BY categoryName
    </CFQUERY>
    <cfreturn qry_Genre>
  </cffunction>
  <cffunction name="getTitles" access="remote" returnType="query">
    <cfargument name="category" type="string" required="yes">
    <CFQUERY NAME="qry_Titles" Datasource="videostore">
      SELECT strVideoTitle, pkVideoID FROM tblTrailers
      WHERE strCategory = '#category#'
      ORDER BY strVideoTitle
      </CFQUERY>
    <cfreturn qry_Titles>
```

```
        </cffunction>
        <cffunction name="getDetails" access="remote" returnType="query">
            <cfargument name="videoID" type="numeric" required="yes">
            <CFQUERY NAME="qry_Details" Datasource="videostore">
                SELECT strVideoTitle, pkVideoID, strDescription, strPoster,
                    strCategory, strVideoTrailer FROM tblTrailers
            </CFQUERY>
            <cfreturn qry_Details>
        </cffunction>
    </cfcomponent>
```

You can point your browser to the *videostore.cfc* file to automatically display the component properties, methods, and so on, as illustrated next.

book.videostore
Component videostore

hierarchy:	WEB-INF.cftags.component book.videostore
path:	C:\CFusionMX\wwwroot\book\videostore.cfc
properties:	
methods:	getDetails, getGenre, getTitles

* - private method

getDetails

remote query **getDetails** (*required numeric videoID*)

Output: enabled
Parameters:
  videoID: numeric, required, videoID

getGenre

remote query **getGenre** ( )

Output: enabled

getTitles

remote query **getTitles** (*required string category*)

Output: enabled
Parameters:
  category: string, required, category

NOTE

You will need your RDS login and password to access the page.

We can test our component using the following ColdFusion MX code:

```
<cfinvoke component="book.videostore" method="getGenre"
  returnvariable="qryResultSet1">
</cfinvoke>
<cfdump var=#qryResultSet1#>
<cfinvoke component="book.videostore" method="getTitles"
  returnvariable="qryResultSet2">
  <cfinvokeargument name="category" value="action">
</cfinvoke>
<cfdump var=#qryResultSet2#>
<cfinvoke component="book.videostore" method="getDetails"
  returnvariable="qryResultSet3">
  <cfinvokeargument name="videoID" value="45">
</cfinvoke>
<cfdump var=#qryResultSet3#>
```

The resulting browser screen is shown next. *<cfdump>* is a very handy tag for debugging. It outputs the elements, variables, and values of most kinds of ColdFusion objects. You can display the contents of simple and complex variables, objects, components, user-defined functions, and other elements.

query

	CATEGORYID	CATEGORYNAME
1	2	action
2	1	comedy
3	4	drama
4	3	family
5	0	featured
6	5	scifi

query

	PKVIDEOID	STRVIDEOTITLE
1	22	Charlie's Angels
2	45	Gladiator
3	49	Minority Report
4	47	Tailor Of Panama
5	46	The Mummy Returns

query

	PKVIDEOID	STRCATEGORY	STRDESCRIPTION	STRPOSTER	STRVIDEOTITLE	STRVIDEOTRAILER
1	45	action	Russell Crowe is cast as Maximus, general and confidante to Emperor Marcus Aurelius (Richard Harris.) When the Emperor is murdered by his son Commodus (Joaquin Phoenix), Maximus is banished from Rome, only to return as the mightiest of gladiators, intent on avenging the Emperor's death.	/trailerchooser/posters/gladiator.jpg	Gladiator	gladiator.swf

As you can see, the component is working and can be activated using ActionScript in Flash MX as shown in the next section.

Flash Remoting ActionScript

We will discuss Flash Remoting in Chapter 6, but right now we'll quickly show you the basic ActionScript code required to call our ColdFusion MX components in order to retrieve all the dynamic content for our dynamic video store application. The relevant ActionScript code to call the *videostore* component *getGenre* method (Main Page) is shown next:

```
#include "NetServices.as"
#include "DataGlue.as"
// set the default gateway URL
NetServices.setDefaultGatewayUrl(
    "http://localhost:8500/flashservices/gateway");
// connect to the gateway
gateway_conn = NetServices.createGatewayConnection();
// get a reference to a service
myVideoStore = gateway_conn.getService("book.videostore", this);
// clear out ListBox
lb_dynamic.removeAll();
if (isInit == null) {
    // do this code only once
    isInit = true;
    // make a call to videostore component getGenre method
    myVideoStore.getGenre(qryResult);
    // set dynamic text header
    subHdr.text = "Select a Genre:";
    // back button not needed in Main Page
    buttonBack.setEnabled(false);
    buttonBack.setLabel("Back");
}
```

In a nutshell, the *NetServices.as* include file is required for using Flash Remoting, and the *DataGlue.as* include file is for the DataGlue object (see Chapter 6). Most of the code is self-explanatory (comments in the code listing).

When successfully calling a component method, Flash MX returns to the *methodName_Result* (for example, *getGenre_Result*) function if there is one in your movie. In our example, we have:

```
function getGenre_Result(result) {
    DataGlue.BindFormatStrings(lb_genre, result,
        "#categoryName#", "#categoryName#");
}
```

The DataGlue object is for Flash Remoting use only and has functions that let you bind RecordSet objects to Flash MX UI components. DataGlue offers a way to format data records for use in a ListBox, ComboBox, or other UI component.

Dynamic Text and ListBox Components

Since we are using one frame to represent both the *Main Page* and *Titles Page*, we will dynamically modify the *subHdr* dynamic text object and *lb_dynamic* ListBox component (see illustration that follows).

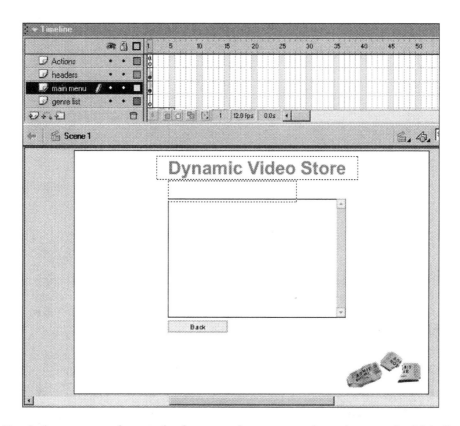

Here's the sequence of events that happens when a user navigates between the *Main Page* and *Titles Page*:

1. **Main Page**   *subHdr* object is loaded with "Select a Genre:" text, and *lb_dynamic* is loaded with the result of the call to *getGenre* (see the following illustration).

2. **Titles Page**   *subHdr* is loaded with "Select a Title:" text, and *lb_dynamic* is loaded with the result of the call to *getTitles* (see next illustration).

3. **Details Page**   When a title is selected from the *Titles Page*, we go to Frame = 5 and load the dynamic text objects with content from the query. The dynamic components are illustrated next (not very interesting as it gets loaded dynamically) followed by the populated version.

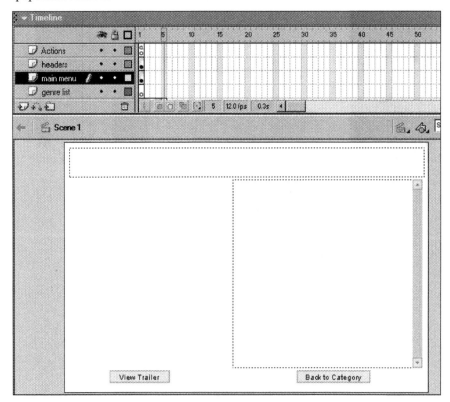

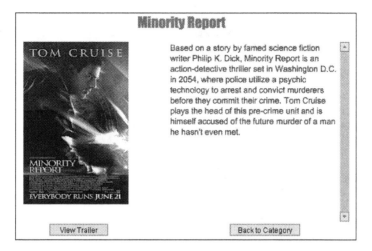

We will cover the *Video Page* in the next section.

Code snippets for some of the actions just described are shown next with their respective comments:

```
//// for Main Page ////

// process query result and populate ListBox with genres
function getGenre_Result(result) {
   DataGlue.BindFormatStrings(lb_dynamic, result,
   "#categoryName#", "#categoryName#");
}

function getGenreDetails() {
   // selecting a genre from the ListBox will result in a call to the
   // component videostore getTitles method
   myVideoStore.getTitles(lb_dynamic.getValue(),qryResultT);
}

//// for Titles Page ////

// process query result and populate ListBox with titles
function getTitles_Result(resultT) {
   // load instruction to dynamic text object subHdr
   subHdr.text = "Select a Title:";
   // populate ListBox with titles
   DataGlue.BindFormatStrings(lb_dynamic, resultT,
      "#strVideoTitle#", "#pkVideoID#");
   // update ListBox change handler
   lb_dynamic.setChangeHandler("getAllTitles");
   // update back button
   buttonBack.setEnabled(true);
   buttonBack.setLabel("Back to Main");
   buttonBack.setClickHandler("back2Main");
}
```

```
function getAllTitles() {
   // selecting a title from the ListBox will result in a call to the
   // component videostore getDetails method
   myVideoStore.getDetails(lb_dynamic.getValue(),qryResultD);
}

// used to go back to Main Page from Titles Page
function back2Main() {
   // load instruction to dynamic text object subHdr
   subHdr.text = "Select a Genre:";
   // update ListBox with genres
   myVideoStore.getGenre(qryResult);
   // update ListBox change handler
   lb_dynamic.setChangeHandler("getGenreDetails");
   // update back button
   buttonBack.setEnabled(false);
   buttonBack.setLabel("Back");
}


//// for Details Page ////

// called after returning from getDetails query
function getDetails_Result(resultD) {
   gotoAndStop("Details");
   // load video title to dynamic text object detTitle
   detTitle.text = resultD.items[0].strVideoTitle;
   // load video description to dynamic text object detDesc
   detDesc.text = resultD.items[0].strDescription;
   // create movie clip for displaying JPG video poster image
   _root.createEmptyMovieClip("imgObj",9);
   _root.imgObj._x=30;
   _root.imgObj._y=60;
   imagePath = "http://localhost:8500/book" + resultD.items[0].strPoster;
   _root.imgObj.loadMovie(imagePath);
   // load the global variable so we can go back to the correct
   // category titles page from the current details page
   _global.back2cat = resultD.items[0].strCategory;
   // load the global variable so we can pop up the appropriate
   // video trailer SWF file
   _global.trailer = "http://localhost:8500/book/" +
      resultD.items[0].strVideoTrailer;
}

// used to go back to Titles Page from Details Page
function back2Titles() {
   gotoAndStop("Main");
   // remove dynamic JPG image
   _root.imgObj.removeMovieClip()
   // update ListBox with titles
   myVideoStore.getTitles(_global.back2cat,qryResultT);
}
```

With dynamic text, there is an additional option (*Character...*) seen on the Property inspector that impacts what the published text looks like (see following illustration).

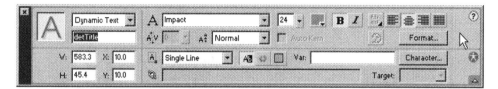

When you use a font installed on your system in a Flash movie, Flash embeds the font information in the Flash SWF file, ensuring that the font is displayed properly in the Flash Player. Not all fonts displayed in Flash can be exported with a movie. You can selectively embed font outlines for all characters or only some of them, as illustrated next.

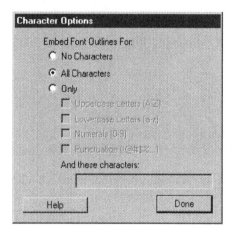

QuickTime Video Publishing

The *Video Page* is technically a dynamic SWF file—many of them, in fact. Each QuickTime movie (**.mov*) trailer will be published as its own SWF file. This is because of a restriction of Flash MX for linked QuickTime video. A linked QuickTime movie imported into Flash does not become part of the Flash file. Instead, Flash maintains a pointer to the source file. If you link to a QuickTime video, you *must* publish the movie as a QuickTime movie. We did not want to publish the movie as a QuickTime movie since we wanted navigational control and interactivity (pause, play, fast forward, close movies, and so on). Instead, we've chosen to embed the QuickTime movie into the Flash file and publish it as a Flash movie (SWF).

On the *Details Page*, we will now arrange a new movie (*Video Page*) to appear when the user clicks the *View Trailer* PushButton. The ActionScript code for this is shown next:

```
function openVideo(){
    Selection.setFocus(_root);
    _root.createEmptyMovieClip("popup",10);
    _root.popup._x=50;
    _root.popup._y=30;
```

```
_root.popup.loadMovie(_global.trailer);
_root.popup._alpha=0;
_root.disableMain();
_root.fader=setInterval(_root.fadeInt,50,1,"popup",35);
}
```

An example of a movie trailer is shown in the illustration that follows.

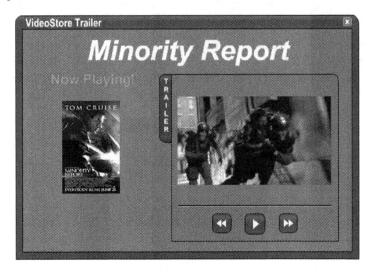

The published SWF file also contains a preloader movie in a separate scene to indicate how much of the video trailer is loaded dynamically. Preloaders are tiny movies that load quickly and tell your viewers to wait. You would create a preloader as follows:

1. Create two scenes, the first for your preloader, and the second for your main movie (a video trailer in our example). The scenes *must* be in the same movie. You can view the different scenes using the Scene selector (Window | Scene) as illustrated next.

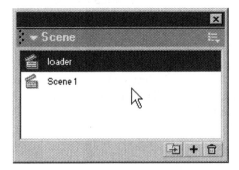

2. You use ActionScript to do the calculation based on information available to the Flash MX client. For example, *_framesloaded* and *_totalframes*. Or use the methods *getBytesTotal* and *getBytesLoaded*, as shown here:

```
//Get total bytes
onClipEvent(load){
    _parent.totalKB=Math.round(_parent.getBytesTotal()*.001);
}

//Update status
onClipEvent(enterFrame){
    _parent.loadedKB=Math.round(_parent.getBytesLoaded()*.001);
}
```

3. On the *last* frame of your preloader scene, make sure the movie clip is completely loaded and play the main movie using ActionScript. For example:

```
onClipEvent(enterFrame){
    _parent.loadedKB=Math.round(_parent.getBytesLoaded()*.001);
    if(_parent.loadedKB>=_parent.totalKB){
    }
}
```

Here is what the preloader looks like for our example video trailer (*Minority Report*).

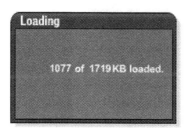

JPEG Images

We have decided to dynamically load JPEG files (movie posters in our example) into our movie during run time using the *loadMovie* method (see the following code snippet):

```
// create movie clip for displaying JPG video poster image
_root.createEmptyMovieClip("imgObj",9);
_root.imgObj._x=30;
_root.imgObj._y=60;
imagePath = "http://localhost:8500/book" +
resultD.items[0].strPoster;
_root.imgObj.loadMovie(imagePath);
```

Thus the content (image) is dynamic, and that's how the movie poster is displayed in the *Details Page*.

Movie Explorer

We want to introduce the Movie Explorer that we find very useful. The Movie Explorer provides an easy way to view and organize the content of a Flash document. It contains a display list of currently used elements, arranged in a hierarchical tree that is easy to navigate in. For display, you can filter which categories of items in the document to show within the Movie Explorer—for example, you can pick from text, graphics, buttons, movie clips, actions, and imported files, and then select these elements for editing and modification. The Movie Explorer view of our dynamic video store is shown next.

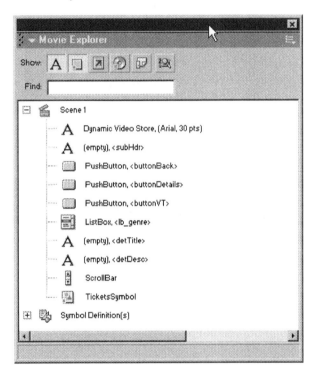

Static Versus Dynamic Video Store Application

Now that we have gone through designing a major portion of the static video store and the full implementation of the dynamic video store, let's summarize in Table 3-3 what the differences in frames, file types, and so on are between them.

   The dynamic video store uses only two frames versus 66 for the static video store (with a 30-movie selection or inventory). Any time modifications (updates or additions or deletions) are made to the inventory, you have to edit the static video store FLA file, retest, republish, and redeploy. Of course, the SWF file size changes, too. One can easily conclude that using databases and server-side code with client-side code is the best way to go when designing Flash MX applications!

Static Video Store	Dynamic Video Store
Main Page (frame 1)	Shared *Main/Titles Page* (frame 1)
Titles Page (frame 5) – e.g., Action	Shared *Main/Titles Page* (frame 1)
Details Page (frame 10) – e.g., Gladiator	*Details Page* (frame 5)
Video Page (frame 15) – e.g., Gladiator embedded video	*Video Page* served dynamically from server (gladiator.swf)
Not needed	RDBMS
Any Application Server	ColdFusion MX
Not needed	Flash Remoting
Titles Page (frame 6) – e.g., Comedy	Shared *Main/Titles Page* (frame 1)
Details Page (frame 11) – e.g., Shrek	Shared *Main/Titles Page* (frame 1)
…and so on.	…and so on.

Table 3-3   *Static Versus Dynamic Design*

Deployment

Deploying to different application servers is a rather involved process and we won't cover it sufficiently here to do justice. However, we will show a bare-bone deployment to the ColdFusion MX server by copying the relevant HTML, SWF, and image files to the web server directory. With ColdFusion MX server, the web root folder is located at:

```
C:\CFusionMX\wwwroot
```

and referred to by the browser as:

```
http://localhost:8500/
```

Our dynamic video store files (HTML, SWF) are located in the *book* subdirectory, and the JPEG images are located in the subdirectory *book\\trailerchooser\\posters*:

```
C:\CFusionMX\wwwroot\book
C:\CFusionMX\wwwroot\book\trailerchooser\posters
```

and referred to by the browser as:

```
http://localhost:8500/book
```

NOTE

You don't deploy your *.fla files, of course.

File Type	Size
Source FLA file (e.g., dyn_video.fla)	316KB
Published SWF file (e.g., dyn_video.swf)	136KB
Published HTML file (e.g., dyn_video.html)	1KB
Movie Trailers files (e.g., minorityreport.swf)	1624KB

Table 3-4   *Deployment File Sizes*

Our example dynamic video store will have the following files deployed:

▶   **/book**   *dyn_video.html, dyn_video.swf, gladiator.swf, minorityreport.swf, …*

▶   **/book/trailerchooser/posters**   *gladiator.jpg, minorityreport.jpg,*

The database is usually deployed into the *C:\CFusionMX\db* directory.
Table 3-4 above shows the file sizes for our dynamic online video store.

NOTE

Please refer to your respective application server documentation on a deployment strategy.

Summary

We have just gone through a quick tutorial using Flash MX to create a rich Internet application. We started from our video store blueprint application and then mapped that to a static stand-alone Flash MX application. The static video store is terrific for prototyping and client presentations to validate requirements and spur design ideas. However, it lacks flexibility and scalability. To do it right, we extend the static video store application by introducing databases, ColdFusion MX, and Flash Remoting, into the fold. The resulting dynamic video store application is much more compact and interactive, extensible, and easily maintained. You can add more genres, change digital assets (images and trailers), and modify video offerings by working with the databases alone. We have also deployed these files to an application server environment. We now have a working prototype of a dynamic Flash application, albeit with less design work. In Chapter 4, we will discuss user interfaces, design rules, usability, style guides, and other Flash design concepts, as well as focus on designing for mobile devices.

PART II

Building Skills for Multichannel Mobile Applications

OBJECTIVES

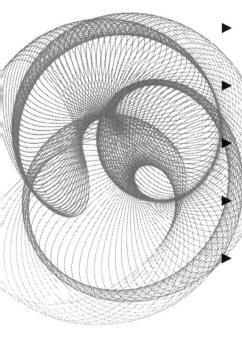

▶ Design mobile user interfaces and integrate animation and multimedia

▶ Explore Macromedia Flash Remoting and Server-Side ActionScript

▶ Review the use of Flash MX with J2EE, .NET, and ColdFusion

▶ Tackle mobile architecture with Flash MX for device detection and session management

▶ Learn the basics of Flash Communication Server and its client-side and server-side objects

Designing Mobile User Interfaces

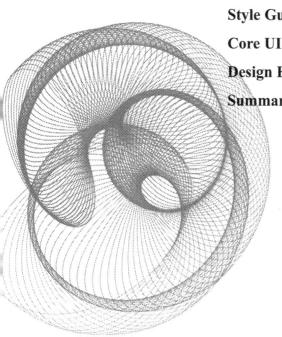

I n this chapter, we look at how to design effective user interfaces (UI) for mobile applications using the Macromedia Flash MX authoring environment. Again, we will take on the route that many designers and developers follow and dissect the key issues of building intuitive Flash user interfaces for mobile devices. We will review the design and development process, contrasting the workflow for Internet and mobile applications. We will examine ways to enhance usability by looking at the qualities of useful mobile applications and the guidelines used for building them. After that, we will drill down into specific details, such as page layout, screen size, typography, input methods, and items that are of practical use. After we address the usability of mobile Flash applications in generic terms, we then review the study guides of designing Flash applications for Microsoft Pocket PCs and the Nokia 9200 Communicator Series. We conclude by summarizing the Macromedia Flash MX Core UI components and look at an example of how to take advantage of them for mobile applications.

Design and Development Process

In a way, the process for designing and developing mobile applications is very similar to building Internet applications in general. All the sound planning and useful guidelines do apply. However, there are a few key points that make this endeavor different that you must bear in mind and comply with, in order to be successful. Besides the usual trappings of bandwidth and user interface limitations, mobile applications may have to run on multiple devices with different form factors and capabilities (browsers and processor speed). Also, your users are now mobile, as opposed to bound to a desktop computer. The mobile user case, user interface, and content will necessarily differ from those of regular Internet applications. In building your mobile applications, you need to decide not only what to show in terms of content and application logic, but also how to use it in terms of user interface, site organization, and navigation.

Your mobile content and business logic are different because your mobile Macromedia Flash application should only present web content that is relevant (and personal) to the user—at the right time and at the right location. Your mobile site organization and navigation must adjust to the device and network limitations, as well as the use case itself. Device limitations may include a simplified user interface, while network limitations might include slower download speeds and an intermittent connectivity. Equally important perhaps is the fact that your mobile user is no longer solely focused on your application, as in the case of a desktop application. While your users may have a task in mind, they are probably eager to complete it as fast as possible—and aren't in the mood (or position) to do much browsing. Hence, the organization and navigation of your mobile application needs to take that into account.

Presentation Layer and Client-Side Issues

To build a mobile rich Internet application—based on Flash—you must plan the user interface and the navigation of the application with a consideration for smaller screen sizes, limited input capability, reduced processing power, and of course, slower connection speed. While you build the front end of the rich application, you must work with the back end. These issues have a direct impact on how you build the user interface, therefore you must be careful when building the back end and writing the scripts.

▶ **Screen size** has an impact on font size and different aspect ratios.

▶ **Low bandwidth** has an impact on how large the file size of your movie should be, how it should be embedded, and how you should stream and download the movie.

▶ **Input capability** has an impact on what primary input method your Flash movie should use and how you can toggle between primary and secondary methods (mouse, keyboard, stylus, pointer buttons, and so on).

▶ **Reduced CPU and memory capability** have an impact on the code (and therefore the user interface you present) as well as how your movie can be loaded and run in conjunction with your applications and resources.

These factors simply demand a clean separation of the presentation layer from the business logic and data layers of your application.

So, when Macromedia Flash MX comes along with a cleaner separation between presentation and the rest of the application (the business logic and the data layer), it's a big step forward in creating mobile presentations independent of the back-end layers. Building user interfaces in Macromedia Flash MX simplifies the server development of web applications by cleanly separating design of the presentation layer in Macromedia Flash from the implementation of business logic on the application server. Interactions between the client, the Macromedia Flash Player, and the back-end, the database and other content sources, can be done via the middle tier—the application server whose functions include management of the business logic and data exchange, as well as providing instructions on its presentation format.

Let's review the mobile development workflow before we dive into the actual details of designing mobile UI.

Mobile Flash Development Workflow

In Chapter 3, we discuss the different roles and workflows related to building Flash Internet applications. As mentioned earlier, the distinct and uniform way of building Macromedia Flash MX applications makes it particularly suitable for mobile development.

Indeed, the mobile workflow for the client-side designer and developer is interesting as they must deal with multiple devices and designs. This may affect how you create digital assets and page designs. For example, you will need to work with the Information Architect and make necessary adjustments due to the limitations in screen size and new navigational aids.

While the mobile workflow is no different from the regular Flash development workflow in that you need to have storyboards, assets, and prototyping, mobile Flash involves other things that regular Flash development doesn't have. Again, it is illuminating to contrast

HTML and Flash. The roles and workflows involved in a Macromedia Flash application project are similar to those in an HTML project, except for one major difference—the clean separation of presentation and business logic in Macromedia Flash MX.

What does it mean when you say "separating the design of the presentation layer from the development of the business logic"? Simply this: the basic design (presentation) of the application is built independently of the back end (logic and data); therefore any changes in the back end do not affect the front end.

Once the server-side developers and Flash client-side developers agree on the structure and content of the messages sent between the tiers, they have thereby drawn clean boundaries between their areas of responsibility.

Designers and client-side developers can build additional features and optimize for different client devices—independently, albeit in conjunction with the server-side engineer. So, you have designers create user interfaces, while client-side Flash developers build the technical ActionScript, and server-side developers connect the front end with databases and application logic flow.

This approach has been advocated and promoted for some time. However, many approaches, especially with HTML, suffer from an intermingling of logic and presentation code. You may find business logic merged into the presentation layer, sometimes including the use of proprietary tags.

There are several benefits to this trait in Flash. First, since the bulk of the user interface is developed in Macromedia Flash rather than HTML, less HTML and coding skills are required of the designer. Flash designers can focus on creating world-class designs and digital assets, and tying them together in an intuitive user interface. Second, a cleaner boundary between the responsibilities of client- and server-side developers mean both teams can work separately but closely together. Client-side developers can concentrate on the client-side logic and presentation formatting in their coding efforts, while the server-side developers can focus on writing code to query databases and delivering application logic, without mixing it with page formatting. They just need to write code that can interpret client-side requests and respond with data messages. No more formatted HTML pages.

For the Flash designers, Macromedia Flash MX has built-in special features to facilitate their work. You can customize Flash to best suit your design workflow. For example, you can set up your default movie properties to the settings you most often use, making your movies consistent, not to mention saving you time! For devices with different screen sizes, you can, of course, use the templates for Pocket PC and Nokia 9200 devices that are shipped with Macromedia Flash MX. You can implement other capabilities in Macromedia Flash MX, too, such as form processing core UI components and leveraging the object-oriented approach offered by Macromedia Flash MX.

When to Use Flash

Wow! When do you use Flash? You almost have to ask the flip side of the question: when shouldn't you? Because of the visual development environment, Macromedia Flash MX is unusually approachable for building *mobile* applications. And Macromedia Flash MX provides an alternate paradigm for constructing mobile Internet application user interfaces due to its clean separation of presentation and logic! Typical mobile applications are based on a markup language (WML), and its user environment includes linked pages and discrete downloads. Indeed, the logic of many e-commerce applications are based on a click-for-a-page model that requires frequent downloads of new pages. A Macromedia Flash user interface offers a unified experience in an uninterrupted manner. You only load the data from the server and the Flash Player will format it accordingly, minimizing download file sizes and reducing the burden on your application server.

Okay, on the flip side: Many of the issues related to Flash web sites are directly applicable to mobile Flash development. The first and foremost question is: can I use Flash and add value? If it is strictly for style, as opposed to performance improvement or other reasons, then you are making a trade-off based strictly on design. It's perfectly fine to do that—however, you must understand how this will affect the user experience. Will your users like it? Will it be a positive experience? One important lesson many of us have learned is the "Flash strictly for fancy design" approach. Many web sites were equipped with lengthy and flashy introductions built with Flash. Since some of them were long and lacked substance, they led to a "user revolt" on Flash as the intro, and helped popularize the use of the now infamous "skip intro" link in many Flash movies. In general, Flash is great for bringing down bandwidth requirements in rich applications. But if your text-based mobile application is doing well using minimal bandwidth, say 9.6 kbps or less, and your device isn't powerful enough to handle much ActionScript, then forget about using Flash!

Usability Issues

Here, we focus on the usability issues as related to mobile Flash applications since there are already numerous resources addressing overall Flash usability and user experience. We will first look at the quality characteristics of enhancing usability in mobile applications. Then, we will review a few usability tips for Flash web sites that still apply to mobile flash applications.

Qualities of the Mobile Flash User Interface

Creating a familiar and consistent user experience for mobile devices involves more than just the user interface, or addressing the presentation layer alone. It involves a comprehensive approach that ensures the overall presentation, application logic, and content are tailored to the needs of the user and adjusted for the constraints by the environment. Presentation issues include site organization, navigation, design, style, and responsiveness. Application logic addresses usability issues such as customization and location-based services (LBS), as well as how streamlined the information flow is. Finally, the content (or data) issues entail the choice of personalizing information, offering content in text or graphics, as well as the amount and complexity of animation and other multimedia content. Many qualities attributed to creating usable Flash Internet applications also apply to the mobile environment. Others may be entirely related to mobile applications when developing with Macromedia Flash MX. Let's review what a mobile Flash application with great usability should possess.

Presentation:

▶ **Organization**   Needless to say, you must have a well-organized mobile web site or application with all those limitations in mobile devices and networks. However, letting your users know how your applications are organized, essentially a big picture viewpoint, could improve the overall user experience. With mobile devices, this becomes a challenge as you must manage the smaller screen and fonts while providing a highly interactive interface.

▶ **Navigation**   Mobile applications must have streamlined navigations that are self-evident and do not involve deep page hierarchy and lengthy sections. A balance is made between how deep and how wide the navigation becomes. Useful mobile applications find ways to simply show users the path they want to follow and the choices they intuitively can expect. Also, users shouldn't lose focus when they progress through various stages of a process (for example, checking out). Jumping from one point to another within the mobile application may cause them to lose interest or their focus, if not both. Allowing your user to go anywhere is okay on an Internet application, but it's not recommended in mobile. Linear navigation, on the other hand, is much more easily understood and implemented in mobile applications. The fine line in linear and non-linear navigation with rich Internet applications is more tilted towards "clear and straightforward" in guiding the users to accomplish what they want!

▶ **Design**   Consistent and functional designs are much preferred. A consistent design provides familiarity and builds confidence for your users. Again, keep the interface simple and functional, and your users can appreciate the self-explanatory aspect of your design and learn by themselves.

▶ **Style**   It is useful to adhere to the style guide of the underlying mobile device. For example, a successful mobile Flash application for the Nokia 9200 Communicator phone must find ways to not only use, but also take advantage of its navigational keys. On the other hand, you may need to design your mobile application to be aligned with your corporate style guide.

▶ **Responsiveness**   A great deal can be said about speediness and responsiveness of mobile applications and the so-called "page refreshes." With Flash, you have the advantage of Flash's client-side processing in the Flash Player and an efficient exchange of data between Flash Player and the back end. The key is to match or exceed user expectation. For example, your users may tolerate and even expect longer download time at the outset, but would expect, or can be delighted with, speedy refreshes on calendar updates or client-side calculations, using Flash Player.

Application Logic:

▶ **Customization**   Every user is different in terms of navigation and application needs that impact the overall experience. Successful mobile applications allow for these differences and provide means to customize usage either on the device itself, or on the server that offers the application logic. The use of presets or predefined settings (either system enforced or user) can help here.

▶ **Location awareness**   Mobile users are at different places at different times. That means they are not necessarily desk-bound. The most successful mobile applications offer location-aware or location-based services that cater to the needs of their users. A restaurant guide for San Francisco is simply no help for users who are currently in London looking for a fine British meal.

▶ **Logic flow and context**   Your users should be able to navigate freely and not be in danger of getting lost. Offering a simple logic flow and providing contextual menus will help. You can also reinforce the user focus by restricting choices and providing obvious UI options.

▶ **Error handling**   As with running applications on PCs, your users may encounter errors while using Flash applications on Pocket PCs or Nokia smart phones. For example, the processing of complex ActionScript within a Flash movie could tax the CPU of your handheld device and occasionally cripple it. You don't want your users to see the infamous "blue screen of death" as a result. Hence, you should build in error-handling capabilities and messages to assist your user when an error occurs. Some of the error messaging capabilities are already available from the devices themselves. Within Nokia, for instance, an error dialog pops up when a movie takes too long to process.

Content and Data Layer:

▶ **Personalization**   Deriving the best user experience involves understanding and providing personalized services to the mobile users. While customization deals with the use of presets (settings made by the users), personalization is driven by the data layer (and the application logic) to make the experience both seamless and tailored to the users' needs. For example, the ability to skip login steps or prefill address fields for billing information is a great way to simplify and streamline your mobile user experience.

▶ **Text or graphics**   Successful mobile applications deliver content in the most appropriate format, be it text or graphics. While the capabilities and limitations of mobile devices may constrain the use of graphics, the successful handling (and speedy download) of graphics, such as icons, can convey the message of your application faster and sometimes more efficiently. Besides presentation options, remember you also have the option of using simplified content.

▶ **Animation and multimedia**   To take this to the next level, the offering of animation and multimedia also involves a decision on content, in addition to presentation or style. Animation can be useful for navigation purposes. But the use of streaming video and animation must justify the trade-off in processing and downloading burden. If so, your users will appreciate the rich content, which is why you build mobile applications with Flash in the first place!

Usability Tips

For now, let's review some quick tips on usability before looking at several items in detail. In general, the following usability tips are crucial for mobile devices:

▶ **Organize information in chunks**   Split long documents into chunks, or simply avoid long documents. If you can't shorten things, create indexes or other means to help whenever possible.

▶ **Keep it simple**   Well, the "Keep It Simple Stupid" (KISS) lesson is never truer than it is here, with "it" being the user interface. Cluttered or fancy interfaces just make it harder for anyone to learn and use. Remember, if it takes time for people to learn something, they may never spend the time to do so. For instance, it's hard to adjust to new interfaces and styles. And witness how long it takes people to accept 100 percent Flash for Internet applications.

▶ **Input methods**   Leverage the default input methods of your target device, but also offer convenient alternatives that are consistent across devices. For text inputs, remember to avoid any keyboard-intensive steps as they lead to errors or inaccuracies, not to mention a slow and tedious user experience.

▶ **Navigation**   Give your mobile users an easy and obvious exit from each section or page. Support back button navigation by including a Flash-based Back button. Avoid multiple or big pop-up menu components that tend to lose your users.

▶ **Make judicious decisions on graphics**   As mentioned before, use icons and pixel fonts where appropriate (more on this later). Use graphics to aid navigation, presentation, and interactions, unless it's too taxing on the processor or download speed.

▶ **Bandwidth**   Obviously, a smaller SWF file will make the download faster. As mentioned in Chapter 3, you must decide whether to create one Flash movie, or break them into several Flash movies. This has an impact on download and/or application speed. If your initial download is greater than 50 kb or so, you probably should provide some indication of the download progress. With some planning, your mobile applications should leverage built-in capabilities of the Flash Player, and the smart use of caching data can lead to less network traffic. Compressing your SWF files streamed to the Flash Player can lead to efficient use of network bandwidth and better experience.

▶ **Processor efficiency and caching**   Optimizing the runtime of Flash applications is the other side of the optimization equation (versus optimizing the file size). We will cover that in detail in Chapter 5.

▶ **Allow customization or personalization**   Provide means for users to enter preset values for customization and store them in your data repository. Your applications should be able to prefill forms with this data, and your applications, leveraging robust server capabilities, should be able to personalize the user experience. This way, your applications won't have to explicitly ask for inputs every time.

▶ **Use local images or built-in icons**   Reduce the burden of transmitting images and icons over the air by building them into your applications and referring to them in your pages.

▶ **Focus on content, not display**   Keep it simple and elegant. Use only supported elements and components. Obviously, the content is the reason your users are using the mobile application. Make your design fit the content, not the other way around. Customize content specifically for the targeted user and target only information that is essential.

▶ **Animation**   Avoid animations if possible. Use animations only to convey a message or aid in navigation. Avoid full-screen wipes and fades as they strain CPU (central processor unit) cycles and can render your applications rather sluggish. More on performance in the "Style Guide" section later.

We will now go into the details of some of the other usability issues for mobile devices, including page layouts, typography, and so on.

Desktop and Mobile Applications

Intuitively, you know the page layout must differ between desktop and mobile Flash applications. Don't simply serve your Flash movies designed for desktop PCs onto a smart phone screen or Pocket PC touch screen and expect to have a seamless user experience. Besides having a bad user experience due to the mismatch in screen size and aspect ratio, you can run into some problems.

For once, spawning new browser instances is not possible on Pocket PCs. And there is no stand-alone player with the Pocket PC. All mobile Flash movies must be viewed within the Pocket PC Mobile Internet Explorer. This means your Flash movies must be embedded within accompanying HTML pages for Pocket PCs. However, this is not true for the Nokia 9200 Communicator, which is shipped with a stand-alone Flash Player.

Perhaps equally significant is the fact that desktop Flash applications are designed to have several panels. These panels may allow quick updates and non-linear interactivity. On a smaller screen, you may not be able to view them clearly. And if some of them use rollovers and your mobile device doesn't support rollovers, your Flash application will be severely crippled, if not entirely useless.

To illustrate these points further, we will start by looking at the three most popular PDAs on the marketplace—Pocket PC 2002, the Nokia Communicator, and the Palm/Handspring. Currently, the Palm/Handspring platform doesn't have Flash Player support. However, it is reasonable to expect the market will bring Flash to this hugely popular PDA as the new operation system, OS 5, takes shape in the marketplace.

Navigation, Page Layout, and Screen Size

User navigation is generally based on the eye movement pattern of your mobile device user. As a result, the general path is from the top to the bottom of the screen, and for western societies, from left to right. The navigational elements are the most important to a user as you want to keep the user oriented and guide them to the next action step at all times. Thus, navigational elements should be on the top of the screen, and primary content elements below the navigational elements (see the following illustration). All these elements (navigation and content) should be "above the fold"—that is, the mobile user should never have to use the horizontal or vertical scroll bar of a browser (embedded SWF) to view the full content.

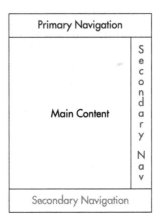

On the Pocket PC 2002 platform, the general screen size is 240 pixels (width) by 320 pixels (height) display resolution. Since there is no stand-alone Flash player currently available, the Flash movie (SWF) must be embedded inside an HTML page and displayed though Microsoft Pocket Internet Explorer (Pocket IE). With this restriction, the mobile user is further subjected to an optional address bar, dynamic scroll bars (vertical and horizontal), captions, and menu bar (see Figure 4-1). Taking all this into account, the "guaranteed" display area is only 230 pixels (width) by 255 pixels (height)!

There are third-party tools available (for example, FlashAssist from Ant Mobile Software) that allow you to run the SWF file in full-screen mode. But a mobile application developer cannot assume that a majority of the mobile device users have this running unless it becomes part of the Pocket PC OS or Macromedia makes it part of the Flash Player installation kit. More details on content publishing can be found in the portion of the upcoming "Style Guide" section devoted to the Pocket PC 2002.

The Nokia Communicator series of smart phones (for example, 9210i) has a 640 × 200 (width × height) pixel display resolution. The Flash Player on the Nokia Communicator is a stand-alone player and the movie can be played in full-screen mode (the shortcut is CTRL-T). However, full-screen mode is not the default, so most applications will run within the "application" area (see Figure 4-2) of 490 pixels (width) by 165 pixels (height) with an indicator and command button area on the display.

More details on content publishing can be found later in the "Style Guide" section on Nokia Communicators.

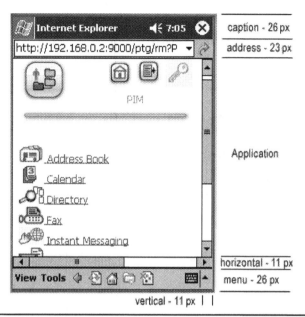

Figure 4-1   *The Pocket PC 2002 displayable area*

In general, the Palm has a 160 × 160 pixel display resolution (color or monochrome) but only 153 × 144 pixels of that are usable for content due to the title display and scroll bar (see Figure 4-3). But there are Palm devices with increasingly higher resolutions, like the

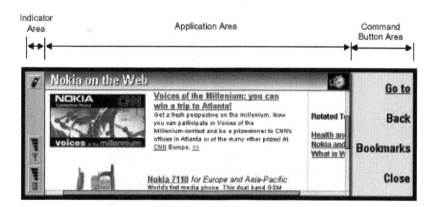

Figure 4-2   *The Nokia Communicator displayable area*

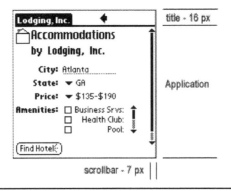

Figure 4-3   *The Palm OS displayable area*

Sony CLIÉ NR70V, which has a 320 pixel (width) by 480 pixel (height) 65,536-color display resolution.

So far, we have only been talking about displaying the content in the default orientation by design—portrait (230 × 255 pixels) for Pocket PC and landscape (490 × 165 pixels) for Nokia. What if we wanted to display in landscape orientation for Pocket PC? For example, let's say we are streaming a video trailer (for example, *The Lord of the Rings—The Two Towers*) to a Pocket PC form factor that only has a width of 230 pixels (see following illustration). As a result, the left and right side of the trailer is cropped!

With a little help from ActionScript, we can rotate the original video (or any objects on the stage like the header static text object) 90 degrees counterclockwise and fit it into the landscape orientation of the Pocket PC form factor (see next illustration).

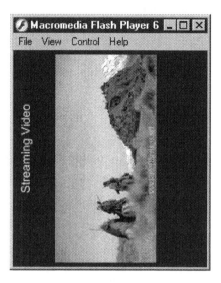

The code snippet would look as follows:

```
// streamingVideo - instance name of embedded video object
// header - instance name of static text object
// rotate video object counterclockwise 90 degrees
streamingVideo._rotation = -90;
// re-position reference corner of video frame
streamingVideo._x = 50;
streamingVideo._y = 245;
// rotate static text object counterclockwise 90 degrees
header._rotation = -90;
// re-position reference corner of text object
header._x = 5;
header._y = 200;
```

More details on how to create streaming videos can be found in Chapter 11.

Typography

One important consideration when bringing your Macromedia Flash experience onto mobile devices is quite obviously the physical legibility of your text. The smaller screen with fewer pixels only engenders this challenge. Because the screens are typically only centimeters wide, legibility would be a problem even if you use the same pixel counts from your desktop

Flash applications. The amount of readable information may be drastically reduced. Remember, a scaled-down version of an 800 × 600 Flash application won't show very well on a handheld device. Instead, you should offer a simpler UI and place fewer elements onscreen at any given time. A few simple icons describing the use of the application can sometimes work as well as text. Icons also have an advantage because they are not language-dependent. If you design your icon system well, you can use icons regardless of language preferences.

Anti-aliasing, the smoothing of pixels, is used in many Flash applications to make edges less jagged and, to some, more aesthetically pleasing when you scale your Flash movies up and down for desktop PCs.

NOTE

Anti-aliasing is a technique that smoothes the edges of diagonal lines on the screen. Without anti-aliasing, diagonal lines often have a "jaggy" appearance caused by the stair-step effect of the pixels. Anti-aliasing blurs the edges of the lines.

As a result, many mobile Flash applications use pixel fonts. Pixel fonts are designed for use with limited screen resolution and size, and they will remain aliased in Flash, regardless of the movie quality. Although pixel fonts are also called bitmap fonts, it is noteworthy that these pixel fonts only emulate bitmaps and are based on vector outlines. As a result, pixel fonts can be efficiently embedded in Flash movies.

The use of pixel fonts can be crucial for mobile applications because legibility and screen economy are the biggest typographic concerns due to small screen sizes. The economy of pixel fonts can make the difference between a clean and legible expression of your content, and a fuzzy looking screen. Plus, your users may not even notice you're using bitmap or pixel fonts unless you deliberately design them that way. For more information on the use and design of pixel fonts for Macromedia Flash MX, a good resource is Craig Kroeger's web site at http://www.miniml.com.

NOTE

Beware that when you set your movie quality to low quality, Flash will automatically make everything aliased.

Also, when you create text, you can specify that the Flash Player use device fonts to display certain text blocks, so that Flash does not embed the font for that text (see the following illustration). This can decrease the file size of the movie and increase legibility at text sizes below 10 points.

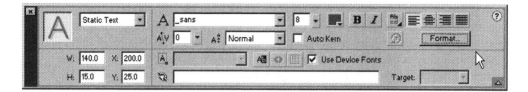

Flash includes three device fonts: _sans (similar to Helvetica or Arial), _serif (similar to Times Roman), and _typewriter (similar to Courier). The Flash Player uses whatever font on the local computer most closely resembles the device font. However, because device fonts are not embedded, if users do not have a font installed on their system that corresponds to the device font, text may look different than expected on a user's system.

NOTE

If your Flash movie is being used in an HTML page, make sure the frame setting window is set to the exact pixel value. If the movie is scaled in any way, the fonts will be anti-aliased.

Color and Contrast

Mobile devices like the Pocket PC and Nokia Communicator can display anywhere from 4,096 to 65,535 colors, or from 4 to 16 levels of gray scale. Unless you are designing exclusively for a specific mobile device and want to maximize the effects, you may want to limit the colors to 12 bits or 4,096 colors. Even then, you should test extensively as many devices may not have screens that are as advanced as desktop monitors which can accurately produce the color effects desired.

A way to compensate for the restriction in colors is through contrast. When designing for mobile devices, you want to select highly contrasting colors because mobile screens may not faithfully reproduce your colors, and inherently have low contrast. Through palette selection, you can create images that are crisp in detail.

Input Methods

Because mobile devices rarely deal with mouse-based inputs, no actual cursor exists. In fact, the position of the user's pointing device isn't known until the mobile user actually taps on the screen. For handheld devices, the user input has been mostly reduced to two methods: tapping and dragging. Tapping by nature is not too precise, and your interface should account for tapping by stylus as well as fingers or fingernails. Your design and button spacing should be far enough apart that it would be difficult to miss the target and hit something else.

Typing is to be *avoided* as much as possible. The Pocket PC has a built-in soft keyboard, and the Nokia Communicator has a physical keyboard (see illustrations that follow). However, most users are not accustomed to browsing or typing with their handheld devices. Unless absolutely necessary, let your mobile user use the keyboard for text input—for example, entering a ticker symbol. If not, use Flash MX UI components like check boxes, radio buttons, sliders, or listboxes to build your input frame.

The UI components of Macromedia Flash MX (check boxes, radio buttons, sliders, combo boxes, and listboxes) let you add this functionality to Flash movies with a minimum amount of authoring and scripting. The Checkbox control provides a simple and widely used method for users to choose Boolean values. Radio Buttons allow users to select a single option amongst those available to them in that context. Slider control gives you a simple way to pick from a range of values. Your mobile users can drag the slider around or simply tap the spot (on the slider) to pick the value. Through the Combo Box control, you can provide a scrollable drop-down list of items which your mobile users can pick and choose from. We will look at a simple example to illustrate how a wizard will ask for input information (with minimal, if any, keyboard input) from a mobile device user. First, the use of check boxes, radio buttons, and a listbox for the first step of the wizard, is shown next.

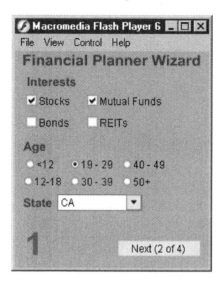

Notice that the "Next (2 of 4)" button which serves as a navigation aid and informs the users where they can navigate to next! Second, the use of a combo box for selecting a list of stocks of interest to the mobile user, all without having to type a single ticker symbol (as shown next).

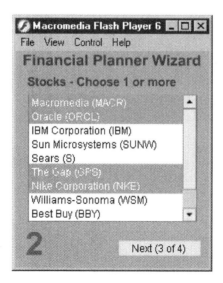

Also, the page number 2 is shown on the lower left corner. You can replace that with an icon if your signpost is number-oriented since icons are a great way to convey meaning while conserving space. Given the screen sizes of mobile devices, developing effective icon systems is advantageous to both the designer and the user. Remember, a good icon should be easily understood, easily recognizable, and easy to remember. If you use icons, simplify and uniformly stylize icons to work as a set.

Menus and Rollovers

In desktop PCs, you can access a contextual menu by right-clicking an item. On a Pocket PC, where there is no mouse, Macromedia offers an equivalent action to the user by holding down the stylus on the device screen. Previously, Macromedia had disabled the contextual menus in Flash 4 Player for Pocket PC because they interfered with file dragging operations on the Pocket PC screen.

Now, the mobile user can invoke the right-click Flash menu on a Pocket PC device. However, if the stylus is held down over a button, the right-click menu will not be activated. This step allows you to have dragging capabilities in your Flash movie while still providing access to the right-click menu.

On the other hand, mouse rollover events are more of a challenge and can be easily mishandled. Because there is no mouse (the Pocket PC doesn't have a cursor), it is important not to make your application rely too heavily on cursor position information. And given the absence of a mouse, mouse rollovers shouldn't be implemented.

NOTE

We recommend you avoid the use of rollovers.

Publishing File Types

One last item to note when publishing for mobile devices is the impact of the Publish Settings (see illustration that follows). Under the HTML tab, two settings of concern are *Dimensions* and *Quality*. Make sure Dimension is set to *Match Movie* so that anti-aliasing is not automatically applied.

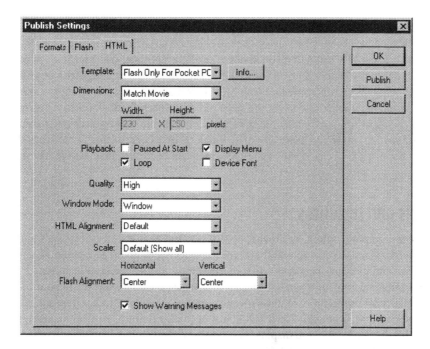

Quality is a trade-off between processing time and applying anti-aliasing, both crucial issues for mobile devices. Anti-aliasing requires a fast CPU to smooth out each frame of the Flash movie prior to its rendering to the screen. Hence, you are left with the choice between choosing a value based on appearance or speed. The default setting for Quality is *High* and that enables anti-aliasing and sets appearance as its priority. A setting of *Low* favors playback speed over screen quality and appearance. It disables anti-aliasing. Yet another setting that may be a good compromise is *Auto High*. Here, playback speed and appearance are *equally* favored, but the tie breaker is for playback speed if needed. Anti-aliasing is enabled at first. But when the frame rate drops below a specified rate—for instance, 10 frames per second in the Flash Player—anti-aliasing will shut off to restore playback speed.

NOTE

Always test the application on the devices to ensure the desired playback.

Forms

Unlike forms in HTML that require different code for different browsers, Macromedia Flash MX offers a platform that supports uniform form processing across browsers. This means you can view any Flash movie and see the same thing no matter what browser your users are using. This way you just have to write one version of the movie.

Masking

Macromedia Flash MX can add distinctive styles to normal images via masks. For example, a common usage is to apply an oval (or round-edged) mask to a rectangular image through client-side scripts with Macromedia Flash MX. This makes it very easy to apply the same effect to additional images and saves the steps of having to individually edit the effect into these new images. You just publish these original images onto your server environment. A point of caution: masking, especially that which involves a large area, could introduce a great number of CPU cycles during run time which can tax your Flash Player. You need to test your applications on the target devices.

Symbols and Instances

A *symbol* is a graphic, button, or movie clip that is created once in the Flash MX authoring environment and reused throughout that same Flash movie or in other movies. Accordingly, this symbol automatically becomes a part of the library for the current Flash file.

An *instance* is a copy of a symbol located on the stage. Using symbols in your movies dramatically reduces the file size, thus speeding movie playback. Rather than storing each instance you use, Macromedia Flash MX stores one definition for the symbol and only refers to that definition each time you display an instance of the symbol. This greatly improves the scalability and the playback speed. Of course, you can convert a group of static objects into symbols. You may be able to reduce your file size even when you use the symbol only once.

Style Guide

We will now focus on the two most popular mobile platforms that have Flash players already available—the Pocket PC and Nokia Communicator. Macromedia has already published individual style guides for both these platforms and has made them available as Content Development Kits (CDK) on their web site at the Flash Device Resource Center (http://www.macromedia.com/software/flashplayer/resources/devices/). What we will be discussing here is strictly the latest Flash Player characteristics for each platform, and how content should be developed for them. Since only Flash 5 Player is currently available for these two platforms as of this writing, the same restrictions will probably apply to Flash 6 (MX) Player when it is made available.

In general, due to processor limitations, try to avoid large amounts of animation and tweening for these mobile devices. Also, because Macromedia Flash uses vectors to display content in Flash Player, the device processor must work extra duties to render graphics and animations.

Pocket PC

Let's go straight to Flash 5 Player on the Pocket PC 2002 platform. Here are the main characteristics of the player:

▶ The Flash movie (SWF) *must* be embedded inside an HTML page and displayed through Pocket Internet Explorer (Pocket IE). No stand-alone player exists.

▶ FSCommand is *not* supported.

▶ When specifying the height and width of the Flash movie in the HTML, the dimensions must be expressed as pixels, not as a percentage (it will be ignored otherwise).

▶ When publishing your content, the presence of the *<OBJECT>* tag is *mandatory*; otherwise the SWF movie won't play. The ID attribute of the *<OBJECT>* tag is required. The value of the attribute does not matter, however. Additionally, between the start and close of the *<OBJECT>* tag there must be a *<PARAM>* tag with the MOVIE attribute pointing to the actual file name of the SWF file. Otherwise, the SWF movie won't play.

▶ Notice that the CODEBASE attribute is not required because Pocket IE will not download ActiveX plug-ins from the Internet that are already installed.

▶ Flash 5 Player for the Pocket PC 2002 is not affected by the "Fit to Screen" option.

The following example code shows what the HTML should look like in order for your embedded Flash movie to play within the Pocket IE.

```
<OBJECT
    classid="clsid:D27CDB6E-AE6D-11cf-96B8-444553540000"
    WIDTH="230" HEIGHT="250" id="ui" ALIGN="">
    <PARAM NAME="movie" VALUE="ui.swf"
    <PARAM NAME="quality" VALUE="high"
    <PARAM NAME="bgcolor" VALUE="#FFFFFF">
    <EMBED src="ui.swf" quality="high" bgcolor="#FFFFFF"
        WIDTH="230" HEIGHT="250" NAME="ui" ALIGN=""
        TYPE="application/x-shockwave-flash"
        PLUGINSPAGE="http://www.macromedia.com/go/getflashplayer">
    </EMBED>
</OBJECT>
```

Content development for the Pocket PC platform should follow these guidelines:

▶ When using a Pocket PC 2002 keyboard, part of your Flash content may be covered by the onscreen keyboard (see previous "Usability Issues" section). You may be able to cope with this by offering a custom, yet smaller, keypad.

▶ If "Hide Pictures" is selected in Pocket IE, Flash movies will not be displayed.

▶ As discussed before, buttons are treated differently with Pocket PC. Because Pocket PC does not use a mouse and has no cursor, a stylus tap takes the place of a mouse for interaction. You should avoid a rollover state and make sure that the hit zones on the buttons are large enough. More often, users can tap inaccurately, or a finger (with short nail) is used for that purpose.

▶ Another pitfall when running mobile applications on the Pocket PC may be that the Flash movie can become defocused. A way to rectify that is to provide a "tap here" button to start the interaction and bring the application and the Flash Player back into focus.

▶ Flash 5 Player for the Pocket PC 2002 includes four built-in fonts: Tahoma (variable width), Courier (fixed width), Bookdings, and Frutiger Linotype. Verdana is a device-friendly font that renders well on bitmap displays at all resolutions, making it suitable for use on mobile devices. Another good screen face is the Geneva font, which now serves as one of the standard fonts on certain handheld devices. In general for devices, most sans fonts display better than serif fonts. Serif fonts tend to lose their details on screens that aren't as sharp as average desktop monitors.

▶ For mobile devices, the less sound the better. Sound requires large amounts of processing power to decompress the sound data, and it also consumes precious power resources.

▶ Flash 5 Player for Pocket PC 2002 follows the existing security model of the Flash Player. For security reasons, a Flash movie playing in a web browser cannot access data residing outside the web domain from which the SWF originated. This parameter applies to any ActionScript command or object that may send or receive data, including loadVariables.

▶ As mentioned earlier in the previous section, "Usability Issues," the "guaranteed" display area is only 230 × 255 pixels due to the optional address bar, dynamic scroll bars (vertical and horizontal), caption, and menu bar (see Figure 4-1).

The Nokia Communicator

Although the Nokia 9200 Communicator Series currently includes the 9210, 9210i, and 9290, for convenience I'll generally refer to all these handheld devices as the Nokia 9200 Communicator. Here are the main characteristics of the player:

▶ Flash 5 Player for the Nokia Communicator is a stand-alone player. Therefore, Flash movies embedded within HTML pages are not accessible. Any Flash movies within an HTML page will be ignored by the browser and will not be displayed. No visual indication of the movie will be displayed within the HTML page.

▶ The largest file that the player can open is approximately 800 to 900 kb; however, this file size may vary slightly depending on the current state of the operating system.

▶ Even though Flash movies can only be run through the Flash Player (and not a web browser on the Nokia Communicator), it is still possible to do server-side device detection. See Chapter 9 for more details.

▶ FSCommand is *not* supported, with the exception of the FullScreen command and Quality setting.

▶ Any nonsupported ActionScript commands encountered by the Flash Player when processing a movie will be ignored.

Content Development for the Nokia Communicator platform should follow these guidelines:

▶ Because the CPU of the Nokia Communicator is significantly slower than the processor on the Microsoft Pocket PC or desktop PC, it is extremely important to take playback performance into consideration when you build and optimize your Flash movies.

▶ As mentioned earlier in the "Usability Issues" section, the "guaranteed" display area is only 490 × 165 pixels (due to the indicator and command button sections) when not in full-screen mode (see Figure 4-2). Scroll bars will appear otherwise, indicating that the entire movie is not visible.

▶ Mono sound is the only supported MP3 sound output. The quality of the playback depends primarily on the CPU utilization of the Flash movie when the sound is played. Because of this, Stereo MP3 may sound choppy at times due to the inadequate CPU processing. It is recommended that when using MP3 sounds, employ only mono sounds exported at 8 kbps. We'll talk more about this in Chapter 5.

▶ Flash 5 Player for the Nokia Communicator includes two built-in fonts: _sans (fixed width) and _typewriter (standard spaced).

▶ The Nokia 9200 Communicator features a full-blown keyboard and supports hot keys. However, a number of hot keys in Flash 5 Player have been added or changed to conform to the Nokia standard. New keys include CTRL-C (Copy), CTRL-X (Cut), CTRL-V (Paste), CTRL-A (Select All), and CTRL-Q (Toggle Cursor).

▶ The following are useful hot keys: CTRL-T (Full Screen mode) and CTRL-E (Exit). Notice that CTRL-Q (Exit) and CTRL-F (Full Screen) for Flash 5 Player are now CTRL-E (Exit) and CTRL-T (Full Screen) for the Nokia 9200 Communicator, respectively.

▶ The primary means of navigation within the Flash movie is through the use of the cursor, which is controlled by the Nokia Communicator arrow keypad located on the bottom-right of the keyboard. While navigating through the virtual pointer interface of Nokia—pointer or keypad—may be similar to using a mouse, they don't work the same way and, in fact, only support limited functions.

▶ Two features—Pause Button and Volume Control Dialog—are specific to the Nokia 9200 Communicator, at the moment. Using these features will improve usability on Nokia devices, but will render your Flash movies incompatible with other formats.

▶ It is sometimes better to use bitmaps as opposed to bitmaps because vectors can be animated with less processor strain. This is particularly important with the slower processors in the Nokia Communicator series. Using bitmaps will produce larger files, however, so be sure to find the right balance of processor and memory requirements, along with file size and target download speed for the particular project. Apply anti-aliasing to a bitmap to smooth its edges for better display. You will have to make the final decision regarding the trade-off in quality when using bitmaps (size) or vectors (performance). Your best bet is to test them on some target devices.

▶ Complex ActionScript can severely grind the CPU to a halt and crash the application. If the Flash Player "times out" when taking too long to process a Flash element, the Flash Player will launch a dialog box to inform the user of the problem. This gives users the option to disable the processing of ActionScript in the movie.

▶ Flash 5 Player follows the existing security model of Flash Player.

▶ No right-click menu is supported on the Nokia 9200 Communicator. Some of the functions are provided through the menu key on the Nokia 9200 Communicator keyboard. Some of the control capabilities of the Flash 5 Player, such as Forward, Backward, Loop, and Print, are not supported either.

Flash MX for Mobile Devices

With Macromedia MX technology, the fusion of ColdFusion MX, Flash MX, Flash Communication Server, and Flash Remoting, most of the processing required on the mobile devices is offloaded to the servers. Flash MX is theoretically a thin, yet smart, client to Flash mobile applications! Even mobile devices with slow processors and small memory can run Flash mobile applications as long as they have a Flash MX player available. And Macromedia has been doing an excellent job on that front! Processors and memory will improve over time, and so will wireless broadband. It can only serve to benefit Flash mobile applications in the future.

A point harkens back to presentation and logic. The Flash client-side developer and designer should focus on the user interface and presentation of content/data on the Flash MX client. The server developer should focus on the heavy-duty number crunching, business logic, and database access available on both the ColdFusion MX and Flash Communication Server. Flash Remoting will form the transparent link between the Flash MX client and these remote servers.

Core UI Components: A Summary

Components are complex movie clips that have predefined parameters, which are set during document authoring, and a unique set of ActionScript methods that allow you to set parameters and additional options at run time. Flash MX includes seven Flash UI components: CheckBox, ComboBox, ListBox, PushButton, RadioButton, ScrollBar, and ScrollPane, as shown next. You can use these components separately to add simple user interaction to Flash movies, or together to create a complete user interface for web forms or applications.

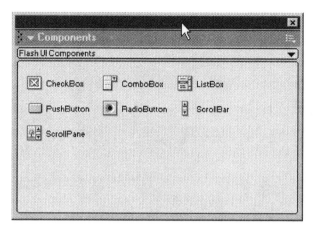

You can download additional components from the Macromedia Exchange for Flash web site. As of this writing, a second set of Flash UI components, Charting components, and Communication components (for use with the Flash Communication Server) are available for download (see the following illustrations, respectively).

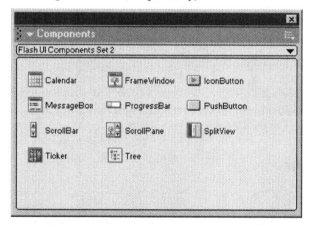

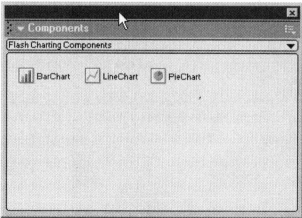

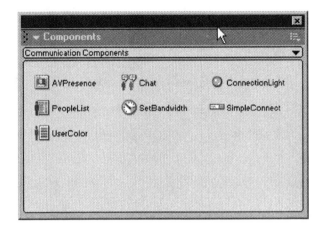

The advantages of using Flash MX UI components for application development are significant because they

► Provide standardized APIs for strict control of appearance and functionality.

► Enable component reuse across the entire application with one or minimal download.

► Make prototype efforts and API test projects incredibly easy to carry out.

► Come fully tested and ready to use.

You use the Components panel to view components and add them to a document during authoring. You can view properties for components that have been added to a document using the Property inspector or the Component Parameters panel.

Core UI Components

These UI components come in very handy for developers of mobile Flash applications because they're easy to use and require a minimal learning curve and scripting skills. In addition, they help standardize your components: format and coding. But, most importantly, these UI components will minimize the amount of data entry required of your mobile user. Here's a brief summary of the core Flash UI components:

► **CheckBox**   Lets you add check boxes to Flash movies with a minimum of authoring and scripting.

► **ComboBox**   Lets you add scrollable single-selection drop-down lists to Flash movies with a minimum of authoring and scripting.

► **ListBox**   Lets you add scrollable single- and multiple-selection listboxes to Flash movies.

▶ **PushButton**   Lets you add simple push buttons to your Flash movie. The PushButton component accepts all standard mouse and keyboard interactions, and has an *onClick* parameter that allows you to easily specify a handler to execute actions when the button is released.

▶ **RadioButton**   Lets you add groups of radio buttons to your Flash document. The *groupName* parameter logically groups radio button instances together and prevents more than one radio button in the same group from being selected at the same time.

▶ **ScrollBar**   Provides drag-and-drop functionality for adding vertical and horizontal scroll bars to dynamic and input text fields. The ComboBox, ListBox, and ScrollPane components use the ScrollBar component.

▶ **ScrollPane**   Lets you add window panes with vertical and horizontal scroll bars to display movie clips in Flash documents. The ScrollPane component is useful for displaying large areas of content without taking up a lot of Stage space. The ScrollPane component only displays movie clips.

NOTE

The ComboBox and ListBox components use a zero-based index, where index 0 is the first item displayed.

Design Example

We will now apply some of the tips and guidelines in this chapter to extend our dynamic video store example (see Chapter 3) to the Pocket PC and Nokia Communicator platforms. This example is pretty straightforward, but we will extend it to a full-fledged mobile commerce application in the future. We'll briefly discuss that after going through the application on both of the mobile devices.

The Pocket PC Video Store

We now show our dynamic video store from Chapter 3 by making it Pocket PC friendly. Here are some features of our application done specifically for the Pocket PC form factor:

▶ **Flash UI components**   ListBox and ScrollBar components used.

▶ **Icons/Buttons**   Clip art or picture icons used for all action buttons with simple colors.

▶ **Layout**   Navigation in the main content area where appropriate, Back button on bottom of screen, and secondary navigation on right side of screen.

▶ **Symbols**   Since we are reusing many graphic images (background) and buttons across different frames within the movie, they are converted to symbols, and multiple instances are used.

Here's a typical user scenario.

1. **Select a Genre**   When the mobile user first uses the application, they select the movie genre they're interested in, as shown next. Let's choose *Action* movies.

2. **Select a Movie**   After selecting the movie genre, the mobile user is presented with a list of movie titles to pick from, as shown next, and is also given a Back button that is Flash-based. Let's choose *Minority Report*.

3. **Movie Details**   A brief description about the movie is shown next (see the following). There are many links on this screen to Critic's Review, Purchase Tickets, Watch Trailer, and View Movie Poster. There is also a Back button. Let's view the movie poster next.

4. **View Movie Poster**   The movie poster is displayed, as shown next. On this screen, the mobile user can buy the movie poster shown. There is also a Back button.

That concludes a typical mobile user scenario. We will touch on mobile commerce at the end of this section.

The Nokia Communicator Video Store

Next, we'll show the dynamic video store by making it Nokia Communicator friendly. Here are some features of our application, designed specifically for the Nokia Communicator form factor:

▶   **Flash UI components**   ListBox and ScrollBar components used.

▶   **Icons/Buttons**   Clip art or picture icons used for all action buttons with simple colors.

▶ **Layout**   Navigation in the main content area where appropriate, Back button on bottom of screen, and secondary navigation on right side of screen.

▶ **Symbols**   Since we are reusing many graphic images (background) and buttons across different frames within the movie, they are converted to symbols and multiple instances are used.

▶ **Music**   MP3 sound output is supported on the Nokia Communicator, albeit mono MP3. The sound files should be exported at 8 Kbps.

Here's a typical user scenario.

1. **Select a Genre**   When the mobile user first uses the application, they select the movie genre they're interested in, as shown next. Let's choose *Action* movies.

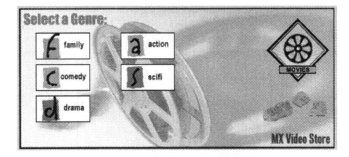

2. **Select a Movie**   After selecting the movie genre, the mobile user is presented with a list of movie titles to pick from (as shown next) and also a Back button that is Flash-based. Let's choose *Minority Report*.

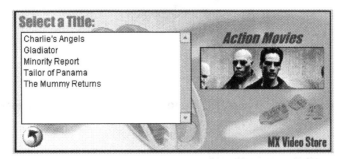

3. **Movie Details**   A brief description about the movie is shown next (see the following). There are many links on this screen, such as to Critic's Review, Purchase Tickets, Watch Trailer, View Movie Poster, or Listen to Tunes. There is also a Back button. Let's take a look at the movie poster and critic's review next.

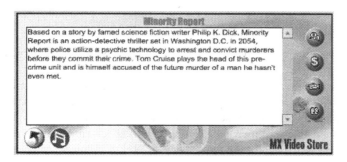

4. **View Movie Poster and Critic's Review**   The movie poster and critic's review is displayed, as shown next. On this screen, the mobile user can buy the movie poster shown, view the trailer, or buy movie tickets. There is also a Back button.

5. **Sample Music CD Tunes**   Let's say the mobile user decides to listen to sample tunes from the movie soundtrack. (The screen is shown next.) On the Nokia Communicator, you can play MP3 files. Afterward, if the mobile user desires, they can purchase the music CD.

This concludes a typical mobile user scenario. We will touch on mobile commerce next.

Mobile Commerce

Mobile Commerce on a mobile device can usually be done in two different ways:

▶ **Billed to carriers** The simplest way is to bill, so that anything purchased on the mobile device becomes part of your telephone bill. This requires a complex business relationship between any online merchant and the telephone company, thus resulting in a very limited choice of merchants. But easy billing is attained with a password, and all the information is available on the physical SIM card and thus is automatically sent to the merchants on checkout.

▶ **Billed to credit cards** Any merchant who has a mobile presence can conduct business. The only feasible way is to set up an account with the merchant using a nonmobile device like a desktop PC to enter the relevant information using a keyboard instead of a mobile device. You would create a user ID and password and log in from the mobile device. All the billing, shipping, and credit card information would already reside on the merchant's server. Once you log in from a mobile device, you can perform the transaction easily from there on.

In our Pocket PC and Nokia Communicator example, you can buy movie tickets and movie posters, and in the case of the Nokia Communicator, you can also buy a music CD from, for example, CDNow or Amazon or whoever your business partner is. Multiple merchants can be involved (for example, Century Theatres for movie tickets, AllPosters.com for movie posters) or you can maintain your own shopping cart and act as the clearinghouse to fulfill your customer orders.

Here's a typical user scenario for transacting in mobile commerce:

1. **Add to Cart** The mobile user adds an item (movie tickets, movie poster, music CD) to the shopping cart.

2. **Login** If the mobile user has not logged in yet, they will be asked to provide a user ID and password. The user ID may already be prefilled, using information from a local SharedObject.

3. **Shopping cart** The selected item is added to the shopping cart. Meanwhile, the application can either display a list of items in the shopping cart or have some indicator (icons or text summary showing number of items in cart) that tells the mobile user that the item has been successfully added to the shopping cart.

4. **Checkout** On checkout, the mobile user will be taken through a series of steps to make sure the merchandise is correctly billed and shipped to the mobile user.

5. **Billing address** Our assumption here is that the mobile user has already preregistered at the merchant or carrier site and entered all the necessary information to facilitate a smooth and painless transaction using a desktop PC. The billing address is now displayed to the mobile user for verification or modification.

6. **Shipping address and shipping method**   The shipping address is now displayed with the shipping method (UPS, FedEx, the U.S. Postal Service, Airborne) to the mobile user for verification or modification.

7. **Billing method**   The credit card number (showing the last four digits is sufficient) and expiration date is now displayed to the mobile user for verification or modification.

8. **Completion**   You're done. Present an Order Summary (OS) with tentative delivery date *and* also send an e-mail or SMS of the OS for the mobile user records.

9. **Back to shopping**   Present a button to take the mobile user back to your desired frame within the movie.

The critical point here is that you preregister *before* using mobile commerce. You can also provide a way to register but that would be too exhaustive a task for the mobile user with limited input methods.

Summary

We have shown you how to design effective user interfaces for mobile applications using the Macromedia Flash MX authoring environment. We went through the design and development process and examined ways to enhance usability for typical handheld devices and provided specific details on page layout, screen size, typography, input methods, and items of practical use. We also went through the style guides of designing Flash applications for Microsoft Pocket PCs and the Nokia 9200 Communicator Series. We concluded by summarizing the Macromedia Flash MX Core UI components and looked at examples of how to take advantage of them for mobile applications.

Integrating Animation and Multimedia

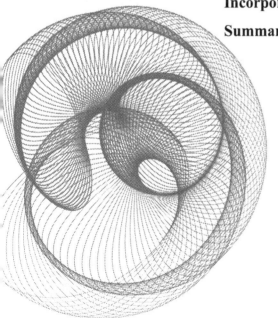

In this chapter, we introduce the various animation and multimedia techniques of Macromedia Flash MX that make it such a compelling platform for building rich mobile applications. We will discuss the basics of incorporating animation, sound, and video into Flash movies, and discuss areas that you should pay attention to when using such capabilities as tweening, streaming, and linking (QuickTime movies). We briefly cover the bandwidth and processing constraints and discuss how you can optimize your Flash movies and the underlying elements for the best mixes of playback and download performance.

Incorporating Animation

Why incorporate animation? Well, if you must ask, the answer would be: If you don't plan to use animation, then why use Flash in the first place? Animation is probably one of the most compelling reasons to use Macromedia Flash MX for mobile devices in the first place. Due to its heritage as an animation tool, Macromedia Flash has become a predominant platform of rich media web site development over time. But, for mobile application development, Macromedia Flash MX lends itself to being a very sophisticated and comprehensive environment for animation and audio-visual presentations and applications.

For once, the appropriate use of animation and multimedia capabilities within Macromedia Flash MX can greatly enhance the usability of your mobile applications without a significant trade-off in file size and download speeds. Subtle or not-so-subtle touches, like simple sound effects for pressing a button and the fading in or out of UI components, can make your applications not only engaging, but downright fun to use.

Macromedia Flash MX offers developers several advantages for creating animations and rich media files, including its outstanding visual, client-side development environment, and its unique cross-platform compatibility. In general, we see a number of reasons why you want to incorporate animations into your mobile Flash applications. They include

- ▶ **Branding**   Many corporate logos and branding elements simply involve animation and sound. For example, the immensely successful "Intel Inside" logo entails both.

- ▶ **Accent and emphasis**   You can also use animation to accentuate a point, such as reaching a goal or winning points in an interactive game, and you can put emphasis on certain actions, such as the pressing of a button or the sliding of the slider.

- ▶ **Instructions and visual effects**   You may be using animation to illustrate the path and the method that the mobile user should follow, be it for driving directions or for operating instructions. Having an animated effect simply helps convey the information more effectively.

- ▶ **Motion**   Quite obviously, if you must describe how objects move and even collide, as in a game or in online presentations of traffic and insurance events, nothing beats animation in getting the "picture across!"

► **Emotion** Besides motion graphics, you can also use animation for what? That's right. Cartoons. With subtle or intense animation, you can deliver the emotion of the characters in your cartoon, perhaps in conjunction with the use of certain audio effects.

There are numerous other reasons why you want to use animation. Regardless of the reason, Macromedia Flash MX offers an excellent platform to achieve these goals, versus other alternatives.

Due to its use of vector objects, animation based on Macromedia Flash can be very dynamic, yet smooth and efficient. Because the Macromedia Flash MX authoring environment is easy to use, you can create more sophisticated animation that would be much harder to create using JavaScript alone. When compared to JavaScript, Macromedia Flash MX gives you a consistent environment with full control over all properties across many platforms (Internet Explorer, Netscape Navigator, Pocket Internet Explorer, and a host of other Flash Players). This way, you can simply animate once by controlling the properties of your screen objects.

Another tool many developers compare Macromedia Flash with is Java Swing. While Java Swing offers excellent design interfaces for creating animation, Swing and Flash take different approaches in insuring platform consistency. Swing is a graphical user interface (GUI) component kit, part of the Java Foundation Classes (JFC) integrated into Java 2 Platform, Standard Edition (J2SE). Swing simplifies "deployment of applications" by providing a complete set of user-interface elements written entirely in the Java programming language. From a UI standpoint, Swing components permit a customizable look and feel without relying on any specific windowing system. It provides facilities for creating animation that blends in with the delivery platform, and is subservient to the look and interface of the platform itself. On the other hand, Macromedia Flash is designed to offer consistent rich media, including fine multimedia details across platforms. These are choices that the designers and developers must make as they approach the decisions of platforms and tools when building mobile solutions.

For mobile applications, animation is a two-edged sword—as it can greatly improve usability and user satisfaction via engaging content; you also could increase your file size many times and even expose limitations of your processor. Before we discuss these issues and explore ways to deal with them, let's review the basics of creating animation with Macromedia Flash MX.

Basics

As discussed earlier, there are many reasons or categories of animation in Flash, but the majority of animation graphics in Flash falls into several areas—user interface, motion, and character animation. Using Flash, you can bring animated motions to objects and symbols, altering such properties as size, shape, color, and opacity. You can make them appear to move across the Stage and follow a deliberate path, while fading in and out of focus. As a Flash designer, you have all the capabilities to make these animation actions in concert with, yet independent of, other changes.

For eBusiness applications, you can use Flash to build interactive charts and animated graphs. In cases like business intelligence applications, your mobile users can easily and quickly visualize complex data, instead of reading through text and numbers. Let's look at what options we have for creating Flash animation sequences.

There are three methods for creating an animation sequence in Flash:

▶ **Frame-by-frame animation**   You can create animation the old-fashioned way, by building it frame by frame, much as the cartoonists at Disney did decades ago (and still do—albeit electronically). This approach, however, can generate a rather large SWF file and does not lend itself to mobile Flash development.

▶ **Tweened animation**   You can make animation by creating keyframes (starting and ending frames) and allow Flash to build the frames in between. For animated objects, tweened animation is an effective way to create the effects of motions and spatial changes over time while keeping your file size to a minimum. The reason is that Flash only stores the values for the changes between frames in tweened animation, much like many video compression techniques.

▶ **ActionScript**   You can also build animation effects through programming—that is, through Flash ActionScript. You have the leeway to alter the properties of the symbols, objects, and their instances.

Tweening

In tweening, keyframes are the starting and ending frames; key moments in the Timeline that Flash uses to calculate the in-between frames automatically. Thus, tweening means less work and smaller file sizes. In frame-by-frame animation, every frame is a keyframe. In tweened animation, only the first and last frames of a tween sequence are keyframes.

So how do you use it? How much is feasible with mobile devices? Let's go through them in sequence, starting with the two methods for creating tweened animation sequences in Flash:

▶ **Motion tweening**   You can change the size, rotation, and of course, position of an instance group, and type in time, and then apply a motion tween along a path to another point in time. Flash can tween the color of instances and type, creating gradual color shifts or making an instance fade in or out. It, therefore, can easily handle animation along *any* path you create.

▶ **Shape tweening**   You can define a shape at one point in time, and then draw a different shape at another point in time, letting Flash interpolate the values in between (a process also known as *morphing*). Make sure you test the effects of the shaped tween since you may want to add an extra frame (or "hint") to help shape the interpolation values.

To review your sequences, you can look at how your animation plays on the stage by setting options in the Property inspector. To tween the changes in properties of instances, groups, and type, use motion tweening. Flash can tween position, size, rotation, and skew instances, groups, and types. Remember, you must turn your groups or types into symbols to tween their color. Also, if you want to just animate individual characters within a block of text, you should put each character in a separate text block (layer).

Movie clips are symbols that can play animation in a Flash movie. They are the only data type that refers to a graphic element. Considering this, a frequent question arises: How is an animated graphic symbol different from a movie clip? The answer lies in the Timeline. Animated graphic symbols are bound to the movie Timeline in which they are placed, whereas movie clip symbols carry their own independent Timelines. As a result, you can see how the animated graphic symbols behave in movie-editing mode in accordance with the same Timeline as the main movie, whereas movie clip symbols are static and do not show animations on Stage within the Macromedia Flash authoring environment.

NOTE

You can only tween an instance, group, or text block.

Motion Tweening

You can create a motion tween using either of these methods:

▶ **Starting and ending keyframes**   This is the typical way of creating a motion tween. Here, you simply provide the first and last keyframes for the sequence and enable the Motion Tweening option in the Property inspector.

▶ **Starting keyframe only**   You create the first keyframe for the animation and tell Macromedia Flash how many frames you want on the Timeline. Then create the motion tween by moving the object to the ending location on the Stage. This way, you can use Flash to generate the ending keyframe for you.

Let's go through a simple motion tween example next. We will create a starting and ending keyframe and let Flash fill in the rest. Our ending keyframe should look like the following illustration.

Mobile Flash MX

The starting keyframe can be anything you fancy—such as the jumble effect, shown next.

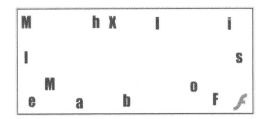

Follow these steps to create our example:

1. Create a new layer (name it **Motion Tween**) and add the following static text to it: **Mobile Flash MX**. Center it both vertically and horizontally on the stage.

2. You can insert other graphic images to another layer (name it **background** this time) for background or static objects. We inserted the Flash MX logo to our library and added an instance here.

3. Select the static text object from the Motion Tween layer, right-click the mouse, and from the menu, select Break Apart, as illustrated in the following.

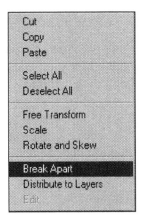

4. Your static text object is now broken apart and looks something like the following illustration.

5. Once again, select the static text objects from the Motion Tween layer, right-click the mouse, and select Distribute to Layers from the menu, as illustrated next.

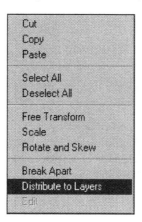

6. You should now have many additional layers, one for each text character of the "Mobile Flash MX" text string, as shown in the following.

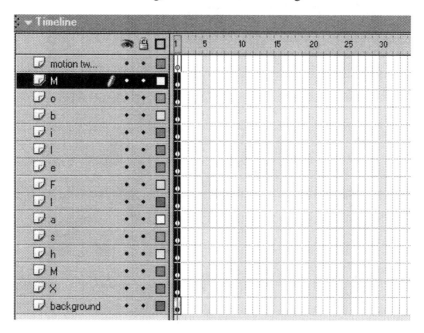

7. For any of the distributed layers (for example, *M*), select frame 30 and insert a keyframe. Your stage will now only show the letter *M* at frame 30. Select any frame on that layer

between 1 and 30 (for example, 15). In the Property inspector for that frame, select Motion for the Tween attribute, as shown next.

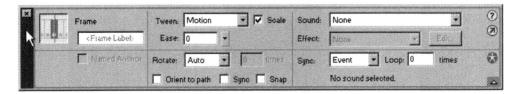

8. Repeat Step 7 for all the distributed layers. When finished, your Timeline should resemble the illustration that follows, and your tweened frames should have a black arrow with a light-blue background. If you get a dashed line instead, your tween is broken. If this is the case, check to make sure the final keyframe is not missing or incomplete.

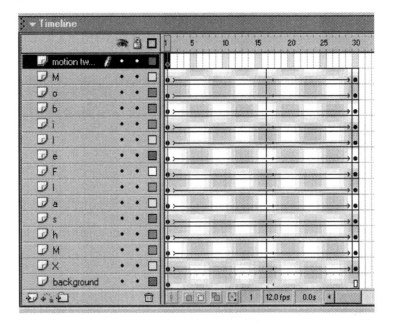

9. Go to frame 1. Select one of the distributed layers and move any of the letters around to jumble it. This is how your movie will start off. It will unjumble itself on frame 30. Move your playhead to any frame between 1 and 30 on the Timeline and you should see motion tweening in action as shown in the sequence of frames illustrated next.

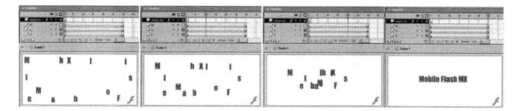

That's it! You've just learned how to create motion tweening.

Shape Tweening

By tweening shapes, you make one shape appear to change into another over time. Flash can tween the position, size, and color of the shapes. It's recommended, however, that you tween one shape at a time in order to yield the best results. Let's look at an example of shape tweening next.

1. Create a new layer (name it **shape tween**). Add the static text **CA** onto the Stage at frame 1. Break it apart twice (the shortcut is CTRL-B)—once to break it into two letters, a second time to turn those letters into shapes.

2. Set the playhead on the Timeline to frame 20. Add the static text **AZ** onto the Stage. Again, break it apart twice.

3. Select any frame on that layer between 1 and 20 (for example, 15). On the Property inspector for that frame, select Shape for the Tween attribute. Your tweened frames should now have a black arrow with a light-green background.

4. Move your playhead to any frame between 1 and 20 on the Timeline and you should see shape tweening in action, as shown in the sequence of frames illustrated next. You can, of course, use shape hints to mold the course of the morphing.

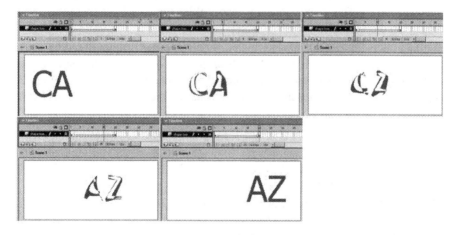

That's it! You've just learned how to create shape tweening.

Of course, you probably have seen or used a great deal of animations based on more intense motion tweening, perhaps those even applied to photographic elements. For mobile devices, these complex effects can be difficult to pull off, as they are processor intensive. Other effects, such as alpha and transparency, could present problems as well. Nonetheless, dynamic animations, even for cartoons, can be created for use in Pocket PCs and other mobile devices—that is, if guidelines are followed and you choose storytelling methods smartly. Let's review the issues and tips for building animations for mobile applications.

Issues and Tips for Mobile Applications

In general, you can't simply bring your desktop Flash animation, with 800 × 600 pixel resolution, to the handheld environment. There is a dilemma that current devices and Flash Players are limited in terms of CPU speed, memory and screen size, as well as connectivity speed, but we have to build for current audiences and plan for better capabilities and more complex animation and effects. Also, you must account for the various versions of devices and players. Hence, when making great animation for devices, it's useful to think about the lowest common denominator in terms of playback and small screen size.

Several features unique to Macromedia Flash animation make possible continuous movement, property changes (such as brightness, tint, opacity, scale, and position), and animation of any object.

When animating content, keep in mind the CPU limitations of the device in order to prevent the movie from slowing down or accidentally dropping frames. The following are some general guidelines to keep in mind when animating content for mobile devices:

▶ **Frame rates**   In general, we recommend a frame rate of 12 frames per second. If you need to provide intense animation, experiment with dynamically changing the movie's quality settings. This change may noticeably affect the visual quality of the movie, so be sure to thoroughly test it.

▶ **Alpha effects**   Limit the number of simultaneous tweens. Alpha effects on symbols are too CPU intensive, and they should be used judiciously. In particular, it is generally not a good idea to tween symbols and adjust their alpha levels at the same time. Avoid such intensive effects as extensive gradients, masks, extensive motion, and alpha blending.

▶ **Use ActionScript**   In some cases, animating via ActionScript may produce more desirable results. Nevertheless, you should avoid intense ActionScript. Experiment with combinations of tweens, key frame animations, and ActionScript-driven movement to produce the most desirable results.

▶ **Photos and special effects**   Complex photos are challenging since raster images can bulk up your SWF files, as can special effects like panoramic view, zooms, and pans. To produce the desirable results, play with different combinations of methods, such as key frame animations, tweens, and ActionScript programming instead. The trick is to experiment and find the right balance between download bandwidth, the device's processor speed, and player performance. If they absolutely have to use these effects, try to lighten the load on your device CPU by using simple backgrounds and other symbols.

▶ **Separating and singling out effects**   To avoid overwhelming your CPU, another trick is to isolate and separate more complex effects and movements by simply drawing them one at a time with different layers. This way, your processor will have a better chance to build the frames and service the requests accordingly.

▶ **Different speeds**   If you can't avoid a moderate amount of animation and tweening, another trick is to vary the tweening in accordance with how fast the underlying processor is and how great its capabilities are. If you detect a faster device, you can serve up a different SWF that takes advantage of the faster processor speed. You can use this in conjunction with dynamically changing the extent of tweening and animation effects at different parts of the movie. We will cover device (and Flash Player) detection in Chapter 9 and look at how to serve up the appropriate SWF file based on the device capability.

It may sound discouraging that you have to abandon or scale back these techniques and effects to make it work in Pocket PCs and Nokia phones. However, devices are getting more powerful, and bandwidth is improving immensely. So, be patient and try out those animation sequences, and use mostly simple motions and strong actions first. Test your target devices frequently under a number of configurations and situations (for example, try running Macromedia Flash Player and your web browser simultaneously).

NOTE

Use close-ups and larger characters when building cartoons, just as you might optimize a video movie recording by using digital cameras (with a lower resolution of, say, 320 × 200 pixels).

Optimizing Animation

As mentioned throughout this book, mobile devices have significantly slower processors and smaller memories compared to desktop PCs. With that in mind, here are some general guidelines on how to optimize your movies or animation:

▶ Use symbols for every element that appears more than once, especially bitmap images.

▶ Use tweened animations whenever possible. This takes up less file space than a series of keyframes.

▶ Limit the area of change in each keyframe and make the action take place in as small an area on Stage as possible.

▶ Use vector graphics instead of bitmap graphics for faster playback. Avoid animating bitmaps and photos if possible.

▶ Limit the use of gradients and minimize the number of simultaneous gradients in any given frame.

Incorporating Audio

While digital audio can be cumbersome to download or transmit over slow wireless connections, it is nevertheless fruitful to build it into your mobile applications. In many Internet applications, sound effects are added as afterthoughts. But for Flash applications, sound is an integral part of the rich media experience. Let's go into more detail on the basics since the variables can greatly affect both the performance and functionality of those mobile Flash applications equipped with audio.

The Basics

Let's start off with several audio terms and parameters you should know:

▶ **Sampling rates** When digital audio is recorded, the signal (sound) is registered at a specific frequency or sampling rate. The higher the sampling rate, the better the sound quality. Unfortunately, the higher the sampling rate, the bigger the file size. As a reference point, the sampling rate of your CD music recording is generally 44.1 kHz.

▶ **Bit depth** Besides recording rates, the dynamic range of recorded sound—that is, fidelity—is controlled by the bit depth. The higher the bit depth, the more expansive the range of the recorded audio, and the higher the fidelity. Typical sound is recorded at a bit depth of 8 bits or higher (16 and 24 bits are common).

▶ **Codec** Codec is the type of compression and decompression that audio (and video) engineers apply to media sources, generally for transport and storage purposes. Most codecs are proprietary encoding and decoding routines. You compress your audio (and video) files to transmit over the Internet as streaming media, for example, or you store your sound more effectively, at the expense of overall sound quality. After it arrives at the destination device, the codec will decompress the file and convert it back to audio signals you can listen to. You may decompress during playback while keeping the file in a certain format. An example is MP3. You can convert your music into the MP3 format. Then, when you play it back, it's converted into audio music that plays through your speakers. You nonetheless store your music in the same MP3 format, however. Hence, the codec allows better transmission and smaller file sizes. It should be noted that you can record a sound at a certain range, and through codec, play it back at another.

▶ **Mono versus stereo** Audio files are recorded in either stereo or mono. Stereo meaning two sound channels, while mono meaning only one. Because of this, stereo sound files are double the size of those in mono. If you play mono sound on devices

(MP3 players) that have two stereo speakers, however, each channel (speaker) will play the same mono sound.

Planning and Recording

For all practical purposes, we recommend mixing and composing sound at a sampling rate of 22 kHz with an 8 bit depth or better. Recording at this level or higher allows you to compress it further if needed, and resample to a lossy rate to accommodate the target bandwidth. After you have recorded the audio at a high sampling rate, you can archive, edit, and reuse the source audio.

Currently, you can import WAV (Waveform Audio File Format, Windows only), AIFF (Audio Interchange File Format, Macintosh only) and MP3 (Windows or Macintosh) file formats into Macromedia Flash. If you have QuickTime 4 or later installed on your system, you can import AIFF, Sound Designer II, QuickTime (MOV) Sound, Sun AU (Windows or Macintosh), AVI, MPG/MPEG, and Windows Media File formats (WMV and ASF).

NOTE

When you import an audio file, Macromedia Flash stores it in the Library along with bitmaps and symbols. Similar to symbols, you only need one sound file to use and reuse in your movie.

Because codecs require raw computing power for the decompression of the sound file, pay special attention to which encoding format to use. On slower CPUs, you may not want to use any audio compression during active sequences (motion tweening, keyframe animation) in the Flash movie. Macromedia Flash supports Default, ADPCM, MP3, Raw, and Speech as shown next:

► **Default** Uncompressed; as is.

► **ADPCM** Adaptive Differential Pulse Code Modulation. The greater the compression, the lesser the sound quality. You can convert stereo into mono to reduce file sizes. Available sampling rates are 5, 11, 22, and 44 kHz. You can choose from 2, 3, 4, or 5 bits.

► **MP3** An efficient compression algorithm. You can convert stereo to mono with a bit rate of your choice, ranging from 8 kbps to 160 kbps.

► **Raw** Exports the sound with no compression. You can convert stereo into mono and choose the same sampling rates as for ADPCM.

► **Speech** Exports the sound with compression techniques designed for speech. You can choose the same sampling rates as for ADPCM.

You can use the Sound Properties dialog box to change any properties (compression, quality, and so on), as shown next.

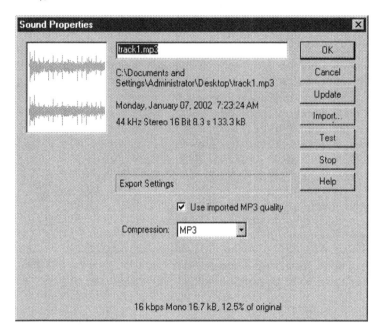

NOTE

The Nokia Communicator will not play higher than 8 kHz.

Because Flash 4 and later support MP3, it seems automatic to use this type of sound compression. MP3 provides smaller file sizes, greater audio clarity, and higher audio fidelity. But sometimes it makes sense to resist using it when deploying content to devices. The problem is that MP3 sound compression dedicates much of a device's processor to decompress and play the audio. Because MP3 draws down on the processor, it can negatively affect an animation's playback. Frames are either dropped to keep up with the sound, or the playback of the animation frame rate declines dramatically. As a result, you should reconsider using ADPCM, the other audio compression format, in cases when your device processor needs a lighter load.

NOTE

Flash supports 8- and 16-bit audio only. When you set your audio to ADPCM in a Flash movie, Flash will convert the sound to 16 bit before applying the compression.

Embedding and Linking

Many devices are not connected directly to the Web and instead get files by synchronizing with a desktop PC. But if it's not bandwidth that hinders us, then it's the limited storage! Many handhelds only have 8–64 MB of built-in storage space, so there isn't too much room for big files.

NOTE

Flash can't sample a sound at a higher rate than its original imported rate. You can always downsample an imported sound (from 44 kHz to 22 kHz) if necessary.

Here's a description of the synchronization options for imported sound files:

▶ **Event**   Flash will initialize the specified sound when the assigned keyframe is played. Regardless of further playback, the sound will continue to play until it has finished. This means you can have a stop action for any frame after the sound keyframe, and the sound will still play. If the keyframe is played again *before* the sound is finished, Flash restarts the sound.

▶ **Start**   Flash will play the sound when its first keyframe plays and will continue to play it until complete. If the keyframe is played again *before* the sound is finished, Flash will *not* start the sound again.

▶ **Stop**   Stops the sound.

▶ **Stream**   Flash will try to synchronize the sound with the animation. It will drop frames or add them to match the sound's length.

You can set the sound parameters in the Property Inspector for the sound on the Stage, as illustrated next.

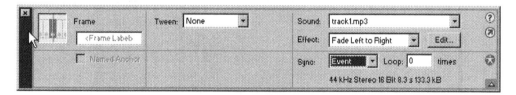

Optimizing Audio

The following are general guidelines for optimizing audio:

▶ Event sounds have the benefit of being stored only once in the SWF file. You can use many instances of the same sound resource without any significant increases in file size. This is especially useful for creating sound effect or background beat tracks for your Flash movie. You can import just a few short sound files and compose a lengthy soundtrack without creating a large SWF file.

NOTE

An event sound needs to be fully downloaded before it's played.

▶ Use small looping sound clips under the animation and insert shorter musical effects for specific emphasis. Background music can be created by looping short sounds. Keep in mind, however, that loops, and especially nested loops, are not very processor friendly.

NOTE

You may have a synchronization problem between a sound event and a move with complex animations, if the Pocket PC slows down the frame rate of the movie to display each frame.

▶ With the Stream Sync option, Flash Player will play all its timelines in synchronization with the playback of the specified sound. It will strictly follow the frame rate as set. But if Flash Player skips frames and causes unwanted jumps in animations, you may want to stream your audio, which is particularly useful for animation with lip-sync to the characters in your Flash movie. Be sure to preload more than five seconds of the streaming track. Flash will start to play the sound as soon as the five-second sound buffer is filled.

▶ Unlike streamed video, Flash movies are, in reality, progressive downloads. That means files are cached in the web browser's cache folder.

NOTE

When you set a sound to stream in Flash, any custom compression settings in the library are ignored.

▶ Use MP3 compression whenever possible. This is best suited for small to mid-length audio files. It is possible to have the first movie with higher compression than the second.

▶ Some mobile users might prefer to use the Pocket PC 2002 Windows Media Player for audio and video files (WMV, MP3, and so on) rather than using Flash. You can easily launch the Window Media Player from Flash using the following ActionScript code snippet:

```
// local files
getURL("file:///My%20Documents/audio/track1.mp3");

// remote files
getURL("http://dell-tom:8500/book/track1.mp3");
```

We are, of course, making the assumption that your audio and video file extensions are already associated with the Windows Media Player by default.

▶ For situations where your mobile user may not want audio from your Flash applications, you should provide a quick option (button) to mute the sound.

Incorporating Video

With the latest release of Macromedia Flash MX, you can embed video into your Flash movies. Previously, video could only be simulated with a series of bitmap or vector images (or frame-by-frame animation). Now you can import video clips in various formats, including MOV (QuickTime), AVI (Audio Video Interleave), and MPEG (Motion Picture Experts Group) directly into the Flash movie. Additional video formats may be supported depending on the codecs installed on your system—not all codecs are compatible with Macromedia Flash MX, however.

NOTE

You can also import Flash video files (FLV), video that's been compressed in the native video format for Flash MX, normally used for streaming.

Embedded video is compressed with the Sorenson Spark video codec, a video compression technology which Macromedia and Sorenson Media developed exclusively for Flash. Sorenson Spark can produce high quality video at small file sizes, and allows you to scale, rotate, and mask embedded video as well as control it using ActionScript. During playback, Flash *natively* decompresses the video clip. Since this codec is built into Flash MX, you don't need any additional plug-ins or software.

The Basics

The following are several video terms and parameters you should know:

▶ **Frame rate**   This is the number of frames per second (FPS) at which an animation is played. A frame rate of 12 FPS usually gives the best result. QuickTime MOV and AVI movies normally have a frame rate of 12 FPS.

▶ **Spatial compression**   Spatial compression is applied to a single frame of video, and compresses the video image much as single JPEG images are compressed. The degree of spatial compression affects the overall video quality.

▶ **Temporal compression**   This compression technique takes advantage of the fact that consecutive frames of video content often have much of the same pixel data. By identifying pixel differences between consecutive frames, and storing just those frame differences in a compressed file, temporal compression has dramatically reduced video data size. Frames compressed with temporal compression are called interframes.

▶ **Video keyframe**   A complete frame of video, not just the computed differences between two frames. Keyframes are used as reference points for subsequent interframes.

▶ **Keyframe interval**   Determines how frequently a full frame of the source video is preserved in the Timeline. For example, a keyframe interval of 24 will insert a video keyframe every 24th frame in the Timeline. Each new keyframe is used as a reference point for any subsequent frame differences (interframes) that follow it. Smaller interval values result in more keyframes and a larger file size; larger intervals result in fewer keyframes and a smaller file.

The Sorenson Spark codec included in Macromedia Flash MX uses a combination of spatial and temporal compression techniques. As of this writing, this codec is supported in Flash Player 6, which is not ported to the Pocket PC 2002 or Nokia 9200 Communicators yet. Be sure to check for its support before building it into your mobile Flash movies.

Planning and Recording

If you already have video files that you want to import into Flash, then skip to the next section on how to import them. If not, here are a few issues to consider:

▶ **Medium**   This could be a VHS or Digital Video tape, or an MPEG file recorded on your digital camera. The higher the recording resolution, the better. If you are using a video camera or web cam with the Flash Communication Server (see Chapter 11), you can record the stream and save it as an FLV file. Make sure the camera mode is set to capture in the highest resolution (for example, 640 × 480) as the camera object has a default setting of 160 × 160.

▶ **Sound**   For most recording, a 44 kHz sampling rate is sufficient. You can scale it down from here for mobile devices, as discussed in the previous section titled "Incorporating Audio."

▶ **Output format**   It's best to write out a video format of QuickTime MOV or Windows AVI with the original codec of your captured footage along with the correct width and height you plan to use in your Flash movie. Again, if you are using a video camera or web cam with the Flash Communication Server, the output file format is FLV.

Embedding and Linking

When you import video into Flash, the video can be imported in two different ways:

1. **Embedded**   The video is embedded into the Flash file, just like bitmaps. When the Flash movie is published as a SWF file, the embedded video plays back in the Flash

MX player. The embedded video is compressed upon import based on the Import Video Settings dialog box as shown next.

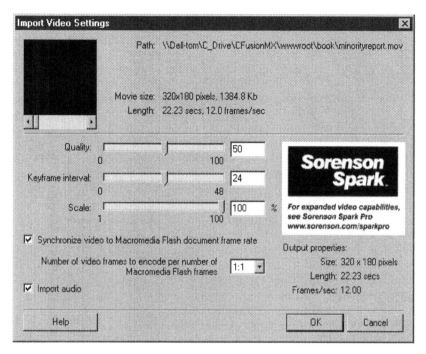

A few settings to note here. The *KeyFrame Interval* setting of 24 is acceptable for video that does not have a great deal of quick actions and motions. Checking the Synchronize Video To Flash check box will match the playback rate of the imported video to Flash's frame rate. Flash Player will drop frames if the imported rate is faster than that of your Flash movie. If the check box is *not* checked, Flash will assign one frame of video to each frame in the Timeline. The result is that the imported video plays slower than it should if it has an inherent frame rate that is faster than Flash's.

2. **Linked**   The video is linked to an external QuickTime (MOV) video file. The QuickTime movie is imported as a linked file. You can then add animation or interactivity to the video using the Flash MX authoring environment. Afterward, you *must* export it from Flash as a QuickTime movie.

When you add an instance of a video object to the Stage, either by dragging it from the Library or importing it directly to the Stage, Macromedia Flash MX determines how many frames are required to display the entire clip. You will be asked if you want that number of frames inserted automatically. The number of frames inserted is equal to the video duration multiplied by the frame rate of Flash. A ten-second video imported into a Flash document with a frame rate of 12 FPS will require 120 frames to display.

Embedded and linked videos appear in the Library as symbols. You can view and set properties of a video symbol by selecting it in the Library and choosing *Properties* from the Library pop-up panel or by double-clicking the symbol in the Library. From the Embedded Video Properties dialog box shown next, you can update an imported video (if it is modified externally), import another video for replacement, or export the embedded video as a macromedia Flash Video file (FLV). You can import the FLV file in another document without having to recompress the video.

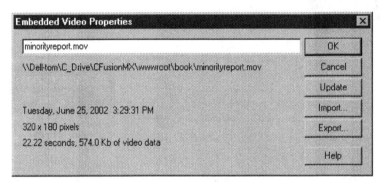

Optimizing Video

Video can add considerable size to a Flash movie. Keep in mind your target device's connection speed when publishing SWFs that contain embedded video. The following are some guidelines for optimizing video:

▶ Keep video clips short. Unlike video streaming, a frame of embedded video does not get discarded from memory after being displayed. Very long video clips may eventually affect the performance and stability of the playback system.

NOTE

Movie clips must download completely before they can play back. To take advantage of the streaming capabilities of the Flash Player, embedded video must reside on the main Timeline of the movie that contains it.

▶ With video compression, the most important factor to remember is variability from frame to frame. That is, how much and how often does your subject matter change? In general, the best results can be achieved with video compression if the subject matter does not move randomly or wildly.

▶ Publish one video per SWF file. Publish the same video, with different compression settings, in separate SWF files. Let your users choose the appropriate movie for their Internet connection. The *loadMovie* action lets you load external Flash movies during playback.

▶   The Flash Player must decompress a frame of video before that frame can be displayed. If the video clip contains a sound track, the Flash Player will drop frames to keep pace with the sound track if it cannot decompress the video fast enough.

Summary

In this chapter, we showed you the basics of animation, including motion and shape tweening. We also discussed the basics of audio and video compression, and how they can be used in Flash movies, embedded or linked. More importantly, we've reviewed tips and guidelines on how to optimize various properties of Flash movies for delivery to, and playback on, mobile devices. Having become more aware of the effects and implications of preparing and publishing multimedia to mobile Flash devices, let's move on to the next chapter.

CHAPTER
6

Server-Side Flash

IN THIS CHAPTER:

Server-Side Scripting

What Happened to Flash Generator?

Flash Client to Server Communication

Introducing Macromedia Flash Remoting

Flash Remoting Components

Server-Side ActionScript

Summary

F lash content without any remote connection would be pretty static. As we have shown in Chapter 3, server-side scripting, along with database queries, can add a great deal of interactivity and transactional capabilities to your Flash movies. Without server-side capabilities, you will have to package everything into the SWF files and download these large files onto the client Flash Player. With server-side Flash, the Flash client can communicate with the server back-end and receive dynamic content while keeping the deployed files small. In this chapter, we will touch on a few popular server-side scripting languages, introduce Flash Remoting, and examine the new objects available for use with Flash Remoting that will help you create exciting and compelling Flash applications.

Server-Side Scripting

Since you are interested in server-side application development, you're probably aware of Active Server Pages (ASP) from Microsoft, JavaServer Pages (JSP) from Sun Microsystems, and ColdFusion Markup Language (CFML) from Macromedia. We will briefly go through these three scripting languages next as Flash Remoting is optimized for use with ASP.NET, JSP, and ColdFusion.

Active Server Pages

Active Server Pages is a server-side scripting technology that can be used to create dynamic and interactive web applications. An ASP page is an HTML page that contains server-side scripts that are processed by the web application server before being sent to the user's browser. You can combine ASP with Extensible Markup Language (XML), Component Object Model (COM), and Hypertext Markup Language (HTML) to create powerful interactive web sites.

ASP.NET is the latest version that runs on the .NET environment from Microsoft. It is a programming framework built on the Common Language Runtime (CLR) that can be used on a server to build powerful web applications. ASP.NET is fully API-compatible with traditional ASP, except for the following three exceptions:

► **Request()**
► **Request.QueryString()**
► **Request.Form()**

For all three, ASP returns an array of strings, while ASP.NET returns only a single string. ASP.NET pages also have several semantic changes from existing ASP pages:

► **Languages**   ASP.NET pages only support a single language. ASP allowed multiple languages to be used on a single page, which was useful for script library scenarios.

▶ **Script blocks**   ASP.NET page functions must be declared in <script runat=server> blocks. In ASP, page functions can be declared within <% %> blocks.

▶ **Page-render functions**   ASP.NET does not support page-render functions.

Macromedia Flash MX comes with new APIs for client/server application development, including support for ASP.NET within the Flash Remoting Architecture (see section titled "Introducing Macromedia Flash Remoting").

JavaServer Pages

JavaServer Pages™ is the Java™ 2 Platform, Enterprise Edition (J2EE) technology for building applications that generate dynamic web content, such as HTML, DHTML, XHTML, and XML. The JSP technology enables the easy authoring of web pages with maximum power and flexibility.

The JSP technology is platform independent in its dynamic web pages, its web servers, and its underlying server components. JSP pages may be authored on any platform, run on any web server or web-enabled application server, and accessed from any web browser. Server components, meanwhile, can be built on any platform and run on any server.

The JSP technology emphasizes the use of reusable components such as JavaBeans™ components, Enterprise JavaBeans™ components, and tag libraries. These components can be used with interactive tools for component development and page composition, yielding considerable time savings in development. In addition, they provide the cross-platform power and flexibility of the Java programming language or other scripting languages.

Macromedia Flash MX comes with new APIs for client/server application development, including support for J2EE within the Flash Remoting Architecture.

ColdFusion Markup Language

Macromedia ColdFusion MX is a rapid scripting and server environment for creating rich Internet applications. ColdFusion MX includes an easy-to-learn, tag-based scripting language, CFML, with connectivity to enterprise data and powerful built-in search and charting capabilities. ColdFusion MX enables developers to easily build and deploy dynamic web sites, content publishing systems, self-service applications, commerce sites, and more.

With CFML, you can enhance standard HTML files with database commands, conditional operators, high-level formatting functions, and other elements to rapidly produce easy-to-maintain web applications. However, CFML is not limited to enhancing HTML. For example, you can create Macromedia Flash MX applications consisting entirely of Flash elements and CFML. Similarly, you can use CFML to create Web services for use by other applications.

With ColdFusion MX, you can extend CFML further by creating custom tags or user-defined functions (UDFs), or by integrating COM, C++, and Java components (such as JSP tag libraries). You can also create ColdFusion components, which encapsulate related functions and properties and provide a consistent interface for accessing them. All these features let you easily create reusable functionality that is customized to the types of applications or web sites you are building.

We will be using both ColdFusion MX and JavaServer Pages for many examples in this book. We will also include a few examples that use ASP.NET, where appropriate (for example, with Flash Remoting).

What Happened to Flash Generator?

Macromedia Generator is a web server application that can dynamically combine text, graphics, and sound to build rich media content and deliver the final product in a variety of animated or static formats. Flash Player 6 *does* support Generator content *but* you can no longer edit or add new Generator content with the Macromedia Flash MX authoring environment. Let's take a quick look at what Generator is, what's been replaced within Flash MX, and how we can work around the Generator content.

History

Flash developers have used Generator's authoring extensions (Generator objects) to create templates (*.swt*). These templates contain variable elements to be replaced with content provided by various data sources including text files and databases. The data can be sport scores, stock quotes, news headlines, and so on. The Generator template has placeholders for text, graphics, and sound which are filled dynamically by Generator. This generated content can be played back as movies, whether it be JPEG, animated GIF, or QuickTime (MOV) using the client's Flash Player.

Generator authoring extensions, when used alone, create static SWF, GIF, JPEG, PNG, and MOV files that can be uploaded to a web server. With the offline and online server components of Generator, the Generator authoring extensions are used to create graphical front ends for sophisticated server-side applications.

Generator is being replaced with Flash Remoting and its integration with ColdFusion MX, J2EE application servers, and Microsoft .NET platforms. Additionally, Flash MX also includes something called Components (more on this in section titled "Flash Remoting Components") that can be used to perform some of the server functions previously provided by Generator.

What to Do with Generator Content

As mentioned, you can edit Generator-enabled FLA files with Flash MX, but the Generator content itself can no longer be edited. Any Generator objects on the Stage will have an X through them, indicating they cannot be edited. Also, new Generator content cannot be added in Flash MX as there are no Generator authoring extensions for Flash MX. It is also not possible to publish SWT template files from Flash MX.

The simplest solution is to replace Generator objects with new Flash MX objects like the Charting components or other UI components. For other objects, you will need to redesign your server-side code to work with the new Flash Remoting architecture and generate your dynamic elements differently using other third-party technologies or applications.

If you have ColdFusion MX, you can use the charting and graphing capabilities of this application server to generate and serve up dynamic charts and graphs. ColdFusion MX has expanded its support for charting, increasing the number of charts, the available formatting options, and enabling offline chart generation (similar to Generator). In addition to bar charts, pie charts, and line graphs, ColdFusion MX now supports eight additional chart types, including the capability to mix different types in the same chart (for example, a bar chart with an overlaid line graph). Finally, the charting engine now allows developers to use batch scheduling to save generated chart images to disk. This is particularly useful for reports that do not need real-time data access or for high-volume applications.

Flash Client to Server Communication

With Flash 5, the only way for the Flash client to communicate with a remote server is through the XML and the XMLSocket objects, as well as the *loadVariables* action. Now, with Flash MX and Flash Remoting, this can be done a lot easier, simpler, and faster. While the XML and XMLSocket objects are still available, and in fact, vastly improved, the *loadVariables* action has been superceded by the LoadVars action. We will discuss these three items next.

The XML Object

As you've probably guessed by its name, you can use the methods and properties of the XML object to load, parse, send, build, and manipulate XML document trees. In Macromedia Flash MX, the XML object has become a native object (it was previously interpreted during run time). As such, you will experience a dramatic improvement in performance. However, you must use the constructor *new XML()* to create an instance of the XML object before calling any of the methods of the XML object. The available methods are shown in Table 6-1.

Method	Description
appendChild	Appends a node to the end of the specified object's child list
cloneNode	Clones the specified node
createElement	Creates a new XML element
createTextNode	Creates a new XML text node
getBytesLoaded	Returns the number of bytes loaded for the specified XML document
getBytesTotal	Returns the size of the XML document in bytes

Table 6-1 *XML Methods*

Method	Description
hasChildNodes	Returns *true* if the specified node has child nodes; *false* otherwise
insertBefore	Inserts a node in front of an existing node in the specified node's child list
load	Loads a document from a URL
parseXML	Parses an XML document into the specified XML object tree
removeNode	Removes the specified node from its parent
send	Sends the specified XML object to a URL
sendAndLoad	Sends the specified XML object to a URL and loads the server response into another XML object
toString	Converts the specified node and any children to XML text

Table 6-1   *XML Methods* (continued)

The XML object also has numerous properties associated with it, as shown in Table 6-2.

Property	Description
contentType	Indicates the MIME type transmitted to the server
docTypeDecl	Sets and returns information about an XML document's DOCTYPE declaration
firstChild	References the first child in the list for the specified node
ignoreWhite	When set to true, text nodes that only contain white space are discarded during the parsing process
lastChild	References the last child in the list for the specified node
load	Checks if the specified XML object has loaded
nextSibling	References the next sibling in the parent's node child list
nodeName	Returns the tag name of an XML element
nodeType	Returns the type of the specified node (XML element or text node)
nodeValue	Returns the text of the specified node if the node is a text node
parentNode	References the parent node of the specified node
previousSibling	References the previous sibling in the parent's node child list
status	Returns a numeric status code indicating the success or failure of an XML parsing operation
xmlDecl	Sets and returns information about an XML document's document declaration

Table 6-2   *XML Properties*

The XMLSocket Object

XMLSocket can send data to the client at a time initiated by the server (push). The XMLSocket object implements client sockets that allow the computer running the Flash Player to communicate with a server computer identified by an IP address or domain name.

To use the XMLSocket object, the server computer must run a daemon that understands the protocol used by the XMLSocket object. The protocol is as follows:

▶ XML messages are sent over a full-duplex TCP/IP stream socket connection.

▶ Each XML message is a complete XML document, terminated by a zero byte.

▶ An unlimited number of XML messages can be sent and received over a single XMLSocket connection.

The XMLSocket object is useful for client-server applications that require low latency, such as real-time chat systems, since the XMLSocket maintains an open connection to the server. This allows the server to immediately send incoming messages without a request from the client.

Setting up a server to communicate with the XMLSocket object can be challenging. If your application does not require real-time interactivity, use the *loadVariables* action, or Flash HTTP-based XML server connectivity (*XML.load, XML.sendAndLoad, XML.send*), instead of the XMLSocket object. To use the methods of the XMLSocket object, you must first use the constructor, *new XMLSocket*, to create a new XMLSocket object.

Because the XMLSocket object establishes and maintains an open connection to the server, the following restrictions have been placed on the XMLSocket object for security reasons:

▶ The *XMLSocket.connect* method can connect only to TCP port numbers greater than or equal to 1024. One consequence of this restriction is that the server daemons that communicate with the XMLSocket object must also be assigned to port numbers greater than or equal to 1024. Port numbers below 1024 are often used by system services such as FTP, Telnet, and HTTP, thus the XMLSocket object is barred from these ports for security reasons. The port number restriction limits the possibility that these resources will be inappropriately accessed and abused.

▶ The *XMLSocket.connect* method can connect only to computers in the same subdomain where the SWF file (movie) resides. This restriction does not apply to movies running off a local disk.

The XMLSocket object also has numerous properties associated with it, as shown in Table 6-3.

Property	Description
close	Closes an open socket connection
connect	Establishes a connection to the specified server
send	Sends an XML object to the server

Table 6-3   *XMLSocket Methods*

NOTE

We recommend using the Flash Remoting objects as that will simplify your design and development of mobile applications significantly. Additionally, we also recommend using the Flash Communication Server (details can be found in Chapter 11) and the use of Real-Time Messaging Protocol (RTMP) communication instead of XMLSocket. If those objects are not sufficient, then by all means use the XMLSocket object.

The LoadVars Object

The LoadVars object is an alternative to the *loadVariables* action for transferring variables between a Flash movie and a server. You can use the LoadVars object to obtain error information, progress indications, and stream data while it downloads. The LoadVars object works much like the XML object; it uses the methods load, send, and sendAndLoad to communicate with a server. The main difference between the LoadVars object and the XML object is that LoadVars transfers ActionScript name and value pairs, rather than an XML DOM tree stored in the XML object. The LoadVars object follows the same security restrictions as the XML object. You must use the constructor new LoadVars() to create an instance of the LoadVars object before calling its methods.

The LoadVars object has numerous methods associated with it, as shown in Table 6-4.
The LoadVars object also has two properties associated with it, as shown in Table 6-5.

Method	Description
load	Downloads variables from a specified URL
getBytes	Returns the number of bytes loaded from a load or sendAndLoad method
getBytesTotal	Returns the total number of bytes that will be downloaded by a load or sendAndLoad method
send	Posts variables from a LoadVars object to a URL
sendAndLoad	Posts variables from a LoadVars object to a URL and downloads the server response to a target object
toString	Returns a URL encoded string that contains all the enumerable variables in the LoadVars object

Table 6-4   *LoadVars Methods*

Property	Description
contentType	Indicates the MIME type of the data
load	A Boolean value that indicates whether a load or sendAndLoad operation has completed

Table 6-5   *LoadVars Properties*

Introducing Macromedia Flash Remoting

Macromedia Flash Remoting provides the infrastructure that lets you connect to remote services exposed by application servers and Web services (see Figure 6-1). Flash Remoting simplifies the Flash application development process by providing a programming mode and runtime support for connecting ActionScript directly to remote server objects.

By storing information in a database and retrieving it, you can create dynamic and personalized content for your Flash movies. For example, you could create a message board, personal profiles for users, or a shopping cart that keeps track of a user's purchases so it can determine the user's preferences.

Flash Remoting supports object-based access, such as ColdFusion components or Java objects, and XML document processing to exchange data with any remote service, including ColdFusion components or pages, an Enterprise JavaBean (EJB), a Java class, an MBean, or a .NET application page.

Architecture

Developing Flash applications with Flash Remoting consists of building application server functionality and exposing that functionality through the Flash Remoting service, the server-side component of Flash Remoting (shown in Figure 6-1). Using the Flash Remoting ActionScript classes, Flash applications call functions on remote services named *service functions* in ActionScript.

Using Flash Remoting to connect to remote services requires two distinct areas of knowledge:

▶ **Interacting with Flash Remoting services in ActionScript**   Using the Macromedia Flash MX authoring environment, Flash developers call functions on remote services using the Flash Remoting ActionScript classes, including the NetServices, NetConnection, NetDebug, and RecordSet classes.

▶ **Exposing remote services to Flash**   Macromedia Flash Remoting supports the following application servers:

  ▶ Macromedia ColdFusion MX

  ▶ Microsoft .NET

  ▶ Java 2 Enterprise Edition (J2EE) application servers, including Macromedia JRun 4 and IBM WebSphere 4

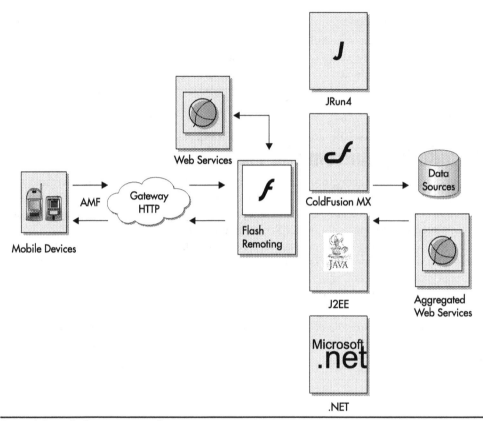

Figure 6-1 *Flash Remoting Architecture*

Flash's Action Message Format (AMF) provides a high-performance, optimized binary protocol that runs over HTTP and enables ActionScript to invoke and use data and logic hosted on an application server, or an XML Web service out on the Internet. AMF provides an object-based remote procedure call (RPC) mechanism, and supports passing both simple and complex data types between Flash ActionScript and any server-side programming language.

Integration with ColdFusion MX, J2EE, and .NET

To use the Macromedia Flash Remoting service with Macromedia ColdFusion MX, you build ColdFusion pages and components, or deploy Java objects. In ColdFusion pages, you use the Flash variable scope to interact with Flash applications (ColdFusion components natively support Flash interaction). In addition, you can use ColdFusion's server-side ActionScript functionality, which lets you query databases and perform HTTP operations in ActionScript files on the server. The public methods of Java objects are also available to the Flash Remoting service. We will discuss this in detail in Chapter 7.

To use Macromedia Flash Remoting with Microsoft .NET, you use the Flash Remoting custom server control. You can use server controls in Microsoft ASP.NET pages or you can bind the data defined by Active Data Objects (ADO) to server controls. In addition, you can use .NET Web services with Flash Remoting. Like other .NET applications, you can use any programming language that .NET supports, including C#, Visual Basic .NET, and JScript.

To expose functionalities that you build in Java 2 Enterprise Edition (J2EE) application servers to Macromedia Flash movies, you build public Java methods in your Java applications, save the class files to the WEB-INF directory of your application, and call the public methods in ActionScript. Macromedia Flash Remoting supports the following Java application types:

► Java classes (stateless)

► JavaBean objects (stateful)

► Enterprise JavaBeans (EJB; stateless session, stateful session, and entity beans)

Again, more on this in Chapter 7.

Flash Remoting Components

In this section, we will specifically cover objects for communicating between the Flash MX client and server back-ends. A few other traditional, non-Flash Remoting objects like XML and XMLSocket were covered earlier in this chapter.

To interact with application servers using Macromedia Flash Remoting, you must connect to the application server Flash Remoting service, call service functions and pass parameters, and handle the results returned to Flash. To connect to an application server Flash Remoting service and call a service function, you use the NetServices and NetConnection ActionScript classes.

NetConnection is an ActionScript class that manages a bidirectional object for connecting to remote resources. NetServices serves as a layer of abstraction to NetConnection that simplifies ActionScript coding for typical Flash Remoting usage patterns.

To debug Flash Remoting applications, you also use the NetDebug and NetDebugConfig classes. If you return record sets from an application server, including database query results, you use the RecordSet class to work with and manipulate the returned record sets in ActionScript. In addition, the DataGlue functions are available to bind RecordSet objects to Flash MX user interface (UI) components.

When used together, the Flash Remoting–related ActionScript classes provide functions to connect, interact, and manipulate data on the client.

NOTE

Flash Remoting doesn't push information to the client. Therefore, you should use XMLSocket instead.

The NetServices Object

The NetServices object is a collection of functions that helps you create and use connections to services using Flash Remoting. In addition, it helps you create and use NetConnection objects.

NOTE

The NetServices object is for Flash Remoting use only.

To use NetServices, you must first import the NetServices.as file in the first frame of the Flash movie with the *include* command, as follows:

```
#include "NetServices.as"
```

The available methods are shown in Table 6-6.
Here's a code snippet used when establishing a service connection:

```
#include "NetServices.as"
NetServices.setDefaultGatewayUrl("http://localhost:8500/
    flashservices/gateway");
var gw = NetServices.createGatewayConnection();
```

NOTE

The Flash movie only connects when you actually make a Flash Remoting service function call.

By default, Macromedia Flash MX assumes you are connecting to Flash Remoting using the non-secured HTTP protocol. Otherwise, you will need to explicitly specify the HTTPS secured protocol, as in the following:

```
NetServices.setDefaultGatewayUrl("https://www.mygateway.com/
    flashservices/gateway");
```

You can then make a service function call through Flash Remoting like:

```
ServiceObject.functionName
```

We will show you how to make a service function call next.

Method	Description
createGatewayConnection	Connects to Flash Remoting
setDefaultGatewayURL	Sets the default URL to connect to Flash Remoting

Table 6-6   *NetServices Methods*

The NetConnection Object

The NetConnection object manages a bidirectional connection between the Flash Player and the Flash Remoting service. The NetServices functions use the NetConnection object to call functions on and return results from application servers.

The available methods are shown in Table 6-7.

NOTE

The Action Message Format (AMF) is a lightweight binary messaging format that the Flash MX Player and the Flash Remoting gateway have agreed upon. It is also geared towards supporting ActionScript objects.

Here's some ActionScript code to call the *HelloNokia* service function:

```
#include "NetServices.as"
NetServices.setDefaultGatewayUrl("http://localhost:8500/
   flashservices/gateway");
var gw = NetServices.createGatewayConnection();
var serviceObject = gw.getService("com.macromedia.book.HelloNokia",
   new Result());
serviceObject.sayHello();
```

In this example, the *getService* references the HelloNokia component in the /com/macromedia/book directory. Then it calls the serviceObject *sayHello* function. We will discuss how to create server-side ColdFusion MX components in Chapter 8.

NOTE

ColdFusion MX components are referenced by both their name and location. This is equivalent to namespace management on the server.

Method	Description
addHeader	Adds a context header to the Action Message Format (AMF) packet structure
call	Invokes a command or method on the server
close	Closes the connection with the server
connect	Connects to an application on the application server
getDebugConfig	Retrieves the NetConnection object's debugging identifier
getDebugID	Retrieves the NetConnection object
getService	Creates a Flash Remoting service object
setCredentials	Sends authorization credentials to Flash Remoting
setDebugID	Sets a debug identifier for a NetConnection object
trace	Sends a client trace message associated with the NetConnection to the NetConnection Debugger

Table 6-7 *NetConnection Methods*

The RecordSet Object

The RecordSet object lets you manipulate RecordSet objects returned from Flash Remoting or create client-side RecordSet objects. A record set is a list of records, with functions for fetching, accessing, and manipulating the list of records in various ways.

NOTE

The RecordSet object is for Flash Remoting use only.

RecordSets created on an application server usually consist of database query results. Each record in a RecordSet object is represented by an untyped ActionScript object. In a RecordSet object, individual records are identified by an index number. The index starts at zero. When the RecordSet is sorted, or a record is added to or deleted from the RecordSet, the index changes.

Each field of the record is represented by a field in the object. For a RecordSet object that originated from an application server, the field names are the same as the names of the fields as defined by the server-side RecordSet. For local RecordSet objects, the field names are as defined in the original call to the new RecordSet() function.

To use the RecordSet object, you must use the *include* command to import the NetServices ActionScript class file, which also includes the RecordSet ActionScript class, in the first frame of a Flash movie, as shown next:

```
#include "NetServices.as"
```

The available methods are shown in Table 6-8.

Method	Description
addItem	Inserts a record into the RecordSet object
addItemAt	Inserts a record into the RecordSet object at the specified index
addView	Defines an object that will receive notifications when the RecordSet object changes
filter	Creates a new RecordSet object that contains selected records from the original RecordSet object
getColumnNames	Returns the names of all the columns of a RecordSet object
getItemAt	Returns a record if the index is valid and the record is immediately available
getItemID	Returns the record ID

Table 6-8   *RecordSet Methods*

Method	Description
getLength	Returns the number of records in a RecordSet object
getNumberAvailable	Returns the number of records that have been downloaded from the server
removeAll	Removes all records from the RecordSet object
removeItemAt	Removes the specified record from the RecordSet object
replaceItemAt	Replaces a record at the specified index
setDeliveryMode	Changes the delivery mode of a RecordSet associated with an application server
setField	Replaces one field of a record with a new value
sort	Sorts all the records through a user-specified compare function
sortItemsB	Sorts all records in the RecordSet object without making a new copy

Table 6-8   *RecordSet Methods* (continued)

The RecordSet object also has two properties associated with it as shown in Table 6-9.

The following code snippet demonstrates a few methods for manipulating the RecordSet object:

```
#include "NetServices.as"
// create RecordSet object
var bookList = new RecordSet(["BookName ","Price","ISBN"]);
bookList.addItem({BookName:"Macromedia Flash MX: The Complete
   Reference",Price :34.99, ISBN:0072134860});
bookList.addItem({BookName:"ActionScript : The Definitive Guide",
   Price :27.97, ISBN:1565928520});
trace("There are " + bookList.getLength() + " books in the your
   shopping cart.");
```

As mentioned earlier, you use the RecordSet class to handle the returned record sets in ActionScript. You will need to use the DataGlue functions to bind RecordSet objects to Flash MX UI components—that's next.

Property	Description
isFullyPopulated	Determines whether a RecordSet object is fully populated or not
IsLocal	Determines whether a RecordSet object is local or associated with an application server

Table 6-9   *RecordSet Properties*

The DataGlue Object

The DataGlue ActionScript functions let you bind RecordSet objects to Flash MX UI components. DataGlue offers a way to format data records for use in a ListBox, ComboBox, or other UI component.

NOTE

The DataGlue object is for Flash Remoting use only.

To use DataGlue, you must first import the DataGlue.as file in the first frame of the Flash movie with the *include* command, as follows:

```
#include "DataGlue.as"
```

The available methods are shown in Table 6-10.

NOTE

The DataGlue functions do not make a copy of the original data provider's data.

The following example binds the *myRecordSet* RecordSet object to the *myComboBox* UI component in a Flash movie:

```
#include "DataGlue.as"
DataGlue.bindFormatStrings (myComboBox, myRecordSet,
  "#theatreName#","#city#, #state# #zipcode#");
```

In this example, *myComboBox* represents a ComboBox component in the Flash movie, and *myRecordSet* represents the RecordSet object. The *theatreName*, *city*, *state*, and *zipcode*

Method	Description
bindFormatStrings	Binds a data provider (for example, a RecordSet object) to a data consumer (for instance, a ListBox UI component) and formats the data in the function call
bindFormatFunction	Binds a data provider (such as a RecordSet object) to a data consumer (for example, a ComboBox UI component) and formats the data using a custom function

Table 6-10   *DataGlue Methods*

variables represent record field names. The Flash movie displays the *theatreName* variable; however, the *city*, *state*, and *zipcode* variables are returned when the user selects the record. You can use the *getValue* function to return the value.

The NetDebug and NetDebugConfig Objects

The NetDebug object lets you trace function calls, parameters, and results among the Flash movie, Flash Remoting, and the application server. You use the NetConnection Debugger panel in the Flash MX authoring environment to view the debugging results.

To use NetDebug, you must first import the NetDebug.as file in the first frame of the Flash movie with the *include* command, as follows:

```
#include "NetDebug.as"
```

The available method is shown in Table 6-11.

The following example sets a trace on the *serviceObject* object:

```
#include "NetServices.as"
#include "NetDebug.as"
NetServices.setDefaultGatewayURL("http://www.mygateway.com/
    flashservices/gateway");
NetServices.createGatewayConnection();
serviceObject = gatewayConnection.getService("myService", this);
NetDebug.trace({level:"testing", message:"Message to NCD via trace."});
```

You can turn on debugging via the NetDebugConfig object and use the NetConnection Debugger (NCD) panel in the Flash MX authoring environment to view the debugging results.

To use NetDebugConfig, you must first import the NetDebug.as file in the first frame of the Flash movie with the *include* command, as follows:

```
#include "NetDebug.as"
```

The available methods are shown in Table 6-12.

Method	Description
trace	Associates a debugging flag to an ActionScript object

Table 6-11   *NetDebug Method*

Method	Description
getDebug	Determines whether debugging is enabled
setDebug	Turns debugging on or off for an ActionScript object

Table 6-12 *NetDebugConfig Methods*

Server-Side ActionScript

Through the Flash Remoting service, Flash developers can leverage their knowledge of ActionScript to access ColdFusion *Query* and *HTTP* features. You will only need to learn two new ActionScript functions that let you perform ColdFusion HTTP and query operations, and a few lines of setup code on the client side. This is a feature that lets you create data-intensive Flash-based applications. Creating ActionScript files that reside on the server helps separate the business logic of your application from the presentation layer.

Coding the ColdFusion query and HTTP operations in ActionScript is straightforward. The *CF.query* and *CF.http* functions provide a well-defined interface for building SQL queries and HTTP operations that is based on the simplicity of ColdFusion. For example, the following is a typical server-side ActionScript function definition that returns query data:

```
// CF.query operation
function myQuery()
{
    mydata = CF.query({datasource:"EMPDB",sql:"SELECT * FROM Employees"});
return mydata;
}
```

There are also some basic client-side and server-side requirements. On the client side, you only need a small piece of code that establishes a connection to the Flash Remoting service and references the server-side ActionScript you want to use. The following is an example of the required client-side code:

```
// Connect to the Flash Remoting service
#include "NetServices.as"

//  Flash Remoting service URL
NetServices.setDefaultGatewayUrl("http://localhost:8500");

// Create a connection
gatewayConnnection = NetServices.createGatewayConnection();

// Reference your server-side ActionScript here
yahooService = gatewayConnnection.getService("yahoo.stock.
   yahooquotes", this);

// Invoke the getQuotes() method defined in SSAS
```

```
yahooService.getQuotes("MACR");

// Once the record set is returned, you handle the results
// Your ActionScript code goes here…
```

NOTE

Client-side ActionScript (CSAS) files use the .as extension, while server-side ActionScript (SSAS) files use the .asr extension, for ActionScript Remote.

To complete our simple example, the following server-side ActionScript builds on the client-side code shown previously:

```
// yahooquotes.asr

// getQuotes method invoked in CSAS
// Accept a single stock quote symbol argument
function getQuotes(symbol)
{
    // Query some data provider for the specified stock quote
    // and return the results
    // Note:
    // getQuotesFromProvider method is defined elsewhere
    data = getQuotesFromProvider(symbol);

    // Returns data to the client
    return data;
}
```

The *getQuotes* function conducts the stock quote request and returns the results of the request to the client as a RecordSet object. We will discuss both these server-side ActionScript functions next.

CF.query

The *CF.query* function lets you populate Flash MX elements with data retrieved from a ColdFusion data source. To pull data into your Flash MX movie from a ColdFusion data source, follow these two steps:

1. Create an SSAS file that performs queries against a ColdFusion data source.

2. Write ActionScript code in your Flash MX movie that references your ActionScript file (*.asr*) on the ColdFusion server.

You create server-side ActionScript that executes the query and returns the data in a record set to the client. You can also use methods in the RecordSet ActionScript object on the client to manipulate data in the record set and present data in your Flash MX movie. The CF.query function, for example, returns a RecordSet object, which is an instance of the RecordSet class of objects. The RecordSet class provides a wide range of functions for handling record set data, as shown in Table 6-13.

Use these methods in the RecordSet ActionScript class in your client-side ActionScript to scrub, manipulate, mine, filter, sort, or change data returned in the CF.query RecordSet. These functions are available for every RecordSet object returned by the CF.query function to the Flash MX client. You invoke these functions as follows:

```
objectName.functionName();
```

For example, in the result function that you create to handle record set data returned by the CF.query function, you can reference the database column names returned in the record set using the *getColumnNames* RecordSet function:

```
function selectData_result (result)
{
    // result holds the query data
    // employeesView is a Flash ListBox
    stringOutput.text = result.getColumnNames();
    _root.employeesView.setDataProvider(result);
}
```

Method	Description
addItem	Appends a record to the end of the specified RecordSet
addItemAt	Inserts a record at the specified index
addView	Requests notification of changes in a RecordSet object's state
filter	Creates a new RecordSet object that contains selected records from the original RecordSet object
getColumnNames	Returns the names of all columns of the RecordSet
getItemAt	Retrieves a record from a RecordSet object
getItemID	Gets the unique ID corresponding to a record
getLength	Returns the total number of records in a RecordSet object
getNumberAvailable	Returns the number of records that have been downloaded from the server
isFullyPopulated	Determines whether a RecordSet object can be edited or manipulated
isLocal	Determines whether a RecordSet object is local or server-associated
removeAll	Removes all records from the RecordSet object
removeItemAt	Removes a specific record
replaceItemAt	Replaces the entire contents of a record
setDeliveryMode	Changes the delivery mode of a server-associated record set
setField	Replaces one field of a record with a new value
sort	Sorts all records by a specified compare function
sortItemsBy	Sorts all records by a selected field

Table 6-13 *CF.query Methods*

The CF.query ActionScript function uses either named arguments or positional arguments. However, the named argument style is more readable than the positional argument style. Although the positional argument style supports a subset of CF.query arguments, it allows a compact coding style more appropriate for simple expressions of the CF.query function.

```
// CF.query named argument syntax
CF.query
({
    datasource:"data source name",
    sql:"SQL stmts",
    username:"username",
    password:"password",
    maxrows:number,
    timeout:milliseconds
})

// CF.query named positional syntax
CF.query(datasource, sql);
CF.query(datasource, sql, maxrows);
CF.query(datasource, sql, username, password);
CF.query(datasource, sql, username, password, maxrows);
```

The arguments are described in Table 6-14.

NOTE:

The named arguments style requires curly braces {} to surround the function arguments. However, do not use curly braces for the positional arguments style.

Argument	Description	Required?
datasource	Name of datasource for query to retrieve data from	Required
sql	SQL statements	Required
username	Overrides the username specified in the datasource setup	Optional
password	Overrides the password specified in the datasource setup	Optional
maxrows	Maximum number of rows to return in the RecordSet	Optional
timeout	Maximum number of seconds for the query to execute before returning an error; only used in named arguments	Optional

Table 6-14   *CF.query Arguments*

CF.http

The *CF.http* ActionScript function lets you retrieve information from a remote HTTP server. HTTP Get and Post methods are both supported. Using the *Get* method, you send information to the remote server directly in the URL. This method is often used for one-way transactions in which CF.http retrieves an object such as the content of a web page. The *Post* method, meanwhile, can pass variables to a form or CGI program, and create HTTP cookies.

The simplest way to use the CF.http function is to use it with the Get method argument to retrieve a page from a specified URL (the default is the Get method). For example, the following server-side code retrieves file content from the specified URL:

```
function basicGet(url)
{
    // HTTP Get of URL
    result = CF.http(url);
    return result.get("Filecontent");
}
```

The CF.http function returns an object that contains properties, also known as attributes, that you reference to access the contents of the file returned, header information, HTTP status codes, and so on. Table 6-15 shows the available properties.

In order to pass HTTP *Post* parameters in the CF.http function, you must construct an array of objects and assign this array to a variable named *params*. As shown in Table 6-16,

Property	Description
Text	A Boolean value indicating whether the specified URL location contains text data
Charset	The character set used by the document specified in the URL
Header	The raw response header
Filecontent	File contents for text and MIME files
Mimetype	The MIME type
Responseheader	The response header
Statuscode	HTTP error code and associated error strings. Common codes include 400: Bad Request 401: Unauthorized 403: Forbidden 404: Not Found 405: Method Not Allowed

Table 6-15 *CF.http Properties*

Parameter	Description
name	Variable name for the data passed
type	Transaction type. Includes URL Formfield Cookie CGI File
value	Value of URL, Formfield, Cookie, File, or CGI variables that are passed

Table 6-16 *CF.http Parameters*

the following arguments can only be passed as an array of objects in the params argument of the CF.http function.

For example, when you build an HTML form using the Post method, you specify the name of the page to which form data is passed. The Post method in CF.http is used in a similar fashion. However, with CF.http, the page that receives the Post does not display anything.

```
function postWithParams()
{
    // Set up the array of post parameters
    params = new Array();
    params[1] = {name:"UserID", type:"FormField", value:"david"};
    params[2] = [name:"Password", type:"FormField", value:"waffle"};
    url = "http://localhost:8100/";

    // Invoke CF.http with the method, url, and params
    result = CF.http("post", url, params);
    return result.get("Filecontent");
}
```

NOTE

ActionScript starts the array index at zero (0), while ColdFusion array indexes begin at one (1).

NOTE:

Due to ActionScript's automatic type conversion, do not return a Boolean literal to Flash from ColdFusion. Return 1 to indicate true, and 0 to indicate false.

Summary

In this chapter, we presented an overview of a few popular server-side scripting languages. We also went into detail regarding Flash MX objects that are available for exchanging XML data with remote servers. Then we introduced you to the powerful Macromedia Flash Remoting module which opened the floodgates to business logic running on ColdFusion, .NET, and J2EE servers. We described in depth the new Flash MX objects (for the client) that are used to integrate with these remote servers; and finally, we covered server-side ActionScript extensively with ColdFusion MX. In Chapter 7, we will show you how to use Macromedia Flash Remoting with these server-side platforms, and look at examples on how to implement remote exchanges of XML data.

Using Flash Remoting

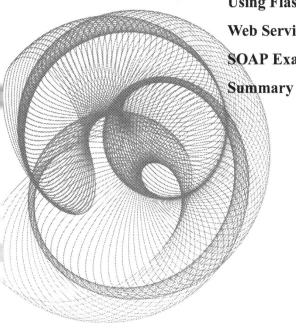

In Chapter 6, we introduced you to Macromedia Flash Remoting and its support for the ColdFusion MX application server, the J2EE application server, and the Microsoft ASP.NET platform. In this chapter, we will discuss how to use Flash Remoting with these server-side capabilities, and introduce you to the exciting world of Web services. Two examples will be shown, illustrating how to build mobile Flash applications with a Flash front end using the popular BabelFish Translation Web Service and Google Search Web Service.

Using Flash MX with ColdFusion MX

To use Flash MX with ColdFusion MX via the Flash Remoting service, you simply build ColdFusion pages and components, or deploy the relevant Java objects. Later, we'll look at how data can be exchanged between the mobile Flash client (Pocket PC) and the application server, depending on what you call on the ColdFusion server side.

ColdFusion Pages

When building a ColdFusion page that interacts with Flash movies, the directory name that contains the ColdFusion page is translated to the Flash service name in ActionScript. The individual ColdFusion page names contained in that directory translate to service functions in ActionScript. You use the *Flash* variable scope to access parameters passed from Flash movies and return values to Flash movies. Table 7-1 shows the variables contained in the Flash scope.

Depending on how the values are passed from Flash, you refer to array values using ordered array syntax or structure name syntax. For example, if you pass the parameters as an ordered array from Flash, *paramArray[1]* references the first value. If you pass the parameters as named parameters, you use standard structure-name syntax like *params.name*. An example follows:

```
<cfset Flash.Result ="Variable 1:#Flash.paramArray[1]#, Variable 2:#Flash.
paramArray[2]#">
```

NOTE

ActionScript array indexes start at zero (0), whereas ColdFusion array indexes start at one (1).

Variable	Description
Flash.Params	Structure containing the parameters passed from the Flash movie
Flash.Result	Return variable to the Flash movie that called the function
Flash.Pagesize	The number of records returned at a time to Flash movie

Table 7-1   *ColdFusion Flash Scope*

ColdFusion Components

ColdFusion components require little modification to work with Flash. The *<cffunction>* tag names the function and contains the logic, and the *<cfreturn>* tag returns the result to Flash. The name of the ColdFusion component file (**.cfc*) translates to the service name in ActionScript.

NOTE

Avoid using non-alphanumeric characters such as the underscore character (_) in component names, method names, and argument names.

The following example illustrates how easy it is to create a ColdFusion component. The ColdFusion code looks like the following (save the file to the root server directory as *flashComponent.cfc*):

```
<cfcomponent name="flashComponent">
  <cffunction name="helloMethod" access="remote" returnType="String">
  <cfset returnMessage ="Hello Mobile Flash MX from CFC">
  <cfreturn returnMessage >
  </cffunction>
</cfcomponent>
```

The client-side ActionScript would look like:

```
#include "NetServices.as"
NetServices.setDefaultGatewayUrl("http://localhost:8500/
   flashservices/gateway");
// connect to the gateway
gatewayConnection = NetServices.createGatewayConnection();
// get a reference to the service
CFCService = gatewayConnection.getService("flashComponent",
   this);
CFCService.helloMethod();

// debug only
function helloMethod_Result(result)
{
   trace(result);
}
```

NOTE

For ColdFusion component methods to communicate with Flash movies, you must set the access tribute of the <cffunction> tag to remote.

Java Objects

You can run various kinds of Java objects with ColdFusion MX, including JavaBeans, Java classes, and Enterprise JavaBeans by using the ColdFusion Administrator to add additional directories to the Java class path. By placing your Java files in the class path, the public methods of the class instance are available to your Flash movie.

For example, assume the Java class *utils.UIComponents* exists in a directory in your ColdFusion class path. The Java file contains the following code:

```
package utils;
public class UIComponents
{
   public String javaHello()
   {
      return "Hello Mobile Flash MX from Java";
   }
}
```

The client-side ActionScript would look like:

```
#include "NetServices.as"
NetServices.setDefaultGatewayUrl("http://localhost:8500/
   flashservices/gateway");
// connect to the gateway
gatewayConnection = NetServices.createGatewayConnection();
// get a reference to the service
JavaService = gatewayConnection.getService("utils.UIComponents ",
   this);
JavaService.javaHello();

// debug only
function javaHello_Result(result)
{
   trace(result);
}
```

Using Flash MX with J2EE

To use Flash MX with Java 2 Enterprise Edition (J2EE) application servers via the Flash Remoting service, you build public Java methods in your Java applications, save the class files to the WEB-INF directory of your application, and call the public methods in ActionScript. Again, we will show you how data can be exchanged between the Flash client and the application server, depending on what you call on the J2EE server side.

Java/JSP Pages

To communicate with Flash Remoting, you declare the file as part of the *flashgateway* package. The public methods are available automatically to Flash movies as ActionScript functions.

For example, create and save the following file to *FlashBean.java* in the *examples* folder of the WEB-INF directory.

```
//names package
package flashgateway.examples;
import java.io.Serializable;

//declares class
public class FlashBean
implements Serializable {
private String message;
   public FlashBean()
   {
      message ="Hello Mobile Flash MX from JavaBean";
   }
   //declares BeanMessage method
   public String BeanMessage()
   {
      return message;
   }
}
```

The client-side ActionScript would look like the following:

```
#include "NetServices.as"
NetServices.setDefaultGatewayUrl("http://localhost:8500/
   flashservices/gateway");
// connect to the gateway
gatewayConnection = NetServices.createGatewayConnection();
// get a reference to the service
J2EEService = gatewayConnection.getService("flashgateway.examples.
   FlashBean",this);
J2EEService.BeanMessage();

// debug only
function BeanMessage_Result(result)
{
   trace(result);
}
```

EJBs

Enterprise JavaBeans (EJBs) are server-side components that encapsulate the business logic of an application. EJBs simplify the development of large, distributed applications being that bean developers focus on business problems and logic, client developers focus on presentation, and new applications can be built from existing beans (portable components).

You build EJBs for Flash Remoting just like any other EJB. When you access the EJB methods exposed through Flash Remoting, you use the JNDI EJB name in the *getService* function. When using Flash with EJB applications, ActionScript functions map to *EJBHome* and *EJBObject* methods.

Using Flash MX with .NET

To use Flash MX with ASP.NET via the Flash Remoting service, you use the Flash Remoting custom server control. As with ColdFusion and Java/JSP, let's look at how data can be exchanged between the Flash client and the .NET server, depending on what you call on the .NET server side.

ASP.NET Pages

You build ASP.NET pages that interact with Flash Remoting just as with any other ASP.NET page. To access parameters sent from Flash, or to return results, use the *flash* custom tag. Table 7-2 contains the available flash custom tag properties.

To build an inline ASP.NET page that interacts with Flash Remoting:

1. Register the custom tag. To import the Flash Remoting assembly into an ASP.NET page, use the ASP.NET *register* command. For example:

```
<%@ Page language="c#" debug="true" %>
<%@ Register TagPrefix="Macromedia"
    Namespace="FlashGateway" Assembly="flashgateway"%>
```

In this example, the *TagPrefix* attribute assigns the initial namespace to all server controls on the page that interacts with Flash Remoting. The *Namespace* attribute calls

Custom Tag Properties	Description
Flash.Params	An IList (collection of objects) containing the parameters passed from the Flash movie
Flash.Result	Return variable to the Flash movie that called the function
Flash.DataSource	The optional ADO data view to bind to Flash Remoting

Table 7-2 *ASP.NET Flash Scope*

the Flash Remoting component definition, while the *Assembly* attribute identifies the Flash Remoting assembly.

2. Use the Flash Remoting custom tag in a page. For example:

```
<%@ Page language="c#" debug="true" %>
<%@ Register TagPrefix="Macromedia" Namespace="FlashGateway"
    Assembly="flashgateway"%>
<Macromedia:Flash ID="Flash" runat="server" />
```

In this example, the *Macromedia:Flash* tag creates an object on the .NET server. The *ID* attribute names the object, and the *runat* attribute tells .NET to execute the script on the server.

3. Build the C# code. When you build the C# code, you use the *flash* custom tag to reference parameters passed from Flash and return results. For example:

```
<%@ Page language="c#" debug="true" %>
<%@ Register TagPrefix="Macromedia" Namespace="FlashGateway"
    Assembly="flashgateway"%>
<Macromedia:Flash ID="Flash" runat="server">
<%
    String message = "Hello Mobile Flash MX from .NET";
    Flash.Result = message;
%>
```

The value assigned to the *Flash.Result* custom tag is the only variable returned to Flash.

4. The ActionScript in the Flash movie would look like the following:

```
#include "NetServices.as"
NetServices.setDefaultGatewayUrl("http://localhost:8500/
    flashservices/*.aspx");
// connect to the gateway
gatewayConnection = NetServices.createGatewayConnection();
// get a reference to the service
ASPNETService =
gatewayConnection.getService("flashservices.examples",this);
ASPNETService.Example1();

// debug only
function Example1_Result(result)
{
    trace(result);
}
```

The reference to the service is a directory containing the ASP.NET pages. Each ASP.NET page in the directory is available as a function of this service. In our example, *Example1.aspx* is used.

ADO.NET Objects

ADO.NET provides an object model for accessing and manipulating data. Using Flash Remoting, you can create dynamic Flash UIs that display query results for ADO.NET applications. Use code-behind authoring to build an ASP.NET page that interacts with Flash Remoting. To build an ASP.NET page with code-behind authoring:

1. Create the ASP.NET page as before except reference the ASPX.CS file instead, which is generated automatically by Visual Studio .NET, using the *CodeBehind* attribute, as in the following example:

```
<%@ Page language="c#" debug="true"
CodeBehind="Example1.aspx.cs"
AutoEventWireup="false" Inherits="examples.ado. Example1" %>
<%@ Register TagPrefix="Macromedia" Namespace="FlashGateway"
    Assembly="flashgateway" %>
```

2. You create an object on the server, named *Flash*, using a custom tag, as in the following example:

```
<form action="Northwind.aspx" runat="server" id="northwindform">
<Macromedia:Flash id="Flash" Runat="Server"></Macromedia:Flash>
<asp:datagrid id="ExamplesGrid" runat="server"
    Font-Names="Arial Narrow" AllowSorting="True">
</asp:datagrid>
</form>
```

3. The ActionScript in the Flash movie would look like the following:

```
#include "NetServices.as"
NetServices.setDefaultGatewayUrl("http://localhost:8500/
    flashservices/*.aspx");
// connect to the gateway
gatewayConnection = NetServices.createGatewayConnection();
// get a reference to the service
ADONETService =
gatewayConnection.getService("flashservices.examples.ado",this);
ADONETService.Example1();

// debug only
function Example1_Result(result)
{
    trace(result);
}
```

Web Services

Besides database queries and server-side scripts, Web services are the latest data sources becoming publicly available. But is it the next big thing, or just the next big hype? We believe Web services are finally starting to fulfill their promises as a useful set of capabilities, as shown by the Google Search Web Service (discussed in the next section). Just about every software maker has embraced Web services and the idea has gained credibility with the support of such industry heavyweights as Microsoft, IBM, Oracle, and Sun Microsystems.

What are Web services? Web services consist of a set of messaging protocols, programming standards, and network registration and discovery facilities that expose business functions to authorized parties over the Internet from any web-connected device. Essentially, they're software components in the network. To put it more simply, a Web service is a discrete business process that:

► Exposes and describes itself

► Allows other services to locate it on the Internet

► Can be invoked

► Returns a response

Web services provide a language- and platform-independent syntax for exchanging complex data using messages. The internals of Web services are implemented using XML, making it easy for any platform to support this technology. The following are three primary components of the Web services platform:

► **UDDI (Universal Description, Discovery, and Integration)**   Provides a way for Web service clients to dynamically locate Web Services.

► **WSDL (Web Services Description Language)**   Syntax to describe the functionality of a Web service.

► **SOAP (Simple Object Access Protocol)**   Protocol used for sending messages and data between applications.

With a Web service, you can make a request to the remote application to perform an action. For example, you can request a stock quote, pass a text string to be translated, or request information from a product catalog. The advantage of Web services is that you do not have to re-create application logic someone else already created; therefore, you can build your applications faster.

NOTE

This section contains an overview of the architecture of Web services. For detailed information, consult one of the many Web services books.

UDDI

How do you find what Web services are out there? As a consumer of Web services, you want to know what Web services are available, and as a publisher of Web services, you want others to be able to find your Web services and easily invoke them. Universal Description, Discovery, and Integration (UDDI) provides a way for Web service clients to dynamically locate Web services that provide specific capabilities. You use a UDDI query to find service providers, while a UDDI response contains information, such as business contact info, business category, and technical details, about how to invoke a Web service.

Once you find a desired Web service and its associated WSDL URL, you can start to consume that service. Let's try and find the BabelFish Translation Service using the XMethods web site. XMethods has a great list of publicly available and "running" Web services. Because Web services are still in their infancy as of this writing, there aren't too many to choose from for development. Follow these steps to find the appropriate WSDL file:

1. Point your browser to http://www.xmethods.com (see Figure 7-1).

2. Scroll down to find the BabelFish Web Service (see Figure 7-2). Click the BabelFish link.

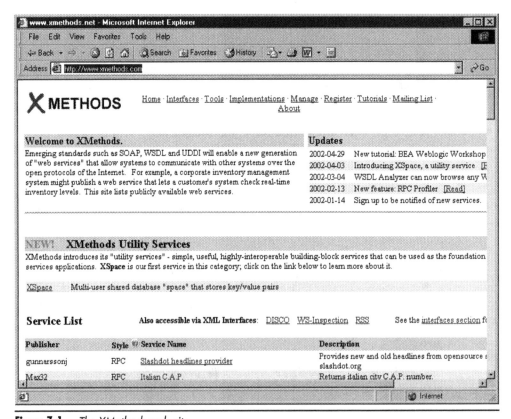

Figure 7-1   *The XMethods web site*

3. You will see details about the BabelFish service (see Figure 7-3). Select the WSDL link (see Figure 7-4) and you'll view full details of the BabelFish Translation Service showing input and output parameters—those are the only things you need to know if you are consuming a Web service using ColdFusion MX. If not, you'll need to understand how to generate your own Web service client in addition to the SOAP endpoint.

You have now successfully used the XMethods pseudo-registry and found a Web service to consume.

WSDL

A WSDL document is an XML file that describes a Web service's purpose, where it is located, and how to access it. The WSDL document describes the operations you can invoke and their associated data types. ColdFusion can generate a WSDL document from a Web service, and you can publish the WSDL document on a URL to provide information to potential clients.

The WSDL file is self-describing. That means a person who makes a Web service available also publishes a description of the API to the Web service as a WSDL file.

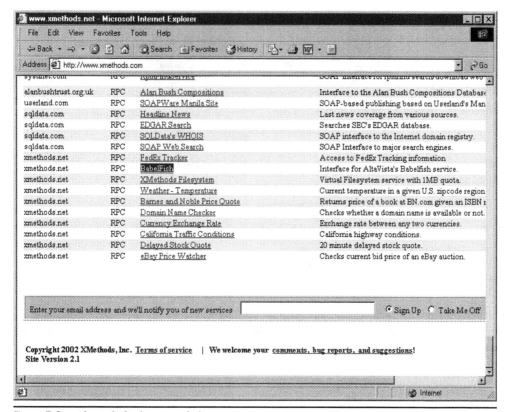

Figure 7-2 *The BabelFish service link*

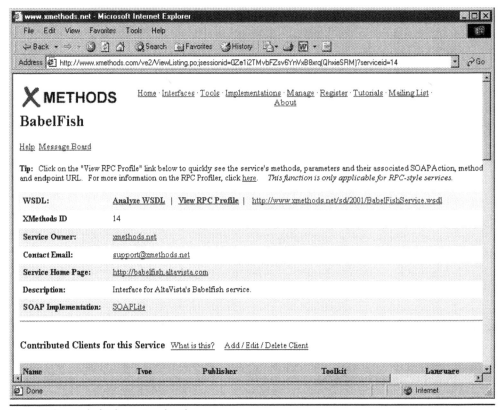

Figure 7-3 *BabelFish service details*

This XML-formatted document includes information about the Web service, such as the following:

▶ Operations you can call on the Web service

▶ Input parameters you pass to each operation

▶ Return values from an operation

SOAP

SOAP provides a standard XML structure for sending and receiving Web service requests and responses over the Internet. Usually, you send SOAP messages using HTTP, but you also can send them using SMTP and other protocols. Macromedia's ColdFusion MX application server actually integrated the Apache Axis SOAP engine to support Web services.

We'll use the ColdFusion MX Application Server for quite a few examples in this book because, in addition to its ease of programming, it's tightly integrated with the Flash MX client. The ColdFusion Web Services Engine performs the underlying functionality to support

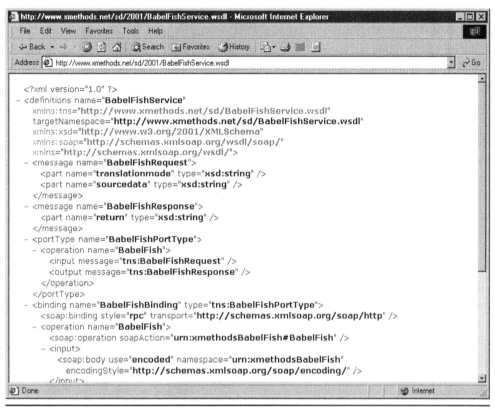

Figure 7-4 *The BabelFish WSDL file*

Web services, including generating WSDL files for Web services you create. In ColdFusion, to consume or publish Web services does not require you to be familiar with SOAP or to perform any SOAP operations. You will see more of this in the chapters to come. You can find additional information about SOAP in the W3C's SOAP 1.1 note at http://www.w3 .org/tr/soap should you choose to use other tools and application servers for your Web services development endeavors.

We will next go into detail about consuming two publicly available Web services using the Flash MX client with Flash Remoting and communicating with the Web services from AltaVista (BabelFish) and Google (Search).

SOAP Examples

Two of the most popular Web services used by developers today are AltaVista's BabelFish Translation Web Service and the Google Search Web Service. Both are freely available but you do need to register with Google to use theirs, and there are limitations to the Web services, as noted in the following sections.

The BabelFish Translation Web Service

In its simplest form, an access to a Web service is similar to a function call. Instead of the function call referencing a library on your computer, it references a remote functionality over the Internet. Consuming Web services typically involves a two-step process:

▶ Parse the WSDL file of the Web service to determine its interface—a Web service makes its associated WSDL file available over the Internet. You need to know the URL of the WSDL file defining the service. For this example, you can access the WSDL file for the BabelFish Web Service at http://www.xmethods.net/sd/2001/BabelFishService.wsdl.

▶ Make a request to the Web service. Using Flash Remoting with Flash MX client ActionScript, we can call the remote Web service.

Details about the BabelFish Translation Web Service are shown in Table 7-3. The ten-thousand-foot view of this example is shown next:

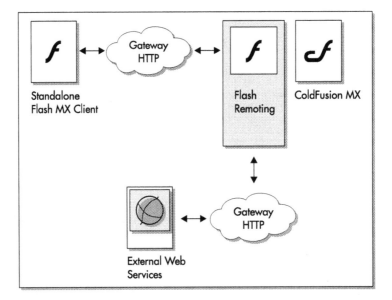

The information in the WSDL file defines the Web service operations and the input and output parameters of each operation, including the data type of each parameter. The following example shows a portion of the WSDL file for the BabelFish Web Service:

```
<message name="BabelFishRequest">
    <part name="translationmode" type="xsd:string" />
    <part name="sourcedata" type="xsd:string" />
</message>
```

```
<message name="BabelFishResponse">
   <part name="return" type="xsd:string" />
</message>
<portType name="BabelFishPortType">
   <operation name="BabelFish">
   <input message="tns:BabelFishRequest" />
   <output message="tns:BabelFishResponse" />
   </operation>
</portType>
```

The operation name used in the examples in this section is *BabelFish*. This operation takes a single input parameter defined as a message of type *BabelFishRequest*. You can see that the message BabelFishRequest contains two string parameters: *translationmode* and *sourcedata*.

Description
The AltaVista BabelFish Translation Web service enables you to translate short passages to and from English to a number of languages, and to and from several specific pairs of languages (for example, German to French, French to German).

Usage

WSDL:
  http://www.xmethods.net/sd/2001/BabelFishService.wsdl
METHOD:
  BabelFish
INPUT:
  translationmode (xsd:string) – see the following
  sourcedata (xsd:string) – text to be translated
OUTPUT:
  return (xsd:string) – translated data
KEY:
  translationmodes are as follows:

Translation	Translationmode
English	French"en_fr"
English	German"en_de"
English	Italian"en_it"
English	Portuguese"en_pt"
English	Spanish"en_es"
French	English"fr_en"
German	English"de_en"
Italian	English"it_en"
Portuguese	English"pt_en"
Spanish	English"es_en"
Russian	English"ru_en"

Table 7-3   *The BabelFish Web Service*

When you call the BabelFish operation, you pass both parameters as input. Our example therefore invokes an operation on the BabelFish Web Service to translate the string passed by the *sourcedata* argument as well as the translation mode passed by the *translationmode* argument.

> **NOTE**
>
> The BabelFish Web Service can translate text strings up to about 4kB, or 640 words in length, from one language to another.

Web service operations often return information back to your application. You can determine the name and data type of returned information by examining the WSDL file for the Web service. The BabelFish operation returns a message of type *BabelFishResponse*. The message statement in the WSDL file defines the BabelFishResponse message as containing a single string parameter named *return*.

The Flash Remoting service lets you call ColdFusion MX pages from a Flash MX client, but it does not let you call Web services directly. To call Web services from a Flash MX client, you use Flash Remoting to call the BabelFish web. The Flash MX client will pass input parameters to the Web service via Flash remoting, which then returns any output data to the Flash MX client.

We have created a simple Flash (*babelfish.fla*) file that interfaces with our BabelFish Web service sized for a Pocket PC Flash client, as shown in Figure 7-5.

One major item to note. The resulting dynamic text box, *translateResult,* does NOT have its font embedded since we are handling multiple languages here. Non-Latin characters will not display, otherwise your results box will be empty or contain garbage. Of course, your system must have the appropriate fonts installed already. For example, let's translate our English text string to Japanese, as shown in Figure 7-6.

Figure 7-5   *The BabelFish Flash MX UI*

Figure 7-6   *BabelFish English to Japanese translation*

Here we have a few dynamic components of interest; their instance names are listed in Table 7-4.

There are two sets of ActionScript required for this example. One is associated with the *submitButton.* The other is for the general Frame. Let's start off with the submitButton. The ActionScript is executed this way when the button is pressed:

```
submitButton.onRelease =function (){
    statusText.text = ">Connecting to BabelFish..."
    flashtestService.BabelFish(cb_types.getSelectedItem().
    data,sourceText.text);
}
```

With the *release* event or button press, we update the status display (Dynamic Text component instance, *statusText*) and call the BabelFish Web Service with the selected

Instance Name	Component
sourceText	Input Text component for string to be translated
cb_types	ComboBox component for selecting translation modes
translateResult	Dynamic Text component for displaying translation results
statusText	Dynamic Text component for displaying status of Web service interactions
submitButton	Button component for submitting request to Web service

Table 7-4   *BabelFish UI Components*

translation mode (from the ComboBox component instance, *cb_types*) and text to be translated (Input Text component instance, *sourceText*). The ComboBox is populated using the Properties window (see Figure 7-7). To get there, double-click *Labels*, then *Data*.

getSelectedItem().data will send the data of the selected item in the ComboBox—for example, "*en_fr*"—to the Web service.

NOTE

Because we are using the new event model for Flash MX, the ActionScript is much cleaner and eliminates the need to scatter code everywhere.

The ActionScript for the general Frame is listed next:

```
#include "NetServices.as"

function BabelFish_Result(result)
{
      translateResult.text = result;
      statusText.text = ">Translation results..."
}


if(inited == null)
{
      // do this code only once
      inited = true;
      // set the default gateway URL
      NetServices.setDefaultGatewayUrl("http://localhost:8500/
            flashservices/gateway");
      // connect to the gateway
      gatewayConnection = NetServices.createGatewayConnection();
      // get a reference to the service
      flashtestService =
            gatewayConnection.getService("http://www.xmethods.net/
            sd/2001/BabelFishService.wsdl",this);
}
```

A brief explanation of the code is needed here. The *include* statement, *setDefaultGatewayUrl*, and *createGatewayConnection* actions are required for using the Flash Remoting service as discussed in the previous sections. The first real code is *getService*, used for establishing a reference with the BabelFish Web Service simply by pointing to the URL of the WSDL file. When the Web service call completes, the function *BabelFish_Result* is invoked with the *result*

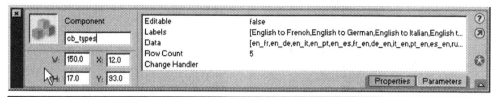

Figure 7-7 *The ComboBox Properties window*

from the Web service passed to it. This is when the Dynamic Text component instance, *translateResult*, gets populated with the value of the parameter *result*. That's it!

Google Search Web Service

Google appears to have achieved the first instances of a functional Web service—something that we, software developers, can actually use. Current uses of the Google Web API include a tool that can, among other things, search the company's database through Instant Messenger or send results of a search via e-mail.

With the Google Web APIs service, you can query more than 2 billion web documents directly from your own software programs. Google uses the SOAP and WSDL standards so you can develop within your favorite environment—be it Visual Studio .NET, Java, ColdFusion Studio, or Perl. To start writing programs using Google Web APIs, point your browser to http://www.google.com/apis and follow these steps:

1. Download the Google Developer's Kit. The Google Web APIs Developer's Kit provides documentation and example code for using the Google Web APIs service.

2. Create a Google account. To access the Google Web APIs service, you need a license key. Your Google account and license key entitle you to 1,000 automated queries per day.

3. Write your program using your license key. Your program must include your license key with each query you submit to the Google Web APIs service.

NOTE

Google Web APIs are a free beta service and are available for non-commercial use only.

Details about the Google Search Web Service are shown in Table 7-5.

Description

The Google Web APIs service is a beta web program that enables developers to easily find and manipulate information on the Web. Developers write software programs that connect remotely to the Google Web APIs service. Communication is performed via SOAP. The Google Web APIs service gives you query access to Google's web search, enabling you to develop software that accesses billions of web documents which are constantly refreshed. Developers can issue search requests to Google's index of more than 2 billion web pages and receive results as structured data, access information in the Google cache, and check the spelling of words. Google Web APIs support the same search syntax as the Google.com site. Google provides each developer who registers to use the Google Web APIs service a limit of 1,000 queries per day.

Usage

WSDL:
http://api.google.com/GoogleSearch.wsdl
METHOD:
doGoogleSearch
INPUT:
  key (xsd:string) – license key
  q (xsd:string) – query string
  start (xsd:int) – index of first result (zero-based)
  maxResults (xsd:int) – number of results per query
  filter (xsd:boolean) – activates or deactivates automatic filtering of similar results
  restrict (xsd:string) – restrict to subset of Google index
  safeSearch (xsd:boolean) – enables filtering of adult content
  lr (xsd:string) – language restrict
  ie (xsd:string) – input character encoding
  oe (xsd:string) – output character encoding
OUTPUT:
  return (xsd:string)

Table 7-5   *Google Search Web Service*

In the BabelFish example, the data returned is a text string. We will now encounter a complex data type returned by the Google Search Web Service. Let's start off by showing what the Google Flash MX client looks like (see Figure 7-8). Again, we have created a simple Flash (*google.fla*) file sized for a Pocket PC.

Again, we have a few dynamic components of interest; their instance names are listed in Table 7-6.

Instance Name	Component
searchString	Input Text component for string to be searched
lbSearchResults	ListBox component for displaying search results
statusText	Dynamic Text component for displaying status of Web service interactions
submitButton	Button component for submitting request to Web service

Table 7-6   *Google Search UI Components*

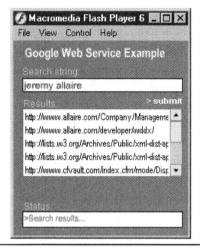

Figure 7-8   *The Google Flash MX UI*

Again, there are two sets of ActionScript required for this example. One is associated with the submitButton. The other is for the general Frame. Let's start off with the submit button. The ActionScript is executed when the button is pressed:

```
submitButton.onRelease =function (){
    statusText.text = ">Connecting to Google..."
    params.q = searchString.text; //this is the search term
    google.doGoogleSearch(params);
}
```

With the *release* event or button press, we update the status display (Dynamic Text component instance, *statusText*) and call the Google Search Web Service with the text string to be searched (Input Text component instance, *searchString*).

The ActionScript for the general Frame is listed next:

```
include "NetServices.as"

function doGoogleSearch_Result(data)
{
    // clear list box
    lbSearchResults.removeAll();
    for(i = data.startIndex-1; i < data.endIndex; i++)
    {
        var fResult = data.ResultElements[i];
        lbSearchResults.setStyleProperty("textSize", 12);
        lbSearchResults.setStyleProperty("textFont","Arial Narrow");
        lbSearchResults.addItem(fResult["URL"]);
    }
    statusText.text = ">Search results..."
```

```
}

//settings for google query
var params = new Object();
//enter your google key here
params.key = "00000000000000000000000000000000";
//the rest are required params - use default
params.start = 0;
params.maxResults = 10;
params.filter = true;
params.restrict = "";
params.safesearch = true;
params.lr = "lang_en";
params.ie = "latin1";
params.oe = "latin1";

// set the default gateway URL
NetServices.setDefaultGatewayUrl("http://localhost:8500/
     flashservices/gateway/");
// connect to the gateway
var gw = NetServices.createGatewayConnection();
// get a reference to the Google API
var google = gw.GetService("http://api.google.com/GoogleSearch.wsdl",this);
```

A brief explanation of the code is needed here. The *include* statement, *setDefaultGatewayUrl*, and *createGatewayConnection* actions are required for using the Flash Remoting service. The first real code is *getService* for establishing a reference with the Google Search Web Service, made by simply pointing to the URL of the WSDL file. When the Web service call completes, the function *doGoogleSearch_Result* is invoked with the *result* from the Web service passed to it. This is when the ListBox component instance, *searchResult*, gets populated with the value of the record set *data*. You can get more information on the structure of the record set from the WSDL file (portions of it are shown next):

```
<xsd:complexType name="GoogleSearchResult">
    <xsd:all>
    <xsd:element name="documentFiltering" type="xsd:boolean"/>
    <xsd:element name="searchComments" type="xsd:string"/>
    <xsd:element name="estimatedTotalResultsCount"
         type="xsd:int"/>
    <xsd:element name="estimateIsExact" type="xsd:boolean"/>
    <xsd:element name="resultElements"
         type="typens:ResultElementArray"/>
    <xsd:element name="startIndex" type="xsd:int"/>
    <xsd:element name="endIndex" type="xsd:int"/>
    <xsd:element name="searchTips" type="xsd:string"/>
    <xsd:element name="directoryCategories"
         type="typens:DirectoryCategoryArray"/>
    <xsd:element name="searchTime" type="xsd:double"/>
```

```
        </xsd:all>
</xsd:complexType>

<xsd:complexType name="ResultElement">
        <xsd:all>
        <xsd:element name="summary" type="xsd:string"/>
        <xsd:element name="URL" type="xsd:string"/>
        <xsd:element name="snippet" type="xsd:string"/>
        <xsd:element name="title" type="xsd:string"/>
        <xsd:element name="cachedSize" type="xsd:string"/>
        <xsd:element name="relatedInformationPresent"
                type="xsd:boolean"/>
        <xsd:element name="hostName" type="xsd:string"/>
        <xsd:element name="directoryCategory"
                type="typens:DirectoryCategory"/>
        <xsd:element name="directoryTitle" type="xsd:string"/>
        </xsd:all>
</xsd:complexType>

<xsd:complexType name="ResultElementArray">
        <xsd:complexContent>
        <xsd:restriction base="soapenc:Array">
        <xsd:attribute ref="soapenc:arrayType"
                wsdl:arrayType="typens:ResultElement[]"/>
        </xsd:restriction>
        </xsd:complexContent>
</xsd:complexType>
```

Notice that the search results are returned as an array of *ResultElements*. You can reference these elements using the *startIndex* and *endIndex*. Once you have referenced the individual ResultElement, you can access each individual property (for example, *URL*, *title*, *snippet*). That's it. Simple, isn't it?

Summary

In this chapter, we have shown you how to use Macromedia Flash MX via Flash Remoting to connect to back-end business logic supported by ColdFusion, .NET, and J2EE servers. We also introduced you to the world of Web services, which can be combined with Flash to provide compelling mobile applications. Finally, we applied all the concepts learned in this chapter in two real-world Web services from AltaVista and Google. With minimal lines of client-side ActionScript and server-side scripts, we were able to create a Flash MX client UI that interacts with remote Web services via the Flash Remoting architecture. In Chapter 8, we will further discuss the use of ColdFusion MX, an application server platform that has been optimized to work closely with the Flash MX client.

CHAPTER

8

Using ColdFusion MX for Mobile Flash

IN THIS CHAPTER:

Why ColdFusion MX?

ColdFusion MX Architecture

ColdFusion Markup Language

ColdFusion Charting/Graphing

ColdFusion Search

ColdFusion Components

ColdFusion Web Services

Server-Side Flash MX Integration

Globalization

Summary

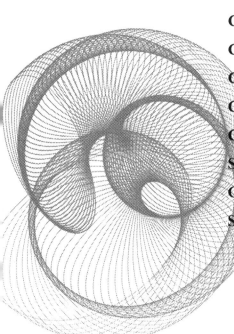

I n the previous two chapters, we have used ColdFusion MX and Flash Remoting as the back end to drive Flash applications, and we have illustrated how simple it is to implement server-side scripting with Flash MX. With ColdFusion MX, Macromedia has made it easy for you to integrate Flash MX with such features as ColdFusion Components, ColdFusion server-side Flash MX integration, and ColdFusion built-in internationalization support. Additionally, publishing and consuming Web services can be a snap through the use of ColdFusion MX and even easier with Dreamweaver MX. We will now go into the architecture and features of this powerful and easy to use server-side scripting platform from Macromedia.

Why ColdFusion MX?

The latest ColdFusion MX release from Macromedia delivers an entirely new run-time architecture and a number of powerful new features for rich Internet applications, including:

▶ **ColdFusion Components** Also known as CFCs, these components make it easy to build reusable code in the ColdFusion Markup Language (CFML). CFCs can be accessed as Web services, Macromedia Flash Remoting services, custom tags, and functions. They're self-describing and generate WSDL files automatically for consumption by all Web services clients.

▶ **XML** Extensible Markup Language (XML) is treated as a native data type, and is easily manipulated and handled with a variety of standard processing functionalities, including XPath and XSLT.

▶ **Web Services** Publishing and consuming Web services has become very approachable with ColdFusion MX. CFCs can be automatically deployed as Web services, providing one of the easiest mechanisms for creating and publishing a Web service. For consumption, ColdFusion MX makes it possible to invoke a Web service with a single line of code (using the <cfinvoke> tag), and then automatically generate custom tags to interface with the methods provided by the service.

▶ **Server-Side ActionScript** Based on the industry-standard ECMAScript, server-side ActionScript allows Flash and ColdFusion developers to work together using languages they are already familiar with.

▶ **Native Macromedia Flash Remoting Services** ColdFusion MX offers native support for Macromedia Flash Remoting. CFCs can be used to automatically deploy services for Macromedia Flash applications, and server-side ActionScript can be used to script services.

▶ **Java Technology Architecture** ColdFusion MX has been entirely rebuilt on a Java technology architecture (see the section titled, "ColdFusion MX Architecture," in this chapter for details). As a result, it can now run stand-alone or be deployed natively on leading Java application servers such as IBM WebSphere and Sun iPlanet. In addition, the environment has strong interoperability with Java and native support for deploying JavaServer Pages (JSP) and Java Servlets.

▶ **Microsoft .NET Support**   ColdFusion MX is built to run on the Microsoft Windows .NET environment. It delivers strong integration with the .NET Framework through support for Microsoft .NET Web services as well as COM.

ColdFusion MX Architecture

Through this release of ColdFusion MX, Macromedia has introduced an innovative new architecture to the ColdFusion environment that merges the *ease of use* and *productivity* of ColdFusion with the power of the J2EE platforms. As a result, you get the benefit of these emerging infrastructure standards *without* the burden of the associated complexity.

Built on an entirely standards-based infrastructure, ColdFusion MX includes an embedded Java server based on Macromedia JRun technology (see illustration that follows). This infrastructure provides the run-time services for ColdFusion applications, including high-performance connectivity to databases, a standards-based Web services engine, and resource management features like database connection pooling, thread management, and security.

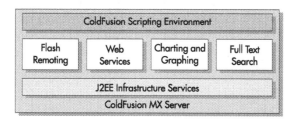

The innovative architecture of ColdFusion MX provides you with much greater flexibility in deploying ColdFusion applications and integrating them with the rest of the enterprise infrastructure. The ColdFusion MX for J2EE Application Server can be deployed on top of leading Java application servers, such as Macromedia JRun, IBM WebSphere Application Server, Sun iPlanet, and BEA WebLogic Server (see following illustration).

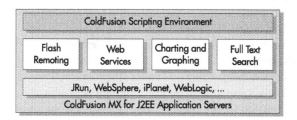

NOTE

Although you can use ColdFusion MX's built-in web server for developing, testing, and debugging ColdFusion applications, Macromedia does not recommend you use it for enterprise deployment.

On top of this powerful infrastructure, ColdFusion MX provides an enhanced version of its rapid server scripting environment and built-in application services that have made ColdFusion so popular. We have already discussed Flash Remoting and the charting/graphing Generator in Chapter 6. The built-in Verity search engine simplifies full-text searching and supports full-text indexing as well. It performs searches against *collections*, a database armed with metadata that describes the documents you have indexed. This indexing process examines a collection and its various types of documents, and creates an index, as a metadata description, to enhance rapid search and retrieval. We will go through the ColdFusion Markup Language, Charting/Graphing, and Verity Search features briefly and will spend more time on ColdFusion Components and Web services.

ColdFusion Markup Language

The ColdFusion Markup Language (CFML) is a *tag-based* language similar to HTML, but uses special tags and functions to enhance standard HTML. Database commands, conditional operators, and formatting functions quickly and easily enhance your web applications.

CFML is similar to HTML in that it includes start and end tags, where each tag is enclosed in angle brackets. All ending tags are preceded with a forward slash (/) and all tag names are preceded with the characters cf. For example:

```
<!-- start tag name -->
<cftagname>
<!-- end tag name -->
</cftagname>
```

CFML also has a "language within a language," *CFScript*, which is similar to JavaScript but easier to use. Unlike JavaScript, CFScript only runs on the ColdFusion Server—it does not run on the client system.

A web page or web application is built with a series of CFML pages. CFML can be extended by using custom tags (reusable CFML pages) or user-defined functions (UDF), or by integrating COM or JSP tag libraries. You can actually mix and match JSP with CFML in the same web page. These applications can also interact with any database that supports a JDBC technology-based driver or ODBC driver.

In terms of an interactive or integrated development environment (IDE), we highly recommend Macromedia Studio MX or Dreamweaver MX even though you could use Notepad, Macromedia HomeSite, or any text editor. Macromedia Studio MX or Dreamweaver MX offers many built-in wizards and extras that simplify your coding.

We have briefly discussed CFML here. Please refer to the *ColdFusion MX CFML Reference Manual* from Macromedia for complete details.

ColdFusion Charting/Graphing

You can create 11 types of charts in ColdFusion—vertical bar, cylinder, horizontal bar, line, area, pie, cone, pyramid, curve, step, and scatter—in 2-D and 3-D formats that are fully customizable. Data is supplied to the chart by using individual data points or from a database query, or through a combination of both. You can even combine multiple data points in a single chart. Most of the graphing capabilities from office applications like Microsoft Excel are available here.

A couple of additional points should be noted. The resulting chart format can be JPG, PNG, or SWF (default), and charts can also be made linkable to URLs, much like image maps in HTML or JavaScript.

We will illustrate a simple charting example here with the following CFML:

```
<cfquery name="get_departments" datasource="cfsnippets">
    SELECT COUNT(Department) AS emp_number, Department
    FROM Employees
    GROUP BY Department
</cfquery>
<cfchart
    xAxisTitle="Department"
    yAxisTitle="Number of Employees">
    <cfchartseries
        type="bar"
        query="get_departments"
        valueColumn="emp_number"
        itemColumn="Department"/>
    </cfchart>
```

The resulting chart, a SWF file, is shown next when viewed by the stand-alone Flash MX Player:

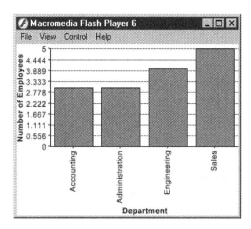

Please refer to the *ColdFusion MX CFML Reference Manual* from Macromedia for complete information.

ColdFusion Search

Macromedia ColdFusion MX includes a restricted version of the Verity K2 Server. ColdFusion can only interact with one K2 Server at a time and can search only a limited number of documents. If you install a fully licensed version of K2 Server and you configure ColdFusion to use the K2 Broker, ColdFusion will not restrict document searches. The Verity K2 Server is a high performance search engine designed to process searches quickly in a high-performance, distributed system. The K2 search system has a client/server model. You can provide a full-text search capability for documents and data sources by enabling the Verity search engine, which is installed with ColdFusion MX by default.

The Verity engine performs searches against *collections*, not against the actual *documents*. A collection is a special database created by Verity that contains metadata describing the documents you have indexed. The *indexing* process examines documents of various types in a collection and creates a metadata description (or the *index*), which is specialized for rapid search and retrieval operations. Collections can be stored anywhere and consist of the following types:

▶ Text files, such as HTML and CFML pages

▶ Binary documents, like MS Word files, Adobe PDF, JPG, TIFF, WAV, MPEG, and others

▶ Record sets returned from database queries

Please refer to the *ColdFusion MX Working with Verity Tools* from Macromedia for complete details.

ColdFusion Components

From our perspective, we believe one of the most important new technologies offered by ColdFusion MX is that you can now easily create component-based applications that take advantage of rich clients and Web services. And this is now done with a more scalable development and deployment model.

Reusability

ColdFusion Components, or *CFCs*, make it easy to create reusable object-based components without requiring complex programming. Note that ColdFusion is *not* an object-oriented language. Using a tag-based syntax to define and encapsulate a component's behavior, the ColdFusion model is immediately accessible to developers familiar with scripting languages, such as CFML, JavaScript, ActionScript, Perl, PHP, and others.

In the strictest sense, *objects* usually have multiple entry points or *methods*. They also provide a mechanism to automatically run initialization code regardless of the entry point—a *constructor*. Constructors, though similar to methods, are not methods, and have no return type. Objects can be adapted and modified or inherited—with *inheritance*, you don't have to rewrite all the code, just leverage the existing code.

Encapsulation

Encapsulating functionality in high-level methods makes sharing functionality between developers more straightforward, since developers need only to understand the component's methods and not the underlying implementation. Let's summarize here the encapsulation aspect of ColdFusion Components.

By encapsulating application functionality in reusable components, you can build more flexible applications as well as work more efficiently within teams. Component methods can automatically be made accessible from a variety of application client types. For instance, the ColdFusion environment automatically handles the plumbing required to invoke components from Web services or from Macromedia Flash (for example, Web service proxy generation), enabling you to focus on building the business logic of your applications.

ColdFusion Components also automatically display documentation about themselves. By simply calling a component via a URL, you can see information about its methods, the parameters those methods require, and the results each method will return. All of this information is generated automatically by ColdFusion MX and displayed on a web page.

Creating a Component

True to ColdFusion, defining a component is extremely easy. Components are files containing CFML code and stored in the web application directory using the new *.cfc file extension. The name of the component is simply the name of the file, and the CFML within it defines the methods it will expose. Thus, the three-step process to creating CFCs unfolds as follows:

1. Create a file with a *.cfc extension (this distinguishes CFCs from ColdFusion templates which have a *.cfm extension).

2. Use the new tags (<cfcomponent>, <cffunction>, <cfargument>, <cfreturn>) to create the components, define their functions and arguments, and return a value.

3. Use any ColdFusion tags, functions, custom tags, components, and so on within the CFC.

Table 8-1 summarizes the new tags. For our example, we will use the Pet Market Blueprint Application (*http://www.macromedia.com/desdev/mx/blueprint*) from Macromedia that demonstrates the power of building rich Internet applications with the Macromedia MX family of tool, server, and client technologies. Created by Macromedia and featured on its web site, Pet Market is a fictitious online pet store that allows users to browse the store's inventory, learn more about specific pets, and purchase pets—the same basic activities that

Tag Name	Description
<cfcomponent>	Defines a ColdFusion Component
<cffunction>	Defines the functions or methods within a CFC
<cfargument>	Defines the arguments or parameters that a function accepts
<cfreturn>	Returns a value or result from a function

Table 8-1   *ColdFusion Component Tags*

any online retailer needs to offer (see following illustration). Pet Market is intended to illustrate how rich Internet applications can be built by extending an existing e-commerce back end without replacing it, simply by delivering significantly more intuitive, responsive, and effective user interfaces and experiences.

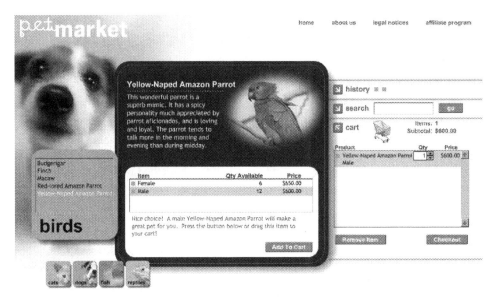

The back end of the Pet Market application is implemented using ColdFusion Components. We will now look at the code snippet from one of them (*catalogservice.cfc*), the CFC that contains the method to get a list of products based on a chosen category:

```
<!--
Code snippet from PetMarket BluePrint Application - Macromedia
-->
<cfcomponent>
   <cffunction name="getProducts" access="remote">
      <cfargument name="categoryoid" required="true" type="numeric">
      <cfquery DATASOURCE="BlueprintDatabase" NAME="listOfProducts">
         SELECT CATEGORYOID, PRODUCTOID, PRODUCTID, NAME, IMAGE, DESCRIPTION
         FROM product
         WHERE CATEGORYOID = #arguments.categoryoid#
         AND locale = 'en_US'
         ORDER BY NAME
      </cfquery>
      <cfreturn listOfProducts>
   </cffunction>
</cfcomponent>
```

The preceding example creates a component (*catalogservice*) with one method (*getProducts*). The <*cffunction*> tag defines the component method. When invoked, the component method queries the *BlueprintDatabase* database and retrieves the products for the given category from the database. The *<cfargument>* tag contains the argument specifying the unique category. The *<cfreturn>* tag returns the query result (record set) and will contain the columns selected by the SQL statement.

Components are self-documenting and can be viewed with the built-in *Component Explorer*. The Component Explorer displays components that are bundled together into packages, depicts inheritances, and shows methods and properties. If the component uses the optional *hint* attribute on the component tags, it will provide documentation for the component. You can browse the Component Explorer at http://localhost:8500/CFIDE/componentutils/componentdoc.cfm.

NOTE

Please modify the port or domain in this URL based on your web server setup. You will also need your RDS login and password to access the page.

By selecting the PetMarket components, we are presented with the following screen:

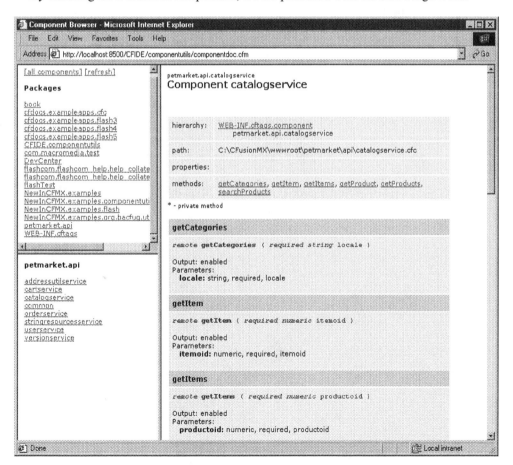

You can see the *getProducts* method description, shown next:

> ## getProducts
>
> *remote* **getProducts** (*required numeric categoryoid*)
>
> Output: enabled
> Parameters:
>   **categoryoid:** numeric, required, categoryoid

Even without the *hint* attribute, it is still very descriptive regarding its usage.

Interacting with a Component

When you build an application that supports multiple client interfaces, care must be taken to make sure the client interfaces can each call the component with ease. Interfaces can call components through Web services, URLs, the <cfinvoke> tag, and using dot notation (for example, objectname.method()).

Interacting with components consists of the following operations:

1. **Invoking a component method**   Use the *<cfinvoke>* tag in ColdFusion pages and components, the HTTP form methods GET and POST, CFScript invocation, Flash Remoting invocation, or Web service invocation.

2. **Passing parameters to a component method**   First, define the parameter in the component method definition, then choose a parameter-passing technique, and finally access the data passed in the parameter.

3. **Returning values from a component method**   Use the *<cfreturn>* tag in the component method definition to specify a variable to return to the client, and access the returned values in the client.

Going back to the example from the previous section, here's the code snippet to invoke the *catalogservice* component method of *getProducts*:

```
<cfinvoke component="petmarket.api.catalogservice"
    method="getProducts" returnvariable="qryResultSet">
    <cfinvokeargument name="categoryoid" value="2">
</cfinvoke>
<cfdump var=#qryResultSet#>
```

You should get a result similar to that shown next:

query						
	CATEGORYOID	DESCRIPTION	IMAGE	NAME	PRODUCTID	PRODUCTOID
1	2	Charming and affectionate, this gentle, silky-coated companion is equally at home as pet or gundog, and is an inseparable friend of children. Cockers are fairly easy to train, and do well with other animals. Moderately active, a small yard is fine.	DG-CS-01.jpg	American Cocker Spaniel	DG-CS-01	26
2	2	These beautiful tri-color coat dogs are gentle, loyal, smartt and easy to train. They are cheerful dogs that love kids and will become a friend for life. These dogs do best with a large fenced yard and exercise.	DG-BM-01.jpg	Bernese Mountain Dog	DG-BM-01	58
3	2	Contrary to their intimidating appearance, these dogs love people. They are gentle, dependable with children, known for courage and excellent guardians. They do well as indoor dogs - apartment life and no yard are fine.	DG-BD-01.jpg	Bulldog	DG-BD-01	46
4	2	Lively and affectionate, this clever dog may try to train the owner! Curious, mischievous, but very devoted to family, they do best with older kids. They are fairly active indoors, but do OK without a yard.	DG-DH-01.jpg	Dachshund	DG-DH-01	42
5	2	Bred to run, this dog has stamina and energy, is playful and sensitive. Enjoys kids, but may be too much for toddlers. Plan to walk or run him often. Very active indoors, best with an average-sized yard.	DG-DL-01.jpg	Dalmatian	DG-DL-01	50
6	2	Handsome and strong, often used as a working dog, this breed is known for courage and loyalty to family. While wary of strangers, they only bark when necessary. They learn quickly, and are almost human in intelligence. They do best with a large yard.	DG-GS-01.jpg	German Shepherd	DG-GS-01	38
7	2	Relaxed but responsive, the versatile, easy-to-train Golden is an ideal family companion and sporting dog, and is most happy around people. Moderately active, they do best with at least a medium sized yard.	DG-GR-01.jpg	Golden Retriever	DG-GR-01	30
8	2	A gentle giant, this dog is dignified, kind, sweet and affectionate with all ages and loves to be around people. It is a good watchdog. Train well. Will do okay in an apartment, but needs plenty of exercise.	DG-GD-01.jpg	Great Dane	DG-GD-01	62
9	2	Perky, merry, intelligent and loving, this dog is absolutely fearless- a BIG dog in a little dog□s body. A strong hunting instinct means they chase, explore, bark and dig. Firm training, terrier experience suggested. Very active indoors and out.	DG-JR-01.jpg	Jack Russell Terrier	DG-JR-01	34
10	2	Hardy, highly intelligent, obedient, and protective, Corgis are devoted little dogs, usually good with kids, and make fine alarm dogs. Very active inside, they do well if exercised and may not need a yard.	DG-PW-01.jpg	Pembroke Welsh Corgi	DG-PW-01	54

Components can also be used as tag libraries. For example, the following code snippet allows you to import the entire component into a tag library and refer to each method as a custom tag:

```
<cfimport component="petmarket.api.catalogservice" prefix="pet">
<pet:getProducts categoryoid="2" result="qryResultSet">
```

Finally, we have a CFScript version of accessing the component as an object:

```
<cfscript>
    Catalog = CreateObject("component", "petmarket.api.catalogservice");
    Catalog.getProducts("2",qryResultSet);
</cfscript>
```

ColdFusion Web Services

Having introduced Web services earlier in Chapter 7, in this section we will delve into how ColdFusion MX can enable you to leverage the power of Web services without being forced to deal with the many low-level details of the technology. In ColdFusion MX, you can create and consume Web services using CFML and ColdFusion Components, and can easily create Web services for reuse by other ColdFusion developers, or by other developers using technologies that support Web services, such as Microsoft ASP.NET and the Java/J2EE platform. Conversely, ColdFusion applications can also consume Web services created using these other technologies.

Consuming Web Services

You will notice that invoking, or consuming, a Web service in ColdFusion MX is done with the same ease as invoking a ColdFusion Component. To do that, you simply specify the location of the service and pass it the appropriate input parameters. ColdFusion MX automatically handles interaction with the SOAP protocol—parsing the interface description associated with the service, generating the necessary client proxies, and marshalling the input and output parameters to and from the service. Taking the BabelFish example from Chapter 7, instead of calling it using ActionScript from within the Flash MX client, we employ the following ColdFusion server-side code:

```
<cfset mode = "en_fr">
<cfset source = "Hello Mobile Flash MX">
<!-- call web service -->
<cfinvoke
    webservice="http://www.xmethods.net/sd/2001/BabelFishService.wsdl"
    method="BabelFish"
    translationmode="#mode#"
    sourcedata="#source#"
    returnVariable="foo">
<cfoutput>#foo#</cfoutput>
```

Using this, you will get the following from the Web service:

```
Bonjour MX Mobile D'Instantané
```

A single ColdFusion tag (*<cfinvoke>*) is all it took to consume or invoke an external Web service! Performing the equivalent task in other programming environments usually involves a lengthier and more complex set of object calls and proxy creation. As a result, working with Web services is more time consuming and the code is harder to maintain.

ColdFusion provides two methods for consuming Web services. The method you choose depends on your ColdFusion programming style and application. We have already illustrated the first way (using the *<cfinvoke>* tag) and will show the equivalent call in our BabelFish example using the second manner: CFScript. The code snippet is shown next:

```
<cfscript>
    BF_WS = CreateObject("webservice",
        "http://www.xmethods.net/sd/2001/BabelFishService.wsdl");
    translatedResult = BF_WS.BabelFish("en_fr", "Hello Mobile Flash MX");
```

```
    writeoutput(translatedResult);
</cfscript>
```

Again, you can simply use one or two lines of ColdFusion code to consume a Web service!

Publishing Web Services

ColdFusion MX also makes it easy to expose functionality built in ColdFusion as a Web service. Once a method is exposed as a Web service, it can be invoked by another ColdFusion application or by any other technology that supports the SOAP standard for Web services, such as ASP.NET, Java, or PHP. As a result, developers using other technologies can take advantage of functionality built by ColdFusion developers without having to know ColdFusion at all.

Creating or publishing Web services in ColdFusion MX is done through ColdFusion Components. Making a ColdFusion Component available as a Web service takes only a *single* step. In the slightly modified example that follows, setting the access parameter to "remote" tells the ColdFusion MX environment to make this function available as a Web service.

```
<cfcomponent>
    <cffunction access="remote" name="English2French" returntype="string">
        <cfargument name="source" type="string">
        <cfinvoke
        webservice="http://www.xmethods.net/sd/2001/BabelFishService.wsdl"
        method="BabelFish"
        translationmode="en_fr"
        sourcedata="#source#"
        returnVariable="foo">
        <cfreturn foo />
    </cffunction>
</cfcomponent>
```

Any component can become a Web service simply by adding the *access="remote"* attribute! What can be simpler? And there is something else you may notice from the preceding example. We've created a Web service out of another Web service—sort of like a hosted-Web service where you can control how the remote or external Web service is accessed, maybe by pay-per-use or a "Lite" version with limited features. In our example, we're providing a BabelFish Lite with only English to French translation service. The calling method is *English2French*, and you can automatically generate a WSDL file by referencing the following URL: http://localhost:8500/book/bflite.cfc?wsdl.

NOTE

We saved the file as bflite.cfc in the web server root book subdirectory.

Your browser should see a WSDL file as shown in the following illustration:

```
<?xml version="1.0" encoding="UTF-8" ?>
- <wsdl:definitions targetNamespace="http://book" xmlns:wsdl="http://schemas.xmlsoap.org/wsdl/"
    xmlns:xsd="http://www.w3.org/2001/XMLSchema" xmlns:wsdlsoap="http://schemas.xmlsoap.org/wsdl/soap/" xmlns:intf="http://book"
    xmlns:impl="http://book-impl" xmlns:SOAP-ENC="http://schemas.xmlsoap.org/soap/encoding/"
    xmlns="http://schemas.xmlsoap.org/wsdl/">
  - <wsdl:message name="English2FrenchRequest">
      <wsdl:part name="source" type="SOAP-ENC:string" />
    </wsdl:message>
    <wsdl:message name="CFCInvocationException" />
  - <wsdl:message name="English2FrenchResponse">
      <wsdl:part name="return" type="SOAP-ENC:string" />
    </wsdl:message>
  - <wsdl:portType name="bflite">
    - <wsdl:operation name="English2French" parameterOrder="source">
        <wsdl:input message="intf:English2FrenchRequest" />
        <wsdl:output message="intf:English2FrenchResponse" />
        <wsdl:fault name="CFCInvocationException" message="intf:CFCInvocationException" />
      </wsdl:operation>
    </wsdl:portType>
  - <wsdl:binding name="bflite.cfcSoapBinding" type="intf:bflite">
      <wsdlsoap:binding style="rpc" transport="http://schemas.xmlsoap.org/soap/http" />
    - <wsdl:operation name="English2French">
        <wsdlsoap:operation soapAction="" />
      - <wsdl:input>
          <wsdlsoap:body use="encoded" encodingStyle="http://schemas.xmlsoap.org/soap/encoding/" namespace="http://book" />
        </wsdl:input>
      - <wsdl:output>
          <wsdlsoap:body use="encoded" encodingStyle="http://schemas.xmlsoap.org/soap/encoding/" namespace="http://book" />
        </wsdl:output>
      </wsdl:operation>
    </wsdl:binding>
  - <wsdl:service name="bfliteService">
    - <wsdl:port name="bflite.cfc" binding="intf:bflite.cfcSoapBinding">
        <wsdlsoap:address location="http://localhost:8500/book/bflite.cfc" />
      </wsdl:port>
    </wsdl:service>
  </wsdl:definitions>
```

When the ColdFusion MX environment encounters the *remote* keyword, it automatically generates the WSDL file for the method. This XML-based document is the interface specification that enables a remote client to understand and invoke the service. Using this information, a developer could invoke the *English2French* Web service from any technology that supports Web services.

Dreamweaver MX

Macromedia offers a visual editing environment (VDE), Dreamweaver MX, that is an editor for designing, coding, and developing web sites, web pages, and web applications. The visual editing features in Dreamweaver MX let you quickly create pages without writing a single line of code. You can view all your site elements or assets and drag them from an easy-to-use panel directly into a document, and still write code manually—Dreamweaver, however, also includes many coding-related tools and features. In addition, Dreamweaver helps you build dynamic database-backed web applications using server languages such as ASP, ASP.NET, CFML, JSP, and PHP.

Next, we will run through an example that uses Dreamweaver MX to consume the same BabelFish Web service we manually coded for, and then display the generated code. We will now show you the workflow for consuming a Web service using Dreamweaver MX. To create a page that consumes a Web service, follow these steps:

1. Determine the URL of the WSDL. In the BabelFish example, it's located at http://www.xmethods.net/sd/2001/BabelFishService.wsdl.

2. Generate a web proxy for the Web service from the WSDL. From the Server Components panel (see illustration that follows), choose Web Service, click the + button, and then select Add Using WSDL. A new window will appear (shown in the second illustration). Enter the URL as in Step 1. Choose ColdFusion MX as the name of the Proxy Generator.

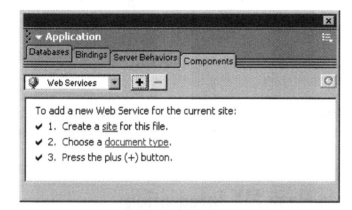

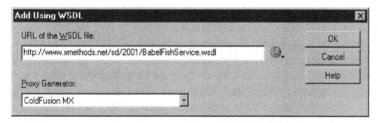

3. After the web proxy is generated, you can add the Web service to a page and edit the necessary parameters and methods to make use of the service's functionality. You should see the BabelFish Service appear in the Server Components panel after expanding on the tree (see the following illustration).

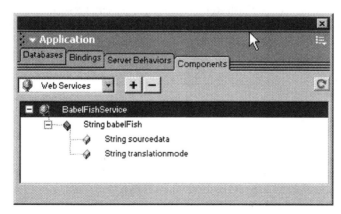

4. You add a Web service to your page by selecting and dragging BabelFish Service from the Server Components panel. The following CFML code is added to your page automatically and you can edit it as appropriate.

```
<cfinvoke
    webservice="http://www.xmethods.net/sd/2001/BabelFishService.wsdl"
    method="babelFish"
    returnvariable="aString">
    <cfinvokeargument name="translationmode"
        value="enter_value_here"/>
    <cfinvokeargument name="sourcedata"
        value="enter_value_here"/>
</cfinvoke>
```

The developer does not even need the <cfinvoke> tag as the code is automatically generated. And the interface to the BabelFish Web service is derived from its WSDL file by Dreamweaver MX.

Server-Side Flash MX Integration

With a widely distributed, rich Internet client in Flash MX and an approachable, standards-based application server like ColdFusion MX with Flash Remoting, what can you expect Macromedia to deliver? Of course, by combining the power of client-side ActionScript with server-side ActionScript and CFML, it virtually becomes a no-brainer in terms of a tightly integrated environment. As shown in Chapter 6, since Flash Remoting works with other enterprise application servers (J2EE and .NET), you're not limited to just ColdFusion MX. But the coding simplicity using CFML (versus Java/JSP or .NET ASP), native connectivity with Flash MX, and ColdFusion MX being implemented in Java give you the best of all worlds! Let's look at how these pieces are pulled together in an integrated fashion.

Flash Remoting

As discussed in Chapter 6, the Flash Remoting service provides a secure, high-performance connection between ColdFusion MX and the Flash MX player. A native part of the ColdFusion MX environment, this service uses a high-performance proprietary binary message format (Action Message Format or AMF) that runs over HTTP/HTTPS to speed the transfer of data between client and server. ColdFusion MX server and the Flash MX client handle encoding and decoding automatically.

CFML

As seen earlier in this chapter, you can invoke any method of a ColdFusion Component from a Flash MX client directly through ActionScript and Flash Remoting. As a result, you can easily create applications to support both standard HTML browsers, as well as rich Flash MX clients, without having to rewrite application logic.

ColdFusion MX also offers you a direct way to send and receive information from the Flash MX client from within standard CFML pages. In Chapter 7, we have seen how three new server variables, *flash.result*, *flash.pagesize*, and *flash.params*, can provide us with a seamless exchange of data between server-side CFML and client-side ActionScript. This way, we can enable easy construction of dynamic Flash applications that rely on data provided by the ColdFusion MX environment.

Server-Side ActionScript

As discussed in detail in Chapter 6, ColdFusion MX provides native support for server-side ActionScript, enabling Flash MX developers to use the familiar ActionScript to connect to ColdFusion MX resources. Using this new capability, Flash MX developers can execute queries against a database, preprocess data before sending it to the client, or invoke Web services via a URL.

Using ActionScript on the server is virtually the same as using it on the client. The only difference is that server-side ActionScript includes several functions not found in client-side ActionScript. For example, *CF.query* allows you to perform queries against ColdFusion data sources. As a result, you can create functions for querying databases or interacting with other server-side resources. Once a function has been defined on the server, it can be called from any Flash MX client using the Flash Remoting service.

Debugging

The Flash MX authoring environment provides a powerful tool for debugging applications that uses the Flash Remoting service, and this tool is tightly integrated with ColdFusion MX. The NetConnect Debugger monitors calls between ColdFusion MX, the Flash MX Player, and the Flash MX application, thus providing a unified view of application behavior—all from within the Flash MX authoring environment.

By monitoring calls as they are processed, you can easily trace the flow of data and quickly correct any errors that may occur in the application. This is one way that Flash MX and ColdFusion MX help simplify the process of developing and testing rich Internet applications.

Globalization

In today's global economy, it is essential to build your rich Internet applications that allow access by users with different language skills. This is essentially important for mobile applications where users may bring their handheld devices and mobile phones across borders and continents. Your applications, with globalization, can therefore accept data inputs using a character set other than the one you use to build your Flash MX applications. Very often, your mobile applications may be written in English, even though your intention was to allow users to submit form data in all common languages. Or perhaps you have built your mobile Flash applications in Japanese (default character set: SHIFT-JIS), but want to allow localized data inputs in dates, currencies, and times based on the user's default client device. Of course, your URL encoding will allow parameters based on character sets different from the underlying language you used for coding!

In a nutshell, your "global" applications should be able to accept inputs, process data, and present results (or pages) in different or mixed character sets. Globalization comprises two parts: internationalization and localization. Let's review them here.

Internationalization

Internationalization generally refers to the practice of making your application logic and functionality language agnostic. Your application should be able to retrieve data from a database, invoke Web services, and compute results regardless of its language representation.

Localization

Localization, on the other hand, is related to the process of enabling the fact that nuances and local customs are implemented with your interfaces and experiences. For example, your applications can certainly handle names, dates, and times in Japanese and English, but local customs may require Japanese family names to be presented first, before the given names. Presentation styles and interfaces are also areas where localization can add a touch of sophistication. For example, doughnut charts, instead of pie charts, are often used for corporate presentations in Japan. By applying a localized interface with this kind of subtlety to your language-neutral business logic can make your rich Internet applications even more compelling to their users.

ColdFusion MX Support

Since ColdFusion MX is implemented in the Java programming language, you can leverage the many globalization features inherent in Java. First and foremost is the data encoding of ColdFusion MX. As in Java, all data strings are stored internally with the Unicode character set. That means you can represent and present any text data in any language by simply using Unicode! In addition, ColdFusion MX ships with tags and functions that allow you to control your outputs in different formats and encoding.

NOTE

Unicode encoding is a standard for representing multilingual plain text for data processing and communications. Because each character of each major language is assigned a unique code — name and numeric value — Unicode encoding offers a consistent way to represent scripts in European, Middle Eastern, and Asian languages. Besides text, Unicode also covers punctuation marks and symbols used in many languages.

Flash MX Support

Flash Players earlier than version 6 do not support Unicode, as Flash movies of that period were created and exported with mixed multi-byte encoding (the Latin-1 character set for European languages, and the SHIFT-JIS character set for Japanese). Flash Player 6 can of course read these earlier Flash movies. However, earlier Flash Players will not be able to read the text or UI strings from Flash MX movies, which are based on Unicode.

Indeed, Flash MX FLA files are created with double-byte character set (DBCS), or UTF-16 encoding, by default. Flash movies published in Flash MX format use UTF-8 encoding. When files are imported into the Flash MX authoring environment, however, text and UI strings are converted into DBCS format for editing.

On the client side, the Flash Player 6 stores characters in both UTF-8 and UTF-16 format. You can use Flash Player 6 to play a Flash movie in a language other than the one used for your operating system. However, you must have the fonts needed for their rendering either preinstalled on your device, or embedded in your movie.

NOTE

There are two common forms of Unicode: UTF-16 and UTF-8. UTF-16, or Unicode Transformation Format-16, uses a two-byte sequence, or a 16-bit format for character encoding. UTF-8 represents each code point as a sequence of up to four bytes.

Naturally, Flash Player 6 can handle XML and server-side scripting based on different languages. Extensible Markup Language format, in Latin-1, SHIFT-JIS, UTF-8, or UTF-16, is supported. Flash Player 6 can also interpret externally loaded ActionScript files, such as those using the #include action. These features open up tremendous opportunities for building distributed mobile applications to run in Flash Player, but are driven by server-side scripts, XML, and Web services.

Summary

We have shown how ColdFusion MX is living up to the same tradition and ease of use that ColdFusion developers have come to love. With only a few lines of code, components and Web services can be reused, extended, consumed, or published! ColdFusion Components, or CFCs, represent the most important feature of this release of ColdFusion MX, and drive the behind-the-scene generation of client proxies and data marshalling for consuming and publishing Web services. All these are done automatically, thus shielding the complexity from developers, who would rather focus more of their time on building the business logic instead.

Tackling Mobile Architecture and Platform Issues

IN THIS CHAPTER:

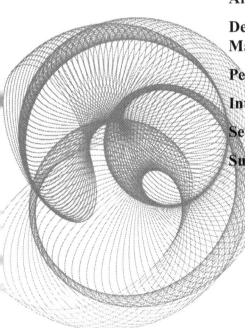

In the earlier chapters, we discuss the use of Macromedia Flash MX for implementing mobile and web-based applications that are rich in nature. We then review the use of server-side capabilities to drive dynamic content and database related transactions. In this chapter, we will build on these foundations and review the basic tenet of dealing with mobile architecture, setting the stage for our discussion of multichannel application development. Much as in Chapter 1, we will discuss the conventional methodology of delivering and supporting mobile data services, using XML and various markup languages, and compare that to the new paradigm unique to Macromedia Flash MX, which uses a rich client–server metaphor. We'll look at ways to tackle platform issues ranging from retrieval of content from different data sources to the support of different devices, as well as how different versions of Flash Player can be detected and how user sessions are managed in a mobile environment. We will briefly survey how mobile Macromedia Flash applications can be enriched by the use of personalization and location-based services for adoption in enterprises and for public consumption.

Architecture and Site Design

As discussed in Chapter 3, the workflow for mobile Flash applications is interesting given that the built-in capabilities of Flash Player, along with its ubiquity, make it easier to support different devices and browsers that inherently are Flash enabled. As a result, web site or application design can be greatly simplified in terms of the overall mobile architecture that would cover any devices, networks, protocols, markups, languages, form factors, Flash Player versions, and modals.

Architecture

While an extensive coverage of the various mobile architectures in use is beyond the scope of this book, we can categorize a robust framework in terms of an n-tier or multitier architecture that comprises a front end, a middle tier, and a back end, as shown next. On the front end, you will need to support various networks, browsers, gateways, and devices, making necessary adjustments to accommodate the contextual and navigational needs as well as limitations in screen size and form factor. On the back end, you would come across such entities as RDBMS, legacy data sources, mainframe or mid-range computers (for example, IBM AS400), and Web services.

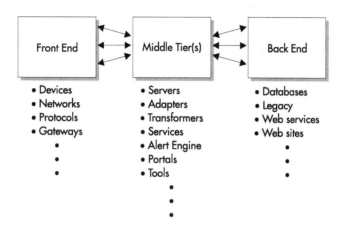

For this chapter, we will focus our attention on the *middle* tier, which could include both the web and application server. Other servers may be present, including mail server, messaging server, content/transaction servers, offline/sync servers, and so on. For a mobile or multichannel architecture, the middle tier(s) may also include other capabilities such as data adapters, device transformers, transcoding servers, applications, services, alert and other engines, portals, and development tool kits. We shall review the elements of this architecture next.

Data Adapters

How would you handle the multitude of data sources and application program interfaces? The most robust way to ensure manageability and scalability is to implement protocol-based adaptation of content from web sites, relational databases, Web services, and other data sources such as web applications. Using adaptation protocols, the middle tier can abstract any content from any data source, yet remain content agnostic. You can also create custom adapters for integrating backend data sources into your applications. Indeed, even for legacy systems, such as the likes of IBM AS400, you can mirror the data with a relational database and abstract content from the database via adapters or APIs!

Device Transformers

On the other side of the middle tier, you must support a plethora of devices and protocols. A conventional framework for mobile implementation would use an XML paradigm to address the needs for serving up multiple markup pages to different devices, as discussed in Chapter 1. Typical mobile applications are based on a markup language (such as WML), and its user environment includes the download of these linked pages as published in that particular markup language.

In this case, you can build device-transformation rules that allow support for any type of device and markup language. Using XSLT style sheets, you can transform XML documents into the appropriate markup language format suitable for the device that makes the page or content request. The reason for this approach, again, is to separate the presentation layer from the application logic. Another advantage is its relatively straightforward way of supporting future devices and markup languages. By adopting XML, you can literally future-proof your applications and infrastructure. In Chapter 10, we'll go deeper into how XML-based applications are delivered at run time using XSLT transforms and other means.

Point Servers and Transcoders

The middle tier(s) may comprise a number of point servers commonly used for Internet applications, mobile applications, and communications. The Flash Communication Server from Macromedia, which we will discuss in detail in Chapter 11, belongs to this category. Within this tier, you may have web and mail servers, data logger, SMS and push servers, as well as tools and integration facilities. The integration of these servers, including offline, push and voice servers, could be rather involved and their discussions are beyond our scope here!

Another common facility, called a transcoding server or transcoder, allows the adaptation of portions of a web site to be repurposed into mobile devices. Through other servers and facilities, you can also tap into personalization and location-based services to build a compelling mobile interface and serve up personal and location-sensitive content!

Applications and Services

Residing in the middle tier are, of course, your mobile applications and services. These applications may be written in XML, or in the case of Macromedia Flash applications, in the form of SWF files—ready to be served up to the requesting device. Other services, such as device management tools and portals, may also be present.

Alert Engines, Portals, and Tools

Inherent in the infrastructure are engines that can push alerts based on application logic, and portals that allow customization or modification of personal profiles! And, of course, tool kits for developers and administrators alike.

Mobile Macromedia MX Differences

With Macromedia Flash MX, you already have a clean separation of presentation and logic—with a paradigm based on a smart client that can be driven by different flavors of application servers (ColdFusion MX, J2EE, .NET) and supplemented by Flash Remoting and Flash Communication Server. The real difference, however, is that you may no longer have to worry about supporting markup languages and protocols if all you want to do is serve SWFs in response to mobile requests. In such cases, you'll have no need for device transformers. But, if you intend to support Flash and non-Flash requests, as well as build multichannel, or even multimodal applications, you may be better off including this approach in your application infrastructure. We will cover this in more detail in Chapter 10 where we discuss a multichannel application development framework. We'll show you how to implement multichannel applications in order to deliver both markups and Flash content in Chapter 12. One thing is certain: you'll need to detect the type of devices and the version of Flash Player if you intend to support Flash applications with or without the use of markup languages. Let's look at that next.

Device and Flash Player Detection and Session Management

In this section, we return to the world of mobile Macromedia Flash, and review how to tackle issues regarding detection of different types of mobile devices as well as the presence (and version) of Flash Player. We'll also study how sessions are managed by many Flash applications and web sites, and how to handle them in a mobile environment.

The focus is on detecting client devices that dictate the form factor of SWF files served by the server to the client. The following is the detection flow logic for devices that can only access Flash content using an HTML page with embedded SWF files.

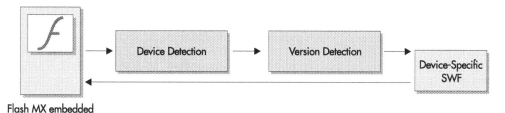

Flash MX embedded
in Web page.

Mobile Devices

The alternative is the detection flow logic for devices that can only access Flash content using a stand-alone SWF file (see next illustration).

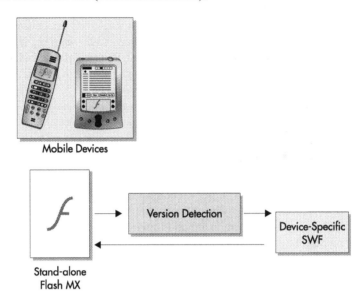

Mobile Devices

Stand-alone
Flash MX

The desktop PC is currently the only device (without additional third-party software) that can access Flash content using both methods just described.

NOTE

Since almost all non-desktop PC devices will not run JavaScript and will not automatically download the Flash Player plug-in (for example, Windows IE with ActiveX control), we shall not use or rely on any of these techniques for detection.

We will go into mobile device detection and Flash Player version detection next.

Detecting Mobile Devices

Detection of mobile devices will be strictly done on the server. To detect the mobile device and serve the correct version of a Flash MX application for the specific form factor requires a database of device properties. The database will contain a lookup table for a specific device or default device. The content in the database will include screen width and height at a minimum.

Here's the control flow from a client request to the server:

1. Client mobile device makes a request to a specific URL of the Flash MX application from a web browser like Pocket IE or Blazer.

2. The server script looks at the HTTP request header and extracts the User Agent information.

3. The server script then does a lookup for the identified device and decides which SWF file to serve to the device.

4. The correct form factor SWF file is served to the client device.

User Agents

In order to determine which mobile device made the request to the server, we need to extract the User Agent information from the HTTP Request header. The User Agent is that part of the HTTP header of a request which contains information about the device. The User Agent information can be easily extracted in ColdFusion using the following CFML code:

```
<cfset userAgent = #HTTP_USER_AGENT#>
```

In Active Server Pages (ASP), the equivalent code is

```
<%
   userAgent = Request.ServerVariables("HTTP_USER_AGENT")
%>
```

In JavaServer Pages (JSP), the equivalent code is

```
<%
   String userAgent = request.getHeader("User-Agent");
%>
```

Table 9-1 lists the common User Agent strings for Pocket PCs and desktop PCs. You'll need to add to and delete from this list for all the devices your application supports.

The User Agent string for the Nokia Communicator is not applicable since the SWF file can only run stand-alone there.

Player Versions

In order to determine which version of Flash Player is being used to make the request to the server, we need to use the following ActionScript code:

```
playerVersion.text = "Player: " + getVersion();
```

We don't really need to worry about Flash Player version 4 or earlier as they do not support the getVersion() script. If you have a stand-alone SWF installed on your device, you're most likely to have the latest version of Flash Player available. If not, the ActionScript code must detect that and take the appropriate actions.

Table 9-2 lists the common version number strings for Nokia Communicator and desktop PCs.

Devices	User Agent String Patterns
Desktop PC Microsoft IE 5.5	Mozilla/4.0 (compatible; MSIE 5.5; Windows NT 5.0)
Pocket PC Pocket IE	Mozilla/2.0 (compatible; MSIE 3.02; Windows CE; 240×320)
Pocket PC 2002 Pocket IE	Mozilla/2.0 (compatible; MSIE 3.02; Windows CE; PPC; 240×320)

Table 9-1   *User Agent Strings*

Devices	Flash Player Version String Patterns
Desktop PC Flash Player	WIN 6,0,50,0
Nokia Communicator	NOK9200 5,0,95,0
Pocket PC plug-in	WINCE 5,0,86,0

Table 9-2 *Flash Player Version Strings*

The Flash Player version string for the Pocket PC is that of the embedded Flash Player since the SWF file can only run embedded within the HTML file, not stand-alone.

Form Factors

With a Flash MX application running on a device, the main concern here is the form factor, not whether it supports XHTML, WML, HDML, and so forth. The form factor is different for the desktop PC, Nokia Communicator, Pocket PC, and other devices your application supports.

The table below lists the common form factors for the Nokia Communicator, Pocket PC, and desktop PC.

Devices	Width (pixels)	Height (pixels)
Desktop PC Flash Player (large)	1024	768
Desktop PC Flash Player (medium)	800	600
Nokia Communicator Full Screen	640	200
Nokia Communicator Normal	463	200
Pocket PC Normal	230	250

Due to the possible presence of an optional address bar, dynamic scroll bars (vertical and horizontal), captions, and menu bar, it is inappropriate to assume we have a full-screen Pocket PC display (see the section titled "Navigation, Page Layout, and Screen Size" in Chapter 4).

Example Scenario

Putting it all together, let's go through a quick example of what happens when a Pocket PC 2002 mobile device like the HP iPAQ makes a request for a Flash MX application using Pocket IE browser. Let's assume we have the device user strings and device form factor information stored in a relational database named "devices." We will be using ColdFusion MX for our server-side scripts. Here's what follows:

1. User selects Internet Explorer from the Start menu (see illustration).

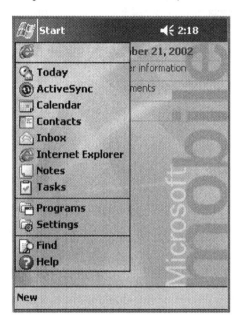

2. User then types in the URL of the example application: **http://localhost:8500/ex1.cfm** (see following). Note that Pocket IE has the Address Bar and Menu Bar visible.

3. The server-side code detects the user agent from the HTTP header (Windows CE; PPC), does a lookup for that device from the database (see Table 9-4 that follows), determines its form factor (230 pixels width × 250 pixels height), and redirects it to a server script (ex1_230 x 250.cfm) that displays the Flash SWF file correctly. The code listing for ex1.cfm (original detection) and ex1_230 x 250.cfm (correct form factor display) is shown next.

```
// extract user agent
<cfset userAgent = #HTTP_USER_AGENT#>

// determine device type
<cfset foundDev = FindNoCase("Windows CE; PPC; 240x320",userAgent)>
   <cfset deviceType = "1"> <!-- Pocket PC 2002 -->
</cfif>
<cfset foundDev = FindNoCase("Windows CE; 240x320",userAgent)>
<cfif foundDev>
   <cfset deviceType = "2"> <!-- Pocket PC -->
</cfif>
<cfset foundDev = FindNoCase("Mozilla/4.0",userAgent)>
<cfif foundDev>
   <cfset deviceType = "3"> <!-- Desktop PC -->
</cfif>


// look up database for form factor
<cfquery name="UA_Query" datasource="agents" maxrows="1">
   SELECT ID,Width,Height
   FROM formFactor
   WHERE ID=#deviceType#
</cfquery>

// redirect to appropriate server script
<cfoutput query="UA_Query">
   <cflocation url="ex1_#Width#x#Height#.cfm">
</cfoutput>
```

Our database table can be as simple as that shown in Table 9-4.

4. The target server script will contain HTML code to display the embedded SWF file with the matching dimensions in the HTML tag and SWF file. The code is shown next.

```
<OBJECT classid="clsid:D27CDB6E-AE6D-11cf-96B8-444553540000"
   codebase="http://download.macromedia.com/pub/shockwave/cabs/
   flash/swflash.cab#version=6,0,0,0"
   WIDTH="230" HEIGHT="250" id="ex1_230x250" ALIGN="">
   <PARAM NAME=movie VALUE="ex1_230x250.swf">
   <PARAM NAME=quality VALUE=high>
   <PARAM NAME=bgcolor VALUE=#FFFFFF>
   <EMBED src="ex1_230x250.swf" quality=high bgcolor=#FFFFFF
      WIDTH="230" HEIGHT="250" NAME="ex1_230x250" ALIGN=""
      TYPE="application/x-shockwave-flash"
      PLUGINSPAGE="http://www.macromedia.com/go/getflashplayer">
   </EMBED>
</OBJECT>
```

ID	Width	Height
1	230	250
2	230	250
3	800	600

Table 9-3   *User Agent Properties*

5. Finally, the Pocket PC display will look like this:

6. You can also add ActionScript code to make sure the correct version of Flash Player is available if you are taking advantage of the newer features of the player. Or display a friendly error message advising the user to download the latest Flash Player.

Managing Sessions

Session management is important because many usability features of dynamic web applications depend on knowing whether a user is online and his/her session is still valid. Here, we shall look at how sessions are managed on web sites and discuss whether that would work for mobile applications in general and mobile Flash applications in particular.

Using Cookies

The old way of managing sessions on a PC was to write a script to set the cookie for Flash and define the expiration date of the cookie. After the cookie has expired, it disappears and is no longer readable by the script. Typical code would break apart any query string or post header sent from Flash, break apart the name/value pairs, and set the name/value pairs as cookies on the user's PC.

You also need to retrieve the cookie set by the server for the current web domain. And, of course, delete them. The scripts first look for all the cookies present and then reset them to have an expiration date of yesterday.

The Mobile or Server-Side Approach

Session management for mobile devices is a unique challenge because not all client devices support cookies. Robust application development and implementation must therefore presume no cookie is supported. To complicate matters, you need to account for applications that must initiate, manage, and terminate user sessions, perhaps in an offline or sporadically connected wireless network.

Upon receiving requests from a user, your application will need to create a session for the user. Unlike in HTTP, where session information is kept by the cookie (through an IE or Netscape browser), all session states are kept in the back end, either through the WAP gateway or the wireless server itself. If the device or the gateway does not support cookies, the middle tier server can use a mechanism called URL rewriting, which basically appends the session ID to the end of the URL through a GET or POST parameter.

When a user session is initiated, the server creates and assigns a session identifier to the instance. Because no cookie is available, the session ID is "coded" on the page sent by the server to the browser. Any subsequent requests will include the session ID to allow the server to recover the session information.

NOTE

The session ID can be rather long and could exceed the 128-character limitation of many mobile devices for URL strings. In such cases, you may have to change the session ID length or limit it to a manageable size.

Personalization and Location-Based Services

Here, let's discuss the personalized, time- and location-sensitive content and services that make mobile applications unique.

Personalization

A mobile device tends to be a personal device with a single user, unlike a PC that may be shared among several users. Because mobile devices are regularly used, perhaps on a daily basis, and are almost always with the user, wireless operators and data service providers are finding it advantageous to exploit time- and location-critical information. By coupling that with personalization features, they can offer a richer user experience for the mobile data services.

Just what is personalization? Personalization, and its close cousin, customization, is a cornerstone of intimate and compelling applications for mobile devices. Personalization means providing information, content, and services that cater to your personal, positional, mobility, and time-sensitive needs. For example, if you plan to travel on a particular stretch of highway, you might need directions, local addresses, and information. Your personalized mobile applications will then serve the content to you in the format and details you prefer. Because your mobile devices are an extension of your lifestyle and work habits, it is no longer a luxury but a prerequisite to present information and applications tailored to your needs and usage of the mobile services—be it specified by you in advance, or automatically determined through algorithms and profiles.

There are various ways of providing personalization, most of which, however, are related to user profiling either at the gateway level, or at the middle tier, as well as through customization by the user or the administrator, as shown next. Data from the content source may be combined and/or filtered to include profiled data and customization presets to tailor to the user's needs. In addition, if location-sensitive services are available, like LBS, you can also build in geocoding and location information to make the mobile services seamless.

We will not address the carrier-based approach at the gateway, but we will expand a bit on our discussion of the application server level (see following illustration).

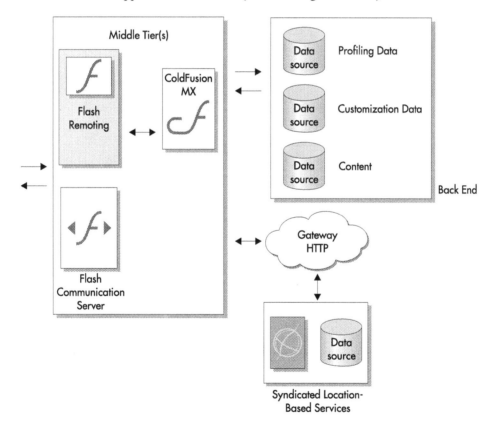

In fact, the data profiling approach relies on the role-based mechanism that associates you with others in the same group of like minds. The customization portal, on the other hand, allows you to define what you would like for your user interface and what personal content would be at your disposal through the mobile device.

Indeed, the customization portal can provide a framework to input preferences, landmarks and alert features that can make your life easier. For example, you can store and query information based on personal location preferences, thereby simplifying inputs on your mobile device (and your life). Of course, you can access these customization features both online through the Internet and via your mobile devices through a wireless connection.

Location-Based Services

As mentioned earlier, location-based services (LBS) can provide spatial information as well as proximity and presence information to you, the mobile user, not to mention the wireless operator. LBS allow you to receive valuable information and content via your mobile device based on your current location. Wireless operators using location-capable products are able to unlock the value of a core strategic asset—the location of their subscribers—by transforming raw location data into new revenue sources (see illustration that follows).

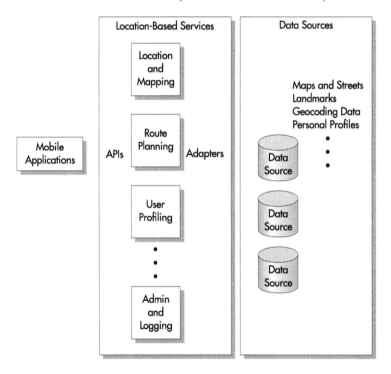

While maps and directions are common usages of LBS, they are by no means all-inclusive— other consumer and enterprise applications may leverage LBS for safety, alerts, promotions, friend finding, as well as asset tracking.

On the consumer side, wireless operators are striving to offer a user interface that is simple enough that practically everyone can easily tap into LBS as needed. With enhanced convenience features, such as call-triggered delivery of Short Message Service (SMS), users can get a text record with details (phone numbers, addresses, special offers) based on their locations and the services they consume.

On the enterprise side, wireless operators are looking to provide location-based call routing and voice-based services to enterprises. These operators want to offer an enterprise customer with a location-enabled phone number that automatically connects callers to the company's nearest location.

Retrieving information based on spatial or "time and distance proximity" to a position, region, or route is very common for dispatch and other vertical applications. You can build LBS applications through modules available from a number of syndicated vendors. They will typically provide you with a suite of customizable features based on proximity analysis, stationary or mobile object tracking, and travel directions. This can be done—around the corner or around the globe—quickly and easily.

How to Hook up LBS

How do you implement LBS in your application? You can start by evaluating, seeking help from, and linking to syndicated LBS providers. This way, you can rapidly build location-sensitive applications by leveraging the data sources and location services prebuilt to serve your application needs. Through data adapters, these services retrieve maps, street information, landmarks, as well as location and user profiles from various data sources. The location services can convert raw network cell coordinates into usable location data, and allow applications like navigation, route planning, and proximity searches. Using geocoding services, your location-aware applications can leverage these modules through APIs, thus allowing you to focus on providing multiple channel support for Flash, voice, SMS, WAP, and HTML applications.

Instead of working with syndicated LBS providers, wireless operators may provide a location management module or "Location Manager" that obtains and supplies their subscribers' locations, if enabled. Typically, wireless operators can derive this kind of presence data from such sources as A-GPS (Assisted GPS), D-GPS (Differential GPS), Cell-ID, AOA (Angle of Arrival), and E-OTD (Enhanced Observed Time Difference), and delivers that data to your LBS and applications. Through APIs, you can pass data and content between your infrastructure and third-party services. This way you can easily integrate location with personalization and application logic, and save time and effort by not having to write code or custom interface.

You can learn more about LBS and its standards at such organizations as Location Interoperability Forum (LIF), Open GIS Consortium's OpenLS initiative, Cellular Telecommunications and Internet Association (CITA), 3GPP, and the WAP Forum.

Internationalization

As discussed in Chapter 8, internationalization is related to the practice of enabling your applications to be language agnostic. Through internationalization, you make sure your applications can serve up the right language user interface and experience. This all depends on the location from which the request was made, and knowing the user's preferences. The methodology is based on localization that can dynamically control the content presentation via multilingual representations. You can implement this feature through server-side support, as well as integrate with, and store, large multilanguage data sets. This is especially useful for location-based services that contain street addresses, directions, points of interest, and dynamic content such as automatic teller machines, gas stations, landmarks, restaurants, and other places.

Security

Security issues concern more than just mobile Macromedia Flash applications, and by themselves deserve coverage well beyond the scope of this book. However, in relation to rich mobile applications, we will briefly discuss issues relevant to mobile devices, and finally, Flash applications themselves.

With souped up microprocessors and increased memories, mobile devices like smart phones and Pocket PCs are becoming more susceptible to security breaches and deliberate attacks. On Pocket PCs, for instance, Microsoft is still addressing the full range of operating system user privacy and system security including user authentication, data encryption, and secure data transport via secure socket layer (SSL) or virtual private network (VPN).

On the Flash side, the key is to focus on security issues related to Flash Player and the integrity of the SWF itself. Many of the security and privacy issues are related to how secure or restricted your Flash applications are when spawning new instances or seeking access to other parts of your mobile devices. This is especially critical because common vulnerabilities arise when rogue programs try to gain access to the other part of your device OS.

For example, prior reports and security bulletins from Macromedia revealed that earlier versions of Flash Player could allow malicious SWFs, working in conjunction with other content on a web server, to read files from your local file systems. These SWFs could then send content back to the web server without your consent or knowledge. Similarly, a hand-edited, malformed SWF header could be exploited to cause a buffer overwrite, leading to execution of malicious code. Also, hackers had the ability to put SWFs from one domain into an HTML page located on a different domain, allowing them to read and transfer data, such as cookies, from the HTML server domain to the Macromedia Flash domain. This was dangerous given that the embedded information in an SWF running in the stand-alone player (EXE) could execute external code, perhaps even launching a virus that could cause extensive damage to user devices.

These are just a few examples of possible vulnerabilities or threats that Flash application developers must be aware of. To the credit of Macromedia, all of these flaws were quickly discovered, reviewed, and rectified or patched, and security alerts were promptly posted. Macromedia is very proactive in this arena to ensure and promote "trustworthy computing." For the latest security alerts, visit **http://www.macromedia.com/security**.

Summary

In this chapter, we introduced you to the architecture and platform issues related to supporting different devices as well as the retrieval of data from different sources. We briefly reviewed personalization and LBS, which can vastly enhance your rich mobile applications. In Chapter 10, we'll address the specific issues of handling single and multiple channels and supporting Flash and non-Flash devices.

CHAPTER 1

Planning and Implementing for Compatibility

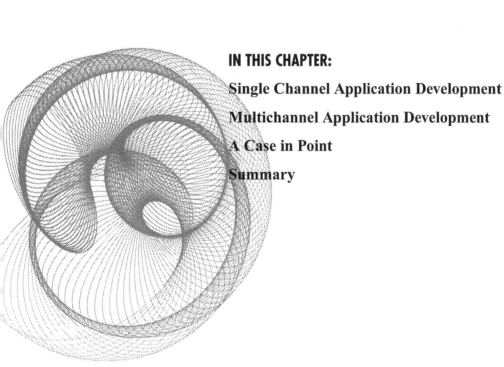

IN THIS CHAPTER:

I n Chapter 9, we looked at the issues related to delivering mobile services with robust infrastructure that supported different platforms. In this chapter, we carry on the discussion and address how you can leverage these resources and build applications for multiple platforms and channels. We will dissect the methodology of single and multiple channel application development, and contrast how mobile development can be carried out with XML/XSLT as well as Macromedia Flash MX.

Single Channel Application Development

Single channel application development refers to building applications for a particular communications channel—for example, the Web, wireless Web, or voice. Here, in the case of rich Internet applications, supporting a single channel that uses different PC or HTML browsers is relatively straightforward as there are only minor variants among browsers, and the number of browsers you need to support are limited. In contrast, supporting mobile applications could prove more challenging owing to the factors we have discussed thus far. For rich mobile applications, delivering services to the smart client of Macromedia Flash may take care of a number of nuances related to operating systems and device platforms. However, you still have to deal with bandwidth, form factor, connectivity, and latency issues. In this section, we will focus on what it takes to build single channel mobile Flash applications, especially for devices and form factors such as Pocket PCs and smart phones.

Focus on Flash MX

Previously, we reviewed a mobile architecture wherein you have a back end of data sources driven by a mid-tier, such as an application server, to support a plethora of devices and channels. In single channel development, you won't have to worry about the content and use case across multiple channels, but you will have to deal with form factors. Unlike HTML web sites and applications, you won't have to worry about browser types. However, you still have to deal with the detection of Flash Player and its version—and whether you run projector or SWF files. Another issue is the changeover of Flash versions, such as when the Flash MX authoring environment is out—but the player is not yet available on all platforms.

In Chapters 6 through 8, we showed you how to combine server-side programming with a Flash client to build single channel applications. For those who are interested in further information on using Java to drive a Flash front end, the Macromedia web site offers a number of resources, including the Pet Market blueprint application.

In Chapter 9, we looked at how you can build detection scripts to determine the device and the Flash Player version. We also showed you how you can go through that and deliver an SWF or HTML file with embedded SWF in response to a request from a client device.

Support for Devices and Form Factors

Once you have determined the preceding issues in supporting different devices for a particular channel, you must decide if the form factor would make a difference among the variants. For example, Nokia Communicator would not have the same form factor and user interface as a Pocket PC, as shown in Chapter 9.

We can also go beyond mobile devices and apply the same methodology to other equipment. How would you modify a device to make it suitable for interactive TV or a Sony Playstation?

Multichannel Application Development

Multichannel has been a buzzword for the retail and e-tail industry for some time. Is it just multidevice? Aren't multidevice and multichannel the same thing? No, not really! Channels traditionally refer to sales channels or communications channels. So, a WAP channel is different from an SMS channel. WAP on different devices is, of course, not multichannel! But supporting WAP, voice, and SMS would *become* multichannel! Besides the obvious differences in protocols and network infrastructures, multichannel applications also involve different use cases! What that means is: you may decide to offer certain content, function, and accessibility to a group of users in a particular channel, while restricting or disallowing these features and use cases in another channel. A good example is e-commerce versus m-commerce. Most e-commerce sites offer extensive merchandising features for browsing. M-commerce sites don't necessarily do that. One reason is the limitation of bandwidth. But a more important reason may be that most mobile users simply don't use their handheld devices or mobile phones for browsing. They use their mobile devices to do something! And they get to them right away, as opposed to browsing online or window-shopping in a retail store.

Now, wouldn't that make the mobile experience very limited? The answer is no. Application features and services will progress along the way. Of course, bandwidth will increase. Despite the hype and the subsequent letdown, it is indeed possible or beneficial for users—for example, consumers or mobile users—to be able to access data, content, and applications through multiple communications channels (or sales channels for retail). For retailers or enterprises, there are very compelling cases where they do want to offer customers or employees access to their web sites and applications. Especially from such channels as the Web, wireless Web, and voice, using the right content and the right user interface.

Very early on, many developers built separate markup pages to support different devices. And they do that for the entire application in WML, compact HTML, and HTML, for instance. As devices and markups begin to grow or change, that creates a support and management issue. Another way to tackle this problem is to use XML for the middle tier, and retrieve data from the back end, presenting results in the correct markup in the front end by using XML and XSLT, as discussed in Chapter 1. This way, your separation of presentation layer from application logic allows for any change in either layer. You can, of course, add support, including Flash, as new devices, protocols, and markups. Plus, you can add new data sources, including Web services, in the back end. Developers are shielded from the complexity of creating and maintaining style sheets for a growing number of devices and ever-changing form factors.

How Do You Do Multichannel?

There are a number of ways to build multichannel applications. Again, you can handle that with XML and markup languages. You can also leverage the power and distribution of Flash Players across multiple devices within different channels. And, of course, you can combine the two and support the best of all.

To build multichannel applications with XML, you obviously can write XML scripts by hand using Notepad or other text editors. Or you can take advantage of a number of development tools in the marketplace. One such tool that is particularly handy for ColdFusion or JavaServer Page (JSP) developers is Where2Net daVinci Studio (see following illustration). Where2Net daVinci Studio offers a unique capability to abstract web page components or objects and provides developers with an easy way to build multichannel pages and applications in a WYSIWYG environment.

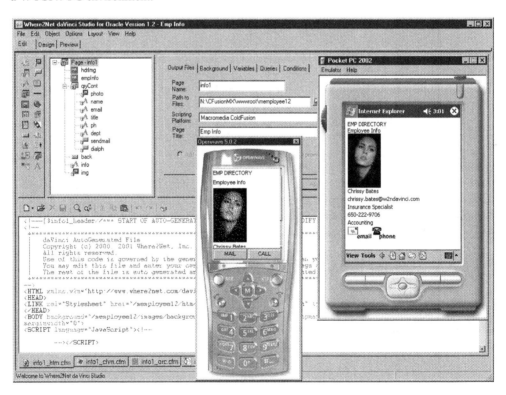

For instance, if you want a dynamic menu driven by a database on your WAP page, you simply select that object and add it to a page using Query Wizard (see illustration that follows).

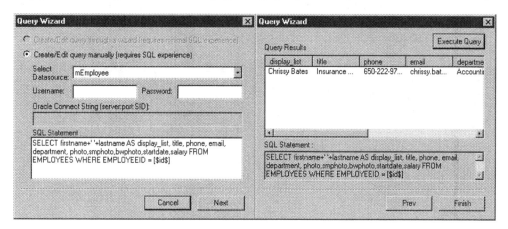

Again, you can achieve that by hand, but then tools are meant to save you time and effort. Let's look at how we can make that happen. By using daVinci Studio, you can automatically generate server-side scripts, XML, and XSL files that form the basic code for various pages of your application. After you are done, you will have a set of files automatically generated and stored in several folders. These include server-side scripts (for example, JSP or ColdFusion), XML, and XSL files. You may also have custom tags or JavaBeans for your application logic. To deploy them, simply move these folders to any server environment. At run time, your application server will execute the scripts and perform transformations to serve up XML or markup pages, as requested by the client devices.

Markups Only

To build multichannel applications, you can use XML/XSLT transformation to achieve that "write once, publish many" goal. We will now take you through one design approach using XML/XSLT and daVinci Studio to build a simple home page or just a presence on the Internet that is available to many devices. This approach is rather generic, and our application will simply apply an XSLT stylesheet to an XML document to generate the correct markup page for the device requesting it. We will support WML, cHTML, or HTML. You can also use a similar approach for other markup languages like VoiceXML.

We will not go into the details of the daVinci Studio rapid application development (RAD) tool here, but will illustrate some simple steps and show you the generated code. You can study that code and come up with your own custom tags in ColdFusion or tag libraries in JSP, or simply implement it any way you want using ASP.NET or PHP. There will only be one URL required for accessing the multichannel application from any device: www.mcapp.com (fictitious). We will be using ColdFusion MX and calling the home page index.cfm—the server will know to serve up index.cfm by using the full URL.

Creating this multichannel application using daVinci Studio is as easy as 1, 2, 3.

1. Start daVinci Studio. Create a new page. The new page wizard (see following illustration) will take the user through all the steps and initialize all the parameters for this page. We will be using ColdFusion MX as our server technology (as opposed to JSP).

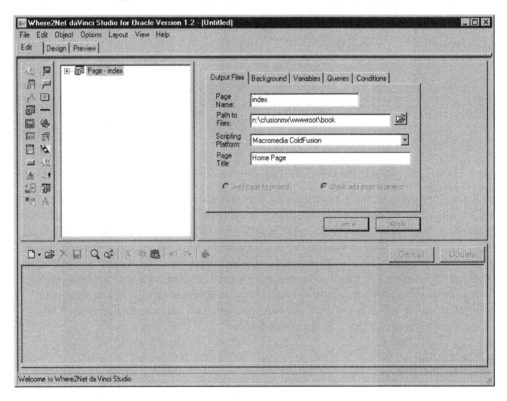

2. Next, we will add some static text and a logo. The static text is added using a "static text object" and the logo is added using a "static image object" (see illustrations that follow).

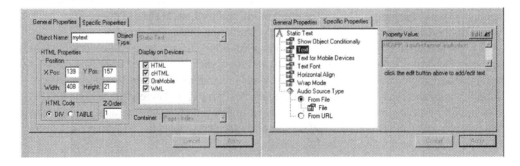

NOTE

We have created multiple image formats for the logo. JPG or GIF would be used for HTML, BMP (black and white only) for WML, and JPG or GIF for cHTML.

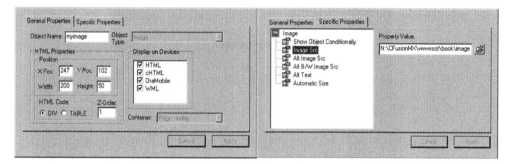

3. Save the design page. daVinci Studio automatically generates all the server code needed for this multichannel application. You can now preview it via device emulators within daVinci Studio, as well as external simulators like Openwave SDK 5.1 Browser or Microsoft Pocket PC 2002 Emulator (see next illustration).

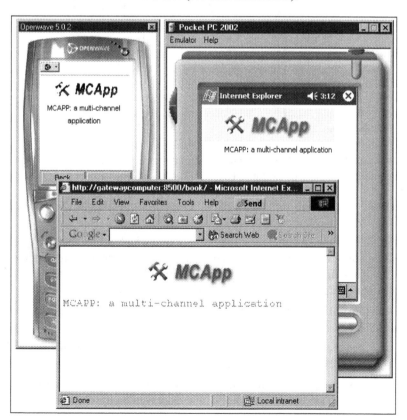

4. You're done generating all the necessary code! In our daVinci Studio implementation, we are using additional code from a custom tag (w2nXSLFilter.cfm) supplied with daVinci Studio. A major portion of this same code is already described in Chapter 9, which discusses detection of devices based on user agents. The custom tags also provide the framework for using XML/XSLT for multichannel applications (see illustration that follows).

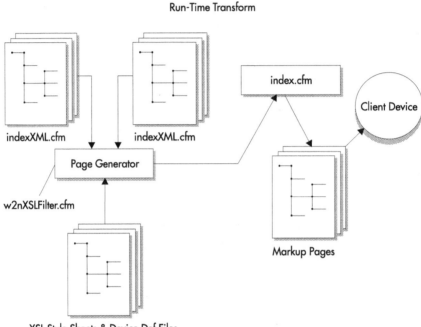

We'll now go into more detail on the action sequences the server goes through when a mobile device references our example URL.

1. ColdFusion server (the Web/App Servers) executes the index.cfm file within the /book directory when a device references the URL.

2. index.cfm calls the custom tag, w2nXSLfilter.cfm, which determines the type of device requesting the content, and prepares the correct HTTP headers for returning the requested data. In our XML/XSLT framework, we have by now determined which XSL stylesheet to use to generate the markup language the device can handle.

3. We load the XML into the server Document Object Model (DOM) by running the indexXML.cfm file.

4. We next load the XSL (and device definition files) into the server DOM—a different one is used for each device detected.

5. Finally, the server performs the XML/XSLT transformation and a resulting markup language page is generated, returned to, and displayed on the client device.

In Chapter 9, we discussed using HTTP_USER_AGENT information from the HTTP header to detect devices. We can also use HTTP_ACCEPT, which tells the server what file types the device browser can accept. Our custom tag actually uses both to get a more precise detection.

Let's have a brief explanation of the three major files—index.cfm, indexXML.cfm, and wmlindex.xsl. index.cfm is the top-level file that acts as a wrapper to detect devices by calling the w2nXSLFilter custom tag. The custom tag also performs the XML and XSLT transformation.

```
<!-- index.cfm -->
<cfset transformedValue="">
<cf_w2nXSLFilter
    XMLTemplateURL="/book/xml/indexxml.cfm"
    r_transformedValue="transformedValue">
<cfoutput>
    #transformedValue#
</cfoutput>
```

indexXML.cfm is the XML content generation file. It's used independently of the devices since we've decoupled the data from the presentation.

```
<?xml version="1.0" ?>
<!-- indexXML.cfm -->
<w2n:Page xmlns:w2n="http://www.where2net.com/davinci">
    <w2n:PageTitle>Home Page</w2n:PageTitle>
    <w2n:PageName>index</w2n:PageName>
    <w2n:Object xmlns:w2n="http://www.where2net.com/davinci">
        <w2n:ObjectType>Image</w2n:ObjectType>
        <w2n:ObjectName>myimage</w2n:ObjectName>
        <w2n:ObjectProps>
            <w2n:Property>
            <w2n:PropName>_ShowCondition_</w2n:PropName>
            <w2n:PropValue>_none_</w2n:PropValue>
            </w2n:Property>
            <w2n:Property>
            <w2n:PropName>Src</w2n:PropName>
            <w2n:PropValue>/book/images/ch10_logo.jpg</w2n:PropValue>
            </w2n:Property>
            <w2n:Property>
            <w2n:PropName>AltSrc</w2n:PropName>
            <w2n:PropValue>/book/images/ch10_logo.jpg</w2n:PropValue>
            </w2n:Property>
            <w2n:Property>
            <w2n:PropName>AltBWSrc</w2n:PropName>
            <w2n:PropValue>/book/images/ch10_logo.bmp</w2n:PropValue>
```

```
        </w2n:Property>
        <w2n:Property>
        <w2n:PropName>AltText</w2n:PropName>
        <w2n:PropValue>[MCApp]</w2n:PropValue>
        </w2n:Property>
        <w2n:Property>
        <w2n:PropName>AutoSize</w2n:PropName>
        <w2n:PropValue>Yes</w2n:PropValue>
        </w2n:Property>
        <w2n:Property>
        <w2n:PropName>HTMLCode</w2n:PropName>
        <w2n:PropValue>DIV</w2n:PropValue>
        </w2n:Property>
    </w2n:ObjectProps>
  </w2n:Object>
  <w2n:Object xmlns:w2n="http://www.where2net.com/davinci">
    <w2n:ObjectType>StaticText</w2n:ObjectType>
    <w2n:ObjectName>mytext</w2n:ObjectName>
    <w2n:ObjectProps>
        <w2n:Property>
        <w2n:PropName>_ShowCondition_</w2n:PropName>
        <w2n:PropValue>_none_</w2n:PropValue>
        </w2n:Property>
        <w2n:Property>
        <w2n:PropName>Text</w2n:PropName>
        <w2n:PropValue>MCAPP: a multichannel
application</w2n:PropValue>
        </w2n:Property>
        <w2n:Property>
        <w2n:PropName>AltText</w2n:PropName>
        <w2n:PropValue>MCAPP: a multichannel
application</w2n:PropValue>
        </w2n:Property>
        <w2n:Property>
        <w2n:PropName>HAlign</w2n:PropName>
        <w2n:PropValue>center</w2n:PropValue>
        </w2n:Property>
        <w2n:Property>
        <w2n:PropName>WrapMode</w2n:PropName>
        <w2n:PropValue>wrap</w2n:PropValue>
        </w2n:Property>
        <w2n:Property>
        <w2n:PropName>AudioSrcType</w2n:PropName>
        <w2n:PropValue>From File</w2n:PropValue>
        </w2n:Property>
```

```
            <w2n:Property>
            <w2n:PropName>AudioSrcFile</w2n:PropName>
            <w2n:PropValue></w2n:PropValue>
            </w2n:Property>
            <w2n:Property>
            <w2n:PropName>AudioSrcURL</w2n:PropName>
            <w2n:PropValue></w2n:PropValue>
            </w2n:Property>
            <w2n:Property>
            <w2n:PropName>HTMLCode</w2n:PropName>
            <w2n:PropValue>DIV</w2n:PropValue>
            </w2n:Property>
        </w2n:ObjectProps>
    </w2n:Object>
</w2n:Page>
```

wmlindex.xsl is the XSLT file for generating WML markup. This file is used to transform the preceding XML file to generate WML for presentation to a client device.

```
<?xml version="1.0" ?>
<xsl:stylesheet
    xmlns:xsl="http://www.w3.org/1999/XSL/Transform"
    xmlns:w2n="http://www.where2net.com/davinci"
    exclude-result-prefixes="w2n" version="1.0">
    <xsl:output method="xml" omit-xml-declaration="yes" indent="yes"/>
    <xsl:template match="/">
        <wml>
            <head>
                <meta http-equiv="Cache-Control" content="no-cache"
                    forua="true" />
            </head>
            <card>
            <xsl:value-of select="//w2n:Script[@id = 'PageHeader']"
                disable-output-escaping = "yes"/>
            <xsl:apply-templates
                select="//w2n:Object[w2n:ObjectName = 'myimage']" />
            <xsl:apply-templates
                select="//w2n:Object[w2n:ObjectName = 'mytext']" />
            <xsl:value-of select="//w2n:Script[@id = 'PageFooter']"
                disable-output-escaping = "yes"/>
            </card>
        </wml>
    </xsl:template>
    <xsl:template match="w2n:PageTitle">
    </xsl:template>
    <xsl:template match="w2n:PageName">
    </xsl:template>
    <xsl:template match="w2n:Script">
```

```
      <xsl:value-of select="." disable-output-escaping = "yes" />
</xsl:template>
<xsl:template match="w2n:Property">
</xsl:template>
<xsl:template match="w2n:ObjectName">
</xsl:template>
<xsl:template match="w2n:ObjectType">
</xsl:template>
<xsl:template match="w2n:Object[w2n:ObjectName/text() = 'myimage']">
   <xsl:value-of select="//w2n:Script[@id = 'myimage_condheader']"
      disable-output-escaping = "yes"/>
   <xsl:choose>
      <xsl:when test="w2n:ObjectProps/w2n:Property/w2n:PropName[. =
         'AltBWSrc']/../w2n:PropValue[. != '']">
         <p>
         <img>
            <xsl:attribute name="src">
               <xsl:value-of select="w2n:ObjectProps/w2n:Property/
                  w2n:PropName[. = 'AltBWSrc']/../w2n:PropValue" />
            </xsl:attribute>
            <xsl:attribute name="alt">
               <xsl:value-of select="w2n:ObjectProps/w2n:Property/
                  w2n:PropName[. = 'AltText']/../w2n:PropValue" />
            </xsl:attribute>
         </img>
         </p>
      </xsl:when>
      <xsl:otherwise>
         <p mode="wrap" align="left">
         <xsl:value-of select="w2n:ObjectProps/w2n:Property/
            w2n:PropName[. = 'AltText']/../w2n:PropValue" />
         </p>
      </xsl:otherwise>
   </xsl:choose>
   <xsl:value-of select="//w2n:Script[@id = 'myimage_condfooter']"
      disable-output-escaping = "yes"/>
</xsl:template>
<xsl:template match="w2n:Object[w2n:ObjectName/text() = 'mytext']">
   <xsl:value-of select="//w2n:Script[@id = 'mytext_condheader']"
      disable-output-escaping = "yes"/>
   <p>
   <xsl:attribute name="align">
      <xsl:value-of select="w2n:ObjectProps/w2n:Property/
         w2n:PropName[. = 'HAlign']/../w2n:PropValue" />
   </xsl:attribute>
   <xsl:attribute name="mode">
      <xsl:value-of select="w2n:ObjectProps/w2n:Property/
         w2n:PropName[. = 'WrapMode']/../w2n:PropValue" />
   </xsl:attribute>
```

```
          <xsl:value-of select="w2n:ObjectProps/w2n:Property/
             w2n:PropName[. = 'AltText']/../w2n:PropValue" />
          </p>
          <xsl:value-of select="//w2n:Script[@id = 'mytext_condfooter']"
             disable-output-escaping = "yes"/>
     </xsl:template>
</xsl:stylesheet>
```

The result of performing the transformation will generate the following WML code that is
viewed on a client device capable of interpreting WML, like the Openwave microbrowser
on most mobile telephones in North America and Europe.

```
<?xml version="1.0" ?>
<!DOCTYPE wml PUBLIC "-//PHONE.COM//DTD WML 1.1//EN"
   "http://www.phone.com/dtd/wml11.dtd" >
<wml>
   <head>
      <meta http-equiv="Cache-Control" content="no-cache" forua="true" />
   </head>
   <card>
      <p>
      <img src="/book/images/ch10_logo.bmp" alt="[MCApp]" />
      </p>
      <p align="center" mode="wrap">MCAPP: a multichannel application</p>
   </card>
</wml>
```

Just Flash Only

If your multichannel strategy includes the need to support Flash, you can of course serve up
the correct SWF file depending on the device requesting it, as shown in Chapter 9. This would
be a multichannel with no markup languages involved—just HTML with embedded SWF or
stand-alone SWF.

Flash Plus Markups

Of course, you may want to support both Flash and non-Flash enabled devices. To do that,
you could opt to do it by providing a jump page, much as a number of web sites have done.
Or, you can use the code snippet described earlier to determine the presence and version of the
Flash Player present. If none is available, you serve up a markup page instead. We'll go into
a complete example of this approach in Chapter 12.

XSL Transforms

As discussed in Chapters 1 and 9, XSL transformations (XSLT) have been used to convert XML
files into a format that can be interpreted by a device or device browser. An XSLT takes an

input document and converts the elements, attributes, and text in that document to an output document, which can contain a completely different set of elements, attributes, and text. The Extensible Stylesheet Language (XSL) is used to express how the XML document will be transformed, which input it expects, and what the output should be.

An XSLT processor is required for the conversion. The XSLT processor reads the XML document and the XSL file, which contains the stylesheet. The rules in the stylesheet are applied to the XML document, and the XSLT processor generates an output document. You can generate HTML, WML, cHTML documents, and even text or binary documents. Using a schema or a DTD, you can create and also validate the document.

Note that there are two approaches to doing the actual XML/XSLT transformation.

▶ **Run-time Transform**   This was what we showed you in the previous section using our multichannel framework. The advantage of this is that you have fewer generated files to maintain, but since the transformation is done during run time, the response may be slower and unnoticeable. You are also limited by the XSLT processor capabilities.

▶ **Design-time Transform**   You can generate the final markup files by doing the transformation during design-time. The advantage is, of course, faster run-time performance, but you trade off in terms of content management, as the number of pages and their mapping could become a challenge depending on the number of supported devices or format. As you will see in Chapter 12, this approach lends itself to better support Flash and non-Flash multichannel applications.

Why Flash for Multichannel?

There are several advantages to using Flash as opposed to using the XML approach. First, developers do not need to have a good understanding of XML/XSLT and all the different markup languages. Not only that, but they don't have to update the DTD and include new tags and attributes for VoiceXML, and so forth. Furthermore, they do not have to keep track of all the changes for both new devices and new markup languages. Also, Flash allows a rich Internet and mobile experience that may be difficult to create via XML/XSLT without extensive work.

Cross-Platform and Cross-Device Flash Support

We have already discussed in detail the many advantages of Flash MX in Chapter 2, including its cross-platform and cross-device support. This is especially applicable to multichannel development! We also talked about Flash MX as a viable alternative to J2ME, which again applies to multichannel development.

Multimodal

Multimodal applications refer to applications that allow users to switch modes during a session—for instance, from wireless data to voice. This type of application is particularly helpful for use cases where users may be preoccupied with other tasks—driving, for example. Another example of multimodal applications may involve multimedia messaging. Specifically, you are online with a voice-based mobile banking session, and a video message comes in. Instead of allowing the video messages to roll into your mailbox, you can switch your banking session to data, and then handle your video message instantly.

To create multimodal applications, you must build your applications so they can handle a session on the server side and yet switch between different modes. Care must be taken to ensure security and scalability, as you may need to avoid having two instances of the session open at the same time.

A Case in Point

Instead of using core example applications, we will briefly discuss two common use cases for multichannel applications. To do this, we'll defer to Chapter 12 where we actually implement a real-world multichannel application. To whet our appetite, let's look at m-commerce and m-promotion, and see what multichannel means in these two cases.

Video Store

In Chapter 3, we examined a video store where you browse for movies and view a trailer. Let's look at what you can do with a video store with multichannel access.

Besides retail stores and product catalogs, multichannel retailers have successfully added an online store to the mix. In many situations, the online store complements the retail store and direct mail channels. Adding wireless into the mix, what can you expect?

In the case of a music store, you can actually expect quite a bit. A wireless channel can provide personal experience with audio (MP3) or video (slim down trailers) clips for review. You can get instant information on the actors and actresses, genre, the whole works—and, of course, location-based services that can guide you to the nearest store, all fully equipped with maps and directions. You may even be able to switch mode into voice, listening to the sound track as you drive to pick up the DVD.

Mobile Sales Promotion

Sales promotions are all about getting consumers to act on a particular offer or proposition, generally a discount or a special deal to try out something new! Promotions in many cases require consumers to clip a coupon and return a rebate form. In other cases, you can expect prizes and points that allow you to redeem products and services.

The mobile revolution has brought numerous opportunities for retailers and brand marketers to communicate with consumers. Through promotions, consumers can get more information, play games, and trade stocks for free (or at a discount) for a limited time. So it should come as little surprise that advertisers are finding ways to squeeze their way onto their handheld devices as well.

Attracted by the prospect of serving you with your personal device, marketers are looking at ways to provide opt-in promotions via mobile channels. The best multichannel approach may involve the use of tent cards to stimulate responses (or a call to action), and use your voice, SMS, or WAP phone to take action.

In Chapter 12, we'll look at a real-life promotion application where you can use wireless channels to check if you've won a prize, enter yourself into drawings, or add points to your account. We'll discuss how the unique capabilities of different communications channels can help marketers sell more or better communicate with their customers.

Summary

In this chapter, we have introduced you to the concept of multichannel application development. You can build Flash-only mobile applications that can be applied to various form factors, or you can combine that with XML/XSLT to support Flash and other markup languages as well. We have shown you a typical framework for multichannel application development, and this will be used as a basis for our discussion later on. Developers can also use this approach to fine-tune their own development efforts.

Flash Communication Server

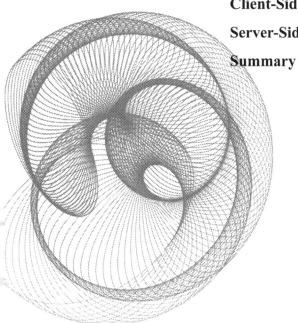

Macromedia Flash Communication Server MX is the easiest way to create rich communication applications in Flash MX. The Flash Communication Server (FCS) enables two or more people to participate in a real-time conversation using text, audio, or video; for example, you can use FCS for net meetings, online communities, customer support, sales support, collaboration, remote training, or instant messaging. FCS is also a platform for streaming live data across networks for delivery to the Internet, mobile devices, interactive TV, and more. You can also use FCS for personal projects like a house intercom, a pet camera, or video publishing. In short, FCS is an essential part of Macromedia's complete solution for database connectivity, directory systems, and presence services.

In this chapter, we will cover application design with FCS and present the client-side and server-side objects made available for use with FCS. We'll conclude by showing you a couple of core examples (building block code) that can be used to build rich multimedia communication applications leveraging FCS and the Flash MX client.

How It Works

FCS is both a development framework and a deployment environment for rich communication applications. You can use Flash MX and FCS to write a communication application, and then use FCS to deploy the application and its scripts. You target Flash Player as your end use interface.

Digital communication typically uses four media types: text, graphics, audio, and video. Communication is either real-time, as with a phone call, or stored, as with e-mail. Communication also ranges from one-to-one interactions, such as phone calls, to one-to-many broadcast interactions, such as television shows. The Flash Communication Server handles all of these data types and interactions with a unified development model. Some examples of the types of application include,

▶ **Rich media messaging** An ideal environment for creating and deploying rich media messaging features, such as live video, audio, or text-based messaging. You can integrate live or recorded streaming video with human-to-human interaction to create new models for communication.

▶ **Real-time collaboration** A rich environment for creating and deploying real-time collaboration features such as team message boards, shared whiteboards, online conference rooms, polling, and much more. Applications can be used offline and synchronized automatically whenever the user is back online.

▶ **Streaming media** Efficient real-time streaming audio and video, coupled with custom user interfaces that integrate seamlessly into a web site, enable dynamic one-to-many presentations. You can synchronize video streams with multimedia content to provide powerful supporting content for presentations.

Client connections to FCS use the Real-Time Messaging Protocol (RTMP), which, unlike HTTP, provides a persistent socket connection for two-way communication between Flash MX clients and the FCS. The FCS may also communicate with an application server via its built-in Flash Remoting module instead of from the Flash movie directly, as illustrated next. FCS is thus acting like a Flash MX client.

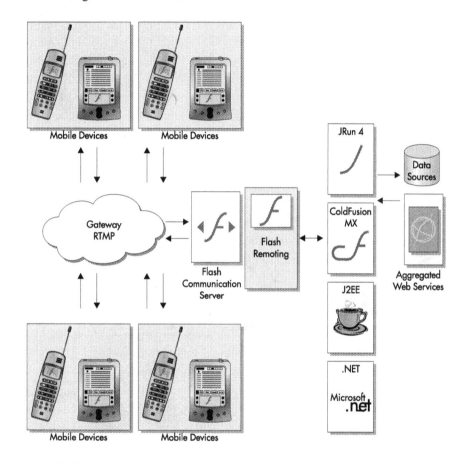

NOTE

With multiple Flash MX clients interacting with the FCS, this minimizes the load on the application server and/or database. With Flash Remoting from the Flash MX client, multiple requests would be made to the application server or database.

Communications pass through the FCS and are delivered to the client, the Flash MX player. When a Flash movie uses FCS, the player connects to the server, which provides a flow of information, called a *network stream*, to and from the client (see following illustration). Other users can connect to the same server and receive messages, data updates, and audio/video streams.

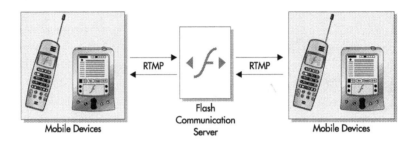

The Flash Communication Server lets you stream live media (audio, video, and data) or record data to be played later, as illustrated next.

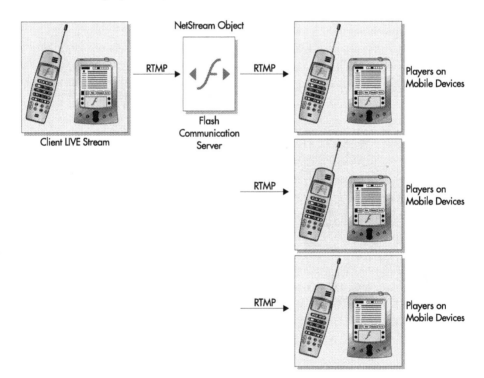

A recorded stream (playback of a FLV file) would look like the illustration that follows.

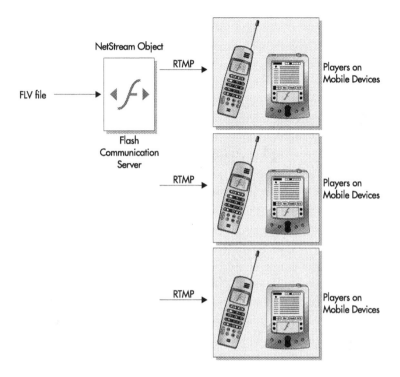

Designing with Flash Communication Server

You create FCS applications that have a client component and, if needed, a server component. The client component is a Flash MX movie (SWF) you develop using Client-Side Communication ActionScript, and the server component is a program you write using Server-Side Communication ActionScript. After you've created the application, register it on the FCS; if there are any server-side scripts, upload them to the FCS. You can then test the application using the Flash Player to connect to the server. While you're testing the movie, you can debug it using the NetConnection Debugger and the Communication App inspector, both part of the Flash MX authoring environment. Once the application works properly, you can deploy it.

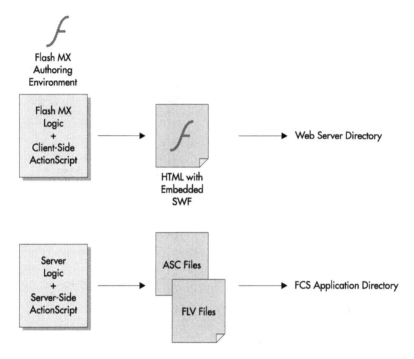

Recorded Streams

When you use methods that record audio, video, or data streams, for example, *NetStream .publish("webcam", "record")*, FCS creates two files, *webcam.flv* and *webcam.idx*, where *webcam* is the string that was passed to the method that recorded the stream. These files are the recorded stream and its associated index file, and are stored in subdirectories of the FCS application directory (automatically created). For example, if the application instance is *WebCam* with an instance name of *MondayInst*, and it records a stream named *webcam*, the *webcam.flv* and *webcam.idx* files will be stored in the following location:

```
$flashcom\applications\WebCam\streams\MondayInst
```

If you want to play back an FLV file that was created by a specialized video application, such as Sorenson Squeeze, or exported from the Flash MX authoring environment of a QuickTime movie, place it in the directory where FCS expects to find it. That is, a subdirectory of a *\streams* directory. When you run the application, FCS will create an IDX file and store it in the same subdirectory.

Client-Side Communication Objects

We will now go through the client-side communication objects available for use with the Flash Communication Server. These are objects associated with the local Flash MX client and used only in client-side ActionScript. Server-side communication objects will be covered at the end of this chapter.

The Camera Object

The Camera object lets you capture video from a video camera attached to the computer that is running the Flash Player. When used with the Flash Communication Server, this object lets you transmit, display, and optionally record the video being captured. With these capabilities, communications applications—such as video conferencing and instant messaging (IM) with video—can be easily developed. Since the Camera object can be used without a server, you can use it to monitor a video feed from a web cam attached to your local system.

The Camera object has the following methods available, as shown in Table 11-1.

The Camera object also has the following properties, shown in Table 11-2.

The *default* camera settings provide a good viewing experience for all bandwidth settings. It can be changed using the following code:

```
cam = Camera.get();
cam.setQuality(bandwidthSpeed,quality)
```

Macromedia recommends using Table 11-3 that follows as a starting point if you wish to experiment with camera settings at different bandwidth speeds.

Method	Description
Camera.get	Returns a Camera object or null if camera not available
Camera.setKeyFrameInterval	Specifies which video frames are transmitted in full
Camera.setLoopback	Specifies whether to use a compressed video stream
Camera.setMode	Sets camera capture mode—height, width, frames per second
Camera.setMotionLevel	Specifies how much motion is required to invoke camera
Camera.setQuality	Sets the maximum amount of bandwidth per second or the required picture quality of the outgoing video feed

Table 11-1   *Camera Methods*

Property	Description
Camera.activityLevel	Amount of motion camera is detecting
Camera.bandwidth	Maximum bandwidth video can use (in bytes)
Camera.currentFps	Rate at which camera is capturing data
Camera.fps	Rate at which you want camera to capture data
Camera.height	Capture height in pixels
Camera.index	Index of the camera
Camera.keyFrameInterval	Indicates which video frames are transmitted in full
Camera.loopback	Camera capturing in compressed or uncompressed mode (Boolean)
Camera.motionLevel	Amount of motion to invoke camera
Camera.motionTimeOut	Amount of time (milliseconds) between no motion detection and invoking camera again
Camera.muted	User has allowed or denied access to camera (Boolean)
Camera.name	Name of the camera as specified by the hardware
Camera.names	An array of strings containing the names of all available video capture devices (includes video cards and cameras)
Camera.quality	Level of picture quality based on the amount of compression applied to each frame
Camera.width	Capture width in pixels

Table 11-2   *Camera Properties*

We've been using a Logitech QuickCam Pro 3000 (see following illustration) for all of our communications application development on the Flash Communication Server.

The QuickCam Pro 3000 has a built-in microphone and a web camera that delivers high-quality images at true 640×480 resolution. As of this writing, Macromedia has tested

Bandwidth	Effect	Code
Modem	Lower image quality, higher motion quality	cam.setQuality(4000,0)
	Higher image quality, lower motion quality	cam.setQuality(0,65)
DSL	Lower image quality, higher motion quality	cam.setQuality(12000,0)

Table 11-3   *Macromedia-Recommended Camera Settings*

Bandwidth	Effect	Code
	Higher image quality, lower motion quality	cam.setQuality(0,90)
LAN	Lower image quality, higher motion quality	cam.setQuality(400000,0)
	Higher image quality, lower motion quality	cam.setQuality(0,100)

Table 11-3   *Macromedia-Recommended Camera Settings* (continued)

and certified the following cameras for use with Flash MX Player as shown in Table 11-4 that follows.

Most video cameras will likely work, so play around and find out!

The Microphone Object

The Microphone object lets you capture audio from a microphone attached to the computer that is running the Flash MX client. When used with the Flash Communication Server, this object lets you transmit, play, and optionally record the audio being captured. With these capabilities, communications applications such as instant messaging with audio and recording presentations can be developed. Since the Microphone object can be used without a server you can transmit sound from your microphone through the speakers on your local system.

The Microphone object has the following methods available, as shown in Table 11-5.

The Microphone object also has the following properties, as shown in Table 11-6.

The Video Object

The Video object lets you display live or recorded streaming video on the stage without embedding it in your SWF file. The video may be a live video stream being captured with the *Camera.get* command, or a live or recorded video stream being displayed through the use of a *NetStream.play* command (see next section).

Manufacturer	Models
3Com	Home Connect
Creative Labs	WebCam Go Plus
D-Link Systems	USB WebCam (DSB-C100)
IBM	UltraPort Camera 2
Intel	Deluxe PC Camera, Easy PC Camera
Irez	Kritter USB, StealthFire
Logitech	QuickCam Traveller, QuickCam Web, QuickCam Express, QuickCam Pro 3000, QuickCam VC
Orange Micro	IBOT Pro FireWire
Veo	StingRay

Table 11-4   *Macromedia-Certified Cameras*

Method	Description
Microphone.get	Returns a Microphone object, or null if microphone is not available
Microphone.setGain	Amount by which the microphone should boost the signal
Microphone.setRate	Rate at which microphone captures sound (kHz)
Microphone.setSilenceLevel	Amount of sound required to activate the microphone
Microphone.setUseEchoSuppression	Uses echo suppression feature of codec

Table 11-5   *Microphone Methods*

The Video object has the following methods available, as shown in Table 11-7.
The Video object also has the following properties, as shown in Table 11-8.

The NetStream Object

The NetStream object opens a one-way streaming connection between the Flash MX client and the Flash Communication Server through a connection made available by a NetConnection object. A NetStream object is like a channel inside a NetConnection object; this channel can either publish audio and/or video data (e.g., *NetStream.publish*) or subscribe to a published stream and receive data (e.g., *NetStream.play*). You can publish or play live (real-time) data and play previously recorded data. You can also use NetStream objects to send text messages to all subscribed clients (e.g., *NetStream.send*).

Property	Description
Microphone.activityLevel	Amount of sound microphone is detecting
Microphone.gain	Amount by which the microphone boosts the signal
Microphone.index	Index of the microphone
Microphone.muted	User has allowed or denied access to microphone (Boolean)
Microphone.name	Name of the sound capture device as specified by the hardware
Microphone.names	An array of strings containing the names of all available sound capture devices (includes sound cards and microphones)
Microphone.rate	Sound capture rate (kHz)
Microphone.silenceLevel	Amount of sound required to activate the microphone
Microphone.silenceTimeOut	Amount of time (milliseconds) between no sound detection and invoking microphone again
Microphone.useEchoSuppression	Determines whether echo suppression is used (Boolean)

Table 11-6   *Microphone Properties*

Method	Description
Video.attachVideo	Specifies a video stream to be displayed on the stage
Video.clear	Clears the image currently displayed

Table 11-7   *Video Methods*

The NetStream object has the following methods available, as shown in Table 11-9. The NetStream object also has the following properties, as shown in Table 11-10.

The NetConnection Object

The NetConnection object manages a bidirectional connection between the Flash Player and a server, which lets you connect to Flash Remoting (see Chapter 6) or to the Flash Communication Server.

The NetConnection object has the following methods available, as shown in Table 11-11.

The SharedObject Object

Shared objects offer real-time data sharing between multiple client movies and objects persistent on the local or remote location. You can think of local shared objects as "cookies" and remote shared objects as real-time data transfer devices. Basic ways to use shared objects are

► Maintaining local persistence

► Storing and sharing data on a server

► Sharing data in real time

Property	Description
Video.deblocking	Amount of sound microphone is detecting
Video.height	Video stream height in pixels
Video.smoothing	Indicates whether video should be smoothed when it is scaled
Video.width	Video stream width in pixels

Table 11-8   *Video Properties*

Method	Type	Description
NetStream.attachAudio	Publisher	Sends audio over the stream
NetStream.attachVideo	Publisher	Sends video over the stream
NetStream.close	Publisher	Stops publishing and frees up stream
NetStream.pause	Subscriber	Pauses or resumes playback of a stream
NetStream.play	Subscriber	Feeds streaming audio, video, and text messages published by Flash Communication Server to clients
NetStream.publish	Publisher	Sends streaming audio, video, and text messages from client to the Flash Communication Server
NetStream.receiveAudio	Subscriber	Specifies whether incoming audio plays on the stream
NetStream.receiveVideo	Subscriber	Specifies whether incoming video plays on the stream
NetStream.seek	Subscriber	Seeks a position in the recorded stream
NetStream.send	Publisher	Broadcasts a message to all subscribing clients
NetStream.setBufferTime	Both	For *publisher*, indicates how long outgoing buffer can grow before dropping frames; for *subscriber*, indicates how long to buffer incoming data before starting to display to stream

Table 11-9   *NetStream Methods*

The SharedObject object has the following methods available, as shown in Table 11-12. The SharedObject object also has the following properties available, as shown in Table 11-13.

Server-Side Communication Objects

We had previously discussed all the client-side objects available with the Flash Communication Server. We will now discuss those available on the server side. One major difference between server-side and client-side ActionScript is naming conventions. When you write server-side ActionScript code, there are certain naming conventions you must use to name your applications,

Property	Description
NetStream.bufferLength	Data currently in buffer (in seconds)
NetStream.bufferTime	Time assigned to buffer (in seconds)
NetStream.currentFps	Frames per second on publisher or subscriber stream
NetStream.time	The time a stream has been playing or publishing (in seconds)

Table 11-10   *NetStream Properties*

Method	Description
NetConnection.call	Invokes a command or method on the Flash Communication Server
NetConnection.close	Closes the connection to the Flash Communication Server
NetConnection.connect	Connects to an application on the Flash Communication Server

Table 11-11   *NetConnection Methods*

methods, properties, and variables. These rules let you logically identify objects so your code executes properly.

▶ **Application Naming**   Flash Communication Server application names must follow the Uniform Resource Identifier (URI) RFC 2396 convention (see http://www.w3.org/Addressing). This convention supports a hierarchical naming system where a forward slash (/) separates the elements in the hierarchy. The first element specifies the application name. The element following the application name specifies the application instance name. Each instance of the application has its own script environment.

▶ **Instance Naming**   By specifying a unique application instance name after an application name, you can run multiple instances of a single application. All users who connect to the same instance name can communicate with each other by referencing the same streams or shared objects.

Method	Description
SharedObject.close	Closes the connection between a remote shared object and the Flash Communication Server
SharedObject.connect	Connects to a remote shared object on the Flash Communication Server
SharedObject.flush	Writes a locally persistent shared object to a local file
SharedObject.getLocal	Returns a reference to a locally persistent shared object that is available to the local client
SharedObject.getRemote	Returns a reference to a shared object that is available to local multiple clients via the Flash Communication Server
SharedObject.getSize	Gets the size of the shared object (in bytes)
SharedObject.send	Broadcasts a message to all clients connected to the remote shared object
SharedObject.setFps	Number of times per second a client's changes to a shared object are sent to the Flash Communication Server

Table 11-12   *SharedObject Methods*

Property	Description
SharedObject.data	A collection of attributes assigned to the data property of the object that will be shared or stored

Table 11-13   *SharedObject Properties*

The Application Object

The Application object contains information about a Flash Communication Server application instance that lasts until the application instance is unloaded. A Flash Communication Server application is a collection of stream objects, shared objects, and clients (connected users). Each application must have a unique name.

The Application object lets you accept and reject client connection attempts, register and unregister classes and proxies, and create functions invoked when an application starts or stops, or when a client connects or disconnects.

The Application object has the following methods available, as shown in Table 11-14.

The Application object also has these properties available, as shown in Table 11-15.

The Client Object

The Client object lets you handle each user, or *client*, connection to a Flash Communication Server application instance. The server automatically creates a Client object when a user connects to an application; the object is destroyed when the user disconnects from the application. Users have unique Client objects for each application to which they are connected. Thousands of Client objects can be active at the same time.

The Client object has the following methods available, as shown in Table 11-16.

Method	Description
Application.acceptConnection	Accepts a connection to an application from a client
Application.clearSharedObjects	Clears all shared objects associated with the current instance
Application.clearStreams	Clears all stream objects associated with the current instance
Application.disconnect	Disconnects a client from the server
Application.registerClass	Registers or unregisters a constructor called during object deserialization
Application.registerProxy	Registers a NetConnection or client object to fulfill a method request
Application.rejectConnection	Rejects a connection to an application

Table 11-14   *Application Methods*

Property	Description
Application.clients	A list of clients currently connected to the application
Application.name	The name of the application instance
Application.server	The platform and version of the server

Table 11-15   *Application Properties*

The Client object also has the following properties available, as shown in Table 11-17.

The NetConnection Object

The server-side NetConnection object lets you create a two-way connection between a Flash Communication Server application *instance* and an application server, another Flash Communication Server, or another Flash Communication Server application *instance* on the same server.

The NetConnection object has the following methods available, as shown in Table 11-18.

The NetConnection object also has the following properties available, as shown in Table 11-19.

NOTE

The server-side NetConnection object is different from the client-side NetConnection object as described in the previous section.

The SharedObject Object

Shared objects let you share data between multiple clients in real time, and can be persistent on the server (objects as real-time data transfer devices). Every shared object is identified by a unique name and contains a list of name-value pairs, called *properties,* just like any other ActionScript object. A name must be a unique string and a value can be any ActionScript data type. All shared objects have a data property, and any property of the data property—known as a *slot*—can be shared.

Method	Description
Client.call	Executes a method on the Flash MX client and returns a value from the client to the server
Client.getBandwidthLimit	Returns the maximum bandwidth the client or the server can use for this connection
Client._resolve	Provides value for undefined properties
Client.setBandwidthLimit	Sets the maximum bandwidth for the connection

Table 11-16   *Client Methods*

Property	Description
Client.agent	The version and platform of the Flash MX client
Client.ip	The IP address of the Flash MX client
Client.readAccess	List of access levels to which the client has read access
Client.referrer	The URL of the SWF file or server where this connection originated
Client.writeAccess	List of access levels to which the client has write access

Table 11-17 *Client Properties*

The SharedObject object has the following methods available, as shown in Table 11-20. The SharedObject object also has the following properties available, as shown in Table 11-21.

The Stream Object

The Stream object lets you handle each stream in a Flash Communication Server application. A *stream* is a one-way connection between the Flash Player and the Flash Communication Server, or between two servers. A user can access multiple streams at the same time, and there can be hundreds or thousands of Stream objects active at the same time.

The Stream object has the following methods available, as shown in Table 11-22.

The Stream object also has the following properties available, as shown in Table 11-23.

FCS Components

There is an initial set of seven FCS communication components shipped by Macromedia for use within the Flash MX authoring environment. Note that building rich communications applications does *not* require the communication components. As a matter of fact, the first two examples in the next section do not use any of these components. The third example is built using only the communication components and no additional authoring and scripting!

Here's a brief summary of the basic communication components:

▶ **SimpleConnect** This component handles connecting a user to FCS and connecting any other specified components in the application to the server.

Method	Description
NetConnection.addHeader	Adds a context header
NetConnection.call	Invokes a command or method on a remote server
NetConnection.close	Closes a server connection
NetConnection.connect	Establishes a connection to a server

Table 11-18 *NetConnection Methods*

Property	Description
NetConnection.isConnected	Indicates whether a connection is made (Boolean)
NetConnection.uri	The URI that was passed by the NetConnection connect method

Table 11-19   *NetConnection Properties*

▶ **PeopleList**   This component displays a list of users who are connected to a communications application. Only users who have supplied a username appear in the list.

▶ **ConnectionLight**   This component provides visual feedback on the state of the client connection. It is green when connected, red when disconnected, and yellow if the latency of the connection is too high.

▶ **UserColor**   This component lets you change the selected colors for components within FCS applications. When you select a color from the pull-down menu, other components that show color, such as Chat components, change color accordingly.

▶ **Chat**   This component shows a regular text chat window. It also supports lurker (moderator or monitor) mode. When you use this component with the SimpleConnect component, lurker mode prevents the display of the input text box and Send buttons if the user has never logged in. The lurker can see other people text chatting. After the user logs in with a username, the user can send text. If you also use the UserColor component, each user has an individual color assigned to his or her text.

Method	Description
SharedObject.clear	Deletes all properties of a shared object
SharedObject.close	Unsubscribes from a shared object
SharedObject.flush	Server is to save the state of a shared object
SharedObject.get	Returns a reference to a shared object
SharedObject.getProperty	Gets the value of a shared object property
SharedObject.getPropertyNames	Gets an array of valid properties in a shared object
SharedObject.lock	Locks the shared object instance
SharedObject.purge	Server removes all deleted properties older than the specified version
SharedObject.send	Sends a message to the client subscribing to this shared object
SharedObject.setProperty	Sets a new value for a shared object property
SharedObject.size	Returns the number of valid properties in a shared object
SharedObject.unlock	Unlocks a shared object instance

Table 11-20   *SharedObject Methods*

Property	Description
SharedObject.name	Name of shared object
SharedObject.resyncDepth	Deleted values of shared object should be permanent with this depth level
SharedObject.version	Version number of shared object

Table 11-21 *SharedObject Properties*

▶ **SetBandwidth**   This component lets users specify their upload and download bandwidths, which then adjusts the quality for the microphones and cameras it manages. It can handle multiple microphones and cameras and prioritizes bandwidth allocation.

▶ **AVPresence**   The AVPresence component lets you send and receive audio and video within your application. The component acts as a presenter seat, which any connected user can use. If a user is sending audio or video (or both) from an instance of the component, the other users see and hear that person's audio and video automatically. The user has controls for sending and receiving, as well as for disabling audio and/or video.

NOTE

Some components provide a user mode that shields the user from other connected users. This mode is called lurker mode, and can be useful, for example, in scenarios that require a moderator or monitor. In lurker mode, a user is not necessarily exposed to other users and might not have full functionality.

Macromedia periodically releases new FCS components at http://www.macromedia.com/software/flashcom/download/components/index.html so please check its web site to get the latest and greatest free components.

Method	Description
Stream.clear	Deletes a stream previously recorded by the server
Stream.get	Returns a reference to a stream object
Stream.length	Returns the length of the recorded stream in seconds
Stream.play	Controls the data source of the stream object
Stream.record	Records all data going into the stream
Stream.send	Sends a call with parameters to all subscribers on a stream
Stream.setBufferTime	Sets the length of the buffer time in seconds

Table 11-22 *Stream Methods*

Property	Description
Stream.bufferTime	Indicates how long to buffer messages before a stream is played
Stream.name	Unique name of the live stream

Table 11-23   *Stream Properties*

FCS Examples

The following steps summarize the sequence of actions required for publishing real-time audio and video using the Flash Communication Server and the Real-Time Messaging Protocol (RTMP):

1. Use *new NetConnection* to create a NetConnection object.

2. Use *NetConnection.connect("rtmp://serverName/appName/appInstanceName")* to connect the application to the Flash Communication Server.

3. Use *new NetStream(connection)* to create a data stream over the connection.

4. Use *NetStream.attachAudio(audioSource)* to capture and send audio over the stream, and *NetStream.attachVideo(videoSource)* to capture and send video over the stream.

5. Use *NetStream.publish(publishName)* to give this stream a unique name and send data over the stream to the Flash Communication Server, so others can receive it. You can also record the data as you publish it, so users can play it back later.

We will go through a few common, yet core, communications applications. You can build on these core applications to create your own full-fledged multimedia communications applications:

▶   Streaming Video

▶   Live WebCam

▶   Live Chat with Audio/Video using components only

Streaming Video

Our first communications application example will be a building block for developing a video-on-demand service. We will show you what you need to do to stream a video file using the Flash Communication Server to a Flash MX client. Macromedia Flash plays a specific video file type: Flash Video (FLV). Let's go through the steps in converting a QuickTime movie into the FLV format and create a Flash MX frame with ActionScript to stream that movie.

1. **Creating a FLV file**   You can make a *.flv* file by importing a video file into the Flash MX authoring environment and exporting it as a **.flv* file. Macromedia Flash can import many common video file types. For our example, we will use the *gladiator.mov* QuickTime

movie file. When you import the video file into Flash, it becomes an embedded video or linked video object. Embedded and linked video appears in the *Library* as Embedded Video and Linked Video symbols, respectively (see illustration that follows).

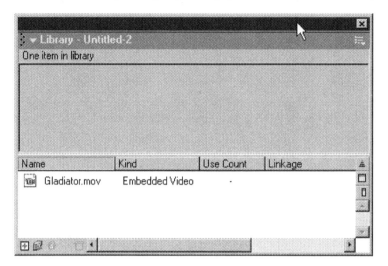

You can view and set properties of a video symbol by selecting it in the Library and choosing Properties from the Library panel's pop-up menu or by double-clicking the symbol in the Library (see following illustration).

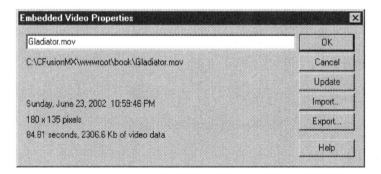

A common mistake is to select the Embedded Video object on the stage and use the Property Inspector window—you will *not* be able to create an FLV file from there. Select *Export...* from the Properties dialog window and save the file as **gladiator.flv** into a new subfolder, *streams/_definst_* (two levels down from book folder). If you do not, the server will not be able to file the FLV file.

2. **Creating a Flash MX frame to stream the video** Now that we have created our FLV file, let's create a frame to stream that video from the Flash Communication Server. First, we create a video object (select *New Video* under *Library* in the upper-right menu) on the stage—this will create an Embedded Video object in the

Library. Drag an instance of the Embedded Video object onto the stage. Select it and name the instance **streamingVideo** (see following illustration). Resize the video to match the size of your FLV file (180×135 in our example).

3. **Writing the ActionScript**   We will now write the appropriate ActionScript code to stream our FLV file to a Flash player. The comments in the code are self-explanatory:

```
// create connection to server
nc = new NetConnection();
nc.connect("rtmp:/book");
nc.onStatus = function(returnObj) {
    if (returnObj.code == "NetConnection.Connect.Success") {
        startVideo();
    }
    // add your code here to handle other situations…
};
function startVideo() {
    // Create input stream
    myInputStream = new NetStream(nc);

    // Attaching stream to the video object
    streamingVideo.attachVideo(myInputStream);

    // set the number of seconds to load before beginning to play
    myInputStream.setBufferTime(10);

    // Play recorded stream
    myInputStream.play("gladiator",0,120,true);
}
```

4. **Deploying the files to the Flash Communication Server**   Before we can stream the video (FLV) file, we need to deploy the appropriate files to the server. The SWF and HTML files will go to your production web server, whereas the FLV files will go to your production flash communication server. You must create a subdirectory that matches your application name (*book* in our example) even though you have no server-side ActionScript files (none in our example). This is because FCS stores any stream or shared object files created by your application in subdirectories of this directory.

5. **Playing the movie**   When deployed, the streaming video application, after a ten-second buffering pause, starts playing the movie and should look as illustrated next (contrast this with the dynamic video store example in Chapter 3 where a user waits for the complete movie to download before playing):

6. **Making final adjustments**   You can extend this streaming video application to include video controls, security, and so on, and turn it into a full-blown streaming media on-demand or pay-per-view application!

Live WebCam

Our second communications application example will be a building block for developing a monitoring or live web cam service. We will show you what you need to do to stream a live video from a web cam using the Flash Communication Server to Flash MX clients. We need to create two FLA files: one for publishing the video (publisher), and one for viewing the video (subscribers). Our web camera will only be connected to the machine doing the publishing, so let's get started.

1. **Creating a Publisher Flash MX frame to stream video**   Let's begin by creating an FLA (*webcam_publish*) with a frame to stream the live video from our web cam to the Flash Communication Server. First, we create a video object (select *New Video* under *Library* in the upper-right menu) on the stage—this will create an Embedded Video object in the Library. Drag an instance of the Embedded Video object onto the stage. Select it and name the instance **liveVideo**. Size the video to be 220×165 (W×H) or any other size as long as it has the same aspect ratio of 640×480 (W×H), our web camera capture resolution. Add a static text header and footer (*Live WebCam* and *Publisher* for example) to top it off (see illustration that follows).

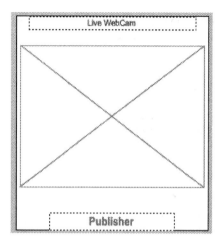

2. **Creating a Subscriber Flash MX frame to stream video**   Next, we create an
    FLA (*webcam_subscribe*) with a frame to stream the live video from the Flash
    Communication Server to Flash MX clients. Then we create a video object (select
    New Video under *Library* in the upper-right menu) on the stage—this will create an
    Embedded Video object in the Library. Drag an instance of the Embedded Video
    object onto the stage. Select it and name the instance **viewVideo**. Size the video to
    be 200×150 (W×H). Add a static text header and footer (*Live WebCam* and
    Subscriber, for example) to top it off (see illustration that follows).

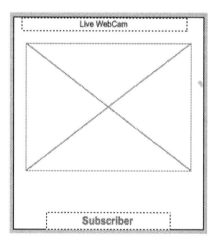

3. **Writing the Publisher ActionScript**   We will now write the appropriate ActionScript
    code to show a live stream from our web cam (which is connected to a local machine)

to the FCS. The comments in the code are self-explanatory, and you can tweak the camera settings for your own situations:

```
// access camera
publisher_cam = Camera.get();
// settings for best quality image
publisher_cam.setQuality(0,100)
// capture at highest resolution
publisher_cam.setMode("640", "480", "15");
// attached to our video object
liveVideo.attachVideo(publisher_cam);
function doConnect() {
    publisher_nc = new netConnection();
    // status debug
    publisher_nc.onStatus = function(info) {
        trace("Level: " + info.level + " Code: " + info.code);
    }
    // connect to webcam app
    publisher_nc.connect("rtmp:/webcam");
    // open connection
    pubStream_ns = new NetStream(publisher_nc);
    // status debug
    pubStream_ns.onStatus = function(returnObj) {
        trace (returnObj.code + " - " + returnObj.level + " - "
        + returnObj.details);
    };
    // attached video to stream
    pubStream_ns.attachVideo(publisher_cam);
    // publish stream to FCS
    pubStream_ns.publish("wc_stream", "live" );
}
// do it
doConnect();
```

4. **Writing the Subscriber ActionScript**   Next, we write the appropriate ActionScript code to show a live stream from the FCS to Flash MX clients. The comments in the code are self-explanatory.

```
function doConnect() {
    subscriber_nc = new netConnection();
    subscriber_nc.onStatus = function(info) {
        trace("Level: " + info.level + " Code: " + info.code);
    }
    // connect to webcam app
```

```
    subscriber_nc.connect("rtmp:/webcam");
    // open connection
    subStream_ns = new NetStream(subscriber_nc);
    // status debug
    subStream_ns.onStatus = function(returnObj) {
        trace (returnObj.code + " - " + returnObj.level + " - "
        + returnObj.details);
    };
    // play stream from FCS
    subStream_ns.play("wc_stream");
    viewVideo.attachVideo(subStream_ns);
}
// do it
doConnect();
```

5. **Deploying the files to the Flash Communication Server**   Before we can stream the
   live video, we need to deploy the appropriate files to the server. The SWF and HTML
   files will go to your production web server, whereas any FLV or server-side ActionScript
   files (none in this example) will go to your production Flash Communication Server.

6. **Publishing WebCam (*webcam_publish*)**   The local machine, where the web cam is
   connected, will ask the user (see following illustration) for access to the camera and
   microphone. Click Allow.

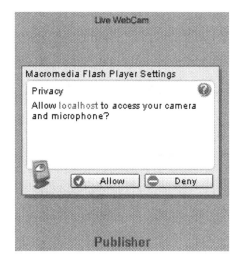

Then the streaming live web cam application will start showing the live images as illustrated next.

Live WebCam

Publisher

7. **Viewing WebCam** (*webcam_subscribe*)   On client machines where the web cam video is being viewed, it will just show the live video as illustrated next. There will be a slight delay depending on your network speed and camera settings for motion and quality.

Live WebCam

Subscriber

8. **Making final adjustments** You can obviously add more features, like selective recording, playback of certain video segments, and so on. We're just providing the basic building blocks for more sophisticated and full-blown communications applications.

Live Chat with Audio/Video

We'll now build a Live Chat application with audio and video support using only the communication components with no additional authoring or scripting. Here's a sneak preview of what the completed mobile flash application should look like, as shown in the Nokia Communicator platform (full screen mode).

To build this application, we've used one of each of the following communication components: Chat, AVPresence, SetBandwidth, PeopleList, SimpleConnect, and ConnectionLight, as shown next.

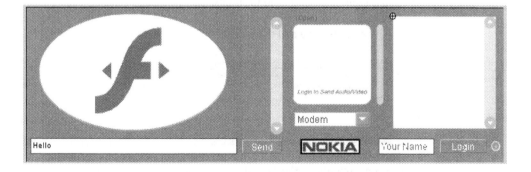

We have given each of these objects on the stage an instance name, as shown in the movie explorer view that follows, so they can be associated with each other.

We have already shown how to use components in your movies in the previous chapters. After placing the desired components on the stage, there are still two more things that need to be done.

1. **SimpleConnect parameters**   You need to supply the application directory, such as *rtmp:/com_test*, and a list of any other communication components you want to connect automatically. In our example, we add them as shown in the following illustration.

2. **Communication components ActionScript**   When you use these communication components, you must use some server-side scripting. But that's already been done for you; see the file named *components.asc* in the script library. All you have to do is create a file called *main.asc* and have it load the components.asc file. The code listing follows:

```
load("components.asc");
```

This *main.asc* file is a server-side ActionScript file that is executed once when the application is loaded. Just save this file in the same directory as your application.

That's it! No coding, no authoring. Just use components, name the instances, and configure them. Publish it and you're up and running! You now have a live chat application with integrated audio and video.

Summary

In this chapter, we introduced you to the powerful Flash Communication Server from Macromedia and the new objects it supports on both the client and server side. Rich communication applications can easily be built using these new objects with minimal ActionScript code. It gets even easier with the out-of-the-box communication components! We showed you how to create the building blocks for a streaming video or video-on-demand application, in addition to the fundamentals of a live web cam application. And we've barely touched on the endless possibilities the Flash Communication Server is capable of enabling— something which could be a separate book by itself!

Creating Flash MX Mobile Applications

OBJECTIVES

- ► Review the skills and knowledge learned and apply to core application development

- ► Implement a multichannel advertising promotion service using Flash and XML

- ► Create an MP3 player for mobile devices based on the Flash MX client

- ► Build a streaming video application for mobile devices using Flash Communication Server and other client- and server-side capabilities

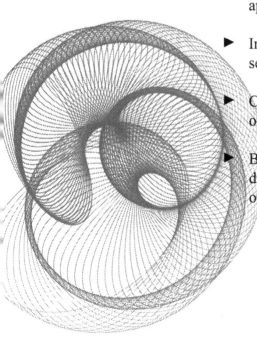

Mobile and Multichannel Ad Promotions

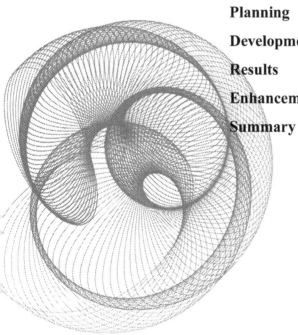

I n this chapter, we'll discuss the design and development of a multichannel, mobile application for advertising promotions. We'll create a back end using a relational database management system (RDBMS) and use XML/XSLT to generate markup pages for HTML browsers for PCs and microbrowsers for mobile devices. We will then create a Flash MX application to support PCs and mobile devices that have Flash Player capability. The mobile promotion (m-Promo) application will leverage the device detection capability to decide whether to serve up markup pages or SWF files. We conclude by discussing how you can enhance this application or modify it to build enterprise multichannel mobile solutions.

Introduction

As shown earlier, this example application illustrates how you can build a multichannel mobile application using both the XML and Flash infrastructure. We'll begin with non-Flash infrastructure (that is, XML/XSLT), and then show you how to migrate the XML application to a Flash-based multichannel mobile application that is easy to use, build, and manage, yet is extensible and scalable.

Why m-Promotion?

For advertisers, promotional campaigns not only build brands and draw customers into a positive relationship with their products, but can take ads one step further through call-to-action promotions using games. Believe it or not, these can actually drive strong sales!

Beyond simple announcements or invitations to enter contests, promotional campaigns with loyalty programs or games can add a level of complexity and interaction that leaves users with a positive feeling and taps into a simple human impulse: the desire to win prizes.

With a mobile game and loyalty program, advertisers get the chance to interact with their customers on the spot with opt-in actions. These kinds of promotions have proven very cost-effective when compared to direct mail, especially when used in context with an integrated marketing program.

Use Case

Here, we are building a mobile and multichannel campaign with a call-to-action along the lines of beer promotion. With ad promo campaigns, you must thoughtfully promote the game. For instance, advertisers, like breweries, can promote their games with tent cards on tables in bars and pubs! Because mobile devices are not a browsing medium, customers (users) must be enticed to seek out the web site (or application) and be directed to the games. Since mobile devices are a lifestyle extension and people carry their phones with them, people can instantly act on our m-Promo offering when at home, using their PC browsers, or when at a pub, using their mobile devices. This will truly create a successful promotion campaign (see following illustration).

Our m-Promo offering also relies on the instant response of mobile users to the caps of the beer bottles. In fact, bottle caps and labels were among the most effective means of promoting the game (see the illustration of the beer bottle cap next)!

The typical scenario of how a beer drinker uses our application is shown in this illustration.

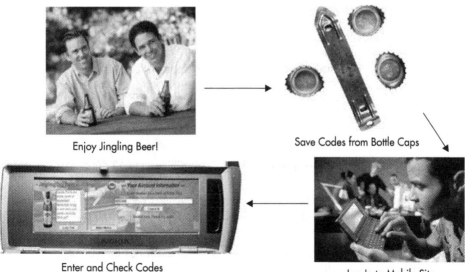

Enjoy Jingling Beer!

Save Codes from Bottle Caps

Enter and Check Codes

Log In to Mobile Site

The usual sequence of events follows:

1. The user is a beer drinker who buys a bottle of beer in a restaurant, bar, or convenience store. User checks the code inside the bottle cap.

2. Using a mobile device, the user can instantly check if the bottle cap is a winner and how many points are earned for merchandise by logging into the redemption web site.

3. Upon login, user enters the code and instantly finds out the status of the game code found inside the beer bottle cap, his/her account status, and more. User can choose to redeem prizes or just log off after registering the code from the bottle cap.

4. Registration on the web site is done on a desktop PC before user can access using his/her mobile device.

The Steps

Before we dive into our application, let's review the steps of our design and development work, which will be used in Chapters 12 through 14.

1. **Requirements**   Define the requirements and features of our application.

2. **Planning**   Identify all the elements and dependencies of our application and plan for implementation.

3. **Development**   Implement the application based on the requirements.

4. **Results**   Review the actual results of our application on your player or device.

5. **Enhancement**   Discuss possible enhancements and modifications, including extension to other applications and use cases.

Requirements

We will briefly describe the requirements from a developer standpoint. This includes the application, the clients (for example, compact HTML browser), the servers (such as ColdFusion MX), the data sources (like RDBMS), and other technologies (Where2Net daVinci Studio Tool, for instance).

Application

Our mobile and multichannel application has the following features:

▶ It runs against a relational database for user login, data storage for user profiles, transactions, and game bottle caps or game cards (we will use game caps and game cards interchangeably hereafter).

▶ It runs as an XML-based application that can generate various markup pages, including HTML, WML, and cHTML.

▶ It runs as a stand-alone SWF file or Projector file, or as an embedded file within an HTML page for devices that support Macromedia Flash.

▶ It runs on a desktop PC, WAP phone, Palm PDA (via cHTML), Pocket PC (via Flash or cHTML), or Nokia Communicator. The user interface should be different for different form factors and markups.

▶ It is capable of detecting device, protocol, and Flash Player automatically and serving the relevant content (data or page).

Clients: Browsers, Micro-Browsers, and Flash Player

Our application will support a plethora of devices and client browsers. For PC browsers, the HTML pages served will work on both Internet Explorer and Netscape Navigator. For WAP browsers, the WML pages created would be compatible with WML 1.2 or later. To support Palm PDAs and Pocket PCs without Flash Player, we will deliver compact HTML pages for their display upon detection. For those devices equipped with Flash Player, we will serve up the SWF file. In the case of markup channels, the application metaphor will be page-based. In the case of Flash channels, we will simply exchange data with the Flash application through Flash Remoting, ColdFusion MX, or another mid-tier infrastructure, which does not necessarily involve serving up a new page.

Tools and Technologies

In developing this application, we will use the following tools and technologies:

▶ **The Flash MX authoring environment**   The Flash MX tool will be used for developing the client-side interface or the end user interface. It will communicate with back-end servers (ColdFusion MX) using Flash Remoting.

▶ **Flash Players**   Relevant Flash clients for Nokia Communicator, Pocket PC, and desktop PC will be supported.

▶ **ColdFusion MX and Flash Remoting**   ColdFusion MX will be used to work with XML files and CF custom tags to perform XSLT transformations. Flash Remoting will be used to communicate between Flash Player and ColdFusion MX.

▶ **Where2Net daVinci Studio or other XML toolkits**   daVinci Studio or other XML integrated development environments can be used to create XML files and provide different style sheets. The XML files will be transformed into the relevant markup pages by applying the correct style sheet(s).

▶ **Browsers, Simulators, and Mobile Devices**   Different HTML, WML, and cHTML browsers are needed for testing and receipt of the markup pages. Simulators and emulators, like a WML browser simulator, can be downloaded at the Openwave web site (**http://www.openwave.com**), while a compact HTML browser can be downloaded at the Microsoft web site (**http://www.microsoft.com**).

Servers: ColdFusion MX

We will use the ColdFusion MX application server to deliver the application as the middle-tier interface between the Flash and non-Flash devices and our application logic and database. A developer version of the ColdFusion server can be downloaded at: **http://www.macromedia.com**.

Likewise, you can use Java-based servers like IBM WebSphere, BEA Systems WebLogic, Sun iPlanet, or Oracle9iAS, to deliver the business logic. Of course, Microsoft .NET will be the other side of the coin if your organization adopts the .NET platform.

Relational Databases

You can build the m-Promotion application with an Oracle database (for instance, version 8.1.6), Microsoft SQL Server 2000, or even Microsoft Access 2000, since the application will be using generic SQL queries. Nonetheless, some minor differences in syntax may still exist. Here, we follow two major steps—setting up the database and writing the ColdFusion code for the native application. We'll show you the data tables built for MS Access later.

Dependent Technology

There are no dependencies for this core m-Promo application.

Planning

Before we start writing our first line of code, we will plan what our user interface would look like and where the content is displayed. This would include creating mockups of the application for the desktop PC, Nokia Communicator, and Pocket PC. We will also partition the amount of work to be done in client-side ActionScript, as well as that done in server-side ColdFusion MX.

Page Layout

The next step in our design process is to create mockups of the application user interface for each of the form factors (desktop PC, Nokia Communicator, PDAs, mobile phone, and Pocket PC). We've made the following assumptions:

▶ **Desktop PC without Flash Player**   The screen size can be 800 pixels by 600 pixels (width × height) or larger. We simply serve up HTML pages individually, not using HTML frames.

▶ **Mobile Phone with WML Browser**   The WAP phone will adhere to the Openwave 5.1 Simulator form factor. There will be no positional layout.

▶ **PDAs with cHTML Browser**   Again, we will stay with Microsoft simulator for the compact HTML browser. There will be no positional layout.

▶ **Desktop PC with Flash Player** Our stage is 800 pixels by 600 pixels (width × height) and can run as a stand-alone SWF file or Projector file (EXE), or an embedded file within an HTML page.

▶ **Nokia Communicator** The SWF file will run in full-screen mode at 640 pixels by 200 pixels (width × height).

▶ **Pocket PC** The HTML page will run the embedded SWF file at 230 pixels by 250 pixels (width × height).

The mockup for the Nokia Communicator is shown next. In this form factor, we have an additional frame to display the game card (or cap) status or account information for the user.

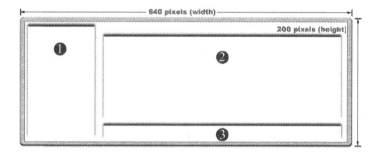

The mockup for the Pocket PC is shown next. Similar to the Nokia, the Pocket PC's smaller form factor has additional frames so as to display the game card or account information for the user. We've kept the navigation on the first frame.

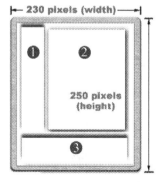

Similar approaches can be taken for all other form factors. Since we are mainly discussing a Flash MX application running on mobile devices, we have focused on the Nokia Communicator and Pocket PC form factors.

Data Flow

Content areas for the stage are populated as follows:

▶ **Brewery or Promotional Logo** Beer bottle logo and branding, and promotional campaign name.

▶ **Main Content area** Game cap information, balance, and code points.

▶ **Navigation** User chooses to enter "Enter Game Code," "Check Balance," and other areas.

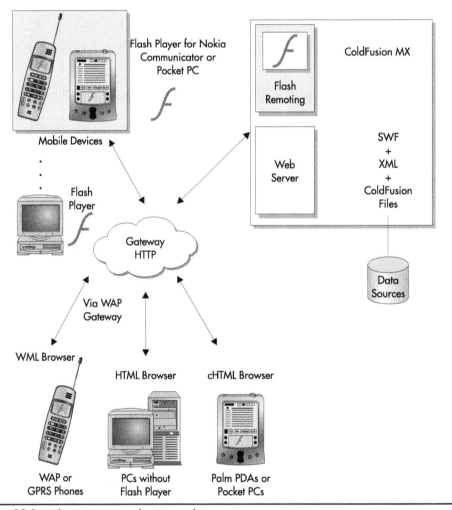

Figure 12-1 *The m-Promo application architecture*

Figure 12-1 shows the basic architecture of our m-Promo application. The ColdFusion MX server acts as the middle-tier server between the multitude of client devices, with or without Flash Player, and the back-end database, XML, and ColdFusion files, XSLT style sheets, ColdFusion custom tags, Flash SWFs, and other components.

Development

Given the requirements, page layouts, and approach discussed in the previous sections, let's start creating the data tables and ColdFusion MX components that will be called to execute XSLT transforms and deliver Flash MX applications to the client.

Data Tables

To create mobile and multichannel promotional applications, you must utilize an RDBMS and create the data tables. With MS Access, you can build these tables by entering the data, or porting them from other sources, like MS Excel. If you are using enterprise RDBMS, you can write code to issue queries with and generate the results for your tables (for instance, use Java code to populate Oracle9*i* Database). In the latter case, you will need to execute the SQL statements to define the schema and populate the tables with data for testing.

The database tables used are as follows (see the next illustration for MS Access):

▶ tblMembers

▶ tblTransactCodes

▶ tblTransactions

▶ tblWinningCards

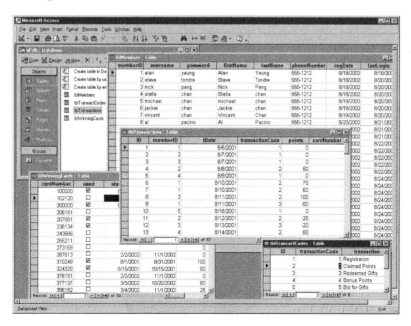

Each member (user) is profiled in a table called *tblMembers*. This table contains the following items:

▶ **memberID**   Unique number identifier of each member of the loyalty and promotion program (for example, 043)

▶ **username**   Username of each member (for example, topdog)

▶ **password**   Password for each member account (for example, topPass123)

▶ **firstName**   First or given name of the member (for example, John)

▶ **lastName**   Last or family name of the member (for example, Smith)

▶ **phoneNumber**   Mobile or fixed line phone number of the member (for example, 4155551212)

▶ **regDate**   Date and time of the member's registration (for example, 08/19/2002 1:42:23 PM)

▶ **lastLogin**   Date and time of the member's latest login (for example, 09/23/2002 11:02:30 PM)

The *tblTransactCodes* table defines the types of user or system transactions allowed in the program. It contains the following items:

▶ **id**   Unique identifier for each transaction code (for example, 1, ...5)

▶ **transactionCode**   Code number for each transaction (for example, 0, 1, ...5)

▶ **transaction**   Name or type of transaction (for example, Claimed Points)

The *tblTransactions* table records and contains all the transactions that took place for the entire m-Promotion campaign. It consists of the following items:

▶ **id**   Unique identifier for each transaction (for example, 12)

▶ **memberID**   Identifier of the owner of this region (for example, 1110)

▶ **tDate**   Date and time of transaction of the user (for example, 12/31/2002 4:02:11 PM)

▶ **transactionCode**   Code number for each transaction (for example, 0, 1, ...5)

▶ **points**   The number of points related to the transaction (for example, 30)

▶ **cardNumber**   Identifier of the game card used for the transaction (for example, 377123)

The vital information related to the winning or valid game cards is contained in the *tblWinningCards* table, which consists of these items:

▶ **cardNumber**   Identifier of the game card (for example, 377123)

▶ **used**   Identifier denoting whether the game card has been used (for example, Yes or No)

▶ **startDate**   Starting date when the game card becomes valid (for example, 8/1/2002)

▶ **endDate**   Date after which the game card is no longer valid (for example, 12/31/2002)

▶ **points**   The number of points awarded for this game card (for example, 100)

XML/XSLT Transformation

Here, we create pages and applications via a WYSIWYG design environment. You can select and add objects (for example, images, menus, and text) to the page. We've used daVinci Studio to create scripts and XML files. During run time, your application server—in this case, ColdFusion MX—can execute these scripts, and the server performs an XML transformation to serve up the content tailored to the form factor and browser required by the requesting device. An example of the XSLT style sheet used for transforming the login XML file into WML markup page (as viewed using Microsoft IE browser) is shown next:

```
N:\CFusionMX\wwwroot\eP\XSL\wml\wmllogin.xsl - Microsoft Internet Explorer

File   Edit   View   Favorites   Tools   Help      Send

<?xml version="1.0" ?>
- <xsl:stylesheet xmlns:xsl="http://www.w3.org/1999/XSL/Transform"
    xmlns:w2n="http://www.where2net.com/davinci" exclude-result-prefixes="w2n" version="1.0">
    <xsl:output method="xml" omit-xml-declaration="yes" />
 - <xsl:template match="/">
  -- <wml>
   - <head>
       <meta http-equiv="Cache-Control" content="no-cache" forua="true" />
      </head>
   -- <card>
       <xsl:apply-templates select="//w2n:Object[w2n:ObjectName = 'welcome']" />
       <xsl:apply-templates select="//w2n:Object[w2n:ObjectName = 'bottle']" />
       <xsl:apply-templates select="//w2n:Object[w2n:ObjectName = 'loginform']" />
       <xsl:apply-templates select="//w2n:Object[w2n:ObjectName = 'desc']" />
      </card>
     </wml>
    </xsl:template>
 - <xsl:template match="w2n:PageTitle">
     <xsl:value-of select="." />
   </xsl:template>
 - <xsl:template match="w2n:Object[w2n:ObjectName = 'welcome']">
  - <p>
   - <xsl:attribute name="align">
       <xsl:value-of select="w2n:ObjectProps/w2n:Property/w2n:PropName[. =
         'HAlign']/../w2n:PropValue" />
      </xsl:attribute>
   - <xsl:attribute name="mode">
       <xsl:value-of select="w2n:ObjectProps/w2n:Property/w2n:PropName[. =
         'WrapMode']/../w2n:PropValue" />
      </xsl:attribute>
       <xsl:value-of select="w2n:ObjectProps/w2n:Property/w2n:PropName[. =
         'AltText']/../w2n:PropValue" />
     </p>
    </xsl:template>
```

XML and Markup Code

We will now discuss the various ColdFusion XML pages. The XML/XSLT portion of the m-Promotion program contains seven pages:

- ▶ **index**   Home page of the m-Promotion web application
- ▶ **login**   Login page
- ▶ **getCardNum**   Obtains game card number
- ▶ **getBalance**   Retrieves point balance of the user's account
- ▶ **validateResult**   Page that verifies if game card is valid and not expired
- ▶ **addTranx**   Adds transaction results
- ▶ **showTranx**   Displays transaction results

There are also four other ColdFusion MX pages used for transactions and validation, but not for page display:

- ▶ **logout**   Confirmation page for logout
- ▶ **application**   Global CF page for custom tags and similar
- ▶ **validateLoginModule**   Module to verify if login is successful (username matches password)
- ▶ **validateCardModule**   Module to verify if game card is valid and unexpired

The ColdFusion MX server code for these pages does all the business logic processing in the background. These four pages will become ColdFusion components that get called as a Web service from the Flash MX client ActionScript for the Flash version of our m-Promo application. We'll discuss this more in the section titled, "Core ActionScript and ColdFusion Components" later in this chapter.

Device and Flash Player Detection

The device, browser, and Flash Player detection follows a certain sequence (see illustration that follows). We have made one decision on user experience: provide the rich Internet experience whenever the device can support it. For example, in the case of Pocket PC, we will force an embedded SWF file with the HTML instead of serving up cHTML if Flash Player is present. If not, cHTML will be served instead.

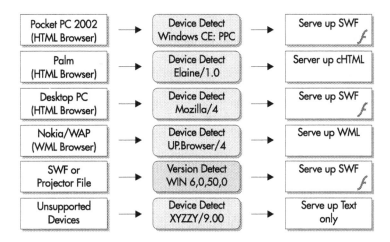

In general, we first determine what devices and browsers the client supports through the request header. Second, we determine if Flash Player is supported for that device. Third, SWF will be served for devices that should support it; otherwise their native markup formats will be served instead. These are all done using JavaScript, ColdFusion, and ActionScript. We have already discussed the device detection code and Flash Player version detection code in Chapters 9 and 10.

Session Management

Here, we use application.cfm to manage the session on the server and use a global ColdFusion variable to register that the user has already logged in. You can, of course, implement this differently. The code is simple, as shown next.

```
<cfapplication name="eP" clientmanagement="Yes"
    sessionmanagement="Yes" setclientcookies="Yes"
    sessiontimeout="20" applicationtimeout="60"
    clientstorage="Registry">
<cfset session.badLoginURL = "/eP/login.cfm">
<cfset session.goodLoginURL = "/eP/index.cfm">
<cfset session.LogInDSN = "ePdb">
<cfset session.LogInTable = "tblMembers">
<cfset session.LogInFieldUserID = "USERNAME">
<cfset session.LogInFieldPassword = "PASSWORD">
<cfset session.LogInFieldAdmin = "ADMIN">
<cfparam name="session.LogInMessage" default="">
```

Content Partitioning or Chunking

When the user requests information on recent transactions, we only deliver the most recent five to ten transactions based on the requesting device. If you are using PC browsers (with or without Flash Player), we deliver ten. If you are using mobile devices, we deliver information on five transactions at a time. We could, of course, have delivered more, but for usability reasons, we don't want a user to have to scroll down the page every time using the uncomfortable and unnatural keys on mobile devices.

With markup protocols, we deliver a new markup page every time. However, with Flash Player and ActionScript, we actually can deliver more than five transactions for mobile devices without the need to refresh.

Core ActionScript and ColdFusion Components

Having discussed the ColdFusion server-side code, we're now ready to show you the ActionScript required to build the front end of our m-Promo Flash MX application. To support our Flash MX application, we need to create a Web service out of our business logic so it can be called from the Flash MX client ActionScript.

The core Web services components are

- ▶ **validateLogin()**   Validates the user ID and password
- ▶ **getBalance()**   Gets the points balance of a validated user
- ▶ **getTransaction()**   Gets a history of all transactions performed by a validated user
- ▶ **getLoggedOut()**   Invalidates a user
- ▶ **getUserInfo()**   Gets the validated user's first name, last name, and member ID
- ▶ **getPoints()**   Checks code and the number of points associated with that code if valid

NOTE
We are using server-side session variables to keep track of a logged-in user.

The ColdFusion MX code for these components is shown next. It's pretty self-explanatory and is documented in the listing.

```
<cfcomponent>
    <cffunction access="remote" name="validateLogIn" output="false"
        returntype="string">
        <cfargument name="userid" type="string">
        <cfargument name="password" type="string">
        <CFQUERY datasource="#session.LogInDSN#" name="FindUser">
            SELECT *
            FROM #session.LogInTable#
            WHERE #session.LogInFieldUserID#='#userid#' AND
                  #session.LogInFieldPassword#='#password#'
        </CFQUERY>
```

```
      <cfif #FindUser.RecordCount# eq 0>
         <cfset session.loggedIn = 0>
         <cfreturn "invalid" />
      <cfelse>
         <cfset session.loggedIn = 1>
         <cfset session.firstName = #FindUser.firstName# >
         <cfset session.lastName = #FindUser.lastName#>
         <cfset session.memberID = #FindUser.memberID#>
         <cfreturn "valid" />
      </cfif>
</cffunction>
<cffunction access="remote" name="getBalance" output="false"
   returntype="string">
   <CFQUERY datasource="#session.LogInDSN#" name="FindUser">
      SELECT SUM(Points) AS Balance
      FROM tblTransactions
      WHERE memberID = #session.memberID#
   </CFQUERY>
   <cfoutput query="FindUser">
      <cfreturn #Balance# />
   </cfoutput>
</cffunction>
<cffunction access="remote" name="getTransactions" output="false"
   returntype="string">
   <CFQUERY datasource="#session.LogInDSN#" name="FindUser">
      SELECT *
      FROM tblMembers, tblTransactions, tblTransactCodes
      WHERE tblMembers.MemberID = tblTransactions.MemberID
         AND tblTransactions.TransactionCode =
            tblTransactCodes.TransactionCode
         AND tblMembers.MemberID = #session.memberID#
      ORDER BY TDate DESC
   </CFQUERY>
   <cfset htmlResult = "">
   <cfoutput query="FindUser">
      <cfset htmlResult = #htmlResult# & "[#TDate#] #Transaction#
         #Points#<br>">
   </cfoutput>
   <cfreturn #htmlResult# />
</cffunction>
<cffunction access="remote" name="getLoggedOut" output="false"
   returntype="string">
   <cfset session.loggedIn = 0>
   <cfreturn />
</cffunction>
<cffunction access="remote" name="getUserInfo" returntype="struct">
   <cfset structUserInfo = structnew()>
   <cfset structUserInfo.firstName = #session.firstName#>
   <cfset structUserInfo.lastName = #session.lastName#>
   <cfset structUserInfo.memberID = #session.memberID#>
```

```
            <cfreturn #structUserInfo# />
        </cffunction>
        <cffunction access="remote" name="getPoints" output="false"
            returntype="struct">
            <cfargument name="code" type="numeric" >
            <cfquery datasource="#session.LogInDSN#" name="checkNum" >
                SELECT points, endDate
                FROM tblWinningCards
                WHERE points > 50 AND endDate > now() AND startDate < now()
                    AND CardNumber = #code# AND used = 0
            </cfquery>
            <cfset structCardInfo = structnew()>
            <cfif #checkNum.RecordCount# eq 0>
                <cfset structCardInfo.points = "0">
                <cfset structCardInfo.endDate = "N/A">
            <cfelse>
                <cfset structCardInfo.points = #checkNum.points#>
                <cfset structCardInfo.endDate =
                    #DateFormat(checkNum.endDate,"mm/dd/yyyy")#>
            </cfif>
            <cfreturn #structCardInfo# />
        </cffunction>
</cfcomponent>
```

A component browser view is shown in the following illustration. These six methods will be called from our Flash MX client ActionScript.

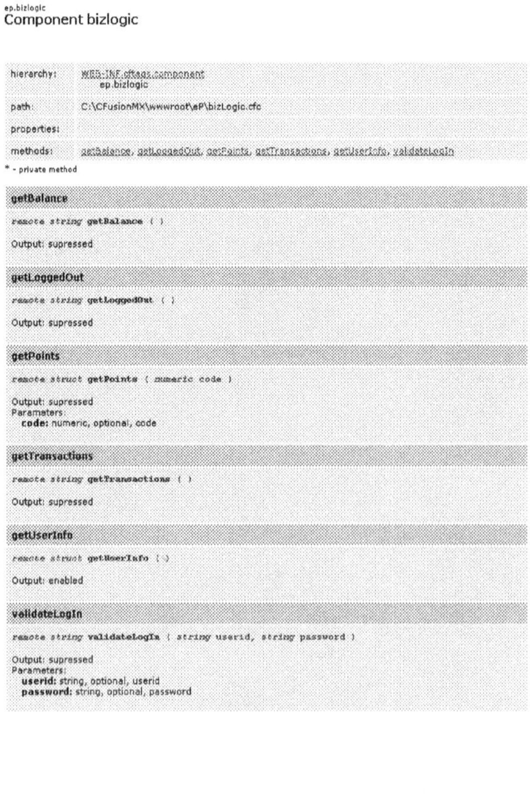

Now that we have our server-side code taken care of, let's describe our client-side ActionScript code. Our start page sets up Flash Remoting with our ColdFusion MX server.

```
#include "NetServices.as"
gatewayConnection = NetServices.createGatewayConnection
   ("http://localhost:8500/flashservices/gateway/");
EPflashService = gatewayConnection.getService("eP.bizLogic", this);
// global variables
gblPoints = "0";
gblEndDate = "N/A";
gblPointsMessage = "";
// buttons
buttonLogIn.onRelease = function (){
   EPflashService.validateLogIn(inUserid.text,inPassword.text);
}
function validateLogIn_Result(result)
{
   if (result == "valid" ) {
      goToAndStop("mainMenu");
   }
   else {
      errorMsg.text = "Invalid User ID or Password. Please try again.";
   }
}
stop();
```

As we move through the frames (see next section for details), we add simple code to handle the buttons and dynamic text. For example, in our main menu frame, we have ActionScript code to display the date and time plus user information (first name, last name, member ID).

```
buttonLogOut.onRelease = function (){
   EPflashService.getLoggedOut();
   goToAndStop("start");
}
function menuAction() {
   switch (listboxObj.getValue()){
      case 1:
         goToAndStop("checkCode");
         break;
      case 3:
         goToAndStop("accountInfo");
         break;
      default:
         goToAndStop("unimplemented");
   }
}
// get date
myDate =new Date();
strDate.text =((myDate.getMonth()+1) + "/" + myDate.getDate() + "/" +
   myDate.getFullYear());
```

```
// get day
myDay =new Date();
switch (myDay.getDay()){
   case 0:
       strDay.text = "Sunday";
       break;
   case 1:
       strDay.text = "Monday";
       break;
   case 2:
       strDay.text = "Tuesday";
       break;
   case 3:
       strDay.text = "Wednesday";
       break;
   case 4:
       strDay.text = "Thursday";
       break;
   case 5:
       strDay.text = "Friday";
       break;
   case 6:
       strDay.text = "Saturday";
       break;
}
// get time
myTime =new Date();
strTime.text =((myTime.getHours()+1) + ":" + myTime.getMinutes());
EPflashService.getUserInfo(result);
function getUserInfo_Result(result)
{
   strFirst.text = result.firstName;
   strLast.text = result.lastName;
   strID.text = result.memberID;
}
```

The rest of the frames only have minor ActionScript code added to handle the buttons. We will discuss the Flash UI components used next.

Flash UI Components

We have used mostly standard Flash UI components here with our design—dynamic text, input text, list boxes, and buttons. They are self-explanatory as most of the business logic is done on the server. We will focus only on the Nokia Communicator form factor for our Flash MX application example since this is the most common usage scenario: a mobile smartphone used in a bar or restaurant when dining or entertaining with friends. The only difference between this platform and that of the Pocket PC or desktop PC is the user interface. Otherwise, the business logic and Web service calls are identical.

Only six frames are involved in our Timeline (see following illustration).

▶ **start**   The login and start frame

▶ **mainMenu**   The first frame seen by a validated user showing menu choices

▶ **checkCode**   Checks to see if the code entered is correct and valid

▶ **accountInfo**   Shows the transaction history of a validated user

▶ **points**   Shows how many points are associated with a valid code

▶ **unimplemented**   A catch-all for future enhancements

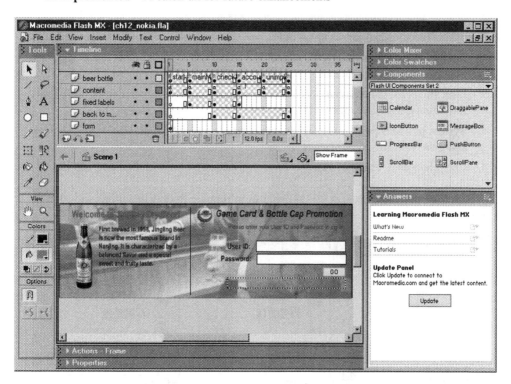

As shown in the ActionScript in the previous section, our application jumps between frames depending on the action chosen from the menu. From the **start** frame, the user logs in. On successful validation, the user is taken to the **mainMenu** frame. They can then choose one of

the menu actions and will be taken to the appropriate frames. For example, if he or she wants to check his or her account history, they will be taken to the **accountInfo** frame. All the dynamic content is served from the ColdFusion MX server via Flash Remoting back to the Flash MX client on the mobile device or desktop PC. The ActionScript only performs navigation and presentation; all the business logic is done on the remote server.

Results

We can now run our m-Promo mobile and multichannel application, either as an XML-based application via ColdFusion MX, a stand-alone Projector file (EXE) or an SWF file, or an HTML page with an embedded SWF file. The following is a typical user scenario.

1. User enters the URL to access the m-Promo home page. All devices use the *same* URL.

2. System prompts the user to log in. User enters a Username and a Password.

3. System accepts and serves up an index page (home page), which presents a menu.

4. User selects from the menu and can enter a game code to add points to his/her account or check the account balance.

5. User enters a Card Number. System accepts the game card number entry and checks for validity. System confirms validity or displays an error message.

6. System provides point results when game card is added to total. User acknowledges and gets real-time point balance.

7. User chooses to check transaction history. System returns with first five transactions.

The screen shots for a Pocket PC 2002 platform running Pocket IE follows (non-Flash, cHTML version):

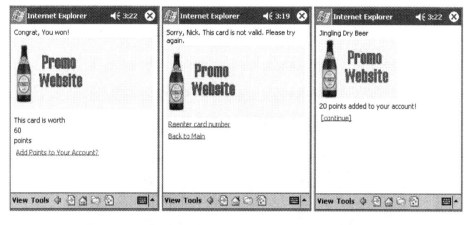

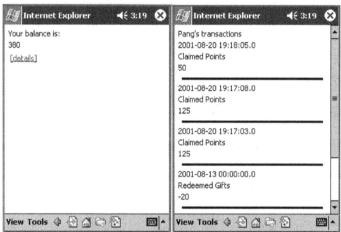

A sample set of screen shots for the Openwave 5.1 SDK Browser follows (non-Flash, WML version):

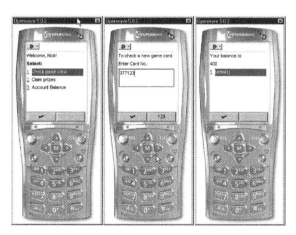

We will now move on to show you the Flash MX version of our application. We will show all the screens available, as this form factor is the most common scenario: mobile. The same could be said for the Pocket PC, which is a subset of the Nokia Communicator because of its smaller form factor. The login, welcome, or home page is shown next.

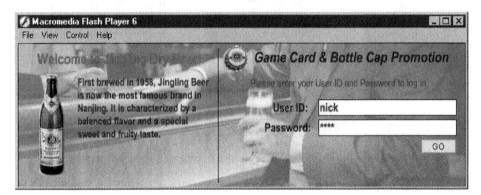

If the login is unsuccessful, the user will be shown an error message and asked to log in again, as shown next.

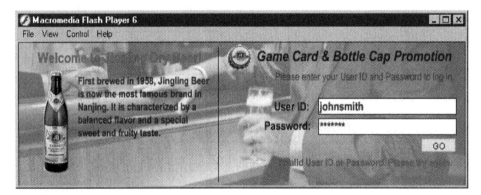

If the login is successful, the user will be taken to a menu frame, as shown next.

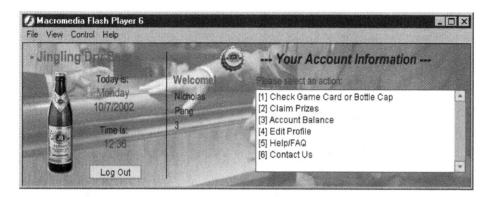

The menu frame is the main menu for user interaction. The menu can be made to be static or dynamic—we have chosen to make it static but have used a list box so that making it dynamic in the future can be easily done in ActionScript. When our Account Balance is shown, the following screen is shown:

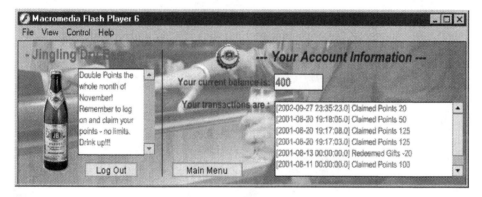

Let's check the code from a card or bottle cap next. Start by entering an invalid or expired code. The user will be told the code is invalid code and asked to try again (see next illustration).

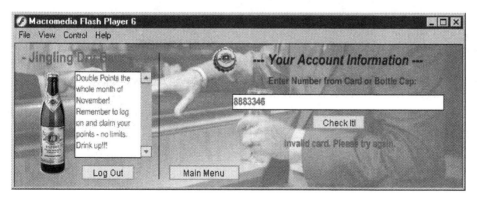

For a valid code, the user can redeem the game card or bottle cap by adding the points to his/her balance. The user can do so any time as long as the code is still valid (see illustration that follows). The user can, of course, wait for double points month (a dynamic promo) before redeeming it, if the validation date permits. Nonetheless, the user may not know if double points month will preceed the expiration date.

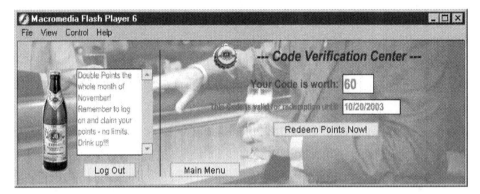

Finally, for unimplemented or coming-soon features, just put a placeholder there (see next illustration).

NOTE

We have allocated portions of the real estate for marketing messages as shown in some of the illustrations. You can also display images (JPEG format) or movie clips for a richer environment.

Enhancements

Many enhancements can be made to improve our application, including:

► **Two-Way SMS Access**   Create an additional access channel using widely available two-way SMS messaging. Send an SMS from any mobile phone with a short code, or simply send in the code, user ID, and password embedded in the message. The server will return with the appropriate response in which the user can interact with. For example, it will show you the points associated with a validated code. Additionally within the message, a user can choose to redeem the points or get their balance. Almost all mobile phones are capable of using this under-utilized channel.

► **Voice Access**   The ability to use any telephone—mobile or landline—to redeem points. Using Interactive Voice Response (IVR) technology and the phone keypad, the server can interact with a user. For example, the user can log in by speaking in his/her own voice or using the keypad on the phone. After being validated, the user can input the code and interact with the server to redeem points or get their balance. User interaction is similar to using a voice mail retrieval system.

► **Redeem Gifts from Other Partners**   We had discussed redeeming points for merchandise from the beverage manufacturer, but merchandise could also be from partners like Amazon, Sony, Nike, and so on. If certain demographics are targeted, the corresponding merchandise should reflect their taste. For example, if Coca-Cola has a promotion for its Cherry Coke, gifts could be targeted towards the appropriate age group (for example, 7 to 19) with merchandise from Sony, Nike, Nintendo, Microsoft, Good Guys, and so forth.

► **Buy Points**   Using a credit card, users can buy extra points in order to redeem a certain prize category or tier. This is common practice for hotel chains (for example, Hilton Hotels International) and airline companies' (such as United Airlines) frequent flyer programs.

► **Play Games**   Interactive games where a user can earn extra points by making it to certain levels or stages and picking up bonuses along the way. While playing these games, the user might be presented (subtly or subliminally) with marketing messages and new products.

Summary

In this chapter, we described in detail how to create a compelling mobile and multichannel application that can deliver both markup pages and Flash MX services! We leveraged the power of ColdFusion application server, XML/XSLT transformations, and utilized many of the new features of the Flash MX. We also showed how to detect channels, devices, protocols, and Flash Players. You can add more channels and optimize the user experience based on the device's capabilities.

The MP3 Flash Audio Player

IN THIS CHAPTER:

Introduction

Requirements

Planning

Development

Results

Enhancements

Summary

I n this chapter, we discuss the design and development of an MP3 Player that does more than just play audio—it enhances the Flash client found in your mobile device. We leverage the information stored within the MP3 binary file and use that to call Amazon.com's Web service to get the album details, then connect to a music database like FreeDB to get the song titles on that particular album. We conclude by suggesting several enhancements you can make to our core Flash MX application.

Introduction

MP3 stands for MPEG Audio Layer 3; MPEG being the acronym for Moving Picture Experts Group. All together that's quite a mouthful! MP3 is a compression technology popular for sharing, downloading, and transporting songs. By compressing raw song files (audio CD) into an MP3 file format, it becomes roughly ten times smaller than the original, with little or no loss in sound quality. The same amount of compact disc space used to store about ten uncompressed songs (~800MB) can now store over 100 MP3 songs. With portable MP3 players from Apple (see the following illustration) like the iPod with a 20GB hard disk (available for both Macintosh and Windows), you can store about 4000 songs or 300–400 CDs!

Major players like Creative Technology are also coming out with innovative MP3 players like the Nomad Jukebox 3 (see the next illustration) with a 40GB hard disk and 11 hours of playback on only a single battery charge!

Why Flash MP3 Player?

While these dedicated MP3 players deliver dynamic music to users, it poses a problem to many mobile users who also carry a mobile phone and PDA/Pocket PC. Instead of lugging along two or three handheld devices, wouldn't it be convenient if the personal digital assistant or mobile phone could also play MP3 music! As we'll discuss later, an audio enabled Flash Player can offer such additional benefits as this to all those road warriors out there who wish to combine business with pleasure.

Use Case

Let's start by building an MP3 player with Flash Player that can leverage distributed data sources and remote resources like Web services. For mobile users, not only can you listen to your favorite music while on the go, you can learn more about the titles, lyrics, and news surrounding it, not to mention where to buy the album, or others like it.

Playlists and Skins

Before we dive into the next step of our design, let's define what playlists and skins are, as you'll run into these digital music buzzwords sooner rather than later.

▶ **Playlist** A collection of songs to listen to. You can usually create custom playlists as well as categorize your favorite tunes by artist, genre, or other personal preference.

▶ **Skin** An interface for your music player. Canned or custom-designed skins can be applied to change the appearance of the player.

Enterprise Use

In the enterprise enhancement, the same "multimedia" client we built from Flash Player allows mobile conferencing, mobile training and support, as well as customer service. Suddenly, broadcasting corporate messages and demonstrating product features becomes truly dynamic and interactive! Now let's delve into what the Flash MP3 Player is all about!

Requirements

First, let's briefly describe the requirements from a developer's standpoint. These include the application, the client (for example, Flash Player 6), the servers (such as ColdFusion MX), the data sources (Web services, for instance), and other technologies (MP3 Players, for example).

The Application

Our Flash MX MP3 application has the following features:

▶ It runs as a stand-alone SWF file or Projector file, or embedded within an HTML page.

▶ It runs on a desktop PC, Nokia Communicator, or Pocket PC. (The user interface should be different for all three form factors.)

▶ It's capable of loading a playlist from an XML file on the server. A playlist is a list of musical selections for the application.

▶ It's capable of consuming Amazon.com Web service in order to get product details based on ID3 tags from the MP3 file.

▶ It's capable of interfacing with a free music database (like FreeDB) to obtain song titles for an album.

▶ It offers rudimentary audio controls like play, stop, and volume.

Clients: Flash Player

In order for our application to work, the end user must be using Flash Player 6.0r40 or later—whether it's a stand-alone Flash Player or an embedded Flash Player within an HTML page. Code can be added to detect the presence of Flash Player in the HTML or by using ActionScript for both the stand-alone or embedded Flash Player. The *Publish* settings of the Flash MX authoring tool can generate the appropriate HTML for the detection and automatic download of the latest Flash Player from Macromedia. Detection of the version number of the Flash Player must be done with ActionScript, however. In any case, the Flash MX application should still play the MP3 audio files on any version of Flash Player (the additional information won't be available).

Tools and Technologies

In developing this application, we'll use the following tools and technologies:

▶ **The Flash MX authoring environment**   The Flash MX authoring tool is used for developing the client-side or end-user interface. It communicates with back-end servers (ColdFusion MX, for instance) using Flash Remoting.

▶ **Flash Player 6**   As mentioned, FlashPlayer 6.0r40 or later can be used in a stand-alone format or embedded in an HTML page.

▶ **ColdFusion MX and Flash Remoting**   Using ColdFusion MX as our back-end server, we'll create ColdFusion components that can be called from ActionScript within Flash Player. These ColdFusion components will consume the Amazon.com Web services and pass the data to the Flash Player. We'll also interface with the FreeDB music web site and pass the data back to the Flash Player.

▶ **The Winamp 3.0 Player**   To edit ID3 tags within an MP3 file, we'll use the freeware, Winamp 3 Player (**http://www.winamp.com**), as a tool. It can handle both ID3v1 and ID3v2 tags (more on v1 and v2 tags later).

Servers: Remote

Our ColdFusion MX server will be the middle-tier interface between the Flash MX MP3 application and remote servers including the Amazon.com Web service and FreeDB web site. A free developer token or license is required to use the Amazon.com Web service. You can apply for one at **https://associates.amazon.com/exec/panama/associates/join/developer/application.html.**

Dependent Technology

Our fully-featured Flash MX application will have only these dependencies:

▶ Amazon.com Web service consumption

▶ FreeDB web site search results

▶ ID3 tags within MP3 binary files

We'll go into more detail on these dependencies next.

The Amazon.com Web Service

With the Amazon.com Web service, you can do the following:

▶ Search for Amazon.com products using any search parameter—such as keywords, author, artist, or ASIN (unique Amazon.com Standard Item Number). In this core Flash application, we'll only use the keywords search method to find the matching album for the MP3 song that is playing.

▶ Add items to an Amazon.com Shopping Cart, Wish List, or Gift Registry.

▶ Access the Amazon.com Web service through either SOAP or XML over HTTP. We'll illustrate how to do it using the SOAP protocol in ColdFusion MX.

The FreeDB Search

The FreeDB web site has an advance search page at **http://www.freedb.org/freedb_search .php** that allows you to specify artist, album title, song name (or track), or a genre to search for. It returns a list of albums in HTML format that match the search criteria. Since there is currently no Web service available from FreeDB, we'll need to parse the HTML results on the web page to retrieve the content. Fortunately, there is a custom ColdFusion tag available, courtesy of MaxFusion (**http://www.maxfusion.co.uk/tags.cfm**). They provide a set of tags that will assist in querying the free version of the CDDB database. The original CDDB is a database to look up CD information using the Internet. With this custom tag, the result of the music search is returned as a query named *AlbumList*.

MP3 ID3 tags

Embedded within every MP3 v1 and v2 binary file is a set of tags (ID3 tags). ID3 tag information may be stored at the beginning or end of an MP3 file. By having access to MP3 song properties, we can leverage that information and complement our MP3 Flash Audio Player with additional features. The entire song must be loaded for the ID3 properties to be available. Once the MP3 file has been completely loaded into the Sound object, you can access the following properties:

- ▶ id3.songname
- ▶ id3.artist
- ▶ id3.album
- ▶ id3.year
- ▶ id3.comment
- ▶ id3.track
- ▶ id3.genre

Besides artist name, album title, release date, comments, track, and genre, available information also includes copyright data, and an encapsulated thumbnail image.

NOTE

The value of genre is an integer, not a name. To use a genre name instead of an integer for the genre property value, you can embed the genre lookup table into the ActionScript of your movie. More details about this can be found in the section titled "Development" later in this chapter

There are actually two variants of the ID3 specification: ID3v1 and ID3v2, and while the potential differences between them are great, virtually all modern MP3 players can handle files with tags in either format. Not only are ID3v2 tags capable of storing a lot more information than ID3v1 tags, but they appear at the *beginning* of the bitstream, rather than at the *end*. This allows for streaming broadcast with servers like the Flash Communication Server. You can display all of this information throughout the duration of the track, not at the end.

It's unfortunate ID3 tags ended up being tagged on the end of MP3 files to begin with. This is one of the reasons why the entire song must be loaded in the Flash MX client for the ID3 properties to be available in your ActionScript.

A new feature available to ActionScript coders with Flash Player 6 version 40 (for example, 6.0r40) and later is its support for MP3 playback and access to ID3 tag properties without having to write native programs. Given its support of MP3 files with ID3 v1.0 and v1.1 tags, you can use Flash Player to retrieve ID3 tag properties from a sound object when an MP3 sound containing an ID3v1 tag has been loaded using the attachSound() or loadSound() method. If a sound does not contain an ID3v1 tag, the ID3 properties will be undefined.

NOTE

Users must have Flash Player 6.0r40 or later in order for the ID3 properties to function. More details about detecting this in the section titled "Development" later in this chapter.

Planning

Before writing our first line of code, we must decide what our user interface will look like and where the content should be displayed. This calls for creating mockups of the application for the desktop PC, Nokia Communicator, and Pocket PC. We'll also partition the amount of work done in client-side ActionScript as well as that done in server-side ColdFusion MX.

Page Layout

Mockups of the application user interface for each of the form factors (desktop PC, Nokia Communicator, and Pocket PC) follow. We've made the following assumptions:

▶ **Desktop PC** With a stage of 800 pixels × 600 pixels (width × height), it can be run as a stand-alone SWF file or Projector file, or as an embedded file within an HTML page.

▶ **Nokia Communicator** The SWF file will run in a full-screen mode of 640 pixels × 200 pixels (width × height).

▶ **Pocket PC** The HTML page will run the embedded SWF file with a mode of 230 pixels × 250 pixels (width × height).

A self-explanatory mockup of the desktop PC stage is shown in Figure 13-1 with the various content and control areas labeled.

The mockup for the Nokia Communicator is shown next. In this form factor, we have an additional frame to display the songs on the album.

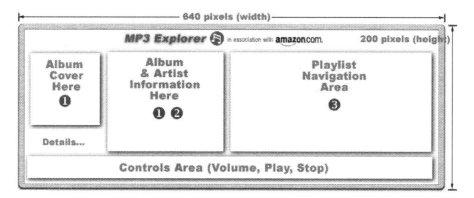

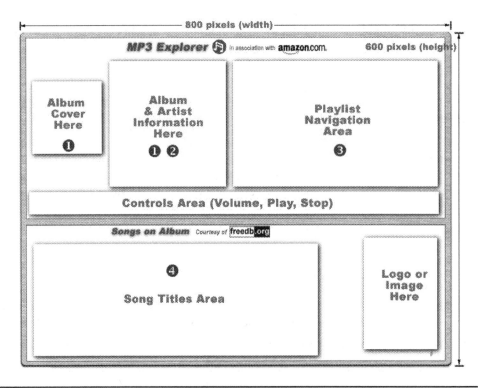

Figure 13-1   *The desktop PC MP3 Flash application*

The mockup for the Pocket PC is shown next. Similar to the Nokia's smaller form factor, the Pocket PC has additional frames to display the songs on the album, as well as the details of each tune. We have kept the navigation on the first frame.

Data Flow

Content areas for the stage (again, shown in Figure 13-1) are populated as follows (corresponding to numbers in the figure):

1. **The Amazon.com Web service**   The album cover, availability, record label, release date, price, and sales rank.
2. **MP3 ID3 tags ActionScript**   Artist name, album name, song name, and genre.
3. **Playlist XML file**   Tree display component showing a playlist. Resides on the web server.
4. **FreeDB web site**   Song titles on album.

Figure 13-2 shows the basic architecture of our MP3 application. The ColdFusion MX server acts as the middle-tier server between the Flash Player and the web services, databases, and XML files.

The Flash MX client will invoke the ColdFusion components as a Web service call from within ActionScript. A ColdFusion wrapper will be created to make the calls to Amazon.com and FreeDB.

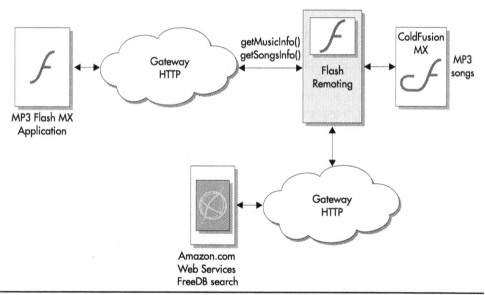

Figure 13-2   *The MP3 application architecture*

Development

Given the requirements, page layouts, and approach as detailed in the previous sections, let's start creating the ColdFusion components that will be called from the Flash MX client to indirectly invoke the external servers and services from Amazon.com and FreeDB.

The Amazon.com Web Service

Before using Amazon.com's Web service, you need to apply for a developer's token. The URL is **https://associates.amazon.com/exec/panama/associates/join/developer/application.html**. Accept the terms and conditions as specified and you'll receive your developer's token in seconds. For our example, we will use DEV01234567890 as the developer token—please replace this with your "*live*" developer token when trying out the examples.

To consume the Amazon.com Web service, we have the following ColdFusion code:

```
<cfscript>
   structKeyWordSearchRequest = StructNew();
   StructInsert(structKeyWordSearchRequest, "devtag","DEV01234567890");
   StructInsert(structKeyWordSearchRequest, "keyword",artist & " " & album);
   StructInsert(structKeyWordSearchRequest, "mode","music");
   StructInsert(structKeyWordSearchRequest, "page",1);
   StructInsert(structKeyWordSearchRequest, "tag","2launch-20");
   StructInsert(structKeyWordSearchRequest, "type","heavy");
   StructInsert(structKeyWordSearchRequest, "version",1.0);
</cfscript>
<cfinvoke
   webservice="http://soap.amazon.com/schemas/AmazonWebServices.wsdl"
   method="keywordSearchRequest"
   returnvariable="structProductInfo">
   <cfinvokeargument name="keywordSearchRequest"
      value="#structKeyWordSearchRequest#"/>
</cfinvoke>
```

The <cfscript> sets up the input parameters required to consume the Amazon.com Web service. Most of them are static except for the *keyword* parameter, which consists of the *artist* and *album* name—both processed by the ActionScript after an MP3 song is loaded into the Sound object.

After consuming the Amazon.com Web service with the keyword search request, we can process the result, extract the required content, and pass the data back to the Flash MX client using a data structure. The code listing is as follows:

```
<cfset structMusicInfo = structnew()>
<cfset structMusicInfo.imageURLMedium =
   #structProductInfo.Details[1].getImageURLMedium()#>
<cfset structMusicInfo.releaseDate =
   #structProductInfo.Details[1].getReleaseDate()#>
<cfset structMusicInfo.ourPrice =
```

```
   #structProductInfo.Details[1].getOurPrice()#>
<cfset structMusicInfo.manufacturer =
   #structProductInfo.Details[1].getManufacturer()#>
<cfset structMusicInfo.availability =
   #structProductInfo.Details[1].getAvailability()#>
<cfset structMusicInfo.album =
   #structProductInfo.Details[1].getProductName()#>
<cfset structMusicInfo.availability =
   #structProductInfo.Details[1].getAvailability()#>
<cfset structMusicInfo.salesRank =
   #structProductInfo.Details[1].getSalesRank()#>
<cfset structMusicInfo.amznASIN =
   #structProductInfo.Details[1].getASIN()#>
```

To finish this up, we wrap the preceding code with <cffunction> to create a ColdFusion component and make the *getMusicInfo* method available.

```
<cfcomponent>
   <cffunction access="remote" name="getMusicInfo" returntype="struct">
      <cfargument name="artist" type="string">
      <cfargument name="album" type="string">
   </cffunction>

   // insert cfscript, cfinvoke, and cfset here

   <cfreturn #structMusicInfo# />
</cfcomponent>
```

Save the preceding code into a file named *amzn.cfc* in an area of your web server directory like C:\CFusionMX\wwwroot. To quickly test this component, use the following ColdFusion code fragment and save it into a file named *test_amzncfc.cfm* in your web server directory.

```
<cfinvoke
   webservice="http://localhost:8500/amzn.cfc?wsdl"
   method="getMusicInfo"
   returnvariable="aStructure">
   <cfinvokeargument name="artist" value="marc anthony"/>
   <cfinvokeargument name="album" value="mended"/>
</cfinvoke>
<cfdump var="#aStructure#">
```

You should see something like this image display on a web browser.

struct	
ALBUM	Mended
AMZNASIN	B000063209
AVAILABILITY	Available
IMAGEURLMEDIUM	http://images.amazon.com/images/P/B000063209.01.MZZZZZZZ.jpg
MANUFACTURER	Sony
OURPRICE	$13.49
RELEASEDATE	21 May, 2002
SALESRANK	361

By making sure our component is functioning correctly using ColdFusion test code, we've removed the need to debug it within the Flash MX client using ActionScript.

The FreeDB Search

The FreeDB version of the CDDB is searchable via MaxFusion's *freedb* custom tags. The main custom tag file, *freedb.cfm*, is listed next.

```
<!-- This will return a query called "AlbumList" with the columns:
    CAT, DISCID and TITLE
-->
<CFHTTP
    url="http://www.freedb.org/freedb_search.php?words=
    #Replace(Attributes.Searchstring,'','+','ALL')#&allfields=NO&
    fields=title&fields=artist&allcats=NO&grouping=cats&cats=misc&
    cats=blues&cats=classical&cats=country&cats=data&cats=folk&
    cats=jazz&cats=newage&cats=reggae&cats=rock&cats=soundtrack"
    method="GET" resolveurl="false">
</CFHTTP>
<CFSET MyText=cfhttp.filecontent>
<CFSET MyStart=1>
<CFSET MyCount=0>
<CFSET myQuery = QueryNew("Cat, DiscID, Title")>
<CFIF Find('A lot of matches found',MyText,1)>
    <CFSET TooMany="Yes">
<CFELSE>
    <CFSET TooMany="No">
</CFIF>
<CFLOOP
condition="Find('freedb_search_fmt.php?cat=',Mytext,MyStart)">
    <CFSET S1=Find('freedb_search_fmt.php?cat=',MyText,MyStart)+26>
    <CFSET E1=Find('&id=',MyText,S1)>
```

```
   <CFSET Cat=Mid(MyText,S1,E1-S1)>
   <CFSET S2=E1+4>
   <CFSET E2=Find('">',MyText,S2)>
   <CFSET DiscID=Mid(MyText,S2,E2-S2)>
   <CFSET S3=E2+2>
   <CFSET E3=Find('</a>',MyText,S3)>
   <CFSET Title=Mid(MyText,S3,E3-S3)>
   <CFSET MyCount = MyCount + 1>
   <CFSET newRow  = QueryAddRow(MyQuery, 1)>
   <CFSET temp = QuerySetCell(myQuery, "Cat", "#Cat#", MyCount)>
   <CFSET temp = QuerySetCell(myQuery, "DiscID", "#DiscID#",
MyCount)>
   <CFIF Len(Title) NEQ 22>
      <CFSET temp = QuerySetCell(myQuery, "Title", "#Title#",
Mycount)>
      <CFSET LastTitle=Title>
   <CFELSE>
      <CFSET temp = QuerySetCell(myQuery, "Title", "#LastTitle#",
Mycount)>
   </CFIF>
   <CFSET MyStart=E3>
</CFLOOP>
<CFSET Caller.AlbumList=MyQuery>
<CFSET Caller.TooMany="#TooMany#">
```

From the *AlbumList*, we get the *DISCID* and *CAT* cross-reference to find the songs on that album from the CDDB database.

```
<CFHTTP
   url="http://www.freedb.org/freedb_search_fmt.php?cat=#Attributes.Cat#&
   id=#Attributes.DiscID#" method="GET" resolveurl="false">
</CFHTTP>
<CFSET MyText=cfhttp.filecontent>
<CFSET MyStart=1>
<CFSET MyCount=0>
<CFSET myQuery = QueryNew("TrackID, TrackTitle, TrackLength")>
<CFSET StartString = '</td><td valign=top>'>
<CFSET TS1=Find('<h2>',MyText,MyStart)+4>
<CFSET TE1=Find('</h2>',MyText,TS1)>
<CFSET DiscTitle=Mid(MyText,TS1,TE1-TS1)>
<CFLOOP condition="Find('#StartString#',Mytext,MyStart)">
   <CFSET S2=Find('#StartString#',Mytext,MyStart)+20>
   <CFSET E2=Find('</td><td><b>',MyText,S2)>
   <CFSET TrackLength=Mid(MyText,S2,E2-S2)>
   <CFSET S1=Find('</td><td><b>',MyText,MyStart)+12>
   <CFSET E1=Find('</b>',MyText,S1)>
   <CFSET TrackTitle=Mid(MyText,S1,E1-S1)>
```

```
    <CFSET MyCount = MyCount + 1>
    <CFSET newRow  = QueryAddRow(MyQuery, 1)>
    <CFSET temp = QuerySetCell(myQuery, "TrackId", "#MyCount#", MyCount)>
    <CFSET temp = QuerySetCell(myQuery, "TrackTitle", "#TrackTitle#",
        MyCount)>
    <CFSET temp = QuerySetCell(myQuery, "TrackLength", "#TrackLength#",
        MyCount)>
    <CFSET MyStart=E1>
</CFLOOP>
<CFSET Caller.DiscTitle=Disctitle>
<CFSET Caller.TrackList=MyQuery>
```

We have added ColdFusion code wrappers around this custom tag to make it a Web service that can be invoked from the Flash MX client. The code is listed next. We call the *freedb* custom tag followed by the *xmcd* custom tag.

```
<cfcomponent>
    <cffunction access="remote" name="getSongsInfo"
            output="false" returntype="string">
        <cfargument name="artist" type="string">
        <cfargument name="album" type="string">
        <cf_freedb searchstring="#album# #artist#">
        <cfif AlbumList.RecordCount GT 0>
            <cfoutput query="AlbumList" maxrows="1">
                <cf_xmcd cat="#CAT#" discid="#DISCID#">
            </cfoutput>
            <cfset htmlResult = "">
            <cfoutput query="TrackList">
                <cfset htmlResult = #htmlResult# & "#TRACKTITLE# -
                    #TRACKLENGTH# [#TRACKID#]<br>">
            </cfoutput>
        <cfelse>
            <cfset htmlResult = "Sorry No Song List Available...">
        </cfif>
        <cfreturn #htmlResult# />
    </cffunction>
</cfcomponent>
```

NOTE

We are returning an HTML string to the Flash MX client from a getSongsInfo Web service consumption.

Finally, we will quickly test this component using the following ColdFusion code fragment and save it to a file named *test_freedbcfc.cfm* in our web server directory.

```
<cfinvoke
    webservice="http://localhost:8500/freedb.cfc?wsdl"
```

```
   method="getSongsInfo"
   returnvariable="HTMLString">
      <cfinvokeargument name="artist" value="marc anthony"/>
      <cfinvokeargument name="album" value="mended"/>
</cfinvoke>
<cfdump var="#HTMLString#">
```

You should see something like this image display on a web browser.

```
Love Won't Get Any Better - 3:39 [1]
She Mends Me - 3:18 [2]
I've Got You - 3:52 [3]
I Need You - 4:13 [4]
Tragedy - 4:10 [5]
I Reach For You - 3:27 [6]
I Swear - 3:47 [7]
Don't Tell Me It's Love - 3:36 [8]
Do You Believe In Loneliness - 4:05 [9]
Give Me A Reason - 3:12 [10]
I Wanna Be Free - 3:59 [11]
Everything You Do - 3:24 [12]
Te Tengo Aquí - 3:51 [13]
Me Haces Falta - 3:52 [14]
Tragedia - 3:46 [15]
```

Again, by making sure our component is functioning correctly using ColdFusion test code, we've removed the need to debug it within the Flash MX client using ActionScript.

The ActionScript Core

The main ActionScript that is core to this application is shown next.

```
#include "NetServices.as"
gatewayConnection = NetServices.createGatewayConnection(
   "http://localhost:8500/flashservices/gateway/");

// set up to get album info from Amazon.com
AMZNflashService = gatewayConnection.getService("amzn", this);
// set up to get song titles from freeDB CDDB
FREEDBflashService = gatewayConnection.getService("freedb", this);

// called after song is loaded and ID3 tags determined
AMZNflashService.getMusicInfo(myTrack.id3.artist,myTrack.id3.album);
FREEDBflashService.getSongsInfo(myTrack.id3.artist,myTrack.id3.album);
```

The two service calls to our ColdFusion components will populate the entire dynamic content on the stage after the artist name and album are determined (see the section titled "ActionScript MP3 ID3" later in this chapter).

On a successful Web service call, the content areas are populated as shown in the following listings:

```
// populate album information including album cover
function getMusicInfo_Result(result)
{
   _root.imgObj.removeMovieClip(); // remove old album cover
   _root.createEmptyMovieClip("imgObj",9); // create empty movie
   _root.imgObj._x=25; // x-coordinate of album cover
   _root.imgObj._y=90; // y-coordinate of album cover
   imagePath = result.imageURLMedium; // medium size album image
   _root.imgObj.loadMovie(imagePath);
   amazonPrice.text = result.ourPrice; // price
   avail.text = result.availability; // availability
   label.text = result.manufacturer; // label name
   releaseDate.text = result.releaseDate; // release date
   salesRank.text = result.salesRank; // sales ranks
   albumASIN = result.amznASIN; // unique item number
   ASIN.text = albumASIN;
}


// populate song titles - result is already in HTML
function getSongsInfo_Result(result)
{
   dtHTML.htmlText = result; // load song titles onto stage
}
```

ActionScript MP3 ID3

So far, we've only shown you the ColdFusion server-side code. Now we're ready to outline the ActionScript required to build the front end of our MP3 Flash MX application. To start off, we'll show you the ActionScript code snippet to load an MP3 song, play it, and obtain the properties from its ID3 tags.

```
// create new sound object
myTrack = new Sound();
//
myTrack.loadSound(this.sampleUrl, false);
//
myTrack.start();
// make sure song is loaded before querying properties
if((myTrack.getBytesLoaded() == myTrack.getBytesTotal())
     && myTrack.duration > 0)
   {
   // get song properties from ID3 tags
```

```
artistName.text = myTrack.id3.artist;
albumName.text = myTrack.id3.album;
songName.text = myTrack.id3.songname;
genre.text = id3_genre[myTrack.id3.genre];
}
```

Note that since the *genre* is a numeric value, we have used ActionScript code to populate a static array in order to do a direct lookup.

```
id3_genre = new Array(
    "Blues", "Classic Rock", "Country", "Dance", "Disco", "Funk",
    "Grunge", "Hip-Hop", "Jazz", "Metal", "New Age", "Oldies", "Other",
    "Pop", "R&B", "Rap", "Reggae", "Rock", "Techno", "Industrial",
    "Alternative", "Ska", "Death Metal", "Pranks", "Soundtrack",
    "Euro-Techno", "Ambient", "Trip-Hop", "Vocal", "Jazz+Funk", "Fusion",
    "Trance", "Classical", "Instrumental", "Acid", "House", "Game",
    "Sound Clip", "Gospel", "Noise", "Alt. Rock", "Bass", "Soul",
    "Punk", "Space", "Meditative", "Instrum. Pop", "Instrum. Rock",
    "Ethnic", "Gothic", "Darkwave", "Techno-Indust.", "Electronic",
    "Pop-Folk", "Eurodance", "Dream", "Southern Rock", "Comedy",
    "Cult", "Gangsta", "Top 40", "Christian Rap", "Pop/Funk", "Jungle",
    "Native American", "Cabaret", "New Wave", "Psychadelic", "Rave",
    "Showtunes", "Trailer", "Lo-Fi", "Tribal", "Acid Punk", "Acid Jazz",
    "Polka", "Retro", "Musical", "Rock & Roll", "Hard Rock", "Folk",
    "Folk/Rock", "National Folk", "Swing", "Fusion", "Bebop", "Latin",
    "Revival", "Celtic", "Bluegrass", "Avantgarde", "Gothic Rock",
    "Progress. Rock", "Psychadel. Rock", "Symphonic Rock", "Slow Rock",
    "Big Band", "Chorus", "Easy Listening", "Acoustic", "Humor",
    "Speech", "Chanson", "Opera", "Chamber Music", "Sonata", "Symphony",
    "Booty Bass", "Primus", "Porn Groove", "Satire", "Slow Jam",
    "Club", "Tango", "Samba", "Folklore", "Ballad", "Power Ballad",
    "Rhythmic Soul", "Freestyle", "Duet", "Punk Rock", "Drum Solo",
    "A Capella", "Euro-House", "Dance Hall", "Goa", "Drum & Bass",
    "Club-House", "Hardcore", "Terror", "Indie", "BritPop", "Negerpunk",
    "Polsk Punk", "Beat", "Christian Gangsta Rap", "Heavy Metal",
    "Black Metal", "Crossover", "Contemporary Christian", "Christian Rock",
    "Merengue", "Salsa", "Thrash Metal", "Anime", "Jpop", "Synthpop"
);
```

NOTE

The genre lookup should be done using a Web service server call if performance is an issue. We did it in ActionScript for simplicity.

ID3 tags reside within the MP3 binary file. You can view and edit these tags using the Winamp Player on Windows and iTunes on Macintosh. Follow these steps to view one of our sample songs:

1. Start the Winamp 3.0 Player application.

2. Load an MP3 song like that with the file name *song_ej_lk.mp3*.

3. From the *Playlist Editor*, highlight "Alison Krauss…" (see following illustration), double-click to start the song, and then do a "View File Info…" from the menu (use the ALT-3 shortcut in Windows).

4. If you don't have the Playlist Editor open, just choose it from the menu as shown next.

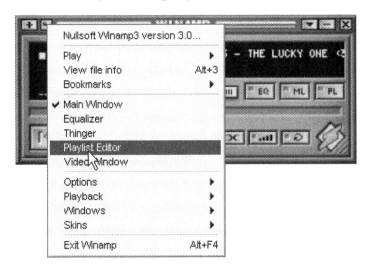

5. You should now see the ID3v1 tag displayed, as shown here.

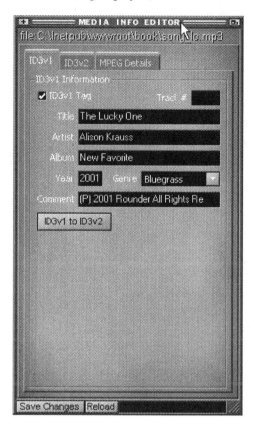

6. You can also tab along and see the ID3v2 tags and MPEG properties of the file, as shown next. ID3v2 tags can contain a lot more information about the album.

Now that you know how to edit ID3 tags using an ID3 editor like Winamp 3.0 player, as well as how to extract that information from within ActionScript, let's move on to developing the Flash MX user interface.

Flash UI Components

So far, we've used mostly standard Flash UI components in our design, such as dynamic text, movie clips, and buttons. One of the newest and least documented components used here is the Tree component, available as part of Flash UI Components Set 2 from Macromedia Flash Exchange. We will go into the details of how we used the Tree component for the XML playlist. The others are self-explanatory.

The Tree component is similar to the ListBox component with the visible difference in terms of hierarchical data display. The Tree display has two types of nodes: branch nodes and leaf nodes. Branch nodes can have subnodes. Leaf nodes cannot have them. Since there is almost no documentation from Macromedia available for this component, we thank Bernhard Gaul for sharing his code and example with us at his web site, **http://www.geocities.com/ bgx_2000/expl/as.htm**.

The tree data comes from our file, *playlist.xml*. This is a standard well-formed XML file that describes the tree display used for navigation. The file content follows:

```
<?xml version="1.0" encoding="UTF-8"?>
<myRoot label="Play Lists">
   <folder label="Latin">
      <sample label="I've Got You - Marc Anthony (sampler 00:30)"
         URL="song_ma1.mp3"/>
   </folder>
   <folder label="Rock">
      <sample label="We Will Rock You - Queen (sampler 00:30)"
         URL="song_queen1.mp3"/>
   </folder>
   <folder label="Soundtrack">
      <sample label="Circle of Life - Elton John (sampler 00:30)"
         URL="song_ej_lk.mp3"/>
   <folder label="BlueGrass">
      <sample label="New Favorite - Alison Krauss"
         URL="song_nf.mp3"/>
      <sample label="The Lucky One - Alison Krauss"
         URL="song_lo.mp3"/>
      <sample label="Maybe - Alison Krauss"
         URL="song_ak_maybe.mp3"/>
      <sample label="Heartstrings - Alison Krauss"
         URL="song_ak_heartstrings.mp3"/>
   </folder>
</myRoot>
```

The ActionScript used to load this playlist and build the XML tree is shown next.

```
// initialization
bg_so = SharedObject.getLocal("bgTree"); // used to save tree state
var t = _level0.bgTree;
var rootNode;
t.setNodeExpansionHandler("saveBranches", _root);
t.setChangeHandler("bgTreeCall", _root);
var cD;

//load the XML
treeXML = new XML();
treeXML.ignoreWhite = true;
treeXML.onLoad = buildTree;
treeXML.load("playlist.xml");

// build XML tree
function buildTree() {
```

```
getRoot();
thisObject = new NodeData(rootNode);
t.setRootNode(new FTreeNode(thisObject.label, thisObject));
sampleArray = rootNode.childNodes;
sampleNode = rootNode.firstChild;
var z = 0;
while (z<sampleArray.length) {
    thisObject = new NodeData(sampleNode);
    t.addNode(t.getRootNode(), new FTreeNode(thisObject.label,
        thisObject));
    folderArray = sampleNode.childNodes;
    folderNode = sampleNode.firstChild;
    var x = 0;
    while (x<folderArray.length) {
        thisObject = new NodeData(folderNode);
        t.addNode(t.getNodeAt(t.getRootNode(), z), new
            FTreeNode(thisObject.label, thisObject));
        folderNode = folderNode.nextSibling;
        x++;
    }
    sampleNode = sampleNode.nextSibling;
    z++;
}
//restore the tree to last saved state
setBranches();
}
```

 NOTE

You need to explicitly set the ignoreWhite property of the tree to true. The default setting is false. Nodes containing white space will be discarded when the XML is parsed. Depending on the editor you used to create the XML, there may be extraneous white space or carriage returns saved in the file—this will take care of it.

The *setBranches* function restores the XML tree to the last saved state using a local SharedObject. The code listing for this is as follows:

```
function setBranches() {
    fL = this.bg_so.data.folderList;
    rO = this.bg_so.data.rootOpen;
    if (fL == undefined) {
        t.getRootNode().setIsOpen(true);
    } else {
        t.getRootNode().setIsOpen(rO);
        for(j=0; j<fL.length; j++){
```

```
            nextNode = t.getNodeAt(t.getRootNode(), j);
            nextNode.setIsOpen(fL[j]);
        }
    }
    t.refresh();
}
```

Supporting ActionScript code for handling the tree navigation follows:

```
// determine the root node to start tree with
function getRoot() {
    rootNode = treeXML.firstChild;
    rootName = rootNode.nodeName;
    var x = 0;
    var y = treeXML.childNodes;
    while (x<y.length) {
        if (rootName == "myRoot") {
            break;
        }
        rootNode = rootNode.nextSibling;
        rootName = rootNode.nodeName;
        x++;
    }
}


// create NodeData object
function NodeData(sNode) {
    this.type = sNode.nodeName;
    this.label = sNode.attributes["label"];
    if (this.type == "sample") {
        this.sampleUrl = sNode.attributes["URL"];
    }
    this.hasUrl = ((this.type == "sample") && (this.sampleUrl.length > 0));
}


// available methods for NodeData object
// load item
NodeData.prototype.loadSample = function() {
    myTrack.loadSound(this.sampleUrl, false);
    poll = setInterval(RockAndRoll, 1000);
    myTrack.setVolume(currentVol);
    debug.text = myTrack.getVolume();
}


// update item
NodeData.prototype.update = function() {
    if (dClick) { // double-click
```

```
            statusHeader.text = "Loading...";
            if (this.hasURL) this.loadSample();
            return;
        }
        playButton._visible = this.hasURL;
        stopButton._visible = this.hasURL;
    }


    // tree node selection
    function bgTreeCall(component) {
        var s = component.getSelectedNode();
        checkDblClick(s);
        //toggle folder state on double-click
        if (s.isBranch() && dClick) {
            toggleOpen = ((s.isOpen()) ? false : true);
            s.setIsOpen(toggleOpen);
            t.refresh();
            saveBranches();
        } else {
            if (!dClick) cD = s.getData();
            cD.update();
        }
    }


    //check if a tree node was double-clicked
    function checkDblClick(s) {
        var clickTime = getTimer();
        dClick = ((clickTime-lastClick<300) && (lastSelected == s));
        lastClick = clickTime;
        lastSelected = s;
    }


    // get tree status when a branch is opened or closed
    function saveBranches() {
        rOpen = t.getRootNode().isOpen();
        bOpen = new Array();
        bArray = t.getRootNode().getChildNodes();
        for (j=0; j<bArray.length; j++) {
            bOpen.push(bArray[j].isOpen());
        }
        this.bg_so.data.folderList = bOpen;
        this.bg_so.data.rootOpen = rOpen;
    }
```

NOTE

The Play and Stop buttons will appear only when an item on the tree display is clicked or double-clicked. If you clicked a non-actionable item like the folder name, they will not appear. Double-clicking is the equivalent of selecting an item by single-clicking and then clicking the Play button.

Once the XML file is read and the tree built, you can double-click it or click the Play button to load and play the selected song. The tree navigation is shown in the next illustration. You'll notice that the folders can be collapsed or expanded, in addition to being able to scroll through them horizontally and vertically.

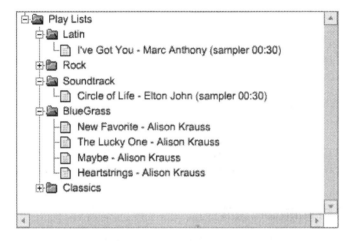

The XML tree state is saved every time you collapse or expand the folders via a local shared object—a process known as rudimentary personalization.

Audio Controls

We've only added a few basic controls here—play, stop, and adjust volume—all of which are done using ActionScript. The code snippet for all these controls is shown in the list that follows.

```
// play song
playButton.onRelease =function (){
   cD.loadSample();
   // cD is the current data depository for the selected tree node
}

// stop song
```

```
stopButton.onRelease =function (){
   myTrack.stop();
}

// adjust volume by +/- 5
upVolButton.onRelease =function (){
   setVol = myTrack.getVolume()+ 5;
   myTrack.setVolume(setVol);
   currentVol = setVol;
   debug.text = setVol; // show current volume on stage
}

downVolButton.onRelease =function (){
   setVol = myTrack.getVolume()- 5;
   myTrack.setVolume(setVol);
   currentVol = setVol;
   debug.text = setVol; // show current volume on stage
}
```

You can double-click the tree display to play the selected song or just press the Play button. You can also select any song to play without having to press the Stop button first.

eCommerce at Amazon.com

We have a button on the application that can redirect the user to the Amazon.com web site to look at detailed buying information on the displayed album. The code is simple, as shown next.

```
// buy button
buyButton.onRelease =function (){
   buyAmazon();
}
// redirect to Amazon.com web site
function buyAmazon(){
   affiliateURL = "http://www.amazon.com/exec/obidos/ASIN/" +
```

```
    albumASIN +"/ref=ase_2launch-20";
    getURL(affiliateURL,"_blank"); // new window
}
```

A separate browser window is launched for the specific item. The content on the Amazon.com web site should match that on our application unless the Amazon.com web service is unavailable or untimely in its content.

Detecting the Flash Player Version

You can add code to detect the version of the Flash Player and respond appropriately. We have chosen to just display the version number on the stage for the desktop PC version of our Flash MX application. The ActionScript code snippet follows:

```
ver.text = "Player: " + getVersion();
```

A string will be displayed that's similar to the following illustration.

Results

We can now run our MP3 Flash MX application, either as a stand-alone Projector file (EXE) or a SWF file, or embedded within an HTML page. A screen shot of the running desktop PC application (stand-alone) is shown next.

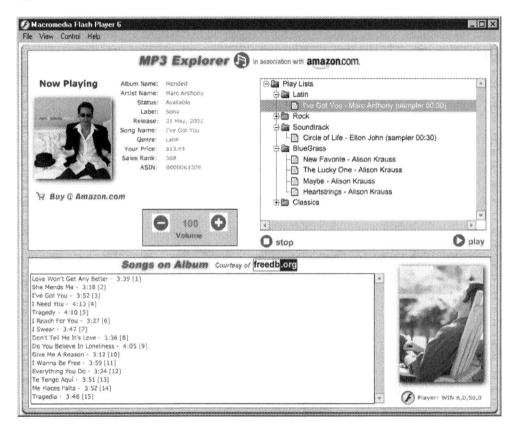

The user selects a song from the fixed playlist in our example. Press the Play button or double-click the song name. Here's the sequence of events that happen when a song plays.

1. After the song is fully loaded, the ID3 tags are read and displayed to the stage.

2. A call is made to the Amazon.com Web service to get the album information. After a successful call where valid data is returned, the data is updated on the stage. This includes the album cover image.

3. A call is made to FreeDB to get the song titles from the CDDB database. Again, after a successful call where valid data is returned, the data is updated on the stage.

4. With all the content fully populated on the stage, the end users sit back and enjoy the song, or adjust the volume to their liking.

5. If they like the song, they can purchase the album from the Amazon.com web site by adding it to their shopping cart. A new browser window pops up separately.

For the Nokia Communicator and Pocket PC form factor, the core of the client-side and server-side code remains the same. The differences are the presentation screen size and the user interface employed to accommodate the content over multiple frames (not just one). The respective Nokia Communicator and Pocket PC versions are shown next. Note that we have just reused the desktop PC version of buttons with some minor skin changes—they can be better modified to suit the appropriate form factors.

The first frame of the Nokia Communicator form factor is shown next. This is similar to the top half of the desktop PC version.

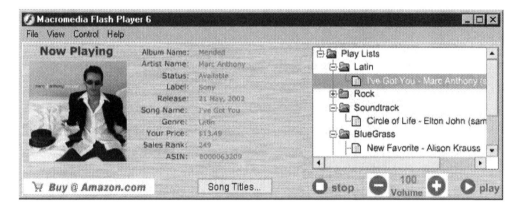

The second frame looks like the following:

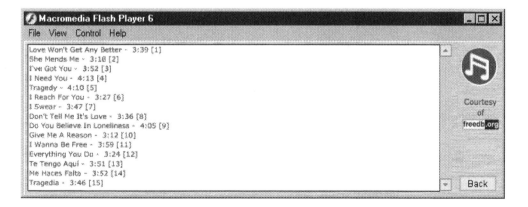

The basic frames for the Pocket PC form factor are shown next.

Clicking the *Buy @ Amazon* button will take you to a detailed page on the Amazon.com web site for the specific album (see the following illustration). The user can then buy the album, read customer reviews, or get items related to the album.

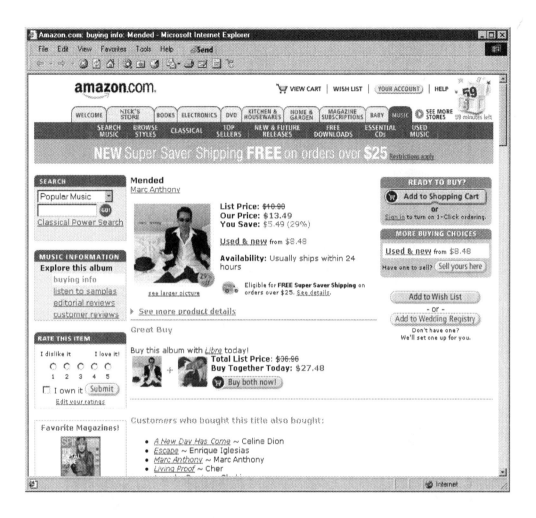

Enhancements

As shown in the previous section, the application user interface and skins are not exactly of "professional" quality, nor can they rival those in MP3 players like Winamp, Windows Media Player, or RealJukeBox. Therefore, many enhancements can be made to improve our application, including:

▶ The capability to add and remove entries to playlists.

▶ Better volume and Timeline control using sliders or the equivalent (see the panel from the Winamp 3.0 player next).

▶ A visual indicator showing time remaining on the song or total time of the song (see the panel from the MusicMatch Jukebox 7.2 Basic player shown next).

▶ A better back-end server interface with a full-featured music database like Gracenote CDDB (the Winamp 3.0 player panel is shown next).

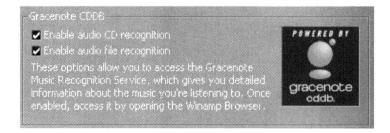

▶ Additional content related to the artist or album, including customer reviews, music videos, news, posters, and fan clubs.

▶ The capability to change skins or have a set of skins or themes (for example, NFL teams, MLB teams, universities) to choose from.

▶ Adding an item or album to the Shopping Cart, Wish List, or Gift Registry on the Amazon.com web site.

▶ Using Macromedia Flash Communication Server to stream MP3 files that are ID3v2-compliant.

▶ Changing the size of the font for the Tree UI Flash component for both the Nokia Communicator and Pocket PC form factors.

Summary

In this chapter, we showed in detail how to create a compelling Flash MX application normally reserved for C++ programmers! We utilized many of the new features of the Flash Player, the Amazon.com Web service, the FreeDB music database, and the complex Tree Flash UI component. Our MP3 Flash MX application is the result of the integration of all these features and client–server technologies. In addition, starting from the desktop PC version, we also created versions for the Pocket PC and Nokia Communicator form factors.

CHAPTER 4

Multimedia Communication, Broadcast, and Surveillance

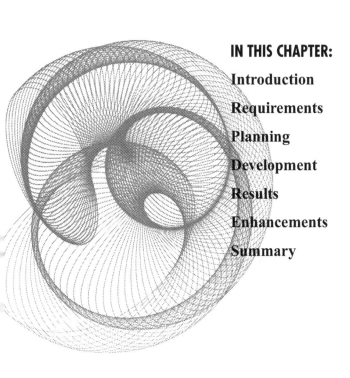

IN THIS CHAPTER:

I n this chapter, we will discuss the design and development of a multimedia communication and broadcast platform that can provide live and recorded videos to desktop PCs and mobile devices. We will apply what we have learned in previous chapters and build a Flash MX application based on ColdFusion MX, Flash MX, and Flash Communication Server. We will then implement the building blocks of a two-way video communication application where two users can engage in audio and video communication in real time using a mobile device like the Nokia Communicator.

Introduction

As discussed in Chapter 11, the Flash Communication Server can be a powerful addition to your middle tier, whether you use ColdFusion, J2EE, or .NET as your application server environment. The capability to deliver streaming multimedia messaging services to Pocket PCs and Nokia Communicators makes it very compelling, especially given that you don't have to write native code to make it happen!

Streaming video or audio alleviates the problems related to limited memory in mobile devices. It enables the distribution of larger media content as well as live communication services, and you can view or display multimedia content with minimal or no delay—and without downloading the entire file.

The Nokia 9210i Communicator is the first Nokia product that supports video and audio streaming in HSCSD (High Speed Circuit Switched Data) networks. A wide variety of streaming services can be made available, including:

▶ **News** Real-time news broadcasts from national or local stations

▶ **Sports** Video highlights of last night's sporting events, or the latest scores

▶ **Music** Excerpts of music tracks from top albums

▶ **Trailers** Movie trailers from the latest releases or rentals

▶ **Web cam** Monitor your child, store, or warehouse—even road and traffic conditions

The growth of bandwidth in mobile networks, a series of ever-improving compression technologies (MPEG-4, H.263, and Flash Communication Server with Sorenson Spark code), and the latest camera and display technologies have combined to enable streaming video for everyday uses. For instance, while GSM technology offers a data speed of 9.6 kbps, HSCSD has increased it to 43.2 kbps, and GPRS has further expanded the rate to 115 kbps. EDGE will increase data speed even more: up to 384 kbps, theoretically; while the introduction of 3G systems could ultimately enable data speeds of up to 2 Mbps. However, with MPEG-4 and H.263 (DivX) technologies it is not possible to deliver the multimedia without having real-time video codecs on mobile devices. Raw video data must be compressed so it can be sent over the narrow-band radio channel and decompressed on the receiver's side, thereafter replayed error-free.

With two-way video communication, content is transferred in both directions, either in real time or non-real time. Two-way communication allows users to create video content at both ends of the communication link and share it with each other, either by delivering and viewing the content simultaneously at both ends, or by creating and viewing it at different times.

Using Flash Communication Server, this can be done easily, without the need for codecs on mobile devices, as long as the client devices have Flash Player 6 and a camera. As of this writing, the built-in cameras from various Nokia mobile phones (for example, Nokia 6650 and 3650 as shown next) are not part of the list of supported cameras compatible with the Flash Communication Server, but this may change soon. Video playback should be here much faster than video capture support in Nokia phones.

Why Multimedia?

Since a picture is worth a thousand words, motion pictures and videos must be worth a great deal more! Besides the rich media experience, multimedia can offer information and efficiency not possible with simple still pictures.

Use Case

To create a full-blown Flash MX application for our multimedia service, we take pieces of the building block code from previous chapters and make them stand-alone applications wrapped within a general user interface (see following illustration). Here, we'll feature the listed news, sports, web cam, music, traffic, and movies services as separate channels (similar to television channels).

Since most of us are familiar with various entertainment channels, perhaps we ought to expand on the use case of web cams.

A web cam can be installed for business use, allowing owners to monitor cash registers, stockrooms, warehouses, and factory floors to prevent theft. Cameras installed in warehouses have reportedly helped eliminate inventory loss. Just one system at the front and back entrances can allow management to keep track of who and what is coming and going. Video security systems, whether highly visible or covert, can be a key element in the prevention, deterrence, and detection of vandalism, thefts, and other improper activities.

On the home use front, you can stop gambling with childcare by evaluating your caregiver's performance through a video camera system. Feel safe and secure when away by seeing how your caregiver interacts with and cares for your children. You can also view cameras on your desktop PC and record it to your hard drive, sending video content over modem or wireless!

In this chapter, we'll focus solely on building a two-way real-time video communication application that can run with Flash Player 6 on a mobile device like the Nokia Communicator (see following illustration). Other designs previously mentioned (the security surveillance camera, for example) can be derived from, or is a subset of, this core video application. Our end user could be running this application while riding in a car, commuting on a train or boat, or while lounging in their local Starbucks coffee shop or Borders book store. Since this application runs with any Flash Player 6 on mobile devices or desktop PCs, we'll leverage the Flash Communications Server "alert" feature (onSync) between callers. That is, if the caller is running this two-way video Flash MX application on her mobile device, the callee should be alerted of the incoming call. The callee will then run the same Flash MX application on his mobile device in order to connect up exclusively in a one-to-one two-way video communication.

The only commercial product available to the consumer that is reasonably priced is the Vialta Beamer (see next illustration). This is a nice piece of communications hardware, but it does not address issues that concern most consumers who already have broadband in their homes, chiefly:

► A telephone connection is required on both ends

► Only a one-to-one connection with required hardware can be used

► Each call made results in telephone toll costs

Our core solution utilizes existing connections and requires no additional hardware or airtime costs. Most important of all, the application can link two people on their mobile phones with cameras (or between a mobile phone and a desktop PC), and can be updated on the server without any hardware changes!

Requirements

We will briefly describe the requirements from a developer's standpoint. This includes the application, the client (Flash Player 6, for instance), the servers (say, Flash Communication Server and ColdFusion MX), the data sources (web sites, file systems, and so forth), and other technologies.

Application

Our Flash MX video communication application has the following features:

▶ It runs as a stand-alone SWF file on a Nokia Communicator or desktop PC.

▶ It has the capability to communicate one-on-one using video and audio, or operate in lurker mode.

▶ It supports MP3 audio to alert the user of an incoming or outgoing call prior to establishing the connection.

▶ It has the capability to solely broadcast audio and video content to online users.

Clients: Flash Player

In order for our application to work, the end user must be using Flash Player 6.0r40 or later. (We previously discussed how you can detect the version number of Flash Player with ActionScript.)

Tools and Technologies

In building this core application, we will use the following tools and technologies:

▶ **The Flash MX authoring environment**   The Flash MX authoring tool will be used for developing the client-side interface or the end-user interface.

▶ **Flash Player**   We'll use Flash Player 6.0r40 or later in a stand-alone format.

▶ **ColdFusion MX and Flash Communication Server**   Our Flash MX application will communicate exclusively with the Flash Communication Server to access live connections between users.

▶ **Wired or wireless web cam**   To broadcast video to desktop PCs and mobile devices, we'll be using web cams (USB or wireless) from end users linked to their connecting devices—for instance, mobile devices or desktop PCs.

Note that no servers or dependent technology is required with this core application.

Planning

As in Chapters 12 and 13, we'll now work on our UI—how the user interface will look and where the content is displayed—before writing our first line of code. This includes creating mockups of the application for a Nokia Communicator. Here, the same form factor can also be used for the desktop PC.

Page Layout

A mockup of the application user interface for the Nokia Communicator is given in Figure 14-1.

We've assumed the SWF file will run in a full-screen mode of 640 pixels × 200 pixels (width × height) on the Nokia Communicator.

Data Flow

As shown in Figure 14-1, content areas for the stage are populated as follows (corresponding to numbers in the figure):

1. **First video camera or web cam**   Audio and video content being streamed
2. **Second video camera or web cam**   Audio and video content being streamed
3. **Online users**   List of people logged in
4. **Login**   Log in as name (real or alias)
5. **Status**   Status indicator (online, offline, incoming call, and so on)

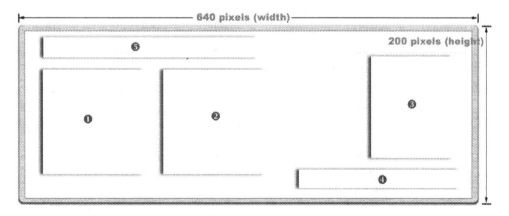

Figure 14-1   *The Nokia Communicator mockup*

As illustrated next, audio and video communications between the two users can be carried out through the centralized Flash Communication Server via the Flash clients.

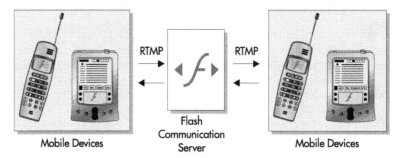

Mobile Devices   Flash Communication Server   Mobile Devices

Development

Given the requirements, page layout, and approach as detailed in the previous sections, let's start creating our application. At the top level, the user gets to select what services or channels they are interested in as illustrated in the *Use Case* section. Each of those channels can be implemented as a button. Once a button is clicked or tapped, we can jump to the correct frame label using ActionScript *goToAndStop* and start that service. For example, goToAndStop("VideoPhone").

NOTE

We recommend that each service or channel be designed separately so that separate SWF files are generated. We want to avoid having a single SWF file that is too big. Additionally, designers and developers can focus on the service or channel they are working on.

While our goal is to build a two-way video and audio communication application, this is just one of the many services or channels that can be offered. You can certainly expand from here.

Flash Communication Server

We'll be using the communication components in the Flash MX authoring environment. With these components, we barely have to write any ActionScript code to leverage the power of the Flash Communication Server. We'll discuss the communication components used and what we did to adapt them to what we are doing in the next section.

Communication between active Flash MX clients will be through a remote shared object (see Chapter 11). The SharedObject *onSync* handler is invoked when any of the SharedObject *data* properties of the remote shared object are changed, as well as the first time a client uses the SharedObject *getRemote* command to connect to a remote shared object on the server. With the onSync handler, individual clients can respond differently depending on the data property changes. More on this in the ActionScript code section.

Flash UI Components

In our application, we will be using the following communication components: SimpleConnect, AVPresence, PeopleList, and ConnectionLight. You can open the Library display window (see following illustration) to view these components.

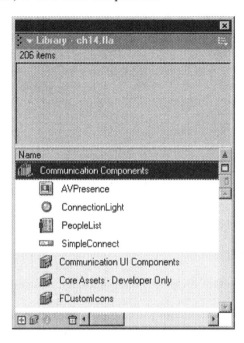

We've already shown how to use components in your movies in the previous chapters. After placing the desired components on the stage, there are still two more things that need to be done.

▶ **SimpleConnect Parameters**   You need to supply the application directory, such as *rtmp:/book*, and a list of any other communication components you want to connect automatically. In our example, we add them (as shown in the following illustration) for the two AVPresence components (av1, av2), the ConnectionLight component (cl1), and the PeopleList component (pl1).

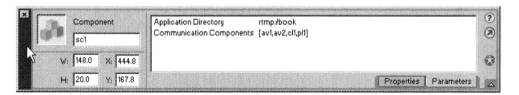

▶ **Communication Components ActionScripts**   When you use these communication components, you *must* use some server-side scripting. But that is already done for you—there is a file named *components.asc* in the script library. All you have to do is create a file named *main.asc* and have it load the components.asc file. The code listing follows:

```
load("components.asc");
```

This *main.asc* file is a server-side ActionScript file that is executed once when the application is loaded. Just save this file in the same directory as your application.

These are the main communication components used. The other components on our stage are basic Flash UI components (for example, dynamic text) and have already been discussed throughout this book in the earlier chapters.

ActionScript Core

The main ActionScript that is core to this application is shown next. We start off by initiating some global variables used for displaying status information on our stage.

```
statusLine.text = "OFFLINE";
callInfo.text = "NONE";
globalCallerIs = "";
globalCalleeIs = "";
```

Next, we create the shared object used in our application. This shared object is how multiple users interact with each other via the Flash Communication Server. We will keep our caller and callee information there so when one user tries to "call" another online user, we can identify who the *caller* and *callee* are and serve up the appropriate audio and visual alerts.

```
nc = new NetConnection();
nc.connect("rtmp:/book/room1");
so = SharedObject.getRemote("users",nc.uri,true);
so.connect(nc);
```

As mentioned earlier, we've modified the PeopleList component such that a single click on any of the entries (names) will activate or initiate a call. Note that the PeopleList component uses a ListBox component for the list display. In order to access and modify the ActionScript code associated with the PeopleList component, first bring up the Library display window (F11 in Windows) and double-click the PeopleList icon (*not* the text). This will open up the PeopleList frame in Scene 1. Open the Actions display and you should see the ActionScript implementation of the PeopleList component, as shown next.

```
 1  /**
 2   * Copyright © 2002 Macromedia, Inc. All rights reserved.
 3   *
 4   * FCPeopleList
 5   * Moving or modifying this file may affect the applications installed on this server.
 6   */
 7
 8  #initclip 1
 9  //
10  function FCPeopleListClass() {
11      this.init();
12  }
13  //
14  FCPeopleListClass.prototype = new MovieClip();
15  //
16  Object.registerClass("FCPeopleListSymbol", FCPeopleListClass);
17  //
18  FCPeopleListClass.prototype.init = function() {
19      this.name = (this._name == null ? "_DEFAULT_" : this._name);
20      this.prefix = "FCPeopleList." + this.name + ".";
21  };
22  //
23  FCPeopleListClass.prototype.onUnload = function() {
24      this.close();
25  };
26  //
27  FCPeopleListClass.prototype.connect = function(nc) {
28      this.nc = nc;
29      if (this.nc.FCPeopleList == null) {
30          this.nc.FCPeopleList = {};
```

Actions - Frame

Actions for Frame 1 of Layer Name Actions

Line 93 of 93, Col 1

NOTE

Exercise caution when editing code here, as it will affect other applications on this server.

Now, let's make changes to our code. In the *connect* function (around line 27 in code listing), insert the list box change handler call function (*lbActivate*) into the *onSync* callback (around line 37) which is located in our top level (use *_root*). The complete code is listed next.

```
#initclip 1
//
function FCPeopleListClass() {
    this.init();
```

```
}
//
FCPeopleListClass.prototype = new MovieClip();
//
Object.registerClass("FCPeopleListSymbol", FCPeopleListClass);
//
FCPeopleListClass.prototype.init = function() {
   this.name = (this._name == null ? "_DEFAULT_" : this._name);
   this.prefix = "FCPeopleList." + this.name + ".";
};
//
FCPeopleListClass.prototype.onUnload = function() {
   this.close();
};
//
FCPeopleListClass.prototype.connect = function(nc) {
   this.nc = nc;
   if (this.nc.FCPeopleList == null) {
      this.nc.FCPeopleList = {};
   }
   this.nc.FCPeopleList[this.name] = this;
   //
   this.so = SharedObject.getRemote(this.prefix + "users",
      this.nc.uri, false);
   this.so.owner = this;
   //
   this.so.onSync = function(list) {
      this.owner.people_lb.removeAll();
      // added line
      this.owner.people_lb.setChangeHandler("lbActivate",_root);
      var totalUsers = 0;
      var totalLurkers = 0;
      for (var i in this.data) {
         if (this.data[i] == " fc_lurker") {
            totalLurkers++;
         } else if (this.data[i] != null) {
            totalUsers++;
            this.owner.people_lb.addItem(this.data[i]);
         }
      }
      this.owner.lurkers = totalLurkers;
      this.owner.users = totalUsers;
      this.owner.people_lb.sortItemsBy("label", "ASC");
   };
   //
```

```
   this.so.connect(this.nc);
   // Need to call connect on our server side counterpart first
   this.nc.call(this.prefix + "connect", null);
};
//
FCPeopleListClass.prototype.close = function() {
   var fullName = "FCPeopleList." + this.name;
   // Let our server side counterpart know that we are going away
   this.nc.call(this.prefix + "close", null);
   //
   this.so.owner = null;
   delete this.so.owner;
   delete this.so.onSync;
   this.so.close();
   this.so = null;
   //
   this.nc.FCPeopleList[this.name] = null;
   this.nc = null;
};
//
FCPeopleListClass.prototype.setUsername = function (newName) {
   this.username = newName;
   this.nc.call(this.prefix + "changeName", null);
   _root.updateStatusLine(newName);
}
//
FCPeopleListClass.prototype.setSize = function (newWidth, newHeight) {
this._xscale = 100;
   this._yscale = 100;
   this.people_lb.setSize(newWidth,newHeight);
}
//
#endinitclip
// B-)
this.setSize(this._width, this._height);
```

Whenever any name on the PeopleList is selected via a single click, our callback is activated. Additional code can be added in a similar manner to customize your usage of this and other Flash components. The code for the change handler is shown next. The code determines which online user is selected and puts the caller and callee information into our server's shared object.

```
function lbActivate() {
   globalCalleeIs = pl1.people_lb.getValue();
   so.data.caller = globalCallerIs;
   so.data.callee = globalCalleeIs;
```

```
      so.data.callactivated = "Y";
      globalActivated = "Y";
}
```

The crucial part of our code is the *onSync* handling when the shared object changes data. The code is shown next.

```
so.onSync = function(list){
    localCaller = so.data.caller;
    localCallee = so.data.callee;
    localCallActivated = so.data.callactivated;
    if (localCallee == globalCallerIs) {
        if (localCallActivated == "Y") {
            _root.imgObj.removeMovieClip();
            _root.createEmptyMovieClip("imgObj",9);
            _root.imgObj._x=15;
            _root.imgObj._y=5;
            _root.imgObj.loadMovie("http://ipaq-2:8500/flashcom/
                applications/book/callinprogress.jpg");
            myTrack = new Sound();
            myTrack.loadSound("song_ej1.mp3", false);
            myTrack.setVolume(50);
            poll = setInterval(RockAndRoll, 1000);
        }
        statusLine.text = "INCOMING CALL";
        callInfo.text = "from " + localCaller;
    }
    if (globalActivated == "Y") {
        if (localCaller == globalCallerIs) {
            _root.imgObj.removeMovieClip();
            _root.createEmptyMovieClip("imgObj",9);
            _root.imgObj._x=15;
            _root.imgObj._y=5;
            _root.imgObj.loadMovie("http://ipaq-2:8500/flashcom/
                applications/book/callinprogress.jpg");
            statusLine.text = "CALLING";
            callInfo.text = "to " + localCallee;
            myTrack = new Sound();
            myTrack.loadSound("song_ma1.mp3", false);
            myTrack.setVolume(50);
            poll = setInterval(RockAndRoll, 1000);
        }
            globalActivated = "N";
    }
}
```

Here is an overview of how the shared object works in our application. A Flash client movie (for example, user A) subscribes to a remote shared object by issuing a *SharedObject.getRemote* command, and provides a *SharedObject.onSync* method with it. The client then connects the remote shared object to the NetConnection object by issuing a *SharedObject.connect* command— *so.connect(nc)* in our code. The Flash Communication Server sends out a synchronization message for the shared object, but no method on the server side is invoked. This synchronization message causes the *SharedObject.onSync* method on the client to be called. When the client, the server, or any other movie instance (for example, user B) makes a change to the shared object, the server again sends out a synchronization message for the shared object. Again, no server method is called, and the synchronization message from the server causes the *SharedObject.onSync* method on each client to be called automatically. This way, we don't have to poll the server routinely. The data flow is illustrated in the following.

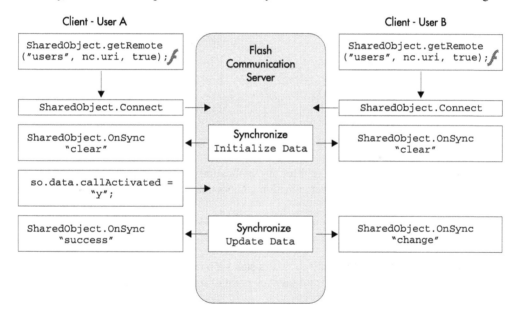

Next, some details on the sound object. In the previous code listing for the *onSync* method, we created a sound object for alert notification. We also called the *RockAndRoll* function after loading the MP3 file. Since we're not streaming, it takes time to load the file and we can't play it until it's fully loaded.

```
function RockAndRoll(){
    myTrack.start();
    if((myTrack.getBytesLoaded() == myTrack.getBytesTotal()) &&
        myTrack.duration > 0){
        clearInterval (poll);
    }
}
```

The ActionScript *setInterval* is calling the *RockAndRoll* function at periodic intervals (every 1000 milliseconds or 1 second in our example).

You can create MP3 files from WAV or other audio formats to make them sound like the ring tones used in today's mobile phone. Be creative—you can easily get good MP3 songs these days so the possibilities are limitless!

Some miscellaneous display-related functions are used in our application. The code is self-explanatory.

```
// display if user is online or not
function updateStatusLine (newName) {
    statusLine.text = "ONLINE";
    callInfo.text = "as " + newName;
    globalCallerIs = newName;
}
// reset button
resetButton.onRelease = function (){
    _root.imgObj.removeMovieClip();
    so.data.callactivated = "N";
    updateStatusLine(globalCallerIs);
    myTrack.stop();
    delete myTrack;
}
```

That is all the ActionScript required for our application. Much of the code is already written for us when we use the communication components.

Results

We can now run our Flash MX application as a stand-alone SWF file. A screenshot of the running application is shown next from the viewpoint of the first user, Jim Caller.

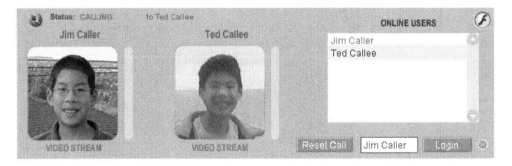

The screenshot from the viewpoint of the second user, Ted Callee, is shown in the following. Notice that the callee is using a lower resolution camera remotely and the screen resolution shows accordingly.

Let's go through the usage scenario after the application is up and running.

1. The user logs into the system and signs in using his name or alias. His name appears on the list (the PeopleList component on the right side of screen) of online users after a successful sign-in.

2. The user (caller) can then select an online user from the people list by using a mouse-click or simply tapping to initiate a call to the callee. The caller web cam does not have to be activated yet. If the caller chose to activate the video being broadcast, it is available to *anyone* who has that application running, including lurkers and the callee (note highlighted status changes in illustration that follows). In our application, when a call is initiated, an MP3 file will play indicating the call is in progress. Again, this can be any MP3 file of your choice, which acts as a ring tone.

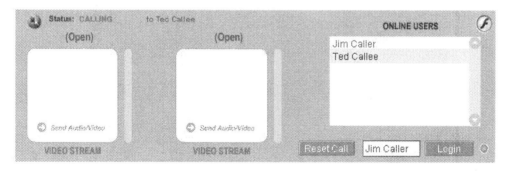

3. The first time a user turns on his web cam, Flash Player will ask for permission from the user (see following illustration) for the Flash Communication Server, which

is running on a server called ipaq-2 (a desktop PC in our case), to access his camera and microphone.

4. The callee will get an audio indicator (another MP3 file will play) in addition to a visual (see next illustration) that is already available if the caller has activated his web cam before initiating the call. The callee can then activate his web cam and start communicating.

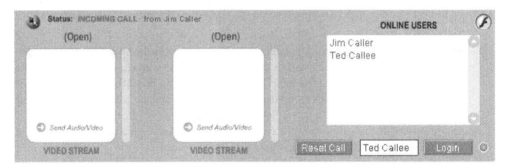

5. With the AVPresence component, any user can pause or stop the video or audio streams any time (see following illustration) by using the mouse or stylus and clicking or tapping the video or audio icons.

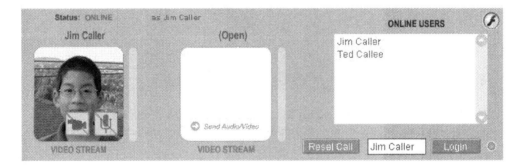

6. When the conversation is completed, the caller and callee will just shut their web cams off by clicking or tapping on the AVPresence component "×" indicator (as shown next) and clicking the *Reset Call* button.

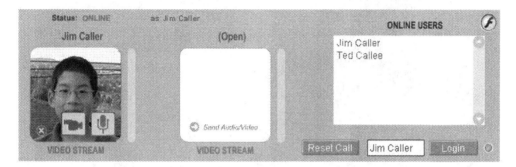

7. That is the basic foundation for building two-way desktop and mobile communication applications. More sophisticated applications can be created on top of this core application—some of which we'll discuss next.

Enhancements

There are certainly many enhancements we can make to improve our core application. For example, we can

▶ Add security features to our two-way communication application so we can have closed and secured one-to-one communications between any two users. Camera displays (AVPresence components) for non-active users can be disabled in ActionScript, and if they try to connect to a user who is already active in the two-way communication, they'll get a busy indication (signal) from the application.

▶ Integrate an address book and personalized ring tones with the application. Using the address book and a ring tone associated with each entry, we can easily build a caller-ID service. As a result, the callee can decide whether or not to take the call without having to check the application display.

▶ Implement video alert features such that users can call anyone—whether the callee(s) are online or not—through SMS or e-mail alerts. The callee(s) can then decide to go online and receive the video call.

The preceding are just some of the enhancements to our web cam core application. New applications, like security surveillance or traffic cam channels (see the following), can be created. As a surveillance application, you can periodically save the streamed video onto the local hard disk as an FLV file. Your web cam application can easily toggle between multiple web cams, and video log files can be produced as well-compressed FLV files accordingly.

Utilizing what you learned from Chapter 11, you can also design the News and Sports channels (see the following) with little effort for streaming news broadcasts or video highlights from sporting events.

Additionally, one potential application we have not yet discussed is having digital pictures taken by a mobile device like the Nokia 7650. The snapshots can be uploaded for viewing on various mobile devices or the Web. Currently, the Flash Communication Server can only save snapshots as FLV files and thus requires an application to utilize the Flash Communication Server (FCS) to view them. If the FCS can save them as JPEG or GIF image formats, many more applications can be developed and made available to a broader Flash and non-Flash audience. Hopefully, this feature will be available in a future FCS release.

Summary

In this chapter, we've shown in detail how to create a compelling multimedia Flash communications application using many of the new features of the Flash Communication Server and Flash Player. You can now do just as much with your Nokia Communicator as you can with your desktop PC. Given the skills and knowledge reviewed in this book, you can go far with this and other core applications. Good luck in your future application designs!

PART

IV

Appendixes

APPENDIX
A

Glossary

357

3G

Acronym for Third Generation. 3G mobile devices and services will transform wireless communications into the always-on, real-time transfer of information, regardless of time and place.

3GPP

Acronym for the Third Generation Partnership Project. A standardization and collaboration forum for creating reports, standards, and interoperable specifications for 3G mobile communications systems.

ActiveX control

A Microsoft implementation of an object that supports a customizable, programmable interface. Using Microsoft Visual Basic, Microsoft Visual C++, and so forth, you can develop ActiveX controls to automate HTML pages by exposing their methods, events, and properties.

actions

Actions are instructions that tell Flash what to do.

ActionScript

The scripting language of Macromedia Flash. You can build interactivity into your Flash movies so they perform certain actions based on user events, such as a stylus tap or a button click.

ADPCM

Acronym for Adaptive Differential Pulse Code Modulation. A technique for digitizing analog information (for example, music) by taking frequent samples of its waveform and expressing them in binary format. ADPCM is used for data storage on a CD-ROM.

AIFF

Acronym for Audio Interchange File Format. An audio file format used in the Apple Macintosh operating system. Also known as Apple Interchange File Format.

AMF

Acronym for Action Message Format. A binary format used by Flash Remoting to deliver purely asynchronous messages over HTTP. Modeled on SOAP, AMF is faster and smaller than standard SOAP in order to optimize event-driven delivery of messages to Flash Players.

anti-aliasing

A technique that smoothes the edges of diagonal lines shown on the screen.

AOA

Acronym for Angle of Arrival. A network-based method used by wireless operators to determine the location of a wireless subscriber (caller). For example, when a wireless caller makes an emergency call through his/her handset, the carrier's cellular towers (antennae) receive the emergency signals and determine the angle from which the signal is coming. The AOA equipment then calculates the location of the handset, by combining the "angle of arrival" data with the location data for the two or more towers that receive the signal.

API

Acronym for Application Program Interface. A set of program capabilities and functions that allow developers to build connectivities between software applications.

ASP

Acronym for Active Server Pages. The server-side scripting language from Microsoft.

ANSI

Acronym for American National Standards Institute. A private, nonprofit organization that administers and coordinates the voluntary standardization and conformity assessment systems in the U.S.

Apache Web Server

Also known as Apache HTTP Server. Used for 63 percent of web sites on the Internet according to the August 2002 Netcraft Web Server Survey, Apache Web Server is an open-source, yet efficient, extensible and secure server that delivers HTTP services over such operating systems as Unix, Windows NT, and Linux.

AVI

Acronym for Audio Video Interleaved. An AVI file, which has an .avi extension, is an audio and video file that conforms to the Microsoft Windows Resource Interchange File Format (RIFF) specification.

base station

A fixed station that is responsible for directly communicating with all cellular phones within its cell. Different base stations are coordinated by a mobile switching center.

Cell-ID

An identifier for an individual cell.

cfc

Acronym for ColdFusion Components.

cHTML

Acronym for compact HTML.

CFML

Acronym for ColdFusion Markup Language.

CTIA

Acronym for Cellular Telecommunications and Internet Association. An organization dedicated to publicizing successful wireless data applications and customer communities. Comprised of wireless operators, device and infrastructure equipment manufacturers, software and hardware vendors, as well as Internet content service providers.

codec

Acronym for compression/decompression. An algorithm or special software that reduces the size of large files or programs, especially to optimize their transport and delivery.

COM

Acronym for Component Object Model. A Microsoft component software model or framework. COM provides a very rich set of integrated services, tools, reusable (client and server) components, and program applications used in the Microsoft environment.

cookies

A piece of information put onto the hard disk of a client device (for example, a desktop PC) by a web site or web server for future use. Cookies provide a mechanism for the server to manage sessions and remember preferences for individual client devices and users.

CSAS

Acronym for Client-Side ActionScript.

CSS

Acronym for Cascading Style Sheet. Provides web developers the ability to position HTML elements—such as images, text, or controls—exactly where they want on an HTML page.

DBCS

Acronym for Double-Byte Character Set.

DHTML

Acronym for Dynamic HTML.

DTD

Acronym for Document Type Declaration. This is a file that defines the format elements for a type of XML document.

EDGE

Acronym for Enhanced Data Rates for Global Evolution. EDGE is an evolution of GSM and US-TDMA systems. This enhanced modulation will significantly increase network capacity and enable data rates up to 473 kbps.

E-OTD

Acronym for Enhanced Observed Time Difference. A network-based method used by wireless operators to determine the location of a wireless subscriber (caller) based on the time differences at which signals are observed (received) by different towers.

EXE

An executable file with an .exe extension. In the context of this book, it is an executable Flash Projector file running on Windows.

FLA

A Flash source file with an .fla file extension.

Flash Generator

A web server application that can dynamically combine text, graphics, and sound to build rich media content and deliver this Generator content to Flash Player. Flash Player 6 does support Generator content but you can no longer edit or add new Generator content with the Macromedia Flash MX authoring environment.

Flash Player

A plug-in, ActiveX, or client-side software that allows Flash movies to be played on various client devices like desktop PCs, Pocket PCs, and smart phones.

Flash Remoting

A Flash infrastructure that allows developers to build remote services exposed by application servers and Web services.

FLV

Acronym or file extension for Flash Video File.

frame

Each screen on the Stage is a frame, just like frames of a movie, and represents a stretch of time.

geocoding

A process for matching the street addresses with geographic location data (longitudes and latitudes). A geocoding software links the records of two databases—street addresses and map coordinates—to support wireless location-based services.

GPRS

Acronym for General Packet Radio Service. GPRS is a wireless data transmission service based on packet transmission. For example, if an e-mail is sent by GPRS, it will be reduced into packets of information. Each individual packet travels to its destination by the quickest possible route. This means the different packets from the same mail can travel separately through foreign networks around the globe in order to avoid obstructions. At the pre-set destination, they are rebuilt and presented to the recipient as a whole. GPRS is a Second and a half Generation (2.5G) service.

GPS

Acronym for Global Positioning System. A system using satellites, receivers, and software that allows users to determine their exact geographic position. It also means a handset-based method used by wireless operators to locate wireless users. Simply put, a wireless handset would receive signals from GPS satellites and calculate the user's position. It then transmits the location data to the cellular towers (antennae) along with the voice signal during emergency calls.

GSM

Acronym for Global System for Mobile communications. GSM is the pan-European standard for digital cellular telephone service. It is also one of the technologies available in the Americas. GSM was designed for markets to provide the advantage of automatic, international roaming in multiple countries. GSM is a Second Generation (2G) service.

guide layer

A layer that is invisible in the final published animation.

H.263

A standard published by the International Telecommunications Union (ITU) to support video compression (coding) for video-conferencing and video-telephony applications. Aimed at video coding for low bit rates (typically 20–30 kbps and above).

HDML

Acronym for Handheld Device Markup Language. It is a specification that allows Internet access from wireless devices such as handheld personal computers and smart phones. This language is derived from HyperText Markup Language (HTML).

HTML

Acronym for HyperText Markup Language. The document format that defines the page layout, fonts, and graphic elements, as well as the hypertext links to other documents on the Web.

HTTP

Acronym for HyperText Transfer Protocol. A protocol or set of rules used for exchanging (requesting and transmitting) web content over the World Wide Web.

HTTPS

Acronym for HyperText Transfer Protocol Secure. A protocol for establishing encrypted connections between browsers and servers on the Internet via strong authentication and HTTP. Typical uses include encrypted connection to an authenticated HTTP server.

IMAP4

Acronym for Internet Message Access Protocol 4. A standard protocol for receiving and accessing e-mail messages at mail servers. It's a more sophisticated protocol than POP3.

i-mode

i-mode is the NTT DoCoMo platform for mobile phone communications that has revolutionized the way millions of people live and work in Japan. With i-mode, cellular phone users get easy access to tens of thousands of Internet sites, as well as specialized services such as e-mail, online shopping and banking, train ticket reservations, and restaurant advice.

instance

An instance in Flash is a usage of a symbol on the Stage.

ISO-OSI Model

Acronym for the International Standards Organization–Open System Interconnect Model. A networking model introduced as guidelines to technology vendors by segmenting communication networking processes, tasks, and services into seven layers: Application, Presentation, Session, Transport, Network, Data Link, and Physical.

J2EE

Acronym for Java 2 Platform, Enterprise Edition. J2EE defines the standard for developing multitier enterprise applications.

J2ME

Acronym for Java 2 Platform, Micro Edition. This is the edition of the Java 2 platform targeted at consumer electronics and embedded devices.

Java Servlet

Java programs that run on a web server to dynamically build web pages for delivery to a client browser.

JavaScript

A scripting language developed by Netscape to add interactivity to HTML pages.

JPEG

Acronym for Joint Photographic Experts Group. A type of compressed, graphical format commonly used for representing digital photographs. A still-image format, JPEG is more compact than bitmap. JPEG files sometimes have a .jpg file extension.

JSP

Acronym for JavaServer Pages. JavaServer Pages technology separates the user interface from content generation, enabling designers to change the overall page layout without altering the underlying dynamic content. JavaServer Pages allows web developers and designers to rapidly develop and easily maintain information-rich dynamic web pages that leverage existing business systems.

keyframe

A keyframe is a frame that defines some change in your animation.

layers

Layers are used to organize objects on the Stage. Layers keep objects separated from each other.

LBS

Acronym for Location-Based Services. A set of services typically provided to mobile data service subscribers (mobile phone users) that are tailored to the time and location of the individual users.

LIF

Acronym for Location Interoperability Forum (**www.locationforum.org**). A global industry initiative to develop and promote common industry solutions for location-based services.

markup language

A meta-language used for marking up or presenting documents using a particular software application or medium, such as a web browser or a micro-browser.

masking

A technique for creating visual effects that hide items through the use of layers or masks.

MIME

Acronym for Multipurpose Internet Mail Extensions. This is an extension of SMTP, the original e-mail messaging protocol, so that web clients and servers can handle additional file types besides ASCII text. New file types include images, audio, video, and application programs.

MMS

Acronym for Multimedia Messaging Service. MMS messages can contain formatted text, graphics, data, animations, images, audio clips, voice transmissions, and video sequences. Sending digital postcards and PowerPoint-style presentations are expected to be among the most popular user applications of MMS. MMS is a Third Generation (3G) service.

MP3

Acronym for MPEG Audio Layer 3. A standard technology and format for compressing audio files into about one-twelfth the size of the original sound or music files without loss of quality when played with an MP3 player.

MPEG-4

Acronym for Moving Picture Experts Group 4. A standard enabling the integration of digital television, interactive graphic applications, and web-based multimedia.

MSC

Acronym for Master Switching Center. A facility used by wireless operators to coordinate activities between different base stations, which in turn control the communications and air interfaces with individual cellular phones (or terminals).

Microsoft IIS

Acronym for Microsoft Internet Information Server or Services. A web server built into (or tightly integrated with) the Microsoft Windows operating systems (for example, NT, 2000, XP), Microsoft IIS provides full-fledged publishing, communication, and administration capabilities for hosting web sites and applications.

.NET

Microsoft .NET is a set of Microsoft software technologies for connecting information, people, systems, and devices. Among other things, it enables software integration through the use of XML Web services via the Internet.

Nokia Communicator

A series of smart phones built and marketed by Nokia.

OOP

Acronym for object-oriented programming. OOP is a newer programming concept based on "objects" and data, as opposed to actions and logic flow.

OS

Acronym for Operating System.

personalization portal

A web site that end users access to select services and configure their device portal. Users access the personalization portal from their desktop computers.

PHP

Acronym for Personal Home Pages. A server-side scripting language that is freely available as an alternative to Microsoft Active Server Pages, Macromedia ColdFusion Markup Language, and JavaServer Pages. Used primarily on many Linux web servers.

PIM

Acronym for Personal Information Management. PIM solutions refer to address book, calendar, messaging, and other personal information management functions that are typically found in PDAs and other digital handheld devices.

pixel font

Designed for use with limited screen resolution and size, pixel fonts remain aliased in Flash, regardless of the movie quality.

plug-in

A program that can be downloaded onto a Netscape browser as a supplement. They're typically used for additional functions, such as viewing PDF files, Flash movies, and other multimedia content.

Pocket PC

A pocket-sized personal computer developed and marketed by Microsoft.

POP3

Acronym for Post Office Protocol 3. A standard protocol for receiving e-mail messages at mail servers. A store-and-forward service.

PNG

Acronym for Portable Network Graphics. An image compression file format that is lossless. Developed to be patent-free (and therefore requiring no licensing fee), PNG is expected to replace the GIF format.

PQA

Acronym for Palm Query Application. Software downloaded to Palm OS-compatible PDAs to partition the query portion of a web application onto the Palm PDAs, allowing their access to web clipping applications over Palm.net.

RAD

Acronym for Rapid Application Development. A concept that applications can be developed more rapidly and be of higher quality through the use of tools, workshops, prototyping, reuse of software components, and other means. Commonly used terms include RAD tools and RAD tool kits.

RDBMS

Acronym for Relational Database Management System. A program that allows you to create, update, and administer relational databases.

Relational Database

A collection of data organized as a set of related tables where data can be accessed and reassembled in different ways without the need to reconstruct or reorganize the tables.

rollover

Action that occurs when the mouse cursor rolls over a button.

RTMP

Acronym for Real Time Messaging Protocol. A Flash Communication Server protocol that accommodates real-time transmittal and receipt of messages.

SGML

Acronym for Standardized General Markup Language. A detailed system, or meta-language, adopted by ISO to allow the markup of documents so their appearance is independent of the underlying software applications. It provides a means of editing, formatting, publishing, and retrieving text or information via an explicit nested structure.

SMS

Acronym for Short Messaging Service. SMS allows mobile phone users to send and receive text messages of up to 160 characters in a cost- and time-efficient manner.

SMTP

Acronym for Simple Mail Transfer Protocol. A protocol for sending e-mail messages between servers. Also used for sending messages from a mail client to a mail server.

SOAP

Acronym for Simple Object Access Protocol. SOAP provides a simple and lightweight mechanism for exchanging structured and typed information between peers in a decentralized, distributed environment using XML.

SQL

Acronym for Structured Query Language. An ANSI standard for accessing database systems. SQL statements are used to retrieve, insert, delete, and update data in a database.

SSAS

Acronym for server-side ActionScript.

SSL

Acronym for Secure Socket Layer. A security scheme for bulk-encrypting data used for private communications between a web server and a client device through HTTPS.

Stage

The Stage is a movie screen where you place objects.

style sheet

An XSLT (eXtensible Stylesheet Language Transformations) instance that implements content presentation for XML documents.

SVG

Acronym for Scalable Vector Graphics. A language for describing two-dimensional graphic objects in XML, including vector graphic shapes, images, and text.

SWF

Acronym for Shockwave Flash. A Flash movie file extension.

symbol

A reusable element that, in the context of Macromedia Flash, you use with a document. Symbols include graphics, buttons, video clips, sound files, or fonts.

TCP/IP

Acronym for Transmission Control Protocol/Internet Protocol. The granddaddy of all protocols used for Internet communications. TCP/IP comprises two layers. Transmission Control Protocol manages the breakdown and reassembly of data in terms of packets used in transmission over the Internet. Internet Protocol provides the addressing rules and methods for routing packets from their origin to final destinations through gateways, switches, and servers over the Internet.

TDMA

Acronym for Time Division Multiple Access. TDMA utilizes GPS satellites to reference a synchronized time, and then divides the channel into time slots. As a result, channel capacity is increased because one channel has now been converted to multiple voice or data transmission vehicles. TDMA is a proven technology in cellular systems used in Europe, the USA, and Japan.

telematics

A technology combining all the possibilities inherent in wireless voice and data communications with GPS location capabilities to deliver location-specific security, information, and productivity-enhancing services to people on the move.

Timeline

A visual representation of the time sequence of a Flash movie, in individual movie frames, as presented within the Macromedia Flash authoring environment.

transformer

Software that converts content from an XML format into the target device format.

tweening

An interpolation technique where an animation program automatically creates extra frames between the key frames that have been manually created. This provides smoother animation without having to draw every frame.

typography

The art and technique of arranging the composition of movable fonts on a document.

UDDI

Acronym for Universal Description, Discovery, and Integration. An XML-based registry for businesses to list their Web services.

UML

Acronym for Unified Modeling Language. It is a language for specifying, visualizing, constructing, and documenting the artifacts of software systems, as well as business modeling and other non-software systems. The UML represents a collection of best engineering practices that have proven successful in the modeling of large and complex systems.

Unicode

Officially called the Unicode Worldwide Character Standard, Unicode is a system to interchange, process, and display language texts. It currently supports 34,168 code characters from 24 written languages.

URL

Acronym for Uniform Resource Locator. A form of Uniform Resource Identifier (URI), a URL that specifies the address of the file or web content accessible on the Internet (for example, www.osborne.com), and the type of protocol needed to access this resource (for example, http://).

UTF-16

One of the standard ways to encode a Unicode character set. It encodes all currently defined characters in exactly two octets, as well as all others likely to be defined in exactly four octets. In UTF-16 encoding, characters are represented by either one or two unsigned 16-bit integers.

vector analysis

The analysis, use, and rendition of images and graphic formats based on vectors and mathematical representations as opposed to pixels.

VPN

Acronym for Virtual Private Network. A method in which a public or shared network, such as the Internet, provides secure, remote access between an organization's data network and its remote workers, partners, branch offices, and so on, by using tunneling protocols and other security procedures. A typical tunneling protocol is the Layer 2 Tunneling Protocol (L2TP), which encrypts data at the origin and decrypts it at the destination through a tunnel that cannot be "breached" by data not properly encrypted.

VoiceXML

A web-based markup language for representing human-computer dialogs that is similar to HTML. VoiceXML assumes a voice browser with both audio output (computer-synthesized and/or recorded) and input (voice and/or keypad tones). VoiceXML leverages the Internet for voice application development and delivery, greatly simplifying these difficult tasks and creating new opportunities.

W3C

Acronym for the World Wide Web Consortium. A consortium promoting interoperability and World Wide Web standards through specifications and reference software products that are free and vendor-neutral.

WAP

Acronym for Wireless Application Protocol. A wireless standard that aims to align industry efforts to bring advanced applications and Internet content to digital cellular phones.

Web Clipping Proxy

A proxy server used to handle translation between the HTML and web clipping application formats, before content is transmitted to and from the Palm PDAs.

Web services

Web services consist of a set of messaging protocols, programming standards, and network registration and discovery facilities that expose business functions to authorized parties over the Internet from any web-connected device. Essentially, they're software components in the network.

WIDL

Acronym for Web Interface Definition Language. A metadata language that defines interfaces to web-based data and services. WIDL enables automatic and structured Web access by compatible applications.

WIDL file

A file written in Web Interface Definition Language that associates input and output parameters with the source content a user wishes to make available in a wireless service.

WML

Acronym for Wireless Markup Language. A markup language optimized for the delivery of content to wireless devices.

WMLScript

Acronym for Wireless Markup Language Script. A scripting language associated with WAP.

WSDL

Acronym for Web Services Description Language. A WSDL document is an XML file that describes a Web service's purpose, where it is located, and how to access it.

WWW

Acronym for the World Wide Web. All the users and resources (for example, servers) that utilize HyperText Transfer Protocol for information exchange.

WTAI

Acronym for Wireless Telephony Application Interface. Defines a set of functions that can be invoked by WML or WMLScript.

WYSIWYG

Acronym for What You See Is What You Get.

XHTML

Acronym for eXtensible HyperText Markup Language. Essentially, a reformulation of HTML in XML, XHTML is a family of current and future document types and modules that reproduce, subset, and extend HTML 4. XHTML family document types are XML-based.

XHTML-MP

Acronym for eXtensible HyperText Markup Language, Mobile Profile. XHTML-MP is a superset of XHTML Basic, which is a simpler version of XHTML. XHTML Basic is intended for smaller, non-computer devices such as mobile phones, personal digital assistants, pagers, and television-based web browsers.

XML

Acronym for eXtensible Markup Language. A flexible markup language that allows tags to be defined by the content developer. Tags for virtually any data item, such as a product, sales representative, or amount due, can be created and used in specific applications, allowing web pages to function like database records.

XSLT

Acronym for eXtensible Stylesheet Language Transformations. A style sheet format for XML documents.

ActionScript Quick Reference

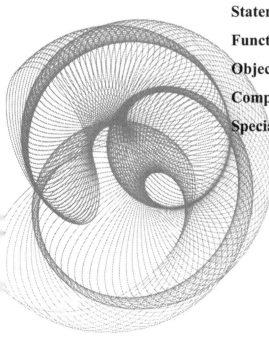

In this appendix, we will categorize all the ActionScript operators, keywords, statements, actions, objects, and components. Macromedia's ActionScript dictionary mixes all these together in an alphabetical manner, which is fine for developers who already know the language; unfortunately novices will find it very user unfriendly. Therefore, for all you beginners out there who know how to program, the category summary we've included here is intended to give you a jump-start on ActionScript programming.

NOTE

The properties and methods for each object or component can be easily located in the ActionScript dictionary and we will not repeat their details here.

We have also removed all deprecated ActionScript elements. We highly recommend using the new Flash MX elements even though deprecated elements are still supported by Flash Player 5.

Operators

Operators are terms that calculate a new value from one or more values. We have categorized them as Arithmetic, Logical, and General (operators which do not fall into the Arithmetic or Logical groupings).

Arithmetic

Operator	Description
--	Decrement
++	Increment
%	Modulo
%=	Modulo assignment
-	Subtraction
*	Multiplication
*=	Multiplication assignment
/	Division
+	Addition
+=	Addition assignment
-=	Subtraction assignment

Logical

Operator	Description
!	NOT
&&	Logical AND
&	Bitwise AND
&=	Bitwise AND assignment
^	XOR (exclusive OR)
^=	XOR assignment
|	Bitwise OR
||	Logical OR
!=	Bitwise OR assignment
~	Bitwise NOT
<	Less than
<<	Bitwise left shift
<<=	Bitwise left shift assignment
<=	Less than or equal to
!=	Inequality
!==	Strict inequality
==	Equality
===	Strict equality
>	Greater than
>=	Greater than or equal to
>>	Bitwise right shift
>>=	Bitwise right shift assignment
>>>	Bitwise unsigned right shift
>>>=	Bitwise unsigned right shift assignment

General

Operator	Description
()	Grouping
,	Evaluate expressions

Operator	Description
.	Methods or properties
?	Conditional
//	Comment delimiter
/*	Comment delimiter
[]	Array
{}	Object initializer
=	Assignment
()	Grouping
instanceof	Determines whether an object belongs to a specified class
new	Creates a new object
super	Invokes the superclass version of a method
typeof	Flash interpreter to evaluate expression
void	Discards the expression value

Keywords

Keywords are reserved words that have special meaning.

Operator	Description
break	Instructs Flash to skip the rest of the *loop* body and stop the looping action
case	Defines a condition for the *switch* action
default	Defines the default case for a *switch* action
this	References an object or movie clip instance

Statements/Actions

Actions are statements that instruct a movie to do something while it is playing.

Actions	Description
call function	Allows you to use parameter fields to call a user-defined function in normal mode in the Actions panel
clearinterval	Clears a call to the *setInterval* function
continue	Causes interpreter to jump around in a *loop* body but not break out of it
delete	Removes a variable or object
do while	Executes the statements, and then evaluates the condition in a *loop* for as long as the condition is true
duplicateMovieClip	Creates an instance of a movie clip while the movie is playing

Actions	Description
else	Specifies the statements to run if the condition in the *if* statement returns false
else if	Same as *else* with the additional condition
#endinitclip#	Indicates the end of a block of component initialization actions
#initclip#	Indicates the start of a block of component initialization actions
for	A *loop* construct that evaluates the initialize expression once, and then begins a looping sequence as long as the condition is true
for in	Loops through the properties of an object or element in an array
fscommand	Allows the Flash movie to communicate with Flash Player or a web browser
function	A set of statements that you define to perform a certain task
getURL	Loads a document from a specific URL into a window
goToAndPlay	Sends the playhead to the specified frame in a scene and plays from that frame
goToAndStop	Sends the playhead to the specified frame in a scene and stops it
if	Evaluates a condition to determine the next action in a movie
#include	Includes the contents of the file specified in the parameter when the movie is tested, published, or exported
loadMovie	Loads an SWF or JPEG file into the Flash Player while the original movie is playing
loadMovieNum	Loads an SWF or JPEG file into a level in the Flash Player while the originally loaded movie is playing
loadVariables	Reads data from an external file and sets the values for variables in a Flash Player level or a target movie clip
loadVariablesNum	Reads data from an external file and sets the values for variables in a Flash Player level
nextFrame	Sends the playhead to the next frame and stops it
nextScene	Sends the playhead to Frame 1 of the next scene and stops it
play	Moves the playhead forward in the Timeline
prevFrame	Sends the playhead to the previous frame and stops it
prevScene	Sends the playhead to Frame 1 of the previous scene and stops it
print	Prints the movie clip
printAsBitmap	Prints the movie clip as a bitmap
printAsBitmapNum	Prints a level in Flash Player as a bitmap
printNum	Prints the level in Flash Player
removeMovieClip	Deletes a movie clip instance
return	Specifies the value returned by a function
set variable	Assigns a value to a variable
setInterval	Calls a function, method, or object at periodic intervals while a movie plays
setProperty	Changes a property value of a movie clip as the movie plays
startDrag	Makes the movie clip draggable while the movie is playing

Actions	Description
stop	Stops the movie that is currently playing
stopAllSounds	Stops all sounds currently playing in a movie without stopping the playhead
stopDrag	Stops the current drag operation
switch	Creates a branching structure for ActionScript statements
toggleHighQuality	Turns anti-aliasing on and off in Flash Player
trace	Evaluates the expression and displays the result in the Output window in test mode
unloadMovie	Removes a loaded movie or a movie clip from Flash Player
unloadMovieNum	Removes a loaded movie from Flash Player
updateAfterEvent	Updates the display when called within an event handler
var	Used to declare local variables
while	Tests an expression and runs statements repeatedly in a loop as long as the expression is true.
with	Allows specification of an object with the object parameter and evaluates expressions and actions inside that object with the statement parameters

Functions

Functions are blocks of reusable code that can be passed parameters which are then used to return values.

Functions	Description
asfunction	A special protocol for URLs in HTML text fields
Boolean	Converts an expression to a Boolean value
escape	Converts the parameter to a string and encodes it in a URL-encoded format
eval	Accesses variables, properties, objects, or movie clips by name
evaluate	Creates a new empty line and inserts a semicolon for writing statements to be evaluated in the Actions panel
getProperty	Returns the value of the specified property for the movie clip instancename
getTimer	Returns the number of milliseconds that have elapsed since the movie started playing
isFinite	Evaluates an expression and returns true if it is a finite number
isNaN	Evaluates a parameter and returns true if the value is not a number
Number	Converts the expression to a number
parseFloat	Converts a string to a floating-point number
parseInt	Converts a string to an integer
String	Returns a string representation of the specified parameter

Functions	Description
targetPath	Returns a string containing the target path of the movie clip object
unescape	Evaluates the parameter as a string, decodes the string from its URL-encoded format, and then returns the string

Objects

Objects are collections of properties and methods. Each has its own name and is an instance of a particular class. Built-in objects are predefined in the ActionScript language. *Methods* are functions assigned to an object, while *Properties* are attributes that define an object.

Object	Description
Accessibility	A collection of methods you can use to create accessible content with ActionScript
Arguments	An object created with every function that contains an associative array of passed parameters, plus references to the caller and callee functions
Array	Lets you access and manipulate arrays
Boolean	A wrapper object with the same functionality as the standard JavaScript Boolean object
Button	Button symbols in a Flash movie
Camera	Used with Flash Communication Server to capture video from a video camera attached to the computer that is running Flash Player
Color	Lets you set the RGB color value and color transform of movie clips
CustomActions	Allow a Flash movie playing in the Flash authoring tool to manage any custom actions registered with the authoring tool
Date	Lets you retrieve date and time values relative to universal time or relative to the operating system on which Flash Player is running
Function	Enables ActionScript code to call a function
Key	Used to build an interface that can be controlled by a user with a standard keyboard
LoadVars	An alternative to the loadVariables action for transferring variables between a Flash movie and a server
LocalConnection	Lets you develop Flash movies that can send instructions to each other
Math	Used to access and manipulate mathematical constants and functions
Microphone	Used with Flash Communication Server to capture audio from a microphone attached to the computer running Flash Player
Mouse	Used to hide and show the cursor in the movie
MovieClip	Provides the same functionality as actions that target movie clips
Number	Wrapper object for the number data type used to manipulate primitive numeric values

Object	Description
Object	Root of the ActionScript class hierarchy
Selection	Manages selection with text fields and movie clips
SharedObject	Allows real-time data sharing between objects that are persistent on the local location
Sound	Controls sound in a movie
Stage	Used to access and manipulate information about the boundaries of a Flash movie
String	Wrapper for the string primitive data type used to manipulate primitive string value types
System	Used to determine the capabilities of the system and Flash Player hosting a Flash movie
TextField	Used to manipulate dynamic and input text fields in a Flash movie
TextFormat	Object that represents character formatting information
Video	Allows display of live streaming video on the Stage without embedding it in your SWF file
XML	Used to load, parse, send, build, and manipulate XML document trees
XMLSocket	Client sockets that allow the computer running Flash Player to communicate with a server computer identified by an IP address or domain name

Components

Components are complex movie clips that have defined parameters and methods.

Component	Description
FCheckBox	Drag-and-drop functionality for adding check boxes to Flash documents
FComboBox	Drag-and-drop functionality for adding scrollable single-selection drop-down lists to Flash documents
FListBox	Drag-and-drop functionality for adding scrollable single-selection and multiple-selection list boxes to Flash documents
FPushButton	Drag-and-drop functionality for adding buttons to Flash documents
FRadioButton	Drag-and-drop functionality for adding groups of radio buttons to Flash documents
FScrollBar	Drag-and-drop functionality for adding scroll bars to dynamic and input text fields in Flash documents
FScrollPane	Drag-and-drop functionality for adding scroll panes to display movie clips in Flash documents
FStyleFormat	Sets or changes properties in the global style format assigned to all Flash UI components by default, or creates new custom style formats to use with Flash UI components

Special Properties

Property	Description
_alpha	Sets and retrieves the alpha transparency of an object
_focusrect	Specifies whether a yellow rectangle appears around the button that has keyboard focus
_global	Creates global variables, objects, or classes
_height	Sets and retrieves the height of an object
_highquality	Specifies the level of anti-aliasing applied to the current movie
_level	A reference to the root movie Timeline of the Nth _level
_parent	Specifies or returns a reference to the movie clip or object that contains the current movie clip or object
_quality	Sets or retrieves the rendering quality used for a movie
_root	Specifies or returns a reference to the root movie Timeline
_soundbuftime	Establishes the number of seconds of streaming sound to prebuffer
_width	Sets and retrieves the width of an object
_x	Sets the x coordinate of an object
_xscale	Determines the horizontal scale of an object
_y	Sets the y coordinate of an object
_yscale	Determines the vertical scale of an object

Tutorial: Relational Databases and SQL

A Relational Database Management System (RDBMS) is a type of Database Management System (DBMS) that stores data in the form of related tables. Relational databases are powerful because they require few assumptions about how data is related or how it will be extracted from the database. As a result, the same database can be viewed in many different ways.

An important feature of relational systems is that a single database can be spread across several tables. This differs from flat-file databases, in which each database is self-contained in a single table. Almost all full-scale database systems are RDBMSs.

Structured Query Language (SQL) is an ANSI (American National Standards Institute) standard for accessing database systems. SQL statements are used to retrieve, insert, delete, and update data in a database. SQL works with database programs like Microsoft Access, IBM DB2, Informix, Microsoft SQL Server, Oracle 8/9, Sybase, MySQL, and many others.

RDBMS

A *database* defines a structure for storing information, typically organized into objects called *tables*, which are collections of related objects. Tables are identified by names (like Automotives, Employees, Orders), and contain columns and rows with data. Rows contain records (like one record for each employee), while columns contain data (like Country, Units, First Name, Last Name, Title, Location, and Phone).

Each row, called a data *record*, corresponds to one manufacturer in the Automotives table. The value of a column within a record is referred to as a record *field*. The following shows an example table, named *Automotives*, containing information about various automotive imports and exports.

ManufID	Manufacturer	Country	Units
1601	BMW	Germany	40000
1602	Mercedes Benz	Germany	35000
1603	Honda	Japan	100000
1604	Nissan	Japan	50000
1605	Mazda	Japan	28000
1606	Audi	Germany	20000
1607	Jaguar	England	15000
1608	Volvo	Sweden	25000
1609	Kia	Korea	60000
1610	Porsche	Germany	17000

ManufID, *Manufacturer*, *Country*, and *Units* are table columns. The rows contain ten records (for four manufacturers). This example uses the *ManufID* field as the table's *primary key* field. The primary key contains a unique identifier to maintain each record's unique identity. Typically, you specify which column contains the primary key when you create a database table.

To read or modify data for the Automotives table, you will use the SQL programming language. For example, the following SQL statement returns all rows from the table where the *ManufID* is *1601*:

```
SELECT * FROM Automotives WHERE ManufID=1601
```

You will receive only one record back (in our example), which is shown in the following illustration:

ManufID	Manufacturer	Country	Units
1601	BMW	Germany	40000

We will cover basic SQL commands in the next section.

NOTE

Some database systems require a semicolon at the end of the SQL statements. Please check with your product documentation.

In many database designs, information is distributed to multiple tables. One advantage of using multiple tables is that you can add tables containing new information without modifying the structure of your existing tables. For example, to add units sold information, you add a new table (*WesternSales*, for instance) to the database where the first column contains the manufacturer's ID and the rest of the columns contain the ZIP code, units, quotas, dealers, and so on. Access to a small table is more efficient than accessing a large table. Therefore, if you want to update the *Units* of a *Manufacturer*, you update only the *Automotives* table, without having to access the *WesternSales* table or other tables in the database.

We will not cover database designs here. There are many excellent books out there you can reference, or you can contact your resident database administrators (DBA) for questions and suggestions. This section is meant to introduce you to one of the dynamic drivers of mobile application development.

SQL

This section introduces the SQL programming language. We will describe basic SQL syntax and show examples of SQL statements. It should provide enough information for you to start developing dynamic mobile applications. However, this section does not contain an exhaustive description of the entire SQL programming language. For complete SQL information, see the SQL reference that ships with your database.

Introduction

As the name suggests, SQL is the syntax used for executing queries. But the SQL language also includes syntax to update records, insert new records, and delete existing records—SQL is an ANSI/ISO standard programming language for writing database queries. A query is a request to a database. The query can ask for information from the database, write new data to the database, update existing information in the database, or delete records from the database.

A SQL statement always begins with a SQL verb. The following keywords identify commonly used SQL verbs (they also form the data manipulation language part of SQL):

▶ **SELECT**   Extracts data from a database

▶ **UPDATE**   Updates data in a database

▶ **DELETE**   Deletes data from a database

▶ **INSERT**   Inserts new data into a database

The following keywords are used to refine the SQL statements:

▶ **FROM**   Names the data tables for the operation

▶ **WHERE**   Sets one or more conditions for the operation

▶ **ORDER BY**   Sorts the result set in the specified order

▶ **GROUP BY**   Groups the result set by the specified select list items

The following are basic operators which perform logical and numeric functions:

Operator	Description
=	Equal to
<> or !=	Not equal to
<	Less than
>	Greater than
<=	Less than or equal to
>=	Greater than or equal to
+	Addition
-	Subtraction
/	Division
*	Multiplication
AND	Both conditions must be met
OR	At least one condition must be met
NOT	Exclude the condition following

Operator	Description
LIKE	Matches with a pattern
IN	Matches with a list of values
BETWEEN	Matches with a range of values

NOTE

In some versions of SQL, the "not equal to" operator "<>" can be written as "!=". Again, check your product documentation.

Here's a simple example: the following SQL statement

```
SELECT Manufacturer FROM Automotives
```

will result in ten records as shown in the following illustration.

Manufacturer
BMW
Mercedes Benz
Honda
Nissan
Mazda
Audi
Jaguar
Volvo
Kia
Porsche

The statement is interpreted as "select column name, Manufacturer, of all rows from the Automotives table."

The data definition language part of SQL permits database tables to be created or deleted. These include the following statements in SQL:

- ► **CREATE TABLE**   Creates a new database table
- ► **ALTER TABLE**   Alters a database table
- ► **DROP TABLE**   Deletes a database table
- ► **CREATE INDEX**   Creates an index or search key
- ► **DROP INDEX**   Deletes an index

Reading from a Database

The most commonly used SQL statement is the SELECT statement. The SELECT statement selects columns of data from a database. The SQL statement has the following syntax:

```
SELECT column_name(s)
FROM table_name(s)
[ WHERE search_condition ]
[ GROUP BY group_expression ]
[ ORDER BY order_condition [ ASC | DESC ] ]
```

The statements in square brackets are optional.

NOTE

The additional options to SELECT are dependent on your database. Please check your product documentation.

The WHERE clause allows you to filter the results of a query and returns only those records that meet a specific criterion. You can also combine multiple conditions using the WHERE clause. For instance, the following example uses two conditions:

```
SELECT ManufID,Manufacturer,Country FROM Automotives WHERE ManufID=1604
   AND Country='Japan'
```

and will result in the record shown in the next illustration.

ManufID	Manufacturer	Country
1604	Nissan	Japan

NOTE

We used single quotes around the conditional values in the preceding example, because SQL uses single quotes around text values. Most database systems will also accept double quotes. Numeric values should not be enclosed in quotes.

The LIKE clause is used to specify a search for a pattern in a column. A "%" sign can be used to define wildcards both before and after the pattern. For example, the SQL statement

```
SELECT * FROM Automotives WHERE Country LIKE '%an%'
```

will result in the record shown in the following illustration.

ManufID	Manufacturer	Country	Units
1601	BMW	Germany	40000
1602	Mercedes Benz	Germany	35000
1603	Honda	Japan	100000

ManufID	Manufacturer	Country	Units
1604	Nissan	Japan	50000
1605	Mazda	Japan	28000
1606	Audi	Germany	20000
1607	Jaguar	England	15000
1610	Porsche	Germany	17000

By default, the database does not sort the records returned from a SQL query. In fact, you cannot guarantee that the records returned from the same query will come back in the same order each time you run the query. This is where the ORDER BY clause comes in. You can write your SQL statement to sort the records returned from the database in a specific order. For example, the following SQL statement returns all the records of the table ordered by the *Country* column in ascending (alphabetical) order, by default:

```
SELECT * FROM Automotives ORDER BY Country
```

ManufID	Manufacturer	Country	Units
1607	Jaguar	England	15000
1601	BMW	Germany	40000
1602	Mercedes Benz	Germany	35000
1606	Audi	Germany	20000
1610	Porsche	Germany	17000
1603	Honda	Japan	100000
1604	Nissan	Japan	50000
1605	Mazda	Japan	28000
1609	Kia	Korea	60000
1608	Volvo	Sweden	25000

You can also combine multiple fields in the ORDER BY clause to perform additional sorting:

```
SELECT * FROM Automotives ORDER BY Country, Units
```

This statement returns rows ordered by *Country*, then by *Units*, as illustrated next.

ManufID	Manufacturer	Country	Units
1607	Jaguar	England	15000
1610	Porsche	Germany	17000
1606	Audi	Germany	20000
1602	Mercedes Benz	Germany	35000
1601	BMW	Germany	40000
1605	Mazda	Japan	28000
1604	Nissan	Japan	50000

ManufID	Manufacturer	Country	Units
1603	Honda	Japan	100000
1609	Kia	Korea	60000
1608	Volvo	Sweden	25000

It should be noted that the AS clause is very useful for repackaging query results. For example, you may have cryptic or undesirable column names you don't want in your SQL statement results, or perhaps you need to generate different reports for various departments that require more meaningful column names. Using our Automotives database, let's rename some of the columns in the following manner as part of the query:

```
SELECT ManufID AS Manufacturer_Code,
    Manufacturer AS Make,
    Country AS Country_Of_Origin,
    Units AS Number_Of_Imported_Vehicles
FROM Automotives
WHERE Country = 'Germany'
```

The results returned by this query are shown in the following illustration.

Manufacturer_Code	Make	Country_Of_Origin	Number_Of_Imported_Vehicles
1601	BMW	Germany	40000
1602	Mercedes Benz	Germany	35000
1606	Audi	Germany	20000
1610	Porsche	Germany	17000

The syntax of the column name alias is

```
SELECT column AS column_alias FROM table
```

Note that you can also have a table name alias, whose syntax is

```
SELECT column FROM table AS table_alias
```

NOTE

Some SQL implementations do not support the AS keyword. Check with your database administrator or refer to the database user's guide for more information.

Modifying a Database

In the previous section, we simply read data from a database, but you can also use SQL to modify a database in the following ways:

► Insert data into a database

► Update data in a database

► Delete data from a database

To insert data into a database, use the SQL INSERT INTO statement to write information to a database. A write adds a new row to a database table. The basic syntax of an INSERT INTO statement is as follows:

```
INSERT INTO table_name(column_names)
VALUES(value_list)
```

where
column_names specifies a comma-separated list of columns - optional
value_list specifies a comma-separated list of values

NOTE

The order of values has to correspond to the order in which you specified column names.

For example, the following SQL statements will insert a new row into the Automotives table, resulting in the table shown in the illustration following:

```
INSERT INTO Automotives
VALUES('1611','Mini','England','20000')
```

ManufID	Manufacturer	Country	Units
1601	BMW	Germany	40000
1602	Mercedes Benz	Germany	35000
1603	Honda	Japan	100000
1604	Nissan	Japan	50000
1605	Mazda	Japan	28000
1606	Audi	Germany	20000
1607	Jaguar	England	15000
1608	Volvo	Sweden	25000
1609	Kia	Korea	60000
1610	Porsche	Germany	17000
1611	Mini	England	20000

If you wish to specify only the columns where you want to insert data, use the following SQL statement, which will offer results like those in the illustration that follows:

```
INSERT INTO Automotives (ManufID,Manufacturer,Units)
VALUES(1612,'Acura','31000')
```

ManufID	Manufacturer	Country	Units
1601	BMW	Germany	40000
1602	Mercedes Benz	Germany	35000
1603	Honda	Japan	100000
1604	Nissan	Japan	50000
1605	Mazda	Japan	28000
1606	Audi	Germany	20000
1607	Jaguar	England	15000
1608	Volvo	Sweden	25000
1609	Kia	Korea	60000
1610	Porsche	Germany	17000
1611	Mini	England	20000
1612	Acura		31000

To update data in a database, use the UPDATE statement in SQL. UPDATE lets you update the fields of a specific row or all rows in the table. The UPDATE statement has the following syntax:

```
UPDATE table_name
SET column_name1=value1, ... , column_nameN=valueN
[ WHERE search_condition ]
```

For example, the following SQL statements will update a row in the Automotives table. The resulting table is shown in the illustration following:

```
UPDATE Automotives
SET Country='Germany'
WHERE ManufID=1611
```

ManufID	Manufacturer	Country	Units
1601	BMW	Germany	40000
1602	Mercedes Benz	Germany	35000
1603	Honda	Japan	100000
1604	Nissan	Japan	50000
1605	Mazda	Japan	28000
1606	Audi	Germany	20000
1607	Jaguar	England	15000
1608	Volvo	Sweden	25000
1609	Kia	Korea	60000
1610	Porsche	Germany	17000

ManufID	Manufacturer	Country	Units
1611	Mini	Germany	20000
1612	Acura		31000

NOTE

There are additional options to the UPDATE clause, depending on your database. Please check your product documentation.

To delete data from a database, use the DELETE statement, which removes rows from a table. The DELETE statement has the following syntax:

```
DELETE FROM table_name
[ WHERE search_condition ]
```

For example, the following SQL statements will delete a row, ManufID = 1612, in the Automotives table. The resulting table is shown in the illustration that follows.

```
DELETE FROM Automotives WHERE ManufID=1612
```

ManufID	Manufacturer	Country	Units
1601	BMW	Germany	40000
1602	Mercedes Benz	Germany	35000
1603	Honda	Japan	100000
1604	Nissan	Japan	50000
1605	Mazda	Japan	28000
1606	Audi	Germany	20000
1607	Jaguar	England	15000
1608	Volvo	Sweden	25000
1609	Kia	Korea	60000
1610	Porsche	Germany	17000
1611	Mini	Germany	20000

NOTE

There are additional options to the DELETE clause, depending on your database. Again, check your product documentation.

We'll now learn about a few more SQL commands that are both powerful and necessary for dynamic application development. The first is the built-in COUNT function. The syntax for the COUNT function is

```
SELECT COUNT(column) FROM table
```

The COUNT(*) function returns the number of selected rows in a selection. For instance, in our previous example, the following SQL statement:

```
SELECT COUNT(*) FROM Automotives
```

would result in the following:

```
11
```

That is, it returned the number of rows without a NULL value in the specified column.

Another SQL command of note is the DISTINCT keyword. DISTINCT is used to return only distinct or different values. The syntax is

```
SELECT DISTINCT column(s) FROM table
```

For example, the following SQL statement will result in the table shown in the next illustration:

```
SELECT DISTINCT Country FROM Automotives
```

Country
Germany
Japan
England
Sweden
Korea

This concludes our quick RDBMS tutorial. For more information, check your local bookstore for books on RDBMS and SQL.

APPENDIX
D

Online Resources

This appendix contains a listing of useful sites and resources for finding information on Macromedia Flash MX, ColdFusion MX, Flash Communication Server, mobile devices, Dreamweaver MX, and more.

The Macromedia Designer and Developer Center

Macromedia's Designer and Developer Center contains complete articles, tutorials, and detailed information on many of Macromedia's products, including Flash MX, ColdFusion MX, Flash Communication Server, Dreamweaver MX, Studio MX, mobile devices, J2EE, and more. This should be your first stop for additional details on anything discussed in this book.

▶ The Macromedia Designer and Developer Center–Home Page
http://www.macromedia.com/desdev/

▶ The Macromedia Flash MX Application Development Center
http://www.macromedia.com/desdev/mx/flash/

▶ The Macromedia ColdFusion MX Application Development Center
http://www.macromedia.com/desdev/mx/coldfusion/

▶ The Macromedia Flash Communication Server Application Development Center
http://www.macromedia.com/desdev/mx/flashcom/

▶ The Macromedia Dreamweaver MX Application Development Center
http://www.macromedia.com/desdev/mx/dreamweaver/

▶ The Macromedia Studio MX Application Development Center
http://www.macromedia.com/desdev/mx/studio/

▶ The Macromedia Mobile Development Center
http://www.macromedia.com/desdev/mobile/

▶ The Macromedia Rich Internet Application Development Center
http://www.macromedia.com/desdev/topics/richapps.html

▶ The Macromedia Web Services Development Center
http://www.macromedia.com/desdev/topics/web_services.html

▶ The Macromedia Java Platform Development Center
http://www.macromedia.com/desdev/java/

▶ The Macromedia ASP.NET Development Center
http://www.macromedia.com/desdev/dotnet/

Weblogs/Blogs

Weblogs or Blogs are web pages made up of short and frequently updated posts that are arranged chronologically like a journal. For more information, take a peek at the following sites.

- Flash MX - Mike Chambers, Flash Community Manager, Macromedia, Inc.
  http://www.macromedia.com/go/blog_mchambers

- ColdFusion MX - Vernon Viehe, ColdFusion Community Manager, Macromedia, Inc.
  http://www.macromedia.com/go/blog_vviehe

- ColdFusion MX Architecture - Sean Corfield, Director of Architecture, Macromedia, Inc.
  http://www.macromedia.com/go/blog_scorfield

- Dreamweaver MX - Matt Brown, Dreamweaver Community Manager, Macromedia, Inc.
  http://www.macromedia.com/go/blog_mbrown

- John Dowdell, Macromedia, Inc.
  http://www.macromedia.com/go/blog_jd

- Waldo Smeets, Macromedia, Inc.
  http://www.waldosmeets.com/

- David Burrows Flash Blog
  http://radio.weblogs.com/0102755/

ActionScript

Here you can find listings of examples, tutorials, source code, and other items related to ActionScript programming.

- Colin Moock
  http://www.moock.org

- ActionScript Toolbox
  http://actionscript-toolbox.com/

- ActionScripts Organization
  http://www.actionscripts.org/

Mobile Devices

The following are resources related to mobile devices.

- The Macromedia Device Resource Center
  http://www.macromedia.com/software/flashplayer/resources/devices/

- Macromedia Flash Player for Pocket PC
  http://www.macromedia.com/software/flashplayer/pocketpc/

- Macromedia Flash Player for Nokia Communicator
  http://www.macromedia.com/software/flashplayer/resources/devices/nokia/

- Nokia Communicator World
  http://www.nokiausa.com/communicator

- ▶ Nokia Developer Forum
  http://www.forum.nokia.com/main.html

- ▶ Microsoft Pocket PC
  http://www.pocketpc.com

- ▶ The Openwave WML Developer Center
  http://developer.openwave.com

- ▶ Microsoft Mobile Devices Developer
  http://www.microsoft.com/mobile/developer/

- ▶ Pocket PC Flash Net
  http://www.pocketpcflash.net/

- ▶ Fonts for Flash
  http://www.fontsforflash.com/

- ▶ Miniml
  http://www.miniml.com

Flash MX/ColdFusion MX

Flash MX, Flash Remoting, and ColdFusion related resources (including free components!) can be found at the following sites.

- ▶ Macromedia Exchange for Flash
  http://www.macromedia.com/exchange/flash

- ▶ Macromedia Exchange for ColdFusion
  http://devex.macromedia.com/developer/gallery/index.cfm

- ▶ Macromedia Exchange for Dreamweaver
  http://www.macromedia.com/exchange/dreamweaver

- ▶ Macromedia Flash Remoting Components
  http://www.macromedia.com/software/flashremoting/downloads/components/

- ▶ FlashCFM
  http://www.flashcfm.com/

- ▶ Flash Kit
  http://www.flashkit.com/

- ▶ Flash Components
  http://www.flashcomponents.net/

- ▶ Flash DB
  http://www.flash-db.com/

- Flash Guru MX
  http://www.flashguru.co.uk/

- Flash Magazine
  http://www.flashmagazine.com

- Flazoom
  http://www.flazoom.com/

- Open SWF
  http://www.openswf.org/

- UltraShock
  http://www.ultrashock.com/

- Robert Penner
  http://www.robertpenner.com/

Web Services

The following is a list of resources related to Web services.

- Google Web APIs
  http://www.google.com/apis/

- Amazon Web Services
  http://associates.amazon.com/exec/panama/associates/ntg/browse/-/1067662

- Web Services Directory
  http://www.xmethods.com/

- The Universal Description, Discovery, and Integration (UDDI) project
  http://www.uddi.org/

Index

INTERNATIONAL CONTACT INFORMATION

AUSTRALIA
McGraw-Hill Book Company Australia Pty. Ltd.
TEL +61-2-9900-1800
FAX +61-2-9878-8881
http://www.mcgraw-hill.com.au
books-it_sydney@mcgraw-hill.com

CANADA
McGraw-Hill Ryerson Ltd.
TEL +905-430-5000
FAX +905-430-5020
http://www.mcgraw-hill.ca

**GREECE, MIDDLE EAST, & AFRICA
(Excluding South Africa)**
McGraw-Hill Hellas
TEL +30-210-6560-990
TEL +30-210-6560-993
TEL +30-210-6560-994
FAX +30-210-6545-525

MEXICO (Also serving Latin America)
McGraw-Hill Interamericana Editores S.A. de C.V.
TEL +525-117-1583
FAX +525-117-1589
http://www.mcgraw-hill.com.mx
fernando_castellanos@mcgraw-hill.com

SINGAPORE (Serving Asia)
McGraw-Hill Book Company
TEL +65-863-1580
FAX +65-862-3354
http://www.mcgraw-hill.com.sg
mghasia@mcgraw-hill.com

SOUTH AFRICA
McGraw-Hill South Africa
TEL +27-11-622-7512
FAX +27-11-622-9045
robyn_swanepoel@mcgraw-hill.com

SPAIN
McGraw-Hill/Interamericana de España, S.A.U.
TEL +34-91-180-3000
FAX +34-91-372-8513
http://www.mcgraw-hill.es
professional@mcgraw-hill.es

**UNITED KINGDOM, NORTHERN,
EASTERN, & CENTRAL EUROPE**
McGraw-Hill Education Europe
TEL +44-1-628-502500
FAX +44-1-628-770224
http://www.mcgraw-hill.co.uk
computing_neurope@mcgraw-hill.com

ALL OTHER INQUIRIES Contact:
Osborne/McGraw-Hill
TEL +1-510-549-6600
FAX +1-510-883-7600
http://www.osborne.com
omg_international@mcgraw-hill.com

www.ingramcontent.com/pod-product-compliance
Lightning Source LLC
Chambersburg PA
CBHW080141060326
40689CB00018B/3812